PUBLIC–PRIVATE PARTNERSHIP MONITOR
INDIA

SEPTEMBER 2024

ASIAN DEVELOPMENT BANK

ADB

Notes:
In this publication, "$" refers to United States dollars.
The fiscal year (FY) of the Government of India ends on 31 March. "FY" before a calendar year denotes the year in which the fiscal year ends, e.g., FY2022 ends on 31 March 2022.
ADB recognizes "Bangalore" as Bengaluru and "Orissa" as Odisha.

On the cover: Clock tower in Gujarat, India as part of the Rajasthan Urban Infrastructure Development Project; the liquid natural gas storage facility in Dahej, Gujarat, India's first LNG import and regasification terminal; the 50.4 megawatts of turbines dominate the landscape around Khanke in Maharashtra, India; urban drainage station at Lohiya College in Churu, Rajasthan; and a lab technician taking blood samples for a patient in Medanta Hospital's lab sample collection in Gurugram, India (photos by Rakesh Sahai, Ian Taylor, and Amit Verma).

Cover page prepared by Claudette Rodrigo.

Contents

Tables and Figures iv

Foreword. ix

Acknowledgments xi

Definition of Terms xii

Abbreviations xix

Weights and Measures xxi

Currency Equivalents xxii

Guide to Understanding the Public–Private Partnership Monitor xxiii

I.   Overview. 1

II. National Public–Private Partnership Landscape 11

III. Sector-Specific Public–Private Partnership Landscape. 63
     A.   Roads 63
     B.   Railways. 77
     C.   Ports 91
     D.   Airports 102
     E.   Energy 113
     F.   Water and Wastewater 128
     G.   Information and Communication Technology. 145
     H.   Social Infrastructure. 156
     I.   Other Infrastructure—Municipal Solid Waste. 167

IV. Local Government Public–Private Partnership Landscape. 177

Appendixes 195
     1.   Critical Macroeconomic and Infrastructure Sector Indicators for India. 195
     2.   World Bank's Ease of Doing Business Parameters for India. 198
     3.   Assessment of Public Financial Management System in India, 2010 201

References 203

Tables and Figures

Tables

1   Estimated Total Investments for the Infrastructure Sector 2

2   Regulations on Public–Private Partnerships at State Level.....................................15

3   Prevalent Public–Private Partnership Models 18

4   Updated Harmonized Master List of Infrastructure Subsectors 19

5   Description and Roles of Entities Promoting Public–Private Partnerships.....................21

6   Guidelines for the Formulation, Appraisal, and Approval of Public–Private Partnership Projects...24

7   Phases of a Public–Private Partnership Project Life Cycle 30

8   Description of Public–Private Partnership Tools 35

9   Compensation Clauses from Model Concession Agreement in the Highway Sector 38

10   Government Support Facilities for Public–Private Partnership Projects.........................48

11   Active Project Sponsors in India, July 2021 to August 2022 60

12   Key Regulations for the Road Sector in India...64

13   Phases and Progress of Projects Under the National Highways Development Project...........66

14   Project Progress Under the Bharatmala Pariyojana Project 68

15   Number of Road and Bridge Projects Across Public–Private Partnership Variants..............73

16   Generic Risk-Sharing Matrix Across Variants of Public–Private Partnerships in the Road Sector 75

17   Key Entities Responsible for the Railway Sector in India......................................78

18   Capital Expenditure Plan for Projects in the Railway Sector Under the National Infrastructure Pipeline 84

19   Number of Railway Projects Across Public–Private Partnership Variants.......................88

20   Key Entities Responsible for the Port Sector in India 93

21   Estimated Expenditure of Initiatives in the Port Sector Under the Sagarmala Program of the Ministry of Ports, Shipping and Waterways...96

22   Number of Port Projects Across Public–Private Partnership Variants 99

23   Key Entities Responsible for the Airport Sector in India 103

24   Foreign Direct Investment Allowed in the Airport and Aviation Sector 105

25   Estimated Capital Expenditure Plan for the Airport Sector
Under the National Infrastructure Pipeline 106

26   Number of Airport Projects Across Public–Private Partnership Variants 110

27   Regulatory Entities in the Energy Sector in India 116

28   Capital Expenditure Plan for the Energy Sector by Segment,
Based on the National Infrastructure Pipeline 118

29   Estimated Year-on-Year Capital Expenditure Plan in the Energy Sector,
Based on the National Infrastructure Pipeline 119

30   Capital Expenditure Plan for the Renewable Energy Sector,
Based on the National Infrastructure Pipeline 120

31   Total Year-on-Year Capital Expenditure Plan for the Energy Sector in India....................121

32   Number of Energy Projects Across Public–Private Partnership Variants 124

33   Number of Energy Projects Based on Subsectors 125

34   Tariffs Set Up by the Central Electricity Regulatory Commission for Energy Projects in India...126

35   Key Entities Responsible for the Water and Wastewater Sectors in India 130

36   Capital Expenditure Plan for the Water Sector, Based on the National Infrastructure Pipeline .135

37   Number of Water and Wastewater Projects Across Public–Private Partnership Variants 138

38   Number of Water and Wastewater Projects Based on Subsectors..............................139

39   Water Tariff for the Hyderabad Metropolitan Water Supply and Sewerage Board..............139

40   Tariff Grid for the Hyderabad Metropolitan Water Supply and Sewerage Board................140

41   Tariff for Wastewater for the Hyderabad Metropolitan Water Supply and Sewerage Board.....140

42   Water Tariff for the Bangalore Water Supply and Sewerage Board............................141

43   Tariff Grid for the Bangalore Water Supply and Sewerage Board 141

44   Tariff for Wastewater for the Bangalore Water Supply and Sewerage Board 142

45   Tariff Grid for Wastewater for the Bangalore Water Supply and Sewerage Board 142

46   Typical Risk Allocation Matrix for Variants of Public–Private Partnership Projects
in the Water and Wastewater Sectors in India 143

47   Capital Expenditure Plan for the Information and Communication Technology Sector
in India 150

48   Number of Information and Communication Technology Projects...........................153

49   Typical Risk Allocation for Public–Private Partnership Projects in the Information
and Communication Technology Sector (Build-Own-Operate-Transfer Model) 154

50   Year-on-Year Capital Expenditure Plan for the Social Infrastructure Sector,
Based on the National Infrastructure Pipeline 162

51   Number of Social Infrastructure Projects Across Public–Private Partnership Variants..........164

52   Number of Social Infrastructure Projects Based on Subsectors 165

53   Applicable Regulations for the Municipal Solid Waste Sector in India 168

54   Key Entities Responsible for the Municipal Solid Waste Sector in India.......................169

55   Number of Municipal Solid Waste Projects Across Public–Private Partnership Variants........173

56   Risk Allocation Matrix for Variants of Public–Private Partnerships
in the Municipal Solid Waste Sector..175

57   Structure and Financial Profile of India's Subnational Governments...........................177

58   Revenues of Urban Local Bodies in India 182

59   Expenditures of Urban Local Bodies in India...183

60   Select Case of Municipal Bond Issues in India 184

61   Salient Features of the Concession Structure 192

62   Construction of Sewage Treatment Plants in Mathura—Project Status
Based on June 2023 Monthly Progress Report...193

A2.1 India Basic Country Profile 198

A2.2 Scores on Doing Business in India, by Categories and Subcategories 199

Figures

1   Public–Private Partnership Projects Financially Closed and Cancelled, 1990–2022 4

2   Status of Public–Private Partnership Across Sectors, 1990–2022................................5

3   Investments in Public–Private Partnerships by Sector, 1990–2022 5

4   Various Modes of Procuring Public–Private Partnership Projects, 1990–2022....................6

5   Public–Private Partnership Projects Under Conceptualization and Development,
2020–2022...6

6   Public–Private Partnership Projects with Government Support, 1990–2022 7

7   Payment Mechanisms for Public–Private Partnership Projects, 1990–2022 7

8   Foreign Sponsor Participation, 1990–2022...8

9   Investment Estimates for FY2020–FY2025,
Based on the National Infrastructure Pipeline 59

10   Sector-wise Breakdown of Investments Proposed
Under the National Infrastructure Pipeline, 2020–2025..60

11   Public–Private Partnership Road Projects Under Conceptualization and Development 69

12   Modes of Procurement for Public–Private Partnership Road Projects...........................70

13   Public–Private Partnership Road Projects Reaching Financial Close 71

14   Public–Private Partnership Road Projects with Foreign Sponsor Participation...................71

15   Government Support to Public–Private Partnership Road Projects 72

16   Payment Mechanisms for Public–Private Partnership Road Projects............................72

17   Public–Private Partnership Railways Projects Under Conceptualization and Development......85

18   Modes of Procurement for Public–Private Partnership Railway Projects 86

19   Public–Private Partnership Railway Projects Reaching Financial Close..........................86

20   Public–Private Partnership Railway Projects with Foreign Sponsor Participation 87

21   Government Support to Public–Private Partnership Railway Projects........................... 87

22   Payment Mechanisms for Public–Private Partnership Railway Projects 88

23   Public–Private Partnership Port Projects Under Conceptualization and Development 96

24   Modes of Procurement for Public–Private Partnership Port Projects........................... 97

25   Public–Private Partnership Port Projects Reaching Financial Close 97

26   Public–Private Partnership Port Projects with Foreign Sponsor Participation.................... 98

27   Government Support to Public–Private Partnership Port Projects 98

28   Payment Mechanisms for Public–Private Partnership Port Projects............................. 99

29   Public–Private Partnership Airport Projects Under Conceptualization and Development 107

30   Modes of Procurement for Public–Private Partnership Airport Projects.......................107

31   Public–Private Partnership Airport Projects Reaching Financial Close 108

32   Public–Private Partnership Airport Projects with Foreign Sponsor Participation................108

33   Government Support to Public–Private Partnership Airport Projects 109

34   Payment Mechanisms for Public–Private Partnership Airport Projects.........................109

35   Public–Private Partnership Energy Projects Under Conceptualization
     and Development...121

36   Modes of Procurement for Independent Power Producers, Public–Private Partnership
     Energy Projects 122

37   Independent Power Producers, Public–Private Partnership Energy Projects Reaching
     Financial Close..122

38   Independent Power Producers, Public–Private Partnership Energy Projects
     with Foreign Sponsor Participation 123

39   Government Support to Independent Power Producers, Public–Private Partnership
     Energy Projects 123

40   Payment Mechanisms for Independent Power Producers, Public–Private Partnership
     Energy Projects 124

41   Public–Private Partnership Water and Wastewater Projects Under Conceptualization
     and Development...135

42   Modes of Procurement for Public–Private Partnership Water and Wastewater Projects........136

43   Public–Private Partnership Water and Wastewater Projects Reaching Financial Close 136

44   Public–Private Partnership Water and Wastewater Projects
     with Foreign Sponsor Participation 137

45   Government Support for Public–Private Partnership Water and Wastewater Projects 137

46   Payment Mechanisms for Public–Private Partnership Water and Wastewater Projects.........138

47   Public–Private Partnership Information and Communication Technology Projects
     Under Conceptualization and Development..150

48   Modes of Procurement for Public–Private Partnership Information
      and Communication Technology Projects 151

49   Public–Private Partnership Information and Communication Technology Projects Reaching
      Financial Close..151

50   Public–Private Partnership Information and Communication Technology Projects
      with Foreign Sponsor Participation 152

51   Payment Mechanisms for Public–Private Partnership Information
      and Communication Technology Projects 152

52   Public–Private Partnership Social Infrastructure Projects Under Conceptualization
      and Development...163

53   Public–Private Partnership Municipal Solid Waste Projects Under Conceptualization
      and Development 170

54   Modes of Procurement for Public–Private Partnership Municipal Solid Waste Projects 171

55   Public–Private Partnership Municipal Solid Waste Projects Reaching Financial Close..........171

56   Public–Private Partnership Municipal Solid Waste Projects
      with Foreign Sponsor Participation 172

57   Government Support to Public–Private Partnership Municipal Solid Waste Projects...........172

58   Payment Mechanisms for Public–Private Partnership Municipal Solid Waste Projects 173

59   Local Government Structure in India...179

60   Hybrid Annuity Model Public–Private Partnership and Financing Mode
      for the Construction of Sewage Treatment Plant in Mathura.................................192

A2.1 Rankings on Doing Business in India by Categories, 2020...................................198

A2.2 Scoring on Doing Business in India by Categories, 2020 198

Foreword

The *Public–Private Partnership Monitor (PPP Monitor),* a key publication of the Asian Development Bank (ADB), presents a detailed review of the current state of public–private partnership (PPP) enabling environment for select countries.

Availability of adequate infrastructure is a measure of a country's ability to sustain its economic growth. For economies across Asia and the Pacific, provision of basic infrastructure services, including water, health, energy, transportation, and communications, is an important role for the public sector. As demand for infrastructure has increased faster than government budgets, the public sector has increasingly considered partnership with the private sector as an alternate modality for financing infrastructure.

ADB estimates that Asia and the Pacific must spend $1.7 trillion a year on infrastructure until 2030 to maintain growth, meet social needs, and address the effects of climate change. That amount is expected to go up. The traditional sources of finance for infrastructure—the government's budgetary allocations—have not been enough to meet such demand. Prior to the coronavirus disease (COVID-19) pandemic, ADB estimated an annual infrastructure gap of $204 billion to be filled through private sector investment. That amount is also now expected to have increased with the fiscal constraints as well as additional needs that have become evident in the social infrastructure.

For the private sector, investment in infrastructure, whether through PPPs or otherwise, represents an investment avenue competing with various other investment options available. To compete and crowd in private capital into infrastructure, governments need to provide a conducive environment to adequately establish and protect the rights of the private sector, and the necessary support to ensure every asset brought into the market provides returns that are commensurate with the risks.

The PPP Monitor provides the investment community with analysis of the enabling environment, policies, priority sectors, and deals to facilitate informed investment decisions. For ADB developing member countries (DMCs), the PPP Monitor serves as a diagnostic tool to identify gaps in their legal, regulatory, and institutional framework. ADB and other international development agencies can also benefit from the PPP Monitor as it could be useful in initiating dialogues to assess a country's readiness to tap PPPs to develop and sustain its infrastructure as well as to develop its private sector.

Building on the success of the previous PPP Monitor editions, the new PPP Monitor has been published online to widen its reach. More country reports and updates will be continually added. The PPP Monitor features an interactive online version, allowing users to compare the key PPP parameters and features across DMCs. The online version of the PPP Monitor may be accessed at http://www.pppmonitor.adb.org.

The PPP Monitor has been upgraded to provide a one-stop information source derived from a consolidation of (i) the previous PPP Monitor; (ii) leading PPP databases of multilateral development banks, such as the World Bank and the International Finance Corporation, and organizations like the Economist Intelligence Unit (Infrascope) and the Global Infrastructure Hub (InfraCompass); (iii) reports of a country's PPP unit; (iv) a country's legal framework; and (v) consultations with leading technical experts and legal firms as well as financial institutions.

The PPP Monitor includes more than 500 qualitative and quantitative indicators to profile the national PPP environment, the sector-specific PPP landscape (for eight identified infrastructure sectors), and the PPP landscape for local government projects. The COVID-19 pandemic has pushed social infrastructure into the forefront of policy and planning; hence, where possible, this PPP Monitor takes a bigger focus on social and municipal aspects like health, education, and affordable housing.

The PPP market environment in most ADB DMCs is still emerging or developing. To accelerate infrastructure development, continuous regulatory reforms and institutional strengthening are required to facilitate further private sector investment in infrastructure and to create a sustainable pipeline of bankable projects. Through the PPP Monitor, ADB provides the analytical basis for DMCs in addressing various infrastructure and PPP-related challenges, in developing sustainable infrastructure projects, and in delivering efficient and effective public services through PPPs. ADB also supports DMCs in improving their investment climates, formulating sound market regulations, and building robust legal and institutional frameworks to encourage private sector participation in infrastructure through technical assistance, project development, advisory services, policy support, and investments.

We hope that this PPP Monitor will pave the way for continued dialogue between the public and private sectors and stimulate the adoption of PPPs in Asia and the Pacific, with the end goal of closing the gaps in the infrastructure sector.

F. Cleo Kawawaki
Head, Office of Markets Development and Public–Private Partnership
Asian Development Bank

Acknowledgments

The *Public–Private Partnership Monitor—India* was prepared by the Asian Development Bank (ADB) Office of Markets Development and Public–Private Partnership (OMDP), in close coordination with the India Resident Mission.

A team of markets development advisory specialists from the OMDP led the effort, refining and streamlining the analytical framework to capture the national, subnational, and sector public–private partnership (PPP)-related landscape presented in this document. Contributions and review by the India Resident Mission and the Infrastructure Finance Secretariat (IFS) of the Department of Economic Affairs in the Ministry of Finance were instrumental in the quality control of this document.

The PPP Monitor uses the data published by the governments of ADB's developing member countries (i.e., official websites, reports, publications, laws, and regulations); the data published by other multilateral development agencies; and the data derived from industry publications and databases such as those of the World Bank, European Bank for Reconstruction and Development, Organisation for Economic Co-operation and Development, World Economic Forum, International Monetary Fund, Inframation Group, IJGlobal, Economist Intelligence Unit (Infrascope Index), Global Infrastructure Hub, TheGlobalEconomy.com, Bloomberg, S&P Global, Trading Economics, and the PPP Knowledge Lab.

ADB partnered with Shivanshu Chauhan (a partner at PwC India), leveraging his extensive knowledge of the Indian PPP market and incorporating his insights into the development of the PPP Monitor for India.

Definition of Terms

Term	Definition
Public–private partnership (PPP)	Contractual arrangement between public (national, state, provincial, or local) and private entities through which the skills, assets, and/or financial resources of each of the public and private sectors are allocated in a complementary manner, thereby sharing the risks and rewards, to seek to provide optimal service delivery and good value to citizens. In a PPP, the public sector retains the ultimate responsibility for service delivery, although the private sector provides the service for an extended time. Within Asian Development Bank operations, all contracts such as performance-based contracts (management and service contracts), lease–operate–transfer, build–own–operate–transfer, design–build–finance–operate, variants, and concessions are considered as various forms of PPP. Excluded are • contracts involving turnkey design and construction as part of public procurement (engineering, procurement, and construction contracts); • simple service contracts that are not linked to performance standards (those that are more aligned with outsourcing to private contractor staff to operate public assets); • construction contracts with extended warranties and/or maintenance provisions of, for example, up to 5 years post completion (wherein performance risk-sharing is minimal as the assets are new and need only basic maintenance); and • all privatization and divestures.
Affermage or lease contracts	Under a lease contract, the private sector developer is responsible for the service in its entirety and undertakes obligations relating to quality and service standards. Except for new and replacement investments, which remain the responsibility of the government contracting agency, the operator provides the service at their expense and risk. The duration of the leasing contract is typically 10 years and may be renewed up to 20 years. Responsibility for service provision is transferred from the public sector to the private sector, and the financial risk for operation and maintenance is borne entirely by the private sector operator. In particular, the operator is responsible for losses and for unpaid consumers' debts. Leases do not involve any sale of assets to the private sector.
Availability- or performance-based payments	Method of investment recovery in PPP projects, when payments to the private party are made by the government contracting agency over the lifetime of a PPP contract in return for making infrastructure or services available for use at acceptable and contractually agreed performance standards.

continued on next page

Table *continued*

Term	Definition
Best and final offer	An incentive mechanism provided by the government contracting agency to the private sector developer initiating a PPP project through the unsolicited proposal route (USP proponent) to be automatically shortlisted for the final bidding round and provide its best and final offer to match other bidders' best offer.
Build–lease–transfer	A PPP type whereby a private sector developer is authorized to finance and construct an infrastructure or development facility, and upon its completion hands it over to the government contracting agency on a lease arrangement for a fixed period, after which ownership of the facility is automatically transferred to the government contracting agency.
Build–operate– transfer (BOT)	BOT and similar arrangements are a specialized concession in which a private firm or consortium finances and develops a new infrastructure project or a major component according to performance standards set by the government. Under BOTs, the private sector developer provides the capital required to build a new facility. Importantly, the private operator now owns the assets for a period set by contract—sufficient to give the developer time to recover investment costs through user charges.
Build–own–operate	A PPP type whereby a private sector developer is authorized to finance, construct, own, operate, and maintain an infrastructure or development facility from which the private sector developer is allowed to recover its total investment, operating and maintenance costs plus a reasonable return thereon by collecting tolls, fees, rentals, or other charges from facility users. Under this PPP type, the private sector developer, which owns the assets of the facility, may assign its operation and maintenance to a facility operator.
Build–transfer	A PPP type under which the private sector developer undertakes the financing and construction of a given infrastructure or development facility and, after its completion, hands it over to the government contracting agency, which pays the private sector developer, on an agreed schedule, its total investments expended on the project, plus a reasonable rate of return thereon. This arrangement may be employed in the construction of any infrastructure or development project, including critical facilities that, for security or strategic reasons, must be operated directly by the government contracting agency.
Commercial close	Indicates the signing of the PPP contract between the government contracting agency and the identified private sector developer. Usually occurs after the terms and conditions of the draft PPP contract are negotiated and agreed between the government contracting agency and the identified private sector developer.
Competitive bidding	A process under which the bidders submit information detailing their qualifications and detailed technical and financial proposals, which are evaluated according to defined criteria—often in a multistage process—to select a preferred bidder. Competitive bidding may also include competitive negotiations and license schemes.
Concession	A PPP type that makes the concessionaire (established by the selected private sector developer) responsible for the full delivery of services in a specified area, including operation, maintenance, collection, management, and construction and rehabilitation of the system. Importantly, the private sector developer is responsible for all capital investment. Although the concessionaire is responsible for providing the assets, such assets are publicly owned even during the concession period. The public sector is responsible for establishing performance standards and ensuring that the concessionaire meets them. In essence, the public sector's role shifts from being the service provider to regulating the price and quality of service.

continued on next page

Table *continued*

Term	Definition
Currency conversion swap fee	A premium paid by the borrower to settle on a swap, in which the parties sell currencies to each other subject to an agreement to repurchase the same currency in the same amount, at the same exchange rate, and on a fixed date in the future.
Direct agreement	An agreement normally made between the concessionaire (established by the private sector developer), the government contracting agency, and the lenders. The agreement usually gives the lenders step-in rights to take over the operation of the key PPP contracts.
Direct government support	Direct government support are government liabilities that directly cover project costs, either in cash or in-kind, and are certain to occur. Direct government support can also be classified as follows: • Capital subsidy: These are cash subsidies for capital investments of the project, that is, to cover the costs of the physical assets during construction. • Revenue subsidy: These are cash subsidies for revenue support, that is, to help the private party recoup its investment during the operational phase of the project.
Direct negotiations	A type of PPP procurement under which the PPP contract is awarded on the basis of a direct agreement with a private sector developer without going through the competitive bidding process.
Dispute resolution	A process to resolve any dispute between the government contracting agency and the private sector developer as agreed in the PPP contract. The possible dispute resolution mechanisms in a PPP contract could include resolution through • discussion between both parties, • dispute resolution board, • expert determination, • mediation or conciliation, or • arbitration.
Environmental impact assessment	A process of evaluating the likely environmental impacts of a proposed project or development, taking into account interrelated socioeconomic, cultural, and human health impacts, both beneficial and adverse.
Feed-in tariff	A policy mechanism designed to accelerate investment in renewable energy technologies by offering long-term purchase agreements for the sale of renewable energy electricity.
Financial close	An event whereby (i) a legally binding commitment of equity holders and/or debt financiers exists to provide or mobilize funding for the full cost of the project, and (ii) the conditions for funding have been met and the first tranche of funding has been mobilized. If this information is not available, construction start date is used as an estimated financial close date.
Financial equilibrium	A mechanism in a PPP agreement for dealing with changes—when such changes in specified conditions and circumstances trigger compensating changes to the terms of the agreement. Some civil law jurisdictions emphasize economic or financial equilibrium provisions that entitle a partner to changes in the key financial terms of the contract to compensate for certain types of exogenous events that may otherwise impact returns. The partner is protected as the economic balance of the contract must be maintained and adequate compensation must be paid for the damages suffered. Unexpected changes that merit financial equilibrium may arise from force majeure (major disasters or civil disturbances), government action, and unforeseen changes in economic conditions.

continued on next page

Table *continued*

Term	Definition
Force majeure	An event that is practically beyond the reasonable control of the affected party, as a result of which, such party's performance of its obligations under the PPP contract is prevented or rendered impossible. Force majeure events may include • war, civil war, armed conflict or terrorism; • nuclear, chemical, or biological contamination, unless the source or the cause of the contamination is the result of the actions of or breach by the concessionaire or its subcontractors; • pressure waves caused by devices travelling at supersonic speeds, which directly causes either party (the "affected party") to be unable to comply with all or a material part of its obligations under the contract; or • any other similar events that are beyond the reasonable control of the affected party and that prevent or render impossible the performance by such party of its obligations under the PPP contract.
Government contracting agency	The ministry, department, or agency that enters into a PPP contract with the private sector and is responsible for ensuring that the relevant public assets or services are provided.
Government guarantee	Agreements under which the government agrees to bear some or all risks of a PPP project. It is a secondary obligation, which legally binds the government to take on an obligation if a specified event occurs. A government guarantee constitutes a contingent liability for which there is uncertainty about whether the government may be required to make payments, and if so, how much and when it will be required to pay. In practice, government guarantees are used when debt providers are unwilling to lend to a private party in a PPP because of concerns over credit risk and potential loan losses. Government guarantees can also be used to benefit equity investors in a PPP company when they require protection against the investment risks they bear.
Government pay (Offtake)	Represents the payment made by the government contracting agency to the concessionaire (established by the private sector developer) for the infrastructure assets provided and services delivered through a PPP project and is also referred to as availability of payments defined above. These payments could be • usage-based—for example, shadow tolls or output-based subsidies; • based on availability—that is, conditional on the availability of an asset or service to the specified quality; and • upfront subsidies based on achieving certain agreed milestones.
Gross-cost contract	A type of PPP contract arrangement in the railway sector under which all revenues (from fares and other sources) are transferred to the government contracting agency, and the risks absorbed by the developer are confined to those associated with the cost of operations.
Hybrid arrangement	A method of investment recovery in PPP projects when payments to the private party are made as a combination of user charges and availability payments over the lifetime of a PPP contract, in return for making infrastructure or services available for use at acceptable and contractually agreed performance standards.
Independent power producer (IPP) scheme	A scheme whereby a producer of electrical energy, which is not a public utility, makes electric energy available for sale to utilities or the general public. A scheme whereby a producer of electrical energy, which is a private entity, owns and/or operates facilities to generate electricity and then sells it to a utility, central government buyer, or end users. The IPP invests in generation technologies and recovers its cost from the sale of the electricity.

continued on next page

Table *continued*

Term	Definition
Indirect government support	Indirect government support are either contingent liabilities (liabilities that may not actually occur as they are contingent on a predetermined event) or government policies that support investment. The categories under indirect government support are as follows: • Payment guarantee: This is when a government agrees to fulfill the obligations of a purchaser (typically a state-owned enterprise) of the infrastructure good in the case of nonperformance by the purchaser. The most common example of this is when a government guarantees the fixed payment of an offtake agreement (e.g., power purchase agreement, water purchase agreement) between a private entity and a state-owned enterprise. • Debt guarantee: This is when a government secures the borrowings of a private entity, that is, a government guarantees repayment to creditors in the case of a default by a private entity. • Revenue guarantee: This is when a government sets a minimum income for the private operator. Typically this income is from user fee payments by end-use customers. This form of guarantee is most common in roads with minimum traffic or revenue set by a government. • Exchange rate guarantee: This is when a government protects a private entity from fluctuations in the value of the local currency. For example, the government will agree to reimburse the private entity for losses on debt services if the value of the local currency dips by, for example, 20% or greater. • Construction cost guarantee: This is when a government protects a private entity from potential cost overruns in the construction phase of a project. • Interest rate guarantee: This is when a government protects a private entity from fluctuations in interest rates. Basically, this is the same concept as an exchange rate guarantee with respect to local interest rates. • Tariff rate guarantee: This is when a government guarantees a minimum tariff level for the project. • Tax deduction or government credit: This is when a government provides a tax incentive or government credit to encourage infrastructure development in a specific sector (often in renewables); however, this is only considered government support if it is specific to the project or type of project. General corporate tax incentives, for example, are not considered government support.
Institutional arbitration	An arbitration process in which a specialized institution intervenes and takes on the role of administering the arbitration process between the government contracting agency and the private sector developer for a PPP-project-related dispute. This institution would have its own set of rules, which would provide a framework for the arbitration, and its own form of administration to assist in the process.
Interest rate swap fee	A premium paid by the borrower for a hedging contract to convert a floating interest rate into a fixed rate. The two parties agree to exchange interest rate payments based on a notional principal amount, with typically one paying a fixed rate and the other generally paying a floating rate.
Joint venture	An alternative to full privatization in which the infrastructure is co-owned and operated by the public sector and private operators. Under a joint venture, the public and private sector partners can either form a new company or assume joint ownership of an existing company through a sale of shares to one or several private investors. The company may also be listed on the stock exchange.
Lender's step-in rights	Lender's rights in project-financed arrangements to "step in" to the project company's position in the contract to take control of the infrastructure project where the project company is not performing.

continued on next page

Table *continued*

Term	Definition
Management contract	A PPP type that expands the services to be contracted out and includes some or all of the management and operation of the public service (i.e., utility, hospital, port authority). Although the ultimate obligation for service provision remains in the public sector, daily management control and authority are assigned to the private partner or contractor. In most cases, the private partner provides working capital, but there is no financing for investment.
Material adverse government action	An action by the government that directly and materially affects the private party of a PPP project in performing its obligations under a relevant PPP contract, which would reasonably be expected to result in a material adverse effect.
Net-cost contract	A type of PPP contract arrangement in the railway sector under which all revenues (from fares and other sources) are retained by the developer, and traffic and revenue risks are absorbed either fully or based on a contractually agreed portion.
Nominal interest rate	An interest rate applicable to a borrowing before taking inflation adjustment into account. In certain cases, nominal interest rate also refers to the advertised or stated interest rate on a borrowing, without taking into account any fees or compounding of interest. Nominal interest rate = Real interest rate + Inflation rate
Nonrecourse or limited recourse project financing	The financing of the development or exploitation of a right, natural resource, or other assets where the bulk of the financing is to be provided by way of debt and is to be repaid principally out of the assets being financed and their revenues.
Output-based aid (OBA)	Development aid strategies that link the delivery of public services in developing countries to targeted performance-related subsidies. OBA provides a way in which international financial institutions can directly structure their financing to benefit poor people, even when the service provider is a private company. OBA is the use of explicit, performance-based subsidies funded by the donor agencies to complement or replace user fees. It involves contracting out of basic service provision to a third party—such as private companies, nongovernment organizations, community-based organizations, and even public service providers—with subsidy payment tied to the delivery of specified outputs. This means that targeted and valuable subsidies to disadvantaged populations are funded through donor funds. The private partner, on the other hand, can only recover this funding by achieving specific performance outcomes.
Project bond financing	An alternative source of financing infrastructure project by placing bonds.
Project development	Indicates the stage of the PPP project life cycle including PPP project identification, preparation, structuring, and procurement up to commercial close between the government contracting agency and the private sector developer.
Project development fund (PDF)	A fund dedicated to reimbursing the cost of feasibility studies, transaction advisers, and other costs of project development to encourage contracting agencies to use high-quality transaction advisers and best practice. PDFs provide the specialized resources needed to conduct studies, design and structure a PPP, and procure the PPP.
Real interest rate	The real interest rate is the interest rate applicable to a borrowing that takes inflation rate into account. Real interest rate = Nominal interest rate – Inflation rate

continued on next page

Table *continued*

Term	Definition
Regulatory framework	A framework encompassing all laws, regulations, policies, binding guidelines or instructions, other legal texts of general application, judicial decisions, and administrative rulings governing or setting precedent in connection with PPPs. In this context, the term "policies" refers to other government- issued documents, which are binding on all stakeholders, are enforced in a manner similar to laws and regulations, and provide detailed instructions for implementing PPPs.
Rehabilitate–operate–transfer	A PPP type whereby an existing facility is handed over to the private sector developer to refurbish, operate, and maintain for a franchise period, at the expiry of which the legal title to the facility is turned over to the government contracting agency.
Risk allocation matrix	Matrix indicating the allocation of the consequences of each risk to one of the parties in the PPP contract, or agreeing to deal with the risk through a specified mechanism, which may involve sharing the risk.
Service contract	A PPP type under which the government contracting agency hires a private company or entity to carry out one or more specified tasks or services for a period, typically 1–3 years. The government contracting agency remains the primary provider of the infrastructure service and contracts out only portions of its operation to the private partner. The private partner must perform the service at the agreed cost and must typically meet performance standards set by the government contracting agency. Government contracting agencies generally use competitive bidding procedures to award service contracts, which tend to work well given the limited period and narrowly defined nature of these contracts.
Social impact assessment	Includes the processes of analyzing, monitoring, and managing the intended and unintended social consequences—both positive and negative—of planned interventions (policies, programs, plans, projects) and any social change processes invoked by those interventions. Its primary purpose is to bring about a more sustainable and equitable biophysical and human environment.
Social infrastructure	Covers social services, including hospitals, schools and universities, prisons, housing, and courts.
State-owned enterprise	A company or enterprise owned by the government or in which the government has a controlling stake.
Swiss challenge	A process in public procurement when a government contracting agency that has received an unsolicited bid for a project publishes details of the bid and invites third parties to match or exceed it.
Tax holiday	A government incentive program that offers tax reduction or elimination to projects and/or businesses. In the context of a PPP project, tax holidays are provided to exempt the concessionaire from making any tax payments during the initial demand ramp-up period to make the project financially viable.
Unsolicited bid	A proposal made by a private party to undertake a PPP project. It is submitted at the initiative of the private party, rather than in response to a request from the government contracting agency.
User charges	A method of investment recovery in PPP projects when payments to the private party are fully derived from tariffs paid by users or offtakers over the lifetime of a PPP contract, in return for making infrastructure or services available for use at acceptable and contractually agreed performance standards.
Viability gap fund	A scheme wherein projects with low financial viability are given grants (or other financial support from the government) up to a stipulated percentage of the project cost, making them financially viable as PPPs.

Abbreviations

AAI	Airports Authority of India
AMRUT	Atal Mission for Rejuvenation and Urban Transformation
BOT	build–operate–transfer
BRTS	bus rapid transit system
COD	commercial operation date
DBFOT	design–build–finance–operate–transfer
DEA	Department of Economic Affairs
EIA	environmental impact assessment
EPC	engineering, procurement, and construction
FDI	foreign direct investment
FY	fiscal year
GDP	gross domestic product
GST	goods and services tax
HAM	hybrid annuity model
ICA	Indian Council of Arbitration
ICT	information and communication technology
IDF	infrastructure debt funds
IFS	Infrastructure Finance Secretariat
IHSDP	Integrated Housing and Slum Development Program
IIPDF	India Infrastructure Project Development Fund
InvIT	infrastructure investment trust
IRCTC	Indian Railways Catering and Tourism Corporation
IT	information technology
ITMS	Intelligent Transit Management System
IWAI	Inland Waterways Authority of India
JNNURM	Jawaharlal Nehru National Urban Renewal Mission
MCA	model concession agreement
MNRE	Ministry of New and Renewable Energy

MOF	Ministry of Finance
MOHUA	Ministry of Housing and Urban Affairs
MORTH	Ministry of Road Transport and Highways
MSW	municipal solid waste
MSWM	municipal solid waste management
NBFC	nonbanking financial company
NHAI	National Highways Authority of India
NHDP	National Highways Development Project
NHIDCL	National Highways and Infrastructure Development Corporation Limited
NIP	National Infrastructure Pipeline
NMCG	National Mission for Clean Ganga
NMP	National Monetization Pipeline
NRP	National Rail Plan
O&M	operation and maintenance
PACM	post-award contract management
PMU	project monitoring unit
PPA	power purchase agreement
PPI	Private Participation in Infrastructure
PPP	public–private partnership
PPPAC	Public Private Partnership Appraisal Committee
PRU	performance review unit
ROB	road over bridge
RUB	road under bridge
SERC	state electricity regulatory commission
SMC	Surat Municipal Corporation
SPV	special purpose vehicle
STP	sewage treatment plant
TAMP	Tariff Authority for Major Ports
TOD	transit-oriented development
TOT	toll-operate-transfer
TRAI	Telecom Regulatory Authority of India
TTO	Telecommunication Tariff Order
UDD	Urban Development Department
ULB	urban local body
VGF	viability gap funding

Weights and Measures

GW	gigawatt
km	kilometer
LPCD	liter per capita per day
Mbps	megabit per second
MLD	million liters per day

Currency Equivalents

(As of 3 July 2023)

Currency Unit	–	Indian rupees (₹)
$1.00	–	₹81.980
₹1.00	–	$0.012

Guide to Understanding the Public–Private Partnership Monitor

The *Public–Private Partnership Monitor* (PPP Monitor), a key publication of the Asian Development Bank (ADB), profiles the current state of the public–private partnership (PPP) enabling environment in ADB's developing member countries (DMCs) in Asia and the Pacific. The PPP Monitor features, for the first time, a data-driven, interactive online version that allows users to compare and contrast the key PPP parameters and features across the featured DMCs. While the featured countries are a small sample, more countries will be continually added in the PPP Monitor, which is expected to become a knowledge base for assessing a country's PPP environment for the government and the business community. The new PPP Monitor builds on the success of the first and second editions of the PPP Monitor.

The PPP Monitor provides a snapshot of the overall PPP landscape in the country. This downloadable guide also assesses more than 500 qualitative and quantitative indicators that have been structured per topic—the national PPP landscape, the sector-specific PPP landscape (for eight identified infrastructure sectors and a separate section for other sectors), and the PPP landscape for local government projects. The PPP Monitor also captures the critical macroeconomic and infrastructure sector indicators (including the Ease of Doing Business scores) from globally accepted sources.

Each of the topics and associated subtopics presented below are characterized by qualitative and quantitative indicators. Qualitative indicators take the form of a question to which "Yes," "No," "Not Applicable," or "Unavailable" answers can be given. Quantitative indicators are represented in the form of numbers, ratios, investment value, and duration.

For each of the DMCs covered, the information and data are organized along the following topic clusters:

Overview

Topic	Subtopics
Overview	• Overview of the public–private partnership (PPP) legal and regulatory framework • Number of PPP projects reaching financial close from 1990 to end of 2022 across sectors • Total investment made in PPPs from 1990 to 2022 across sectors • Features of past PPP projects including the number of PPPs procured through various modes • Number of PPP projects under conceptualization and development • Number of PPP projects supported by government • Payment mechanism for PPPs • Foreign sponsor participation in PPPs from 1990 to 2022 • Major sponsors active in the infrastructure sector in the country • Challenges associated with the PPP landscape in the country

National Public–Private Partnership Landscape Indicators

Topic	Subtopics
National public–private partnership (PPP) legal and regulatory framework	Details on the legal and regulatory framework applicable to PPPs and its evolution since the introduction of PPPs in the country Details on other supporting laws and regulations governing PPPs in the country
PPP types	Details on the PPP types allowed to be used in accordance with PPP legal and regulatory framework In case the PPP legal and regulatory framework does not specify the PPP types, this section provides the details on the specific PPP types, which have been adopted for various PPP projects at various stages of the PPP life cycle.
Eligible sectors	Details on various infrastructure sectors for which projects could be procured through the PPP route in accordance with the PPP legal and regulatory framework
PPP institutional framework	Details on the PPP institutional framework including the availability of a PPP unit; the functions of the PPP unit; the principal public entities associated with PPPs and their respective functions; and the details of the public entities responsible for PPP project identification, appraisal, approval, oversight, and monitoring
Entities responsible for PPP project identification, approval, and oversight	
Entities responsible for PPP project monitoring	
The PPP process	Details on the various stages of the PPP process including PPP project identification, preparation, structuring, procurement, and management, in accordance with the PPP legal and regulatory framework of the country
PPP standard operating procedures, tool kits, templates, and model bid documents	Details on the standard operating procedures and standard templates or model bidding documents available for PPPs (if any) Details on the key clauses in a PPP agreement based on the review of select PPP agreements already executed, and/or the review of the PPP legal and regulatory framework
Lender's security rights	Rights of lenders including the charge of project assets
Termination and compensation	Definition on whether the private player is eligible for compensation in case of PPP project termination due to various reasons
Unsolicited PPP proposals	Details on possibility of submission of unsolicited PPP proposals and their treatment, including potential advantages provided to the unsolicited PPP proposal proponent at the PPP procurement stage
Foreign investor participation restrictions	Definition on whether there are any statutory restrictions on foreign equity investments and ownership in PPP projects
Dispute resolution	Definition of the dispute resolution process and the mechanisms available in the country
Environmental and social issues	Details on whether the legal and regulatory framework governing PPPs stipulates a mechanism for managing the environmental and social impact of a PPP project, including the potential environmental and social issues, which could be caused by a PPP project

continued on next page

Table *continued*

Topic	Subtopics
Land rights	Definition of the various mechanisms through which landownership and/or land use rights could be provided to the private partner with respect to the project site for a PPP project Details on land records and registration, which could be provided to the private partner
Government financial support for PPP projects	Details on the various mechanisms of government financial support available to make PPP projects financially viable Salient features of government financial support mechanisms available
Project development funding support	Details on the various sources through which funding could be availed for the development activities (preparation, structuring, and procurement) of a PPP project Details on stages of the PPP project development during which such funding could be availed and utilized, including payments to transaction advisors
PPP project statistics	Details on key PPP statistics in the country such as the availability of (i) a PPP database showing distribution of PPP projects across sectors and across various stages of the PPP life cycle, and (ii) a national PPP project pipeline and its alignment with the National Infrastructure Pipeline for the country
Sources of PPP financing	Details on the sources of financing for PPP projects in the country Details on typical key financing terms for various sources of financing, banks active in project finance for the last 24 months, active PPP project sponsors in the country for the last 24 months, availability of derivatives market, and availability of credit rating agencies in the country

Sector-Specific Public–Private Partnership Landscape Indicators

To profile the sector-specific PPP landscape, the indicators are grouped into five major categories: (i) sector-specific PPP contracting agencies, (ii) sector laws and regulations, (iii) sector master plan (including sector-specific PPP pipeline), (iv) features of the past PPP projects in the sector, and (v) sector-specific challenges for PPPs. The sectors, which do not appear consistently across the featured countries, are covered under the "Other Sectors" category in the sector-specific PPP landscape.

Topic	Subtopics
Contracting agencies in the sector	Details on which government agencies could act as the contracting agencies for a public–private partnership (PPP) project
Sector laws and regulations	Details on the applicable sector laws and regulations for PPP projects, including the sector regulators and their respective functions
Foreign investment restrictions in the sector	Details on the maximum allowed foreign equity investment in greenfield PPP projects in the sector

continued on next page

Table *continued*

Topic	Subtopics
Standard contracts in the sector	Specification on whether standard contracts are available for PPP projects in the sector
Sector master plan	Details on the master plan and/or road map adopted for infrastructure development in the sector by the national government and the corresponding line ministry Details on the pipeline of PPP projects for the sector aligned with this sector master plan and/or road map Details on the PPP projects under conceptualization and development in the sector
Features of past PPP projects	Features of the past PPP projects based on supporting indicators in terms of the number and value (where applicable) of PPP projects for each supporting indicator
Tariffs applicable to the sector	Details on the indicative tariffs applicable in the sector based on the examples of select PPP or other projects operational in the sector
Typical risk allocation for PPP projects in the sector	Details on the typical risk allocation between the government contracting agency and the private partner based on examples of select PPP projects that have achieved commercial close
Financing details of PPP projects in the sector	Typical financing details based on past PPP projects on the lines of the supporting indicators
Challenges associated with PPPs in the sector	Details on the PPP-related and sector-specific challenges faced by PPP projects in the sector
Typical sector-specific infrastructure indicators for the country	Details on select sector-specific infrastructure indicators for the country

Local Government Public–Private Partnership Landscape

To profile the PPP landscape for local government projects, the indicators are grouped into seven major categories: (i) local governance system, (ii) infrastructure development plans for local governments, (iii) sectors in which local governments can implement PPPs, (iv) revenue sources for local governments, (v) borrowings by local governments, (vi) budgetary allocation to local governments, and (vii) credit rating of local governments.

Topic	Subtopics
Key indicators related to local governments in the country	Details on the local governments using select key indicators: (i) the number and levels of local governments, (ii) the typical expenditure profile and heads, (iii) the typical revenue profile and heads, (iv) the typical debt profile and heads, and (v) grants and transfers from the higher levels of government
Local governance system	Details on the local governance system in the country, including the various levels of local governments; their roles, responsibilities, and functions; and the devolution of powers from the higher levels of government to the various levels of local governments

continued on next page

Table *continued*

Topic	Subtopics
Infrastructure development plan for local governments	Details on the infrastructure development plans prepared by the local governments based on their capital investment projects in the pipeline, and the coverage of such infrastructure development plans
Public–private partnership (PPP) enabling framework for local governments	Details on the PPP enabling framework applicable to local government PPP projects, including PPP legal and regulatory framework, PPP policy framework, and PPP institutional framework
Eligible sectors for PPPs for local governments	Details on the eligible sectors in which PPPs could be undertaken by the local government as government contracting agency
Revenues for local governments	Details on the typical sources of revenue for local governments
Borrowings by local governments	Details on the typical sources of debt financing available for local governments, the purpose for which borrowed funds could be used, the terms of such borrowings, and the borrowing exposure of select local governments
Budgetary allocation to local governments	Details on the budgetary allocations and transfers to the local governments from the higher levels of government
Credit rating of local governments	Details on the precedence of local governments being rated by credit rating agencies in the country, and the details of credit ratings obtained by select local governments in the past
Case study on a local government PPP	A case of a PPP project undertaken by a local government in the past covering details on project background, project assets, PPP structure for the project, risk allocation among the parties for the project, project finance and project revenue details, and key learnings from the PPP project

Critical Macroeconomic and Infrastructure Sector Indicators

This section captures the critical macroeconomic and infrastructure sector indicators (including the Ease of Doing Business scores) from globally accepted sources.

Topic	Subtopics
Critical macroeconomic and infrastructure sector indicators	Details of the select key macroeconomic and infrastructure indicators for the country
Ease of Doing Business	Details on the various Ease of Doing Business parameters for the country based on the World Bank's *Ease of Doing Business* publication

Time Periods

The research was carried out in 2023 with the aim of reflecting the status as of the end of 2022. Therefore, some indicator data may have changed between the said period and the publication date of this report.

In country-level and sector-level sections, quantitative data in relation to the number of projects reflect the cumulative number of projects over the periods 1990–2020, 1990–2021, and 1990–2022. Otherwise, the data represent the status at each individual year.

I. Overview

India's economy has greatly benefited from the infrastructure sector, which has been a crucial driver. Realizing the importance of private investments in India's infrastructure growth, the country has systematically rolled out a public–private partnership (PPP) program to deliver high-priority public utilities and infrastructure. By the turn of the last decade, the scale and diversity of India's PPP program have expanded significantly. According to the Economist Intelligence Unit's 2018 Infrascope report, among the 19 Asian countries ranked, India ranked first in overall investment and business climate and second in terms of financing environment. The country ranked third in institutional maturity, and third overall in having an ideal environment for PPP projects.[1]

Trends in Infrastructure Investment in India

The infrastructure of an economy plays a crucial role in driving its advancement and laying the foundation for future development opportunities. Infrastructure investment in India during fiscal year (FY) 2013 to FY2019 is estimated at ₹56.48 trillion ($688 billion).[2] India's infrastructure investment for FY2022–FY2023 was about ₹7.5 trillion ($91.48 billion) and is expected to be ₹10 trillion ($121.98 billion) for FY2024.

The National Infrastructure Pipeline (NIP) was launched with the projected infrastructure investment of ₹111 trillion ($1.35 trillion) during the period 2020–2025, with the majority of projects in the sectors like energy, roads, urban infrastructure, and railways.[3] It is jointly funded by the central government, the state governments, and the private sector. The central (39%) and state (40%) governments have nearly equal contribution, while the private sector has a 21% share.

According to the 2023 Infrastructure Yearbook of CRISIL Limited (formerly Credit Rating Information Services of India Limited), India will spend nearly ₹143 trillion on infrastructure over 2024–2030, more than twice the estimated ₹67 trillion spent over 2017–2023. Of the total, about ₹36.6 trillion will be green investments, marking a rise of five times compared with FY2017 through FY2023. It also

---

[1]   Economist Intelligence Unit. 2018. *Infrascope—India Country Report.*
[2]   Government of India, Ministry of Finance (MOF), Department of Economic Affairs (DEA). 2019. *National Infrastructure Pipeline.* Volume 1.
[3]   Government of India, MOF, Press Information Bureau. 2021. A Strong V-Shaped Recovery of Economic Activity. *Press release. 29 January.*

highlights that traditional sectors like roads and power are anticipated to sustain their significant roles, with emerging sectors like electric vehicles, solar, wind, and hydrogen poised to gain momentum. Table 1 provides an estimate of infrastructure investments lined up until 2030.[4]

Table 1: Estimated Total Investments for the Infrastructure Sector
(₹ trillion)

	2017–2023	2024–2030
Core infrastructure	50.4	96.8
Roads	18.3	37.3
Railways	12.4	25.6
Urban infrastructure	8.6	18.9
Other infrastructure	11.1	15.0

Source: CRISIL. 2023. India's Infrastructure Spending to Double to ₹143 trillion between Fiscals 2024 and 2030, Compared with 2017-2023. Press release. 17 October.

However, achieving this goal requires substantial investments in infrastructure and the involvement of multiple stakeholders for the overall growth of the society. In recent years, PPPs have been an important source of investment in the infrastructure sector in India. According to the World Bank's Private Participation in Infrastructure (PPI) 2023 Half Year report, India ranked fourth in total investments made by the private sector in infrastructure sector. Much of this could be attributed to various initiatives taken by the Government of India.

Additionally, efforts are being made to improve the infrastructure development trajectory in India. In national highways, a step-up in public outlays as a response has helped increase the pace of construction. In June 2022, the Minister of Road Transport and Highways opened 15 national highway projects worth ₹135.85 billion ($1.7 billion) in Patna and Hajipur, Bihar. The proactive policy efforts have also largely contributed to unclogging stalled projects. Recalibrated PPP models, including the hybrid annuity model (HAM) and toll–operate–transfer (TOT), have since helped crowd-in private investments. Similarly, in renewable energy, supported by largely favorable government policies and market conditions, an 18-gigawatt (GW) capacity was added in 2018 alone, notwithstanding recent headwinds. The Union Minister for New and Renewable Energy and Power has informed that the installed renewable energy capacity in India has increased from 115.94 GW in March 2018 to 172.00 GW in March 2023 (i.e., an increase of about 1.48 times). According to the Central Electricity Authority, 365.60 billion units of electricity had been generated over 2022–2023 from renewable energy sources across the country. Globally, India has the fourth-largest installed capacity of renewable energy, according to the *Renewable Energy Statistics 2023* released by the International Renewable Energy Agency.[5]

---

[4]   CRISIL. 2023. India's Infrastructure Spending to Double to ₹143 trillion between Fiscals 2024 and 2030, Compared with 2017-2023. Press release. 17 October.

[5]   International Renewable Energy Agency. 2023. *Renewable Energy Statistics 2023.* July.

The Electricity Act introduced the franchisee model, which allowed for private sector participation in the distribution of electricity in specified areas, leading to an increase in PPPs in the power distribution sector. While the port sector has witnessed active private participation since the 1990s, the airport sector saw a strong interest in the recent decade. Through several initiatives such as Housing for All and Smart Cities, the government has been working on reducing the bottlenecks that impede growth in the urban and social infrastructure sectors.

The NITI Aayog launched the National Monetization Pipeline (NMP) comprising potential brownfield infrastructure assets. The monetization of operating public infrastructure assets has now been recognized as a key financing option for new infrastructure construction. The total value to be unlocked from the NMP is about ₹6,000 billion ($73.2 billion) for core assets of the central government. The Ministry of Finance (MOF) proposes to create an asset monetization dashboard to track progress and provide visibility to investors. Some important measures for monetization are as follows:

- The National Highways Authority of (NHAI) and the Power Grid Corporation of India Limited have each sponsored one Infrastructure Investment Trust (InvIT) to attract international and domestic institutional investors. Five operational roads, with an estimated enterprise value of ₹50 billion, are being transferred to the InvIT promoted by the National Highways Authority of India. Similarly, transmission assets valued at ₹70 billion will be transferred to the InvIT promoted by the Power Grid Corporation of India Limited.
- In October 2022, the National Highways Infra Trust (NHAI InvIT), an infrastructure investment trust sponsored by the NHAI to support the Government of India's NMP, had raised the sum of ₹14.30 billion ($174.5 million) from domestic and international investors through the placement of its units, to partially fund the acquisition of three additional road projects from NHAI.
- Railways will monetize Dedicated Freight Corridor assets for operation and maintenance (O&M), after commissioning.
- Based on the NMP, 25 airports managed by the Airports Authority of India (AAI) have been earmarked for asset monetization over 2022–2025: Agartala, Amritsar, Bhopal, Bhubaneswar, Calicut, Chennai, Coimbatore, Dehradun, Hubli, Imphal, Indore, Jodhpur, Madurai, Nagpur, Patna, Raipur, Rajahmundry Ranchi, Surat, Tirupati, Trichy, Udaipur, Vadodara, Varanasi, and Vijayawada.[6]
- Other core infrastructure assets that are being rolled out under the asset monetization programme are the following: (i) NHAI operational toll roads; (ii) transmission assets of the Power Grid Corporation of India Limited; (iii) oil and gas pipelines of GAIL (India) Limited, Indian Oil Corporation Limited, and Hindustan Petroleum Corporation Limited; (iv) AAI airports in Tier II and III cities; (v) other railway infrastructure assets; (vi) warehousing assets of central public sector enterprises such as the Central Warehousing Corporation and the National Agricultural Cooperative Marketing Federation of India Limited (NAFED); and (vii) sports stadiums.[7]

---

[6] Government of India, Ministry of Civil Aviation, Press Information Bureau. 2021. 25 AAI Airports Earmarked for Asset Monetization under National Monetization Pipeline; AAI Has Identified 13 Airports for Operations, Management and Development of the Airports through PPP Mode. Press release. 9 December.

[7] Government of India, MOF, Press Information Bureau. 2021. Launch of National Monetization Pipeline for Monetizing Operating Public Infrastructure Assets. Press release. 1 February.

From 1990 to 2022, a total of 1,265 PPP projects for different sectors—such as airports, collection and transport, electricity, information and communication technology (ICT), integrated municipal solid waste, natural gas, ports, railways, roads, treatment or disposal, water, and sewage—achieved financial close.[8] The total investment made in these projects was about $295.56 billion (₹24.23 trillion). During this period, about 3% of the total number of projects (amounting to 5% of the total investment) were cancelled. The road and energy sectors have been the most active, accounting for more than 84% of the total number of projects that achieved financial close. Energy takes up the highest share of total investments in such projects, followed by roads, airports, ports, railways, ICT, and water and wastewater. Figure 1 depicts the number of PPP projects that achieved financial close, while Figure 2 presents the status of projects across various sectors.

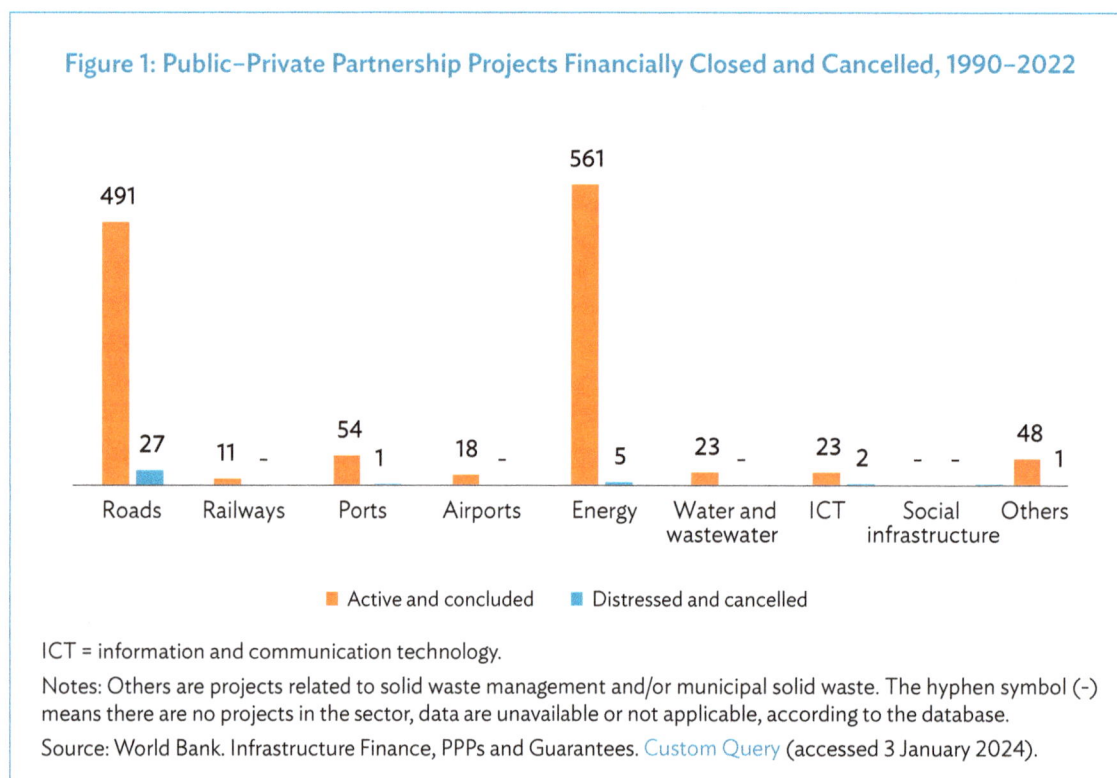

Figure 1: Public–Private Partnership Projects Financially Closed and Cancelled, 1990–2022

ICT = information and communication technology.
Notes: Others are projects related to solid waste management and/or municipal solid waste. The hyphen symbol (-) means there are no projects in the sector, data are unavailable or not applicable, according to the database.
Source: World Bank. Infrastructure Finance, PPPs and Guarantees. Custom Query (accessed 3 January 2024).

The average size of a project that achieved financial close in the airport sector was highest at $816 million (₹66.90 billion), followed by the railways sector at $723 million (₹59.27 billion). Across the sectors, the average size of a project reaching financial close was $302.62 million (₹24.81 billion). Figure 3 shows the total investment in each sector from 1990 to 2022, and the average size of a PPP project in each of the sectors.

---

8   World Bank. Infrastructure Finance, PPPs and Guarantees. Custom Query (accessed 3 January 2024).

Figure 2: Status of Public–Private Partnership Across Sectors, 1990–2022

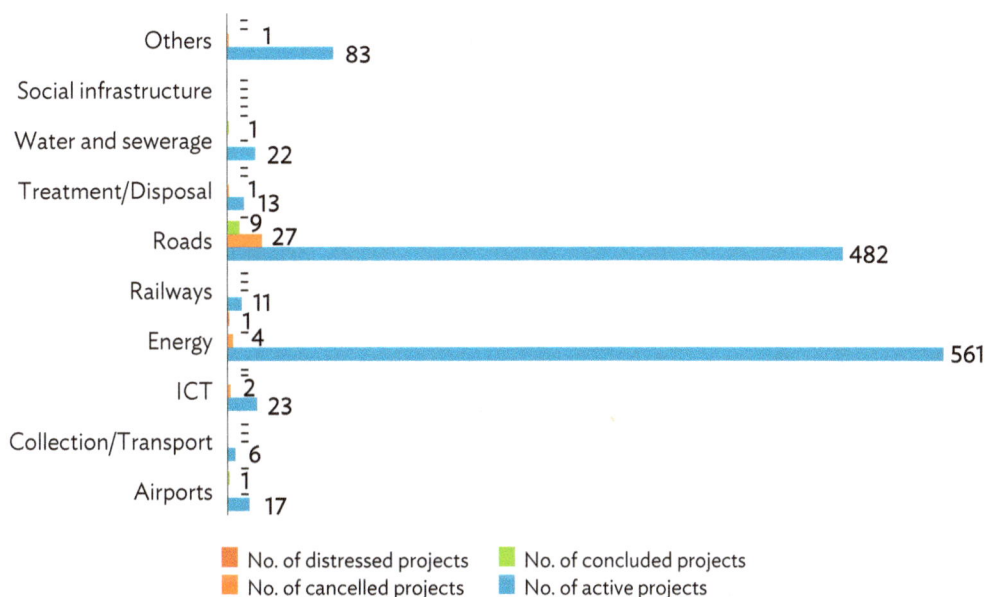

- Others: 1, 83
- Social infrastructure
- Water and sewerage: 1, 22
- Treatment/Disposal: 1, 13
- Roads: 9, 27, 482
- Railways: 11
- Energy: 1, 4, 561
- ICT: 2, 23
- Collection/Transport: 6
- Airports: 1, 17

■ No. of distressed projects   ■ No. of concluded projects
■ No. of cancelled projects   ■ No. of active projects

ICT = information and communication technology.
Notes: Others are projects related to solid waste management and/or municipal solid waste. The hyphen symbol (-) means there are no projects in the sector, data are unavailable or not applicable, according to the database.
Source: World Bank. Infrastructure Finance, PPPs and Guarantees. Custom Query (accessed 3 January 2024).

Figure 3: Investments in Public–Private Partnerships by Sector, 1990–2022
($ million)

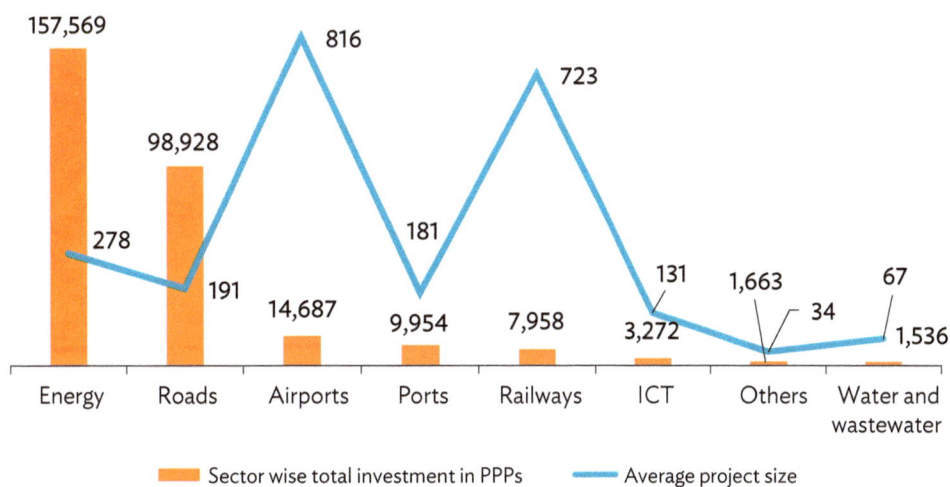

- Energy: 157,569 / 278
- Roads: 98,928 / 191
- Airports: 14,687 / 816
- Ports: 9,954 / 181
- Railways: 7,958 / 723
- ICT: 3,272 / 131
- Others: 1,663 / 34
- Water and wastewater: 1,536 / 67

■ Sector wise total investment in PPPs   — Average project size

ICT = information and communication technology, PPP = public–private partnership.
Note: Others are projects related to solid waste management and/or municipal solid waste.
Source: World Bank. Infrastructure Finance, PPPs and Guarantees. Custom Query (accessed 3 January 2024).

From 1990 to 2022, a total of 200 projects were procured through direct appointment, and 767 projects by way of competitive bidding process, across various infrastructure sectors. Information on 281 projects was unavailable. Figure 4 indicates the number of projects that were procured through different modes.

PPP projects at various stages under conceptualization and development across various infrastructure sectors for 2020–2022 are shown in Figure 5.

Figure 4: Various Modes of Procuring Public–Private Partnership Projects, 1990–2022

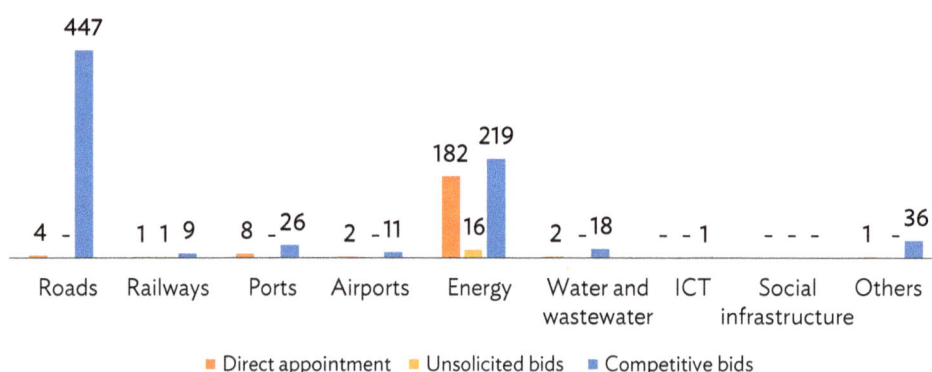

- Direct appointment
- Unsolicited bids
- Competitive bids

ICT = information and communication technology.

Notes: Others are projects related to solid waste management and/or municipal solid waste. The hyphen symbol (-) means there are no projects in the sector, data are unavailable or not applicable, according to the database.

Source: World Bank. Infrastructure Finance, PPPs and Guarantees. Custom Query (accessed 3 January 2024).

Figure 5: Public–Private Partnership Projects Under Conceptualization and Development, 2020–2022

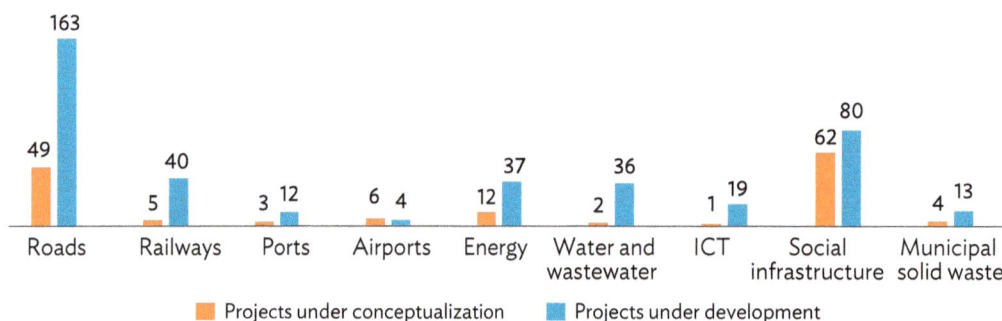

- Projects under conceptualization
- Projects under development

ICT = information and communication technology.

Notes: Projects under preparation and procurement have been extracted from the website of India Investment Grid. Projects in the exhibit include projects under the National Infrastructure Pipeline (NIP) and non-NIP. The NIP is a live and updated repository of infrastructure projects that provides attractive investment opportunities in projects. The non-NIP includes additional project opportunities collated by India Infrastructure Grid.

Source: Government of India, Ministry of Commerce and Industry, Department for Promotion of Industry and Internal Trade, India Investment Grid. Projects under NIP and Non-NIP (accessed 15 July 2023).

From 1990 to 2022, a total of 367 projects received support in the form of viability gap funding from the government and 89 projects received government guarantees. Figure 6 presents the number of projects that received government support across various sectors.

In terms of funding mechanism or payment mechanism, during the same period, 368 projects were awarded on user-charges basis, while 189 projects were on government pay (offtake). Figure 7 shows, by sector, the number of projects under each payment mechanism.

Figure 6: Public–Private Partnership Projects with Government Support, 1990–2022

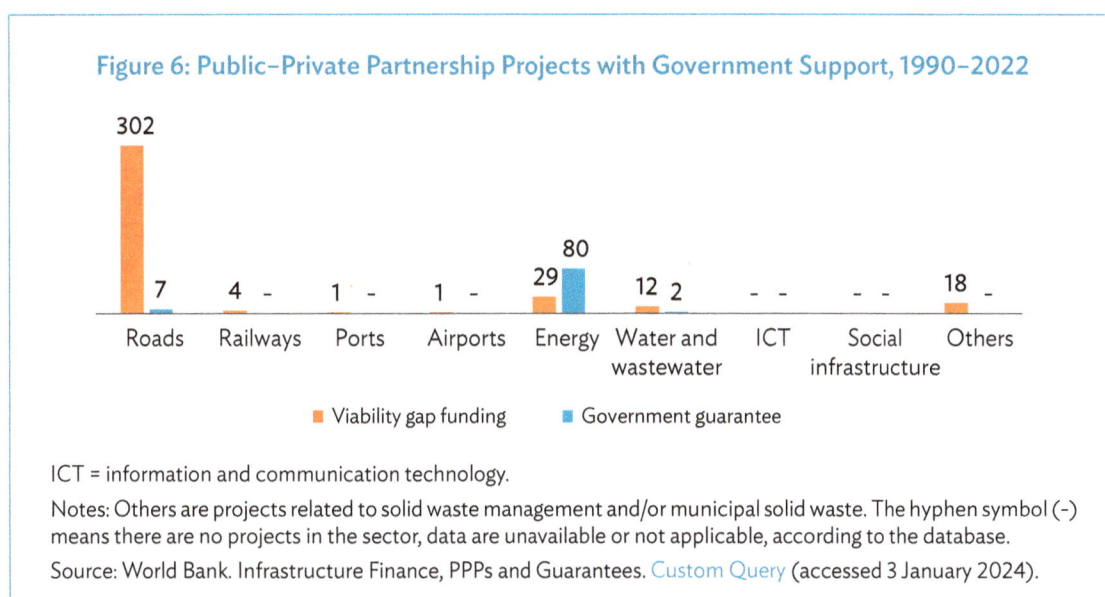

ICT = information and communication technology.

Notes: Others are projects related to solid waste management and/or municipal solid waste. The hyphen symbol (-) means there are no projects in the sector, data are unavailable or not applicable, according to the database.

Source: World Bank. Infrastructure Finance, PPPs and Guarantees. Custom Query (accessed 3 January 2024).

Figure 7: Payment Mechanisms for Public–Private Partnership Projects, 1990–2022

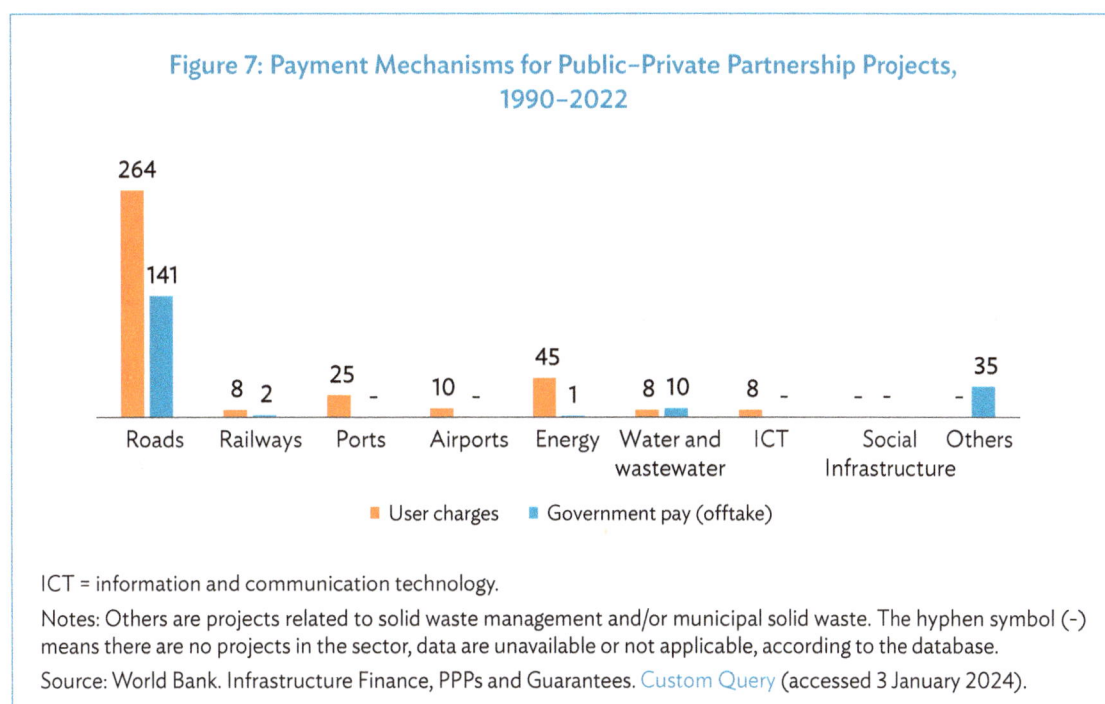

ICT = information and communication technology.

Notes: Others are projects related to solid waste management and/or municipal solid waste. The hyphen symbol (-) means there are no projects in the sector, data are unavailable or not applicable, according to the database.

Source: World Bank. Infrastructure Finance, PPPs and Guarantees. Custom Query (accessed 3 January 2024).

Over 3 decades, India has witnessed active participation of foreign sponsors. A total of 259 projects attracted participation from foreign sponsors, with half of them in the energy sector. Information about 95 projects was either partially available or unavailable from the database. Figure 8 shows the distribution of PPP projects across various infrastructure sectors.

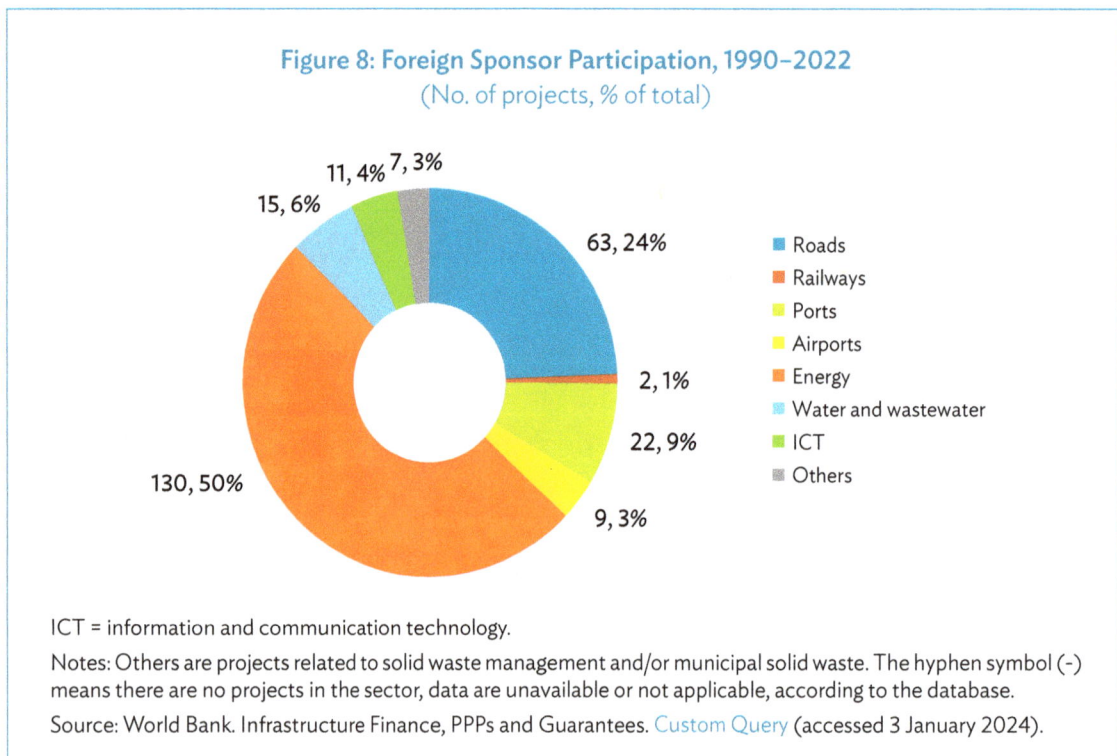

Figure 8: Foreign Sponsor Participation, 1990–2022
(No. of projects, % of total)

Legend: Roads, Railways, Ports, Airports, Energy, Water and wastewater, ICT, Others

63, 24% · 2, 1% · 22, 9% · 9, 3% · 130, 50% · 15, 6% · 11, 4% · 7, 3%

ICT = information and communication technology.
Notes: Others are projects related to solid waste management and/or municipal solid waste. The hyphen symbol (-) means there are no projects in the sector, data are unavailable or not applicable, according to the database.
Source: World Bank. Infrastructure Finance, PPPs and Guarantees. Custom Query (accessed 3 January 2024).

Recent Trends in the Public–Private Partnership Landscape

In the PPP space, India has witnessed the emergence of innovative models aimed at promoting sustainable infrastructure development while addressing a diverse array of socioeconomic challenges. One notable trend involves the integration of technology-centric collaborations, leveraging advancements in digital infrastructure to enhance efficiency and accessibility across multiple sectors. Initiatives such as the Smart Cities Mission and Digital India have catalyzed the adoption of pioneering PPP frameworks, placing a strong focus on intelligent solutions for urban development, e-governance, and digital connectivity. These collaborative efforts prioritize the creation of scalable and inclusive solutions, utilizing private sector expertise and resources to effectively meet societal needs. The growth of the PPP ecosystem in the country is further supported by frameworks that facilitate private investment in critical infrastructure projects, with the goal of optimizing risk-sharing mechanisms, attracting long-term investments, and ensuring the sustainable development of vital infrastructure. As India advances its development agenda, the ongoing evolution of PPPs plays a crucial role in fostering inclusive growth, innovation, and resilience.

Some of the areas where PPPs are emerging are as follows:

(i) **Digital agriculture.** PPPs in the field of digital agriculture establish strategic collaborations aimed at utilizing technology to transform practices within the agricultural value chain. The primary goal is to grant the government access to new technologies, expertise, and innovative ideas, while also providing the private sector with access to the Agri Stack and establishing linkages with government networks in districts and villages. Ultimately, PPPs in digital agriculture aim to modernize conventional farming methods, champion sustainability, minimize environmental impact, and enhance agricultural output to meet the continually growing global demand for food.

(ii) **Urban mobility.** In an effort to meet the increasing mobility demands of the expanding urban population and facilitate the transition from private to public transportation, PPPs play a crucial role in urban passenger rail projects and bus rapid transit systems, and in enhancing last-mile connectivity. These partnerships are instrumental in improving productivity and contributing to the overall social welfare by addressing the evolving transportation needs of urban dwellers.

(iii) **Monetization public–private partnerships.** The NITI Aayog, Government of India has launched the NMP to monetize asset rights, ensure stable revenue streams from brownfield development across existing infrastructure in the country, and develop structured partnerships under defined contractual frameworks with strict key performance indicators and performance standards. PPPs are expected to play a significant role in implementing this strategy.

(iv) **Transit-oriented development.** The transit-oriented development (TOD) through PPP in India has gained momentum with the introduction of a new TOD policy. The TOD policy provides a regulatory framework and incentives to facilitate private investment in TOD projects, seeking to address challenges associated with urbanization, congestion, and environmental sustainability. The TOD policy in India emphasizes mixed-use developments, integrating residential, commercial, and recreational spaces near public transportation hubs. By fostering such synergies, the policy aims to enhance connectivity; reduce traffic congestion; and create livable, pedestrian-friendly environments. As India experiences rapid urbanization, TOD through PPP emerges as a crucial strategy to address the growing demand for efficient and accessible urban spaces, fostering economic growth while prioritizing environmentally conscious and inclusive development.

Way Forward

As India's economy continues to grow rapidly, there is a need for robust physical and social infrastructure to support its development. With a population expected to reach 1.52 billion by 2036, and 70% of them residing in urban areas, there are opportunities to enhance infrastructure services to meet the evolving needs of its dynamic population.[9] To achieve the $5 trillion gross domestic product (GDP) by FY2025, India needs to spend $1.4 trillion on infrastructure, according to an economic survey.[10] It is estimated that India needs to invest $840 billion over the next 15 years into urban infrastructure to meet the needs

9 Government of India, Ministry of Health and Family Welfare, National Commission on Population. 2020. *Population Projections for India and States 2011–2036.* Census of India 2011.
10 *The Economic* Times. 2022. To Achieve $5 Trillion GDP by FY25, India Needs to Spend about $1.4 Trillion on Infra: Eco Survey. 31 January.

of its fast-growing population.[11] Scaling up investment in infrastructure, enhancing allocative efficiency of productive inputs like water, making cities more livable, and stemming the long-term effects of climate change are urgent imperatives for India.

Infrastructure investments in India have shown steady growth. For instance, India is expected to spend nearly ₹143 trillion on infrastructure over FY2024 to FY2030, more than twice the ₹67 trillion spent over FY2017 to FY2023.

The infrastructure sector has become the biggest focus area for the Government of India. India plans to spend $1.4 trillion (₹114.8 trillion) on infrastructure during 2019–2023. The government has proposed an investment of ₹50 trillion ($610 billion) for railways infrastructure over 2018–2030.[12] Several other government initiatives like PM Gati Shakti, National Logistics Policy (NLP), the National Infrastructure Pipeline (NIP), and NMP will help India achieve its economic growth target of $5 trillion by 2025.

The PM Gati Shakti program, launched by the Government of India with an outlay of ₹100 trillion in 2021, aimed at improving infrastructure development and enhancing the efficiency of transportation and logistics networks in the country. It focuses on integrated and multimodal connectivity to boost economic growth and sustainable development driven by seven engines—roads, railways, ports, airports, waterways, mass transport, and logistics infrastructure. These engines are further supported by the complementary roles of energy transmission, ICT, bulk water and sewerage, and social infrastructure.

Also, to complement the PM Gakti Shakti plan, the NLP was launched on 17 September 2022 to drive economic growth and business competitiveness of the country through an integrated, seamless, efficient, reliable, green, sustainable, and cost-effective logistics network by leveraging best in class technology, processes, and skilled labor. This will reduce logistics costs and improve performance. The targets of the NLP are to (i) reduce cost of logistics in India, (ii) improve the Logistics Performance Index ranking (target is to be among the top 25 countries by 2030), and (iii) create data-driven decision support mechanism for an efficient logistics ecosystem. To achieve these targets, the Comprehensive Logistics Action Plan was launched.

Given India's significant infrastructure financing requirements, there is an emphasis on enhancing investments by proactively addressing upstream policy or structural considerations and establishing alternative nonbank financing mechanisms. It presents an opportunity to overcome both financial and nonfinancial barriers to commercial infrastructure financing, paving the way for financing solutions that effectively leverage limited public funding to accelerate the provision of high-quality infrastructure. Additionally, exploring local-level financing and balance street strengthening present promising avenues for further advancement.

---

[11]   World Bank. 2022. India's Urban Infrastructure Needs to Cross $840 Billion Over Next 15 Years: New World Bank Report. Press release. 14 November.
[12]   India Brand Equity Foundation. Infrastructure Sector in India.

II. National Public–Private Partnership Landscape

India's approach to PPPs is decentralized, reflecting diverse frameworks across states. At the central level, the Government of India has developed guidelines, policies, and manuals to promote standardization and best practices in PPP development and implementation. For instance, the *Guidelines for Formulation, Appraisal, and Approval of Central Sector Public–Private Partnership Projects* offer comprehensive guidance for central projects.[13] Additionally, various central regulations, such as the viability gap funding (VGF) guidelines, harmonized list of infrastructure subsectors, the model concession agreements, and the Public Private Partnership Appraisal Committee (PPPAC), contribute to providing a central framework for PPP projects. The PPPAC especially contributes to the standardization of frameworks. Additionally, the Infrastructure Finance Secretariat (IFS) serves as a central institution overseeing the PPP initiatives.

The government has taken measures to strengthen the PPP framework by formulating new innovative PPP models, such as the hybrid annuity model (HAM) and the toll–operate–transfer (TOT) model, to revive the interest of private entities and financial institutions in PPP projects. Additionally, the use of innovative finance mechanisms, such as the VGF, in the development of silos in the food and agriculture sector[14] and in medical colleges and hospitals in the healthcare sector[15] have supported projects that are economically justified but fell just short of financial viability.

National Public–Private Partnership Enabling Framework

1. Public–Private Partnership Legal and Regulatory Framework

Parameter	
Does the country have a national public–private partnership (PPP) law and PPP regulations?	
• Public financial management laws and regulations?	✓
• Sector-specific laws and regulations?	✓
• Procurement laws and regulations?	✓
• Environmental laws and regulations?	✓
• Laws and regulations for social compliance?	✓
• Laws and regulations governing land acquisition and ownership?	✓
• Taxation laws and regulations?	✓
• Employment laws and regulations?	✓
• Licensing requirements?	✓
What are the other components of the PPP legal and regulatory framework?	NA

✓ = Yes, ✗ = No, NA = Not Applicable, UA = Unavailable.

---

[13] Asian Development Bank (ADB). 2019. *Public–Private Partnership Monitor.* Second Edition.
[14] Government of India, MOF, DEA. Viability Gap Funding Scheme. Silos Sector.
[15] Government of India, MOF, DEA. Viability Gap Funding Scheme. Healthcare Sector.

The Government of India has also taken a series of measures to improve the PPP environment in the country:

* Set up in 2006, the India Infrastructure Finance Company Limited provides long-term debt for financing infrastructure projects.
* In 2007–2008, the India Infrastructure Project Development Fund (IIPDF) was created to help finance the cost incurred for developing PPP projects, particularly the costs of transaction advisors. IIPDF supports up to 75% of the project development expenses.
* The Ministry of Finance (MOF) centralizes the coordination of PPPs through the Infrastructure Finance Secretariat of the Department of Economic Affairs (DEA). In 2011, the DEA published guidelines for the formulation and approval of PPP projects. This was part of an endeavor to streamline PPP procedures and strengthen the regulatory framework at the national level to expedite PPP projects' approval. The PPPAC is responsible for PPP project appraisal at the central level.
* The government also created a VGF scheme for PPP projects to help promote the sustainability of infrastructure projects. This scheme provides financial support (grants) to infrastructure projects, normally in the form of a capital grant at the stage of project construction (up to 20% of the total project cost supplemented by another 20% by the respective state governments or statutory authorities).
* A dedicated website managed by the Private Investment Unit (formerly PPP Cell) under the DEA, www.pppinindia.gov.in, provides inventory of all PPP projects including a repertoire of concession agreements signed for the projects.
* To aid ministries in project preparation and decision-making, the government has issued a series of guidance notes and PPP tool kits, which provide sector-specific guidelines for five sectors: state highways, water and sanitation, ports, solid waste management, and urban transport.
* Standardized model bidding documents, such as request for qualification, request for proposal, and model concession agreements for different sectors, have been developed.
* Post-award contract management (PACM) manuals have been made available by the DEA to guide the delivery of PPP projects. The manuals are available for highways, ports, and school sectors.
* In 2015, to further improve private sector participation in the road sector, the government launched HAM primarily to safeguard developers and lenders from the risks or challenges posed by conventional models such as the design–build–finance–operate–transfer (DBFOT) and build–operate–transfer (BOT) models (footnote 13).
* In 2016, the government issued the *PPP Guide for Practitioners* to assist practitioners in managing PPP projects throughout the project life cycle.
* On 21 September 2017, the government announced a new PPP policy to promote private investments in affordable housing. The policy allows central assistance of up to ₹250,000 per house to be built by private builders on private land. It further provides eight PPP options for the private sector to invest in affordable housing sector.
* Apart from HAM, the government has also introduced the TOT model in the road sector, and programs such as the Sagarmala Program for port-led development, the Station Redevelopment Program in the railway sector, and the Regional Connectivity Scheme in the civil aviation sector, to attract private investments (footnote 13).
* In November 2020, the Cabinet Committee on Economic Affairs approved the continuation and revamping of the Scheme for Financial Support to Public–Private Partnerships in Infrastructure (VGF scheme) until 2024–2025, with a total outlay of ₹81 billion ($0.99 billion).

The VGF scheme provides financial support in the form of grants, one-time or deferred, to infrastructure projects undertaken through PPPs with a view to make them commercially viable.

- The DEA has empaneled 12 transaction advisors for PPP projects in the country to support the project sponsoring authorities during the transaction of PPP projects. In July 2022, the DEA published a transaction advisors' manual to be used by the project sponsoring authorities. The manual is a step-by-step guide that project sponsoring authorities can refer to while onboarding a transaction advisor from the DEA's empaneled transaction advisors for their PPP projects.
- The DEA released an updated harmonized list of infrastructure subsectors in October 2022. "Data centers" were categorized under "Communication" and "energy storage systems" under "Energy." The list was originally published in 2009 and has seen several additions of subsectors from time to time.
- In November 2022, the DEA restructured the existing IIPDF as a central sector scheme with a total outlay of ₹1,500 million ($18.3 million) for a period of 3 years, from 2022–2023 to 2024–2025.
- In June 2023, the government also issued a reference guide for setting up state PPP units and a guide for PPP project appraisal.
- In September 2023, the IFS published the Waterfall Framework, which seeks to aid Project Sponsoring Authorities in developing successful infrastructure projects through selecting the appropriate PPP implementation mode.[16]

PPP procurement is governed by a combination of the Constitution of India and certain rules, procedures, and manuals as follows:

- General Financial Rules, 2017;
- Delegation of Financial Powers Rules, 1978;
- Manual for Procurement of Goods, 2017;
- The Central Vigilance Commission Guidelines include guidelines on prequalification criteria, increasing transparency in the procurement process, and integrity pact between the procurer and the prospective bidders.
- The Comptroller and Auditor General, the supreme audit institution in India, has issued the *PPP in Infrastructure Projects, Public Auditing Guidelines, Comptroller and Auditor General of India, 2009* to provide guidance on the auditing processes related to PPP projects in the country (footnote 13).
- The DEA is in the process of preparing a procurement manual that aims to bring together at one place the step-by-step procedures for undertaking PPPs. This manual for procurement embodies the best practices for PPP procurement and aims to provide a guiding document for PPP procurement.

---

[16] Government of India, MOF, DEA, Infrastructure Finance Secretariat. 2023. *Reference Guide for Project Implementation Mode Selection–Waterfall Framework*.

The detailed guidelines for appraisal and/or approval of PPP projects at the central government level, published by the DEA, are as follows:

- Procedure for approval of PPP projects and guidelines for formulation, appraisal, and approval of PPP projects at central level (notification dated 12 January 2006, and further revised, consolidated, and notified in 2013);[17]
- Guidelines for formulation, appraisal, and approval of PPP projects costing less than ₹1,000 million ($13.70 million);
- Guidelines for formulation, appraisal, and approval of PPP projects (i) of all sectors costing more than ₹1,000 million ($13.70 million) and less than ₹2,500 million ($34.24 million), and (ii) under the National Highways Development Project (NHDP) costing more than ₹2,500 million ($34.24 million) and less than ₹5,000 million ($68.48 million); and
- Reference guide for PPP project appraisal dated 14 June 2023 for undertaking systematic due diligence and appraisal of PPP projects.[18]

The procedures defined in the above guidelines are not binding, but the intention is for them to be observed by all central sector projects. These guidelines apply to all PPP projects sponsored by central government ministries or central public sector undertakings, statutory authorities, or other entities under their administrative control.

State-Specific Public–Private Partnership Policies

Many states have specific PPP legislation. Certain states have developed specific legal frameworks to enable PPPs in infrastructure wherein there are dedicated legal PPP instruments (e.g., Andhra Pradesh, Bihar, Gujarat, and Punjab). Few states have specific policy frameworks for private sector participation in infrastructure (e.g., Assam, Karnataka, Maharashtra, and Odisha). Other states, such as Madhya Pradesh, have developed a workflow for PPP project approvals, usually chaired by chief secretaries of the respective states. The Empowered Committees, entities formed specifically to streamline the approval process, typically comprise senior administrative officials. Most states in the country also have an infrastructure board or authority, while many of them also have PPP cells, including Andhra Pradesh, Madhya Pradesh, Kerala, and Punjab, among others.

The Constitution of India divides the responsibility of legislation between the National Parliament and state legislature bodies. The Indian Parliament is competent to make laws on matters listed in the Union List, which includes ports, airports, railways, national highways, inland waterways, telecommunication, oil fields, and mineral resources. The state legislatures are competent to make laws on matters listed in the state list, which includes police services, prisons and corrective facilities, regulation of local government, public health and sanitation, state highways, city roads, and water supply and irrigation (footnote 13). Table 2 shows the states that have an explicit legal framework for infrastructure, including for private investment in public infrastructure.

---

[17]   Government of India, MOF, DEA. 2013. *Appraisal and Approval Mechanisms for Central Sector PPPs.*
[18]   Government of India, MOF, DEA, Infrastructure Finance Secretariat. 2023. *Reference Guide for PPP Project Appraisal.* 14 June.

Table 2: Regulations on Public–Private Partnerships at State Level

State	Relevant Regulation
Andhra Pradesh and Telangana	The Andhra Pradesh Infrastructure Development Enabling Act, 2001
Assam	Policy on PPP, 2008
Bihar	Bihar Infrastructure Development Enabling Act, 2006
Chhattisgarh	Guidelines for Formulation, Appraisal, and Approval of PPP Projects in Chhattisgarh, 2013
Goa	The Goa Policy on PPP; Scheme for Support to PPP in Infrastructure–Goa Infrastructure Project Development Fund, 2010
Gujarat	Gujarat Infrastructure Development Act, 1999 (amended in 2006); Gujarat State Viability Gap Funding Scheme, 2007; Residential Schools of Excellence on PPP Mode, 2021
Karnataka	Guidelines for Procurement of PPP Projects through Swiss Challenge Proposals Route, 2010; Scheme and Guidelines for Financial Support to PPP Infrastructure, 2013; PPP Policy for Infrastructure Projects, 2018
Kerala	Draft Policy for PPP in Kerala, 2014; Kerala Industrial and Commercial Policy (Draft), 2022
Madhya Pradesh	Scheme and Guidelines for Madhya Pradesh Project Development Fund, 2009; Guidelines for PPP Projects, 2009
Maharashtra	Maharashtra State Industrial Cluster Development Programme, 2023
Odisha	The Orissa PPP Policy, 2007
Punjab	The Punjab Infrastructure Development and Regulation Act, 2002; Punjab Infrastructure Development Board Unsolicited Projects Bye-Laws, 2008
Rajasthan	Scheme and Guidelines for Financial Support to PPPs in Infrastructure (Viability Gap Funding Scheme), 2013; Rajasthan Infrastructure Development Fund; Draft PPP Policy, 2020
Tamil Nadu	Tamil Nadu Transparency in Tenders (PPP Procurement) Rules, 2012; Tamil Nadu Infrastructure Development Act, 2012; Tamil Nadu Infrastructure Development Rules, 2012; Tamil Nadu Infrastructure Development Regulations, 2013; Directions for Implementation of Schemes through Public–Private Partnership and Cross-Subsidization via Mixed-Use/Mixed-Income Development and Framing of Detailed Scheme and Guidelines for Land Acquisition and Utilization, 2022
Uttar Pradesh	Uttar Pradesh Infrastructure and Industrial Investment Policy, 2012
Uttarakhand	Uttarakhand Infrastructure Viability Gap Funding Scheme, 2008; Uttarakhand PPP Revised Policy, 2019
West Bengal	Policy on PPP, 2012

PPP = public–private partnership.

Sources: Government of Goa, Department of Finance, Public Private Partnership Cell. 2010. Official Gazette, Government of Goa; Government of West Bengal, Finance Department, Audit Branch. 2012. Notification. No. 6523-F(H). 27 July; Asian Development Bank. 2019. Public–Private Partnership Monitor. Second Edition; Government of Uttarakhand, Uttarakhand Public Private Partnership Cell. 2019. Uttarakhand Public Private Partnership (PPP) Revised Policy, 2019; Government of Karnataka, Infrastructure Development, Ports and Inland Transport Department. Policies and Acts; Government of Rajasthan, Planning Department. 2020. Notice Inviting Public Consultation on Draft PPP Policy, 2020 for the State. Final Version of Draft PPP Policy 2020; Government of Tamil Nadu. Tamil Nadu Infrastructure Development Board; Government of Gujarat, Education Department. Residential Schools of Excellence on PPP Mode, 2021; Government of Tamil Nadu, Housing and Urban Development Department. 2022. Directions for Implementation of Schemes through Public Private Partnership and Cross-Subsidization via Mixed-Use/Mixed-Income Development and Framing of Desired Scheme and Guideline for Land Acquisition and Utilization 2022; Kerala State Industrial Development Corporation. Draft Kerala Industrial and Commercial Policy 2022; and Government of Maharashtra. 2023. Initiatives by the Directorate of Industries.

The Constitution (Seventy-Fourth Amendment) Act, 1992 has decentralized the responsibilities of urban local bodies, which include water supply, urban roads and bridges, public health and sanitation, municipal solid waste, and other public amenities (footnote 13).

Types of Public–Private Partnerships

There are no specific restrictions or exclusions on the types of PPPs that are practiced in India as long as the broad principles of PPPs are followed. The Reference Guide for PPP Project Appraisal provides a detailed write-up on the distinct PPP models (footnote 18), while the Waterfall Framework provides recommendations on the suitability of a PPP model for a particular project type or sector (footnote 16). The PPP models described below are structured on the basis of their characteristics, as well as the distribution of the cardinal risk they pose to both the Project Sponsoring Authority and the private sector participants. These models are as per the DEA booklets.

The following are some of the broad PPP models that are prevalent in project development:

(i) **Limited private sector participation**. Under the traditional public procurement model, government agencies utilize the services of the private sector for well-defined tasks with limited responsibility. These can be implemented in a short time because they are less complex. Limited private sector participation is not applicable for greenfield projects, but it is generally used for existing brownfield infrastructure assets. Three approaches for outsourcing public functions to the private sector are described below. These mechanisms present opportunities to engage the private sector in varying degrees in the maintenance, operation, and management of infrastructure improvements. This may be undertaken by the following types of structures:

(a) **Service contract.** It is a contractual arrangement between a public sector unit and a private sector entity, where public agencies can enter into service contracts with private sector companies for the completion of specific tasks. Service contracts are well-suited to operational requirements and may often focus on the procurement, operation, and maintenance of new equipment including toll collection; installation, maintenance, and reading of meters in the water sector; waste collection; or provision and maintenance of vehicles or other technical systems. Service contracts are generally awarded on a competitive basis and are extended for a relatively short duration like a few months up to a few years. In service contracts, management and investment responsibilities remain strictly with the public sector. While they offer certain benefits, service contracts cannot address underlying management or cost issues affecting poorly run organizations.

(b) **Operation and management contracts.** Public operating agencies utilize management contracts to transfer responsibility for asset operation and management to the private sector. These comprehensive agreements involve both service and management aspects and are often useful in encouraging enhanced efficiencies and technological sophistication. Operation and management contracts tend to be short term but are often extended for longer periods than service agreements. Contractors can be paid either on a fixed fee basis or on an incentive basis where they receive premiums for meeting specified service levels or performance targets. Management contracts have a broader scope involving the management of a series of facilities. In such contracts, responsibility for investment decisions remains with the public authority but some rehabilitation responsibilities can be transferred to the private partner.

(c) **Leasing.** Leases provide a means for private firms to purchase the income streams generated by publicly owned assets in exchange for an upfront payment, fixed lease payment, or revenue share, and to have the obligation to operate and maintain the assets. Lease contracts are usually of medium-term length (5–15 years) and may involve capital investment by the private partner. Lease transactions are different from operation and management contracts in that they transfer commercial risks to the private sector partner, as the lessee's ability to derive a profit is linked with its ability to reduce operating costs, while still meeting designated service levels. Leases are similar to operation and management contracts in that the responsibility for capital improvements and network expansion remains with the public sector owner. However, in certain cases, the lessor may be responsible for specified types of repairs and rehabilitation. Lease contracts are suitable for brownfield infrastructure systems that generate independent revenue streams.

(ii) **Integrated project development and operation opportunities.** Integrated partnerships involve transferring responsibility for the design, construction, and operation of a single asset or group of assets to a private sector partner. This project delivery approach is also known as turnkey procurement and BOT system. From design through operation, BOT contracts can extend for periods of up to 15–30 years. In general, BOT in India are in two modes—BOT annuity and BOT HAM. The BOT HAM model is a variation of the BOT annuity model; the only difference is that the BOT HAM model incorporates a milestone-based payment mechanism during construction.

(iii) **Build–operate–transfer.** The advantage of the BOT approach is that it combines the design, construction, and maintenance functions under a single entity. This allows the partners to become more efficient. The project design can be tailored to the construction equipment and materials to be used. In addition, the private partner is required to establish a long-term maintenance program upfront, together with estimates of the associated costs. The private partner's detailed knowledge of the project design and the materials utilized allow it to develop a tailored maintenance plan over the project life, anticipating and addressing the needs as they occur, thereby reducing the risk of more costly problems. The benefits of this life cycle costing are particularly important as infrastructure owners may spend more money on system maintenance rather than on system development. While there is potential to reap substantial rewards by utilizing the integrated BOT approach, project sponsors must take great care in specifying all standards to which they want their facilities designed, constructed, and maintained; unless needs are identified upfront as overall project specifications, they will not generally be met. It should also be noted that an integrated BOT approach alone does not relieve public sector owners of the burden of financing the related infrastructure improvements.

(iv) **Partnership project development and investment opportunities.** In this type of partnership, the private sector finances projects that would otherwise be fully financed by the public authority. These types of PPP arrangements are particularly attractive for the public authority as they afford all the implementation, operation, and maintenance efficiencies, together with the private investment. These agreements enable a private investment partner to finance, construct, and operate revenue-generating infrastructure in exchange for the right to collect the associated revenues for a specified period of time. Such partnership can be structured for the construction of a new asset or for the modernization, upgrade, or expansion of an existing facility (operation, management, and development agreement model, that is, lease with developmental rights). Concessions often extend for a period of 30 years, or even longer. Under this approach, the ownership of all assets, both existing and new, remains with the public sector (DBFOT model). However, in certain cases, ownership of the assets may be retained with the private party (design–build–finance–own–operate model). Such projects are generally awarded based on criteria such as (i) the end price offered to users (user fee or tariff), (ii) the level of financial support required from the government (VGF), (iii) upfront or recurring revenue-sharing with the government (premium), and (iv) payment by the government for providing infrastructure facilities and services (availability payment, fixed charges, etc.). Table 3 shows broad structures of PPP models with their inherent risks and responsibilities.

Table 3: Prevalent Public–Private Partnership Models

Type	Subtype	Main Activity	Ownership Risk	Design and Construction Risk	Finance Risk	Operation Risk	Indicative Concession Period (years)
Limited Private Participation	Service contract	Performing specific work assigned	Public	Public	Public	Private	A few months to a few years
	Operation and management contracts	O&M	Public	Public	Public	Private	3 to 5
	Lease	O&M	Public	Public	Shared	Private	5 to 15
Integrated Project Development and Operation Opportunities	BOT-Annuity	Build–operate–transfer	Public	Private	Public	Private	15 to 20
	BOT-HAM		Public	Private	Public	Private	15 to 20
Partnership Project Development and Investment Opportunities	OMDA	O&M plus development and expansion	Public	Shared	Shared	Private	30 to 50
	DBFOT	Design–build–finance–operate–transfer	Public	Private	Private	Private	30 to 45
	DBFOO	Design–build–finance–operate–own	Private	Private	Private	Private	30 to 45

BOT = build-operate-transfer; DBFOO = design–build- finance-operate-own; DBFOT = design–build-finance-operate –transfer; HAM = hybrid annuity model; O&M = operation and maintenance; OMDA = operation, management, and development agreement.

Source: Government of India, Ministry of Finance, Department of Economic Affairs, Infrastructure Finance Secretariat. 2023. *Reference Guide for PPP Project Appraisal.*

Eligible Sectors for Public–Private Partnership

PPPs have been employed in a wide range of infrastructure sectors and subsectors in India across the central, state, and local government levels and across various economic and social infrastructure sectors.

In 2009, the Cabinet Committee on Infrastructure prepared a harmonized master list of infrastructure of five main infrastructure sectors (transport, energy, water and sanitation, communication, and social and commercial infrastructure) and 29 infrastructure subsectors. The master list of infrastructure sectors intends to guide financing agencies in preparing short lists based on their objectives. To update the master list regularly, the government has also created an institutional mechanism comprising representatives from DEA, NITI Aayog, Department of Revenue, Chief Economic Adviser, Reserve Bank of India, Securities and Exchange Board of India, Insurance Regulatory and Development Authority, Pension Fund Regulatory and Development Authority, and their respective ministries. The latest update was published in the gazette notification of the central government in October 2022, which added into the list energy storage systems, data centers, and exhibition-cum-convention center.[19] The full master list is shown in Table 4.

Table 4: Updated Harmonized Master List of Infrastructure Subsectors

Category	Infrastructure Subsector
Transport and logistics	• Roads and bridges • Ports[a] • Shipyards[b] • Inland waterways • Airport • Railway track including electrical and signaling system, tunnels, viaducts, and bridges • Railway rolling stock along with workshop and associated maintenance facilities • Railway terminal infrastructure including stations and adjoining commercial infrastructure • Urban public transport (except rolling stock in case of urban road transport) • Logistics infrastructure[c] • Bulk material transportation pipelines[d]
Energy	• Electricity generation • Electricity transmission • Electricity distribution • Oil, gas, and liquefied natural gas storage facility[e] • Energy storage systems[f]
Water and sanitation	• Solid waste management • Water treatment plants • Sewage collection, treatment, and disposal system • Irrigation (dams, channels, embankments) • Storm water drainage system
Communication	• Telecommunication (fixed network)[g] • Telecommunication towers • Telecommunication and telecom services • Data centers[h]

continued on next page

19   Government of India, MOF, DEA. 2022. *Updated Harmonized Master List of Infrastructure Sub-sectors.* 11 October.

Table 4 *continued*

Category	Infrastructure Subsector
Social and commercial infrastructure	• Education institutions (capital stock) • Sports infrastructure[i] • Hospitals (capital stock)[j] • Tourism infrastructure (i.e., three-star or higher category hotels located outside of cities with population of more than 1 million, ropeways and cable cars) • Common infrastructure for industrial parks and other parks with industrial activity such as food parks, textile parks, special economic zones, tourism facilities, and agriculture markets • Postharvest storage infrastructure for agriculture and horticultural produce including cold storage • Terminal markets • Soil-testing laboratories • Cold chain[k] • Affordable housing[l] • Affordable rental housing complex[m] • Exhibition-cum-convention center[n]

[a] Includes capital dredging.

[b] "Shipyard" is a floating or land-based facility with the essential features of waterfront, turning basin, berthing or docking facility, and slipways or ship lifts. It is self-sufficient for shipbuilding, repair, and breaking activities.

[c] "Logistics infrastructure" refers to multimodal logistics park comprising inland container depot with minimum investment of ₹500 million and minimum area of 10 acres, cold chain facility with a minimum investment of ₹150 million and a minimum area of 20,000 square feet, and/or warehousing facility with a minimum investment of ₹250 million and a minimum area of 100,000 square feet.

[d] Includes oil, gas, slurry, water supply, and iron ore pipelines.

[e] Includes strategic storage of crude oil.

[f] Includes dense charging infrastructure and grid scale energy storage systems (ESS) with a minimum qualifying capacity of 200 megawatt-hours, provided that ESS is not being established on a merchant basis.

[g] Includes optic fiber, wire, and cable networks that provide broadband or internet.

[h] Data centers are housed in a dedicated or centralized building for storage and processing of digital data applications with a minimum capacity of 5 megawatts of information technology load.

[i] Includes the provision of sports stadia and infrastructure for academies for training and research in sports and sports-related activities.

[j] Includes medical colleges, paramedical training institutes, and diagnostics centers.

[k] Includes cold room facility for farm level precooling, and preservation or storage of agriculture and allied produce and marine products and meat.

[l] "Affordable housing" is defined as a housing project using at least 50% of the floor area ratio/floor space index for dwelling units with carpet area of not more than 60 square meters.

[m] "Affordable rental housing complex" means a project is to be used for rental purpose only for urban migrant/poor (economically weaker section or low-income group) for a minimum period of 25 years. The project includes basic civic infrastructure facilities such as water, sanitation, sewerage/septage, road, electricity along with necessary social/commercial infrastructure, and the initial rent fixed by local authorities/entities based on local survey of surrounding area where the project is situated. "Project" means a listed project having at least 40 dwelling units of double room or single room or equivalent dormitory units or a mix of all three in any ratio but not more than one-third of the total built up area under double bedrooms units. "Dwelling units" means a unit comprising a double bedroom with living area, kitchen, toilet, and bathroom of up to 60 square meters carpet area, or a single bedroom with living area, kitchen, toilet, and bathroom of up to 30 square meters carpet area. "Dormitory units" means a set of three dormitory beds with common kitchen, toilet, and bathroom in 30 square meters carpet area, meaning 10 square meters carpet area per dormitory bed. The "carpet area" shall have the same meaning as assigned to it in clause (k) of Section 2 of the Real Estate (Regulation and Development) Act, 2016.

[n] "Exhibition-cum-convention center" is defined as exhibition and convention center projects with minimum built-up floor area of 100,000 square meters of exclusively exhibition space or convention space or both combined. Built-up floor area includes primary facilities such as exhibition centers, convention halls, auditoriums, plenary halls, business centers, and meeting halls.

Source: Government of India, Ministry of Finance, Department of Economic Affairs. 2022. *Updated Harmonized Master List of Infrastructure Sub-sectors (Annexure-I).*

Public–Private Partnership Institutional Framework

Parameter	
Does the country have a national public–private partnership (PPP) unit?	✓
What are the functions of the national PPP unit? • Supporting the design and operationalization of the national PPP-enabling framework? • Helping develop a national PPP pipeline? • Supporting the arrangement of funding for project preparation (budgetary allocations, technical assistance funding from multilateral development agencies, operating a dedicated project preparation/project development fund)? • Guiding project preparation and coordination with the government agencies responsible for sponsoring the projects? • Making recommendations to the PPP Committee and/or other approving authorities to provide approvals associated with various stages of the PPP process?	✓ ✓[a] ✓ ✓ ✓

✓ = Yes, ✗ = No, NA = Not Applicable, UA = Unavailable.

[a] The Department of Economic Affairs, Ministry of Finance, Government of India developed the *National Infrastructure Pipeline* (NIP) released in 2019. The NIP comprises both PPP and non-PPP projects and is akin to the national project pipeline. Nevertheless, it is a comprehensive pipeline of all infrastructure subsectors.

There are various entities that have well-defined roles in the process of appraising and approving the PPP projects in the country. A list of the key entities and their roles are briefly described in Table 5.

Table 5: Description and Roles of Entities Promoting Public–Private Partnerships

Institution	Role in Promoting Public–Private Partnerships
Infrastructure Finance Secretariat	The IFS established under the DEA streamlines the process of overseeing policy matters in the infrastructure sector. It has two divisions: the Infrastructure Support and Development Division, and the Infrastructure Policy and Planning Division.
Private Investment Unit, Department of Economic Affairs, Infrastructure Support and Development Division	The PIU (formerly PPP Cell) is responsible for policy-level matters concerning PPPs, including project identification, prefeasibility analysis, coordination with government agencies, procurement, model concession agreements, capacity building, and project operation and management. It is also responsible for matters and proposals relating to clearance by the PPPAC, Scheme for Financial Support to PPPs in Infrastructure (VGF scheme), and the IIPDF.
	The PIU, DEA has developed a PPP India website to enhance the capabilities of implementing agencies in the country for adopting PPPs as the mode for infrastructure development and implementation. It provides key information related to PPP initiatives in India and shares PPP best practices for PPP practitioners from both the government and the private sector. The website is a repository of policy documents, government guidelines, model documents, project information, information on the institutional mechanisms for appraisal of PPP infrastructure projects, schemes developed for financial support to PPP projects, guidance materials, and reference documents.

continued on next page

Table 5 *continued*

Institution	Role in Promoting Public–Private Partnerships
PPP Vertical of the NITI Aayog (formerly Planning Commission of India)	The PPP Vertical is tasked with the (i) formulation of policies to ensure time-bound creation of world class infrastructure; (ii) financing of investment in infrastructure; (iii) promotion of PPPs as the preferred mode for construction and O&M of infrastructure projects; (iv) provision of recommendations on institutional, regulatory, and procedural reforms; (v) standardization of PPP documents; and (vi) appraisal of PPP projects.
IIPDF	The IIPDF is created within the DEA, MOF, Government of India to support the development of PPP projects across central, state, and local governments.
PPPAC[a]	The Cabinet Committee on Economic Affairs, in its meeting on 27 October 2005, approved the procedure for the approval of PPP projects. Pursuant to this decision, the PPPAC was set up. The PPPAC was notified in 2006 as responsible for the appraisal of PPP projects in the central sector. The role of the PPPAC is to provide necessary clearances to the administrative ministry, department, and/or agency based on the appraisal of the projects, and to obtain comments from the other ministries that may be involved in the proposal.
Empowered Institution	The Empowered Institution considers the sanction of projects for VGF of up to ₹1,000 million ($12.2 million) for each eligible project, subject to the budgetary ceiling indicated by the MOF. The Empowered Institution also considers proposals that require funding support of more than ₹1,000 million ($13.70 million) and can forward these proposals to the Empowered Committee.
Empowered Committee	The Empowered Committee considers the sanction of projects for VGF from ₹1,000 million ($12.2 million) up to ₹2,000 million ($24.40 million) upon recommendation by the Empowered Institution for each eligible project, subject to the budgetary ceiling indicated by the MOF. The Empowered Committee provides instructions relating to eligibility of projects for such support as and when requested by the Empowered Institution.

DEA = Department of Economic Affairs, IFS = Infrastructure Finance Secretariat, IIPDF = India Infrastructure Project Development Fund, MOF = Ministry of Finance, O&M = operation and maintenance, PIU = Private Investment Unit, PPP = public–private partnership, PPPAC = Public Private Partnership Appraisal Committee, VGF = viability gap funding.

[a] In 2006, the Government of India notified the appraisal mechanism by setting up of the PPPAC responsible for the appraisal of PPP projects in the central sector.

Sources: Asian Development Bank. 2019. *Public–Private Partnership Monitor.* Second Edition; Government of India, Department of Economic Affairs. About Private Investment Unit (PIU); and Government of India, NITI Aayog. Public Private Partnerships.

Pursuant to the decision of the Cabinet Committee on Economic Affairs dated 27 October 2005, the PPPAC was set up comprising the following:

- Secretary, DEA (acts as the PPPAC Chair);
- Secretary, Planning Commission (Chief Executive Officer, NITI Aayog—the Planning Commission in India has been reconstituted, restructured, and renamed as the NITI Aayog);
- Secretary, Department of Expenditure;
- Secretary, Department of Legal Affairs; and
- Secretary of the Ministry or Department sponsoring a project (footnote 17).

The Cabinet Committee on Economic Affairs may include other experts, as necessary:

- The Committee is supported by the DEA.
- The MOF is the nodal ministry responsible for examining concession agreements from the financial angle, deciding on guarantees to be extended. The MOF assesses risk allocation from the investment and banking perspectives and ensures that projects are scrutinized from the perspective of government expenditure.
- The PPP Vertical of the NITI Aayog (erstwhile Planning Commission) prepares an appraisal note for the PPPAC, providing specific suggestions for improving the concession terms, wherever possible.
- The Ministry of Law and Justice, Department of Legal Affairs is also a part of the PPPAC, as legal scrutiny of the concession agreements is vital.

1. Entities Responsible for Public–Private Partnership Project Identification, Approval, and Oversight

Parameter	
Who is responsible for identifying, preparing, and procuring the public–private partnership (PPP) projects?	Sponsoring ministry and all other levels of government: central government ministries or departments, state governments, municipal or local bodies, public sector undertakings or any other statutory authority
Is there a PPP Committee for providing approvals at various stages of the PPP projects?	✓
Who are the approving authorities other than the PPP Committee for PPP projects?	Secretary, Administrative Ministry; Minister-in-charge, Cabinet Committee on Economic Affairs
Does the country have an independent think tank for various PPP planning, budgeting, and policy decisions?	✓ NITI Aayog[a]
Is there a legislature for the PPP program oversight?	✗

✓ = Yes, ✗ = No, NA = Not Applicable, UA = Unavailable.

[a] The NITI Aayog, a government think tank, comprises Public Private Partnership Vertical, which actively works toward promoting PPPs as the preferred mode for implementing infrastructure projects. The Public Private Partnership Appraisal Unit is part of the Vertical. The Vertical makes policy-level recommendations for institutional, regulatory, and procedural reforms, and works toward the standardization of PPP documents. It also provides transaction structure guidance to implementing agencies, formulates suitable reforms and policy initiatives for consideration by the government, and appraises PPP projects.

Sources: Government of India, Ministry of Finance, Department of Economic Affairs. 2023. *Appraisal and Approval Mechanisms for Central Sector PPPs*; and Government of India, NITI Aayog. Public Private Partnerships.

The DEA has issued guidelines for the formulation, appraisal, and approval of central PPP projects in the country. Projects under the jurisdiction of state governments are undertaken based on the respective state government regulations. The guidelines indicated in Table 6 are pertinent to central government projects and are classified based on the size of the project.

Table 6: Guidelines for the Formulation, Appraisal, and Approval of Public–Private Partnership Projects

Steps Involved	For projects costing less than ₹50 million ($600,000)	For projects costing more than ₹50 million ($600,000) but less than ₹1 billion ($1.2 million) for all sectors	For projects costing more than ₹1 billion ($1.2 million) but less than ₹2.5 billion ($3 million)	For projects costing more than ₹2.5 billion ($3 million) but less than ₹5 billion ($6 million)	For projects costing more than ₹5 billion ($6 million) but less than ₹10 billion ($12 million)	For projects costing ₹10 billion ($12 million) or more
Project Cost Criteria						
Project Identification	Sponsoring Ministry	Sponsoring Ministry	Sponsoring Ministry to undertake interministerial consultations, where required	Sponsoring Ministry to undertake interministerial consultations, where required	Sponsoring Ministry to undertake interministerial consultations, where required	Sponsoring Ministry to undertake interministerial consultations, where required
In-Principle Approval	NA	NA	NA	Sponsoring Ministry to seek in-principle approval by submitting project documents to PPPAC—specifically for sectors that do not have model concession agreements. For sectors where a model concession agreement is available, the PPPAC approval may be obtained before inviting the financial bids.	Sponsoring Ministry to seek in-principle approval by submitting project documents to PPPAC—specifically for sectors that do not have model concession agreements. For sectors where a model concession agreement is available, the PPPAC approval may be obtained before inviting the financial bids.	Sponsoring Ministry to seek in-principle approval by submitting project documents to PPPAC—specifically for sectors that do not have model concession agreements. For sectors where a model concession agreement is available, the PPPAC approval may be obtained before inviting the financial bids.
Appraisal Responsibility	Administrative Ministry	SFC	SFC + 2-member committee	PPPAC	PPPAC	PPPAC

continued on next page

Table 6 continued

Steps Involved						
Project Formulation and Appraisal	Administrative Ministry	The PPP Vertical of the NITI Aayog will appraise the project proposal and forward its Appraisal Note to the Administrative Ministry. The Department of Legal Affairs, the Department of Economic Affairs, and any other ministry/department involved will also forward written comments to the Administrative Ministry within the stipulated time period. The SFC will review the Appraisal Note and the comments of different ministries, along with the response from the Administrative Ministry.	The PPP Vertical of the NITI Aayog will appraise the project proposal and forward its Appraisal Note to the Administrative Ministry. The Department of Legal Affairs, the Department of Economic Affairs, and any other ministry/department involved will also forward written comments to the Administrative Ministry within the stipulated time period. The SFC will review the Appraisal Note and the comments of different ministries, along with the response from the Administrative Ministry.	Approval of the PPPAC shall be sought by the Sponsoring Ministry prior to bidding by submitting draft bid documents and other project documents. The PPP Vertical of the NITI Aayog will appraise the project proposal and forward its Appraisal Note to the PPPAC Secretariat. The Ministry of Law and any other ministry/department involved will also forward written comments to the PPPAC Secretariat within the stipulated time period. The PPPAC Secretariat will forward all the comments to the Administrative Ministry, and the Administrative Ministry shall submit a written response to each of the comments.	Approval of the PPPAC shall be sought by the Sponsoring Ministry prior to bidding by submitting draft bid documents and other project documents. The PPP Vertical of the NITI Aayog will appraise the project proposal and forward its Appraisal Note to the PPPAC Secretariat. The Ministry of Law and any other ministry/department involved will also forward written comments to the PPPAC Secretariat within the stipulated time period. The PPPAC Secretariat will forward all the comments to the Administrative Ministry, and the Administrative Ministry shall submit a written response to each of the comments.	Approval of the PPPAC shall be sought by the Sponsoring Ministry prior to bidding by submitting draft bid documents and other project documents. The PPP Vertical of the NITI Aayog will appraise the project proposal and forward its Appraisal Note to the PPPAC Secretariat. The Department of Legal Affairs, the Department of Economic Affairs, and any other ministry/department involved will also forward written comments to the PPPAC Secretariat within the stipulated time period. The PPPAC Secretariat will forward all the comments to the Administrative Ministry, and the Administrative Ministry shall submit a written response to each of the comments.

continued on next page

Table 6 continued

Steps Involved						
				The concession agreement and any supporting agreements/documents thereof, along with the PPPAC memo, will be submitted for consideration by the PPPAC. The PPPAC will review the Appraisal Note and the comments of different ministries, along with the response from the Administrative/Sponsoring Ministry.	The concession agreement and any supporting agreements/documents thereof, along with the PPPAC memo, will be submitted for consideration by the PPPAC. The PPPAC will review the Appraisal Note and the comments of different ministries, along with the response from the Administrative/Sponsoring Ministry.	The concession agreement and any supporting agreements/documents thereof, along with the PPPAC memo, will be submitted for consideration by the PPPAC. The PPPAC will review the Appraisal Note and the comments of different ministries, along with the response from the Administrative/Sponsoring Ministry.
Invitation of Bids	Financial bids may be invited after obtaining the approval of the competent authority.	Financial bids could be invited after the approval/clearance by the Committee providing final appraisal, but final approval from competent authority is needed before finalizing.	Financial bids could be invited after the approval/clearance by the Committee providing final appraisal, but final approval from competent authority is needed before finalizing.	Financial bids could be invited after the PPPAC conveys its approval, but final approval from competent authority is needed before finalizing.	Financial bids could be invited after the PPPAC conveys its approval, but final approval from competent authority is needed before finalizing.	Financial bids could be invited after the PPPAC conveys its approval, but final approval from competent authority is needed before finalizing.
Project Approval	Administrative Ministry	Secretary (Administrative Ministry)	Minister-in-charge	Minister-in-charge	Minister-in-charge + Finance Minister	CCEA

CCEA = Cabinet Committee on Economic Affairs, DEA = Department of Economic Affairs, NA = not applicable, PPP = public–private partnership, PPPAC = Public Private Partnership Appraisal Committee, SFC = Standing Finance Committee.

Notes: The Ministry of Defence, the Department of Atomic Energy, and the Department of Space will not be covered under the purview of these guidelines. The competent authority is the final contracting authority under the Administrative Ministry.

Source: Government of India, Ministry of Finance, Department of Economic Affairs. 2023. *Reference Guide for PPP Project Appraisal.*

2. Entities Responsible for Public–Private Partnership Project Monitoring

Parameter	
Monitoring of Public–Private Partnership (PPP) projects post commercial close?	✓
Supporting the monitoring and management of fiscal risks and liabilities from PPP projects for the Ministry of Finance?	✓

✓ = Yes, ✗ = No, NA = Not Applicable, UA = Unavailable.

PPP projects are typically based on long-term concession agreements that specify clear and distinct outputs, such as quality of service and quantifiable performance standards that have a direct bearing on the users of such projects. These agreements normally empower the concessionaire to use public assets for building infrastructure projects. The concessionaire is also empowered to levy and collect user charges for the use of public assets. However, the government always remains responsible and accountable for the delivery of services to the users. These projects, therefore, require close monitoring by the government to ensure that the provisions of the respective concession agreements and the applicable laws are enforced. Hence, post-award contract management (PACM) is critical.[20]

The Infrastructure Finance Secretariat (IFS), established under the DEA, MOF, harmonizes policies and initiatives for infrastructure financing and development. The Private Investment Unit under the IFS provides oversight and supports the development of state PPP cells that play a critical role in monitoring projects at the state level. The institutional framework for monitoring the performance of PPP projects comprises the following:

- **Public–Private Partnership Projects Monitoring Unit at the project authority level.** The project monitoring unit (PMU) should be created at the level of project authority or the government department that has granted the concession. The PMU should be operated by at least three officers, wherein at least one of them should have expertise and experience in finance. Each PMU may oversee two or three PPP projects with an aggregate project cost not exceeding ₹25 billion ($342.42 million). The PMU submits monthly reports to the performance review unit (PRU). The monthly report should include compliance status of all the obligations of the concessionaire and the project authority, as specified in the concession agreement. The head of the PMU should be of the rank of director, deputy secretary, or superintendent engineer.
- **Public–Private Partnership Performance Review Unit at the ministry or state government level.** The PRU is headed by an officer not below the rank of a Joint Secretary and should be set up at the central, ministry, state government, and statutory authority levels. The PPP PRU reviews the PPP Projects Monitoring Report submitted by the different PMUs and initiates action for rectifying any defaults or lapses. The PRU, in turn, will submit a quarterly report on the status of PPPs to the competent authority. The respective ministries should send a quarterly compliance report to the NITI Aayog with a copy for the MOF. The NITI Aayog, in consultation with the MOF, will prepare a summary of these reports, along with recommendations for further action and improvement, which would be submitted to the Cabinet Committee on Infrastructure once every quarter for the next 2 years.

[20]   Government of India, MOF, DEA. 2015. *Guidelines for Post-Award Contract Management for PPP Concessions*.

The PPP PMU and the PPP PRU should be associated with the PPP projects, preferably at the project award stage itself. The monitoring must address the two phases of a PPP contract—the construction phase and the operations or operation and maintenance (O&M) phase. PPACM of PPP projects not only deals with transaction and programmatic level but also with the broader fiscal implications such as direct and contingent liabilities.

Further, the DEA has developed a guidance material to improve the PACM of PPPs at the project level. The guidance material aims to provide a structured approach and mechanism for the contracting authorities to monitor the various aspects of compliance and risk management throughout the project life cycle. The guidance material developed for the PACM of PPP concessions has three components:

(i)   The Post-Award Contract Management Guidelines have been developed as a quick reference and strategic road map for contracting authorities and contract managers.
(ii)   The Post-Award Contract Management Manuals have been designed to provide guidance on various activities required to be undertaken by the contracting authority officials at different stages of the project life cycle. The manuals have been developed for PPP projects in three sectors: highways (Volume I), ports (Volume II), and schools (Volume III). Each manual is based on the model concession framework of the Government of India for that sector.
(iii)   The Online Tool kit is a web-based application that provides a quick-reference, interactive, and user-friendly tool kit to understand and manage PPP projects. These tool kits related to project structuring, project appraisals, and contingent liability management are available at https://www. pppinindia. gov.in/, hosted by the PPP Cell, Infrastructure Division, DEA (footnote 20).

The guidelines, manuals, and online tool kit forms the PACM framework for India, which guides all the stakeholders involved in PACM of a PPP project at different levels.

The Public–Private Partnership Process

Parameter	
Does the public–private partnership (PPP) legal and regulatory framework provide for a PPP implementation process covering the entire PPP life cycle?	NA
Feasibility assessment stage • Technical feasibility? • Socioeconomic feasibility? • Environmental sustainability? • Financial feasibility? • Fiscal affordability assessment? • Legal assessment?	✓ ✓ ✓ ✓ ✓ ✓
• Risk assessment and PPP project structuring? • Value-for-money assessment? • Market sounding with stakeholders?	✓ ✓ ✓
Is the PPP procurement plan required to be prepared?	✓
Is there a need to set up a separate PPP procurement committee?	✓

continued on next page

Table *continued*

Parameter	
Is competitive bidding the only method for selection of PPP private developer?	✓
Is the prequalification stage necessary? Or does the PPP legal and regulatory framework allow flexibility to skip the prequalification stage?	Single stage is allowed.
Does the PPP legal and regulatory process provide the option to the preferred bidder for contract negotiations?	✗
Does the PPP legal and regulatory framework allow unsuccessful bidders to challenge the award or submit complaints?	✗[a]
What is the maximum time allowed for submitting a complaint or challenging the award by unsuccessful bidders from the announcement of the preferred bidder?	✗[a]
Does the PPP legal and regulatory framework provide for transparency?	✓[b]
Which of the following are required to be published?[c] • Findings from the feasibility assessment? • Procurement notice? • Outcome of stakeholder consultations from market sounding? • Clarifications to prequalification queries? • Prequalification results? • Clarifications to prebid queries? • Results for the bid stage and selection of preferred bidder? • Final concession agreement to be entered between the government agency and the preferred bidder? And other PPP project agreements executed between government agency and preferred bidder? • Confidentiality?	✓ ✓ ✗ ✓ ✓ ✓ ✓ ✓ ✓

✓ = Yes, ✗ = No, NA = Not Applicable, UA = Unavailable.

[a] The model qualification and bid documents especially take an undertaking from the applicants/bidders that states "I/We acknowledge the right of the Authority to reject our Application without assigning any reason or otherwise and hereby waive, to the fullest extent permitted by applicable law, our right to challenge the same on any account whatsoever."

[b] The existing guidelines, model bidding documents, and tool kits emphasize transparency as a key factor in the PPP implementation throughout the project life cycle.

[c] The guidelines on what to be published are governed by the General Finance Rules 2017 and the procurement manuals published by the Government of India. The contracting agencies, based on internal guidelines and as part of good practices, ensure transparency in the procurement. Typically, the key findings of the feasibility study are shared as an annexure to the bid documents (called project information memorandum). The procurement notice is published in the newspapers as well as uploaded on the e-procurement and the contracting agency's websites. In some cases, the outcomes of market sounding are shared, though it is not often the case. The prequalification and prebid queries and responses are shared with all the bid participants; however, in many instances, contracting agencies do not reveal the name of the entity raising the query. The responses are also typically uploaded on the website. The outcomes of the evaluation are shared to the extent of announcing the winning bidder, followed by a list of qualified bidders in some cases. The database found at www.pppinindia.com also provides copies of the final concession agreements that are signed between the government and the concessionaire.

The Reference Guide for PPP Project Appraisal defines the six broad distinct phases and processes in which PPP projects could be taken up (footnote 18). Each of the six phases are further subdivided into stages, which are indicative and could be overlapping (Table 7). Also, the actual phases and activities undertaken at any stage may vary according to the particular needs of a project.

Table 7: Phases of a Public–Private Partnership Project Life Cycle

Project Identification	Feasibility Analysis	Project Structuring	Project Appraisal	PPP Procurement	PPP Contract Management
• Assessment of preliminary needs • Assessment of strategic needs and alignment • Assessment of potential delivery options • Assessment of prefeasibility study	• Project feasibility studies ✓ Strategic feasibility ✓ Technical feasibility ✓ Legal feasibility ✓ Project management ✓ Environmental and social sustainability	• Contours of PPP structure are finalized ✓ PPP mode selection ✓ Risk assessment ✓ Responsibility framework ✓ Funding assistance ✓ Bid documentation: procurement strategy and planning, EOI, RFQ, RFP, PIM, draft concession agreement	• Feasibility assessment ✓ Strategic feasibility ✓ Technical feasibility ✓ Legal feasibility ✓ Project management ✓ Environmental and social sustainability • Economic viability ✓ Commercial viability ✓ Economic viability ✓ Fiscal viability • Risk and reward balanced ✓ Appraisal of RFQ/RFP ✓ Appraisal of draft concession agreement	• e-procurement • Formation of bid opening and evaluation committee • EOI process • RFQ process • RFP process • Issue of letter of award • Formation of SPV and fulfillment of any precondition • Execution of concession agreement with the SPV	• Formation of contract management team • Conditions precedence • Financial close • Appointed date • Monitoring

EOI = expression of interest, PIM = project information memorandum, PPP = public–private partnership, RFP = request for proposal, RFQ = request for qualification, SPV = special purpose vehicle.

Source: Government of India, Ministry of Finance, Department of Economic Affairs, Infrastructure Finance Secretariat. 2023. *Reference Guide for PPP Project Appraisal.*

Public–Private Partnership Standard Operating Procedures, Tool kits, Templates, and Model Bid Documents

Parameter	
Does the country have public–private partnership (PPP) guidelines/PPP guidance manual?	✓
Does the PPP guidelines/PPP guidance manual adequately cover the process, entities involved, roles and responsibilities of various entities, approvals required at various stages, and the timelines for the various stages of the PPP project life cycle?	✓
What are the templates and checklists available in the PPP guidelines/PPP guidance manual? • Project needs assessment and options analysis checklist? • Project due diligence checklist? • Technical assessment checklist? • Environmental assessment checklist? • PPP procurement plan template?	 ✓ ✓ ✓ ✓ ✓
Does the country have standardized/model bidding documents for PPPs? • Model request for qualification document? • Model request for proposal document? • Model PPP/concession agreement? • State support agreement? • Viability gap funding agreement? • Guarantee agreement? • Power purchase agreement? • Capacity take-or-pay contract? • Fuel supply agreement? • Transmission and use of system agreement? • Performance-based operations and maintenance contract? • Engineering, procurement, and construction contract?	 ✓ ✓ ✓ ✓ ✓ ✓ ✓ ✓ ✓ ✓ ✓ ✓
Does the country have standardized PPP agreement terms?	✓
Does the country have standardized/model tool kits to facilitate identification, preparation, procurement, and management of PPP projects? • PPP family indicator? • PPP mode validity indicator? • PPP suitability filter? • PPP screening tool? • Financial viability indicator model? • Economic viability indicator model? • Value-for-money indicator tool? • Readiness filter?	 ✓ ✓ ✓ ✓ ✓ ✗[a] ✓ ✓
Is there a framework for monitoring fiscal risks from PPPs? • Process for assessing fiscal commitments? • Process for approving fiscal commitments? • Process for monitoring fiscal commitments? • Process for reporting fiscal commitments? • Process for budgeting fiscal commitments?	 ✓ ✓ ✓ ✓ ✓

continued on next page

Table *continued*

Parameter	
Are there fiscal prudence norms/thresholds to limit fiscal exposure to PPPs?	✓
Is there a process for assessing and budgeting contingent liabilities from PPPs?	✓

✓ = Yes, ✗ = No, NA = Not Applicable, UA = Unavailable.

[a] There are no specific tool kits for economic analysis. However, the details considered by the PPP Appraisal Committee for any approval, including in-principle or final approval for projects, seek to understand the economic internal rate of return (IRR) (if computed), though it does not insist on the same. However, specific subsectors and their ministries have issued guidelines for preparing the economic IRR, which is a critical input for approving projects. For example, the Ministry of Housing and Urban Affairs has issued the Appraisal Guidelines for Metro Rail Project Proposals in India, which explains the computation of economic IRR, and wherein economic IRR also becomes a key filter for providing central government assistance for the development of metro rail projects in cities.

As explained in the earlier sections, the government has issued various tool kits, guidelines, and manuals to assist contracting agencies in project preparation, structuring, contingent liability management, PACM, and preparation of model concession agreements (MCAs) and standardized bidding documents.

Concession agreements are contractual documents that govern the relationship between the public and private parties in a PPP transaction. It clearly sets out the terms and conditions of the contract and obligations and rights of the parties involved, allocates the risks between parties, and defines the mechanisms to deal with future events, among others.

An illustrative list of the revised or new MCAs developed and the subsequent changes to MCAs during 2009–2022 is given below:

(i) The HAM-based PPP model and a related MCA (for highways) was notified in 2016 to be used where PPP projects in BOT (annuity/user charge) model are unviable.[21] This model was revised in 2021 to accommodate changes in ownership provisions, shifting of utilities not identified in the original agreement and related reimbursement of costs, maintenance obligations during the construction period if the project timelines get extended for reasons attributable to the Authority, mandating the amounts for which financial close has to be done, change in milestones for payments by the Authority, changes in termination payment schedules and milestone-based termination payments, and introduction of a Dispute Resolution Board and mandated reference to the Board for dispute resolution, among others.

(ii) The MCA for toll–operate–transfer (TOT) model was introduced in 2016 to facilitate the monetization of existing road assets though PPPs. This was amended in 2020.[22]

[21] ADB's South Asia Working Paper Series of December 2019 defines HAM as relating to "projects where the private sector is unable or unwilling to take even the risk of full investments and subsequent annuity payments. A substantial sum of money (40%–60%) is paid during construction stage. The balance of payments are made through contracts based on availability and performance payments over an extended length of time (about 7–10 years post-construction)." R. Peri, C. Chen, and D. Dey. 2019. *Hybrid Annuity Contracts for Road Projects in India. ADB South Asia Working Paper Series.* No. 68. ADB.

[22] Government of India, Ministry of Road Transport and Highways (MORTH). 2022. *Changes in the Model Concession Agreement of TOT.* Circular No. NH-24031/07 t2014-P&P. 3 February.

(iii)   The MCA for BOT (toll) model was introduced in 2000, which was subsequently revised in 2006, 2009, and 2016. This was again updated in 2020 to provide for some critical reforms such as (a) obligations of the National Highways Authority of India (NHAI) to provide vacant access and right-of-way for 90% of the project land as identified in the MCA, (b) review and assessment of the revenue potential every 5 years to capture growth in the originally assessed traffic estimates, and (c) limiting the aggregate liability of either party to 100% of the project cost in cases of default. This was further revised in February 2022 to include (a) the NHAI's rights to order for capacity augmentation subject to certain terms and conditions, (b) cost of such augment to be borne by the NHAI, and (c) amendment relating to toll provisions for such augmentation.

(iv)   The MCA for major ports was first notified in 2008, revised in 2018, and further revised in November 2021, which incorporated changes necessitated by the enactment of the Major Port Authorities Act, 2021 and the dynamics of the market and regulatory conditions. The current MCA includes features such as (a) fixed tariff based on market conditions, (b) compensation for termination payments prior to commercial operation date (COD) in some cases, (c) key performance indicators for the concessionaire, (d) divesture of the equity of original promoters after the expiry of 2 years from the COD, and (e) introduction of the Society for Affordable Redressal of Disputes as part of the dispute resolution mechanism.

As a result of the revised MCAs, there are currently six MCAs across the transport and energy sectors:

(i)   MCA on Hybrid Annuity Model Projects,
(ii)   MCA on Build–Operate–Transfer Projects (Annuity),
(iii)   MCA on Build–Operate–Transfer Projects (Toll),
(iv)   MCA for PPP in Tolling, Operation, Maintenance, and Transfer of National Highways,
(v)   MCA for Multi Modal Logistics Parks under Bharatmala Pariyojana Ministry of Shipping, and
(vi)   MCA for PPP Projects in Major Ports.

In addition to the MCAs notified by the Government of India, the DEA has developed 10 green books or guidelines on the healthcare sector:

(i)   Green book for Diagnostic Centre,
(ii)   Green book for Greenfield Hospital,
(iii)   Green book for Medical College,
(iv)   Green book for Primary Healthcare,
(v)   Green book for Brownfield Hospital,
(vi)   Guide for Practitioners for Diagnostic Center,
(vii)   Guide for Practitioners for Greenfield Hospital,
(viii) Guide for Practitioners for Medical College,
(ix)   Guide for Practitioners for Primary Healthcare, and
(x)   Guide for Practitioners for Brownfield Hospital.

The NITI Aayog, which replaced the Planning Commission in 2015, has also issued several model agreements, green books, and guidelines for various projects. The following is a list of draft concession agreements, green books, and guidelines that have been issued for different sectors:

(i)   Draft MCA for National Highways;
(ii)   Draft MCA for National Highways (Six-Laning);
(iii)   Draft MCA for State Highways;
(iv)   Draft MCA for Operation and Maintenance of Highways;
(v)   Draft MCA for State Ports;
(vi)   Draft MCA for Ports Terminals;
(vii)   Draft MCA for Greenfield Airports;
(viii) Draft MCA for Brownfield Airports;
(ix)   Draft MCA for Airport Terminals;
(x)   Draft MCA for Urban Rail Transit Systems;
(xi)   Draft MCA for Annuity Projects;
(xii)   Draft MCA for Transmission of Electricity;
(xiii) Draft Model Power Purchase Agreement (DBFOT);
(xiv)   Draft Model Power Supply Agreement (DBFOT);
(xv)   Draft Model Agreement for Procurement of Power (Medium-term);
(xvi)   Draft Model Agreement for Supply of Power (Short-term);
(xvii) Draft MCA for Coal Mining;
(xviii) Draft MCA for Exploration and Mining of Coal;
(xix)   Draft MCA for Redevelopment of Railway Stations;
(xx)   Draft MCA for Container Train Operations;
(xxi)   Draft Procurement-Cum-Maintenance Agreement for Locomotives;
(xxii) Draft Model Agreement for Engineering, Procurement, and Construction (EPC) of Civil Works;
(xxiii) Draft Model Agreement for EPC of Railway Projects;
(xxiv) Draft MCA for Storage of Food Grains;
(xxv)   Draft MCA for School Education (Central);
(xxvi) Draft MCA for School Education (States);
(xxvii) Draft documents: Development and Operation of Integrated Solid Waste Management System and Reclamation of Land through Bio-Remediation of Legacy Waste under HAM;
(xxviii) Draft documents: Integrated Development and Operation of Sewage Treatment Plants and Fecal Sludge Management System under HAM;
(xxix) Bidding Documents for PPP in Integrated Solid Waste Management and Integrated Liquid Waste Management;
(xxx)   Draft documents: Operation and Maintenance of Passenger Ropeways;
(xxxi) Draft documents: Operation and Maintenance of Electric Buses in Cities (OPEX Model);
(xxxii) Draft documents: Establishment of a Medical College and Augmentation of Attached Hospital by PPP;
(xxxiii) Draft documents: Setting Up and Operating Automated Inspection and Certification Centers for Transport Vehicles;
(xxxiv) Draft documents: Development and Operation of Eco-Tourism Resort and Supporting Infrastructure; and
(xxxv) Draft documents: PPP for Noncommunicable Disease.

The DEA has also developed a tool kit or a set of PPP tools to improve decision-making processes in PPP projects for contracting authorities and other users. The tool kit, available at www.pppinindia.gov.in, aims to help improve the quality of PPP projects being developed and provide guidance for the entire life cycle of PPP projects. The PPP tools are web-based resources designed to improve decision-making and the quality of infrastructure PPPs in India. The tool kit covers five infrastructure sectors: state highways, water and sanitation, ports, solid waste management, and urban transport (bus rapid transit systems).

The tool kit provides a step-by-step guidance to contracting agencies and practitioners and specific tools for assisting the agencies at various stages. The tools are a set of Microsoft Excel-based worksheets or decision-making charts and guidelines for PPP processes (Table 8).

Table 8: Description of Public–Private Partnership Tools

Name of Tool	Purpose
Family Indicator Tool	Helps the contracting agency quickly see the main PPP mode options available in the selected sector and for a particular project type. The main options are called "families" of PPP modes. The major families of PPP comprise management contracts, lease contracts, concessions, and BOT and its variants. The PPP family indicator is structured as a decision tree.
Mode Validation Tool	Assists the contracting agency in selecting a suitable mode through appropriate risk allocation across various factors listed in the tool. The tool lists 21 risks and allocates a score based on the risk allocation done by the project officer and advises on a suitable mode against the score.
Suitability Filter	Helps the contracting agency check how easy or difficult it is to propose a PPP project. The suitability filter has a set of 29 questions grouped under five major issues that have impact on the suitability of a project for being developed as a PPP. The major elements comprise assessment of public and private sector in terms of regulatory framework and preparedness, capacity assessment, funding scenario, land, time, environment, social and related factors, and project size, among others.
Financial Viability Indicator	A simplified financial model designed to help the contracting agency in evaluating the financial viability of a project in the chosen sector. It is a Microsoft Excel-based model that the project officer could download, fill in with appropriate details, and upload to assess the results and outcomes for subsequent steps.
VFM Indicator Tool	Helps the contracting agency gain an indication of the likelihood that the project will provide VFM as a PPP. This is also a Microsoft Excel-based tool that could be downloaded by the project officer for analysis related to the project. The tool kit also provides a guide and additional information to assist project officers in the process.
Readiness Filter	The readiness filter for each readiness check consists of checklists, each made up of a series of questions. This assists the contracting agency in ensuring that all relevant project details are taken into consideration at the project preparatory stage and that the project is ready for the next stages of the PPP process. The readiness filter is organized into five checklists: (i) project design, need, and justification; (ii) project suitability for PPP; (iii) initial commercial case; (iv) initial risk management strategy; and (v) forward planning.

BOT = build–operate–transfer, PPP = public–private partnership, VFM = value-for-money.
Source: Government of India, Ministry of Finance, Department of Economic Affairs. 2010. *PPP Structuring Toolkit*.

The tool kit also has detailed process charts and guides, providing conceptual understanding and implementation guidance to users.

The DEA has provided a tool kit to guide contracting agencies during PACM. The PPP Post-Award Contract Management Tool kit is a web-based application that has been designed to help improve the contract management and execution of PPP projects in India's infrastructure sector. The tool kit is an efficient guide for public sector entities involved in the execution of these projects. It covers highways, ports, and schools.[23]

The DEA has also developed a web-based application tool that can estimate contingent liabilities arising from PPPs sponsored by line ministries, departments, and state-owned enterprises of central and state governments. The tool is based on relevant understanding of the project risks, the likelihood of their occurrence, and their potential impact on projects. The tool is expected to guide the ministries, governments, and project authorities in measurement, recognition, and disclosure of contingent liabilities arising from their respective PPPs. The tool is a browser-based application designed to estimate contingent liabilities of PPP projects at different stages of their implementation using an in-built contingent liability framework, which is aligned with various provisions relating to termination risks and termination payments provided in the concession agreements.[24]

Other Critical Contractual Provisions and Public–Private Partnership Enabling Considerations

Parameter	
Does the law specifically enable lenders the following rights?	
• Security over the project assets?	✓
• Security over the land on which they are built (land use right)?	✗
• Security over the shares of a public–private partnership project company?	✓
Can there be a direct agreement between the government and lenders?	✗ Only tripartite agreements are in practice.
Do lenders get priority in the case of insolvency?	✓
Can lenders be given step-in rights?	✓

✓ = Yes, ✗ = No, NA = Not Applicable, UA = Unavailable.
Source: Asian Development Bank. 2019. *Public–Private Partnership Monitor.* Second Edition.

The *PPP Guide for Practitioners* issued by the DEA in April 2016 states that in the case of PPP projects, funding is through project finance arrangement, under which lenders generally rely either exclusively or mainly on the cash flows to be generated by the project to recover loans and earn a return on their

---

[23]   Government of India, MOF, DEA. 2015. *Post Award Contract Management Toolkit for PPP Concessions.*
[24]   Government of India, MOF, DEA. 2017. *Contingent Liability Management Tool.*

investments. The arrangement is also known as a nonrecourse or limited recourse funding that has the following features:

(i)   no or limited recourse to the sponsor's assets,
(ii) bankability based on the debt service capacity of the project, and
(iii) debt service capacity based on future cash flows of a single activity.

The Master Circular on "Prudential Norms on Income Recognition, Asset Classification and Provisioning Pertaining to Advances," issued by the Reserve Bank of India on 1 April 2023 states that, in the case of PPP projects, the debts due to the lenders may be considered as secured to the extent assured by the project authority in terms of the concession agreement, subject to the following conditions.[25]

- User charges, tolls, and tariff payments are kept in an escrow account where senior lenders have priority over withdrawals by the concessionaire.
- There is sufficient risk mitigation, such as a predetermined increase in user charges or increase in concession period in case project revenues are lower than anticipated.
- The lenders have a right of substitution in case of concessionaire default.
- The lenders have a right to trigger termination in case of default in debt service.
- Upon termination, the obligations of the project authority are (i) compulsory buyout and (ii) repayment of debt due in a predetermined manner.

Some of the state PPP pieces of legislation and policies provide for facilitation of securitization, wherein the government agency or local authority may facilitate the securitization of project receivables and project assets by the developer, in favor of lenders, subject to terms fixed by the government or state infrastructure authorities.

The DEA PPP guidelines provide for a substitution agreement or tripartite agreement among the lender, the private partner, and the public entity. If a project requires financial assistance from the MOF, then the DEA is party to the tripartite agreement (footnote 13).

Parameter	
Does the law specifically enable compensation payment to the private partner in case of early termination due to	
• Public sector default or termination for reasons of public interest?	✓
• Private sector default?	✓
• Force majeure?	✓
Does the law enable the concept of economic/financial equilibrium?	✓
Does the law enable compensation payment to the private partner due to	
• Material adverse government action?	✓
• Force majeure?	✓
• Change in law?	✓

✓ = Yes, ✗ = No, NA = Not Applicable, UA = Unavailable.

25 Reserve Bank of India. 2023. *Prudential Norms on Income Recognition, Asset Classification and Provisioning Pertaining to Advances.* DOR.STR.REC.3/21.04.048/2023-24. 1 April.

The MCAs designed for various sectors provide the mechanisms for compensation in the event of early termination and event of default by either party, force majeure, and change in law. Table 9 presents extracts from the MCA of a BOT (toll) variant of PPP in the highway sector regarding the compensation payment terms dealing with each of those factors.

Table 9: Compensation Clauses from Model Concession Agreement in the Highway Sector

Factor	Action
Change in Law	If as a result of Change in Law, the Concessionaire suffers an increase in costs or reduction in net after-tax return or other financial burden, the aggregate financial effect of which exceeds the higher of ₹10 million ($0.14 million) and 0.5% of the Realizable Fee in any Accounting Year, the Concessionaire may notify the Authority and propose amendments to this Agreement so as to place the Concessionaire in the same financial position as it would have enjoyed had there been no such Change in Law resulting in the cost increase, reduction in return, or other financial burden as aforesaid.
Authority Default	Upon Termination on account of an Authority Default, the Authority shall pay to the Concessionaire, by way of Termination Payment, an amount equal to (i) Debt Due and (ii) 150% of the Adjusted Equity; provided that the Termination Payment shall not be less than an amount equal to the product of 6 and the average monthly fees actually realized 12 months prior to the Transfer Date.
Concessionaire Default	Upon Termination on account of a Concessionaire Default during the Operation Period, the Authority shall pay to the Concessionaire, by way of Termination Payment, an amount equal to 90% of the Debt Due less Insurance Cover; provided that if any insurance claims forming part of the Insurance Cover are not admitted and paid, then 80% of such unpaid claims shall be included in the computation of Debt Due.
Force Majeure	If Termination is on account of a Nonpolitical Event, the Authority shall make a Termination Payment to the Concessionaire in an amount equal to 90% of the Debt Due less Insurance Cover.
	If Termination is on account of an Indirect Political Event, the Authority shall make a Termination Payment to the Concessionaire in an amount equal to (i) Debt Due less Insurance Cover; provided that if any insurance claims forming part of the Insurance Cover are not admitted and paid, then 80% of such unpaid claims shall be included in the computation of Debt Due; and (ii) 110% of the Adjusted Equity.
	If Termination is on account of an Indirect Political Event and Nonpolitical Event, the Authority shall pay to the Concessionaire, by way of Termination Payment, an amount equal to (i) Debt Due and (ii) 150% of the Adjusted Equity; provided that the Termination Payment shall not be less than an amount equal to the product of 6 and the average monthly fees actually realized 12 months prior to the Transfer Date.

Source: National Highways Authority of India. 2020. *Model Concession Agreement for BOT (Toll) Projects*. 24 August.

Unsolicited Public–Private Partnership Proposals

Parameter	
Does the public–private partnership legal and regulatory framework allow submission and acceptance of unsolicited proposals?	✗[a]
What are the advantages provided to the project proponent for an unsolicited bid? • Competitive advantage at bid evaluation? • Swiss challenge? • Compensation of the project development costs? • Government support for land acquisition and resettlement cost? • Government support in the form of viability gap funding and guarantees?	NA NA NA NA NA

✓ = Yes, ✗ = No, NA = Not Applicable, UA = Unavailable.

[a] The While there is no regulatory framework or law at the central level, the central government actively discourages considering proposals received via unsolicited route. However, some state governments allow unsolicited proposals to be taken up on public–private partnership basis and have issued clear guidelines in dealing with them.

The Government of India generally favors transparent bidding processes to ensure fairness and equal treatment of potential bidders. While it acknowledges the varying approaches across states, such as Gujarat and Andhra Pradesh, which have integrated elements of the Swiss challenge approach and unsolicited proposals into their state PPP acts and policies, it emphasizes the importance of maintaining transparency and fairness throughout the recruitment processes. Similarly, states like Rajasthan and Madhya Pradesh have incorporated such methods into their infrastructure project guidelines. Other states, including Bihar, Karnataka, and Punjab, have also established frameworks for handling unsolicited bids. It is worth noting that these state-level approaches may differ from those of the central government and are applicable to sectors under their jurisdiction (footnote 13).

Foreign Investor Participation Restrictions

Parameter	
Is there any restriction for foreign investors on • Land use/ownership rights as opposed to similar rights of local investors? • Currency conversion?	✓ ✗
Public–private partnership projects with foreign sponsor participation (number)	260[a]

✓ = Yes, ✗ = No, NA = Not Applicable, UA = Unavailable.

[a] Based on the data from World Bank. Infrastructure Finance, PPPs and Guarantees. Custom Query (accessed 3 January 2024). Information on 96 projects is either partially available or not available, and hence excluded.

Source: Asian Development Bank. 2019. *Public–Private Partnership Monitor.* Second Edition.

This section presents the laws and regulations pertinent to land acquisition by foreign investors. According to the Foreign Exchange Management Regulations, 2018 (Acquisition and Transfer of Immovable Property in India), acquisition of immovable property by a foreign investor for carrying on a permitted activity is possible:[26]

- A person resident outside India who has established in India, in accordance with the Foreign Exchange Management Regulations, 2016 (establishment in India of a branch office or a liaison office or a project office or any other place of business), a branch, office, or other place of business for carrying on in India any activity, excluding a liaison office, may be allowed to do the following:
  (i) Acquire any immovable property in India, which is necessary for or incidental to carrying on such activity, provided that
      (a) all applicable laws, rules, regulations, or directions for the time being in force are duly complied with; and
      (b) the person files with the Reserve Bank a declaration in the Form IPI (i.e., a declaration of immovable property acquired by way of purchase in India) as prescribed by the Reserve Bank.
  (ii) Transfer, by way of mortgage to an authorized dealer as a security for any borrowing, the immovable property acquired in pursuance of clause (a) provided that no person from any of the following economies—Afghanistan; Bangladesh; Bhutan; Democratic People's Republic of Korea; Hong Kong, China; Iran; Macau, China; Nepal; Pakistan; the People's Republic of China; or Sri Lanka—shall acquire immovable property, other than on lease and not exceeding 5 years, without prior approval of the Reserve Bank.

- Prohibition on transfer of immovable property in India: No person resident outside India shall transfer any immovable property in India unless
  (i) the Reserve Bank may, for sufficient reasons, permit the transfer, subject to such conditions as may be considered necessary;
  (ii) a bank, which is an authorized dealer, may, subject to the directions issued by the Reserve Bank in this behalf, permit a person resident in India or on behalf of such person to create charge on his or her immovable property in India in favor of an overseas lender or security trustee, to secure an external commercial borrowing availed under the provisions of the Foreign Exchange Management Regulations, 2000 (Borrowing or Lending in Foreign Exchange), as amended from time to time;
  (iii) an Authorized Dealer in India being the Indian correspondent of an overseas lender may, subject to the directions issued by the Reserve Bank in this regard, create a mortgage on an immovable property in India owned by a nonresident Indian or an Overseas Citizen of India, being a director of a company outside India, for a loan to be availed by the company from the said overseas lender provided that
      (a) the funds shall be used by the borrowing company only for its core business purposes overseas; and
      (b) in case of invocation of charge, the Indian bank shall sell the immovable property to an eligible acquirer and remit the sale proceeds to the overseas lender; and

---

[26] Reserve Bank of India. 2018. *Foreign Exchange Management (Acquisition and Transfer of Immovable Property in India) Regulations, 2018.* Notification No. FEMA 21(R)/2018-RB. 26 March.

(iv) A person resident outside India who has acquired any immovable property in India in accordance with foreign exchange laws in force at the time of such acquisition or with the general or specific permission of the Reserve Bank may transfer such property to a person resident in India provided the transaction takes place through banking channels in India and provided that the resident is not otherwise prohibited from such acquisition.

The Foreigners Act (1946), the Registration of Foreigners Act (1939), and the Citizenship Act (1955), together with their rules and amendments, regulate the entry, movement, and stay of foreigners in India. The granting of employment visas by the Indian Bureau of Immigration (under the Ministry of Home Affairs of the Government of India) is allowed only to highly skilled and/or qualified professionals who are being engaged or appointed by a company or organization in India. Furthermore, employment visas shall not be granted for jobs for which qualified Indians are available (footnote 13).

Import of capital goods, machinery, or equipment (excluding secondhand machinery) is allowed subject to the conditions defined in the foreign direct investment (FDI) policy. The Consolidated FDI Policy 2020 provides that a foreign investor in the construction development sector will be permitted to exit and repatriate foreign investment before the completion of a project under automatic route provided that a lock-in period of 3 years, calculated with reference to each tranche of foreign investment, has been completed. However, transfer of stake from one nonresident to another nonresident without repatriation of investment will neither be subjected to any lock-in period nor to any government approval. Lock-in periods do not apply to hotels and tourist resorts, hospitals, special economic zones, educational institutions, old-age homes, and investment by nonresident Indians.

Dispute Resolution

Parameter	
Does the country have a dispute resolution tribunal?	✓
Does the country have an institutional arbitration mechanism?	✓
Can a foreign law be chosen to govern public–private partnership (PPP) contracts?	✗[a]
What dispute resolution mechanisms are available for PPP agreements? • Court litigation? • Local arbitration? • International arbitration?	✓ ✓ ✓
Has the country signed the New York Convention on the Recognition and Enforcement of Foreign Arbitral Awards?	✓

✓ = Yes, ✗ = No, NA = Not Applicable, UA = Unavailable.

[a] Based on the discussion in this publication under the section on Applicability of Foreign Law.

India has regulations related to arbitration and conciliation. The process of arbitration over the last 5 years has been carried out in accordance with the Indian Arbitration and Conciliation Act of 1996. After going through amendments in 2015 and 2018, the government, in March 2021, by assent from Parliament, approved the Arbitration and Conciliation (Amendment) Act, 2021, which replaces the Arbitration and Conciliation (Amendment) Ordinance of November 2020.

The amendment has two primary changes in the Act: (i) Section 36 of the Act that enables automatic stay on awards in certain cases where the court has prima facie evidence that the contract on which the award is based was affected by "fraud" and "corruption," which is deemed effective from October 2015; and (ii) the omission of Schedule VIII and substitution of Schedule 43J from the Act of 1996 with the new section that specifies the regulations, qualifications, experience, and norms for accreditation of arbitrators.[27]

1. Indian Council of Arbitration

The Indian Council of Arbitration (ICA) was established in 1965 as a specialized arbitral body at the national level under the initiative of the Government of India and apex business organizations like the Federation of Indian Chambers of Commerce and Industry. The main objective of the ICA is to promote amicable, quick, and inexpensive settlement of commercial disputes by means of arbitration and conciliation regardless of location. The ICA handles more than 400 domestic and international arbitration cases each year.[28]

According to the *Guidelines for Post-Award Contract Management for PPP Concessions*, the different methods generally followed for dispute resolution listed in the order in which they are generally taken are as follows (footnote 20):

- **Interparty discussions.** Representatives of each party first need to meet and attempt to resolve the dispute in good faith.
- **Mediation or conciliation.** Representatives of the parties should appear before a mediator or a conciliator and attempt to resolve the dispute.
- **Arbitration.** The dispute must be referred to and determined by a Board of Arbitrators to whom the parties make submissions. The process of arbitration must be supported by and should be carried out in accordance with the Indian Arbitration and Conciliation Act.
- **Adjudication.** In case a statutory Regulatory Authority or Commission has been set up, disputes might be settled through its adjudication instead of arbitration. These will not be binding until an appeal against such adjudication has been decided by a court.
- **Accelerated Dispute Resolution Committee.** The dispute must be referred to a committee comprising one or more representatives of each party if resolution in arbitration takes too much time. The committee, in accordance with the procedures or as decided by the committee itself, should set out in the contract attempts to resolve the dispute. Any decision of the committee is usually binding on the parties.

---

[27]   SCC Online Times. 2021. *Arbitration and Conciliation (Amendment) Act, 2021*. Blog. 16 March.
[28]   Indian Council of Arbitration. About Us.

2. Applicability of Foreign Law

Nidumuri (2015) posits that "a conservative argument has been that Indian parties cannot agree to resolve disputes choosing a foreign law, as that would mean contracting out of Indian Law, and therefore opposed to public policy."[29]

> Under the Indian legal framework, parties are free to choose the governing law of their contract, irrespective of the connection between the chosen law and the underlying contract. The limitations to this choice are that the intention of the parties must be expressed bona fide and legal and that the choice should not derogate from the mandatory provisions of Indian law and should not be opposed to public policy of India. The Indian Arbitration and Conciliation Act, 1996 also mandates the application of substantive Indian law when two Indian parties have contractually designated their seat of arbitration to India.[30]

It is thereby inferred that the PPP projects are governed only by laws of India. However, in case of private sector transactions, a recent judgment by the Supreme Court of India confirms that the two Indian parties are entitled to select a foreign seat of arbitration. An article in this order published by legal firm Singhania & Partners LLP states that

> The Court did not find any basis to import the Part I definition of "international commercial arbitration" or impose any nationality requirement in relation to Section 44 of the Indian Arbitration and Conciliation Act 1996. ...The Apex Court has finally resolved the long-term uncertainty by ruling that nothing stands in the way of party autonomy in designating a seat of arbitration outside India, even if both parties are Indian nationals.

India is a signatory to both the New York Convention on the Recognition and Enforcement of Foreign Arbitral Awards (New York Convention) as well as the Convention on the Execution of Foreign Arbitral Awards 1927 (Geneva Convention).[31]

The legal framework for PPP in India ranges from the Constitution of India to rules and regulations notified from time to time by various state instrumentalities. In addition to pieces of legislation relevant to a particular sector, such as the National Highways Authority of India (NHAI) Act (1988), the laws governing normal commercial transactions like the Indian Contract Act (1872), the Sale of Goods Act (1930), and the Negotiable Instruments Act (1881) will also have a bearing on PPP arrangements, as will various statutes.

The Society for Affordable Redressal of Disputes (SAROD) was initiated by the NHAI and the National Highways Builders Federation to settle disputes through arbitration. The objective is to reduce delays and expenses incurred because of disputes between the NHAI and its concessionaires. SAROD has also been applied to the major ports in accordance with the revised Model Concession Agreement of 2018. Under the Major Ports Authorities Act (2021), creation of an Adjudicatory Board has been

---

[29] L. Nidumuri. 2015. Whether Indian Parties Can Choose Foreign Law to Settle Disputes? Indus Law. *Mondaq*. 9 October.
[30] Asian Business Law Institute. 2023. *Choice of Law and Choice of Forum Clauses for Contracts Under Indian Law*. 1 November.
[31] V. Goel and M. Dhankar. 2021. Indian Parties Can Opt for a Foreign Seated Arbitration. Singhania & Partners LLP. *Mondaq*. 29 April.

proposed. The residual function of the former Tariff Authority for Major Ports shall be taken over by the Adjudicatory Board and shall include looking into disputes between ports and PPP concessionaires, reviewing stressed PPP projects, suggesting measures to review stressed PPP projects and revive such projects, and looking into complaints regarding the services rendered by the ports and private operators within the ports.

Environmental and Social Issues

Parameter	
Is there a local regulation establishing a process for environmental impact assessment?	✓
Is there a legal mechanism for the private partner to limit environmental liability for what is outside of its control or caused by third parties?	✓
Is there a local regulation establishing a process for social impact assessment?	✓
Is there involuntary land clearance for public–private partnership projects?	✓

✓ = Yes, ✗ = No, NA = Not Applicable, UA = Unavailable.

1. Environmental and Social Impact Assessment

The Ministry of Environment, Forest, and Climate Change has stipulated that environmental impact assessments (EIAs) are mandatory for infrastructure projects. The EIA notification was first issued in 1994, followed by detailed guidelines and institutional mechanisms published in 2006 via a notification. Subsequently, multiple minor amendments were made with the latest amendment issued in July 2023.

All projects are broadly grouped into two categories, depending on the spatial extent of potential project impacts on human health and on natural and human-made resources. Classifications of projects under Categories A and B are based on the pollution intensity or locational aspects. Category A projects are approved by the central government's Ministry of Environment, Forest and Climate Change. Category B projects are cleared by the State/Union Territory Environmental Impact Assessment Authority. The maximum timeline stated in the EIA Notification for the various stages of obtaining environmental approvals is 210 days, excluding the time required to undertake the EIA study (footnote 13).

In India, a social impact assessment was mandated in 2013 by the Right to Fair Compensation and Transparency in Land Acquisition, Rehabilitation and Resettlement Act. Any major project is required to conduct social impact assessment within 6 months from the project start date. For projects requiring land acquisition, the project developers must obtain consent from the majority of landowners. In the case of PPP projects, consent is required from 70% of landowners. After land acquisition, the project owners are required to compensate the affected individuals with a minimum amount of two times the market rate for urban land and a minimum of four times the value rate for rural land (footnote 13).

The state has legal powers under "the principle of eminent domain" for the acquisition of private property, and this can lead to involuntary displacement of people. The National Resettlement and Rehabilitation Policy (2007) provides for rehabilitation and resettlement of persons affected by the acquisition of land for projects of public purpose or involuntary displacement due to any other reason (footnote 13).

Land Rights

Parameter	
Which of the following is permitted to the private partner: • Transfer land lease/use/ownership rights to third party? • Use leased/owned land as collateral? • Mortgage leased/owned land?	✗ ✗ ✗
Is there a legal mechanism for granting wayleave rights, for example, laying water pipes or fiber cables over land occupied by persons other than the government or the private partner?	✓
Is there a land registry/cadastre with public information on land plots?	✓
Which of the following information on land plots is available to the private partner: • Appraisal of land value? • Landowners? • Land boundaries? • Utility connections? • Immovable property on land? • Plots classification?	✓ ✓ ✓ ✓ ✓ ✓

✓ = Yes, ✗ = No, NA = Not Applicable, UA = Unavailable.
Source: Asian Development Bank. 2019. *Public–Private Partnership Monitor.* Second Edition.

In India, land is subject within the powers of the state government, according to the Constitution of India; hence, property laws in India may differ from state to state. When a person acquires or owns an immovable property, the law also gives that person the right to use, lease, sell, rent, or transfer and/or gift the land. The owner also has a right to mortgage their immovable property as security for loans (footnote 13).

The key regulations governing land in India are as follows (footnote 13):

- The Real Estate Act, 2016 (Regulation and Development), which seeks to protect investors and boost investments in the real estate sector by ensuring that the sale of plots, apartments, buildings, or real estate projects are done efficiently and transparently;
- Right to Fair Compensation and Transparency in Land Acquisition, Rehabilitation and Resettlement Rules, 2015;
- Transfer of Property Act, 1882, which regulates the transfer of property in India;

- Registration Act, 1908, which provides for the procedure for registration of documents related to the transfer of immovable properties with the designated registration authority, and ensures that all documents regarding the sale and purchase of land are recorded and maintained;
- Indian Easements Act, 1882;
- Indian Contract Act, 1872, which determines the circumstances in which obligations of the parties to a contract are legally binding on them; and
- Indian Stamps Act, 1899.

In the case of PPP, the Land Acquisition Act (which applies across nearly all states) provides for the following (footnote 13):

- The appropriate government acquires land for PPP projects, where the ownership of the land continues to be vested with the government.
- When private companies acquire land for PPP projects, the prior consent of at least 70% of affected families shall be obtained through a process, as may be prescribed by the appropriate government.
- Transfer of ownership rights to a third party, use of leased lands as collateral, and mortgage of leased land are usually not permitted under the MCAs of PPP projects.

Government Support for Public–Private Partnership Projects

Parameter	
Project funding support	
Is there a dedicated government financial support mechanism for public–private partnership (PPP) projects?	✓

What are the instruments of government financial support available under this government financial support mechanism?
• Capital grant?
• Operations grant?
• Guarantees to cover[a]
   – Currency inconvertibility and transfer risk?
   – Foreign exchange risk?
   – War and civil disturbance risk?
   – Breach of contract risk?
   – Regulatory risk?
   – Expropriation risk?
   – Government payment obligation risk?
   – Credit risk?
   – Minimum demand/revenue risk?
   – Risk of making annuity/availability payments in a timely manner?
	
	✓
	✓
	
	✗
	✗
	✗
	✗
	✗
	✗
	✗
	✗
	✗

continued on next page

Table *continued*

Parameter	
What are the caps/ceilings for the government financial support under each of the above-mentioned government financial support instruments?	Twenty percent by the central government that could be supplemented by another 20% of total project cost by the state government or respective ministry; for hybrid annuity model projects, 40% of the total project cost in five equal installments linked to project completion milestones
Is there a minimum PPP project size (investment) for a PPP project to be eligible for receiving government financial support?	✗
Are there minimum equity investment requirements the private developer should meet for availing any of the above government support mechanism?	✓[b]
Are there minimum financial commitment requirements for the private developer equity before the government support could be drawn?	✓[c]
Is the government financial support required (usually the bid parameter for PPP projects)?	✓
Are unsolicited PPP proposals eligible to receive government financial support?	✗[d]
Are there standard operating procedures for providing government financial support to PPP projects? • Appraisal and approval process? • Budgeting process? • Disbursement process? • Monitoring process? • Accounting, auditing, and reporting process?	✓ ✓ ✓ ✓ ✓
Who are the signatories to the government financial support agreement?	For viability gap funding, the signatories include lead financial institution, empowered institution, concessionaire, and the owner (contracting agency).
Who is responsible for monitoring the performance of PPP projects availing government financial support? • Independent engineer? • Government agency? • Ministry of Finance?	Lead financial institution
What are the other forms of government support available for PPP projects? • Land acquisition funding support? • Funding support for resettlement and rehabilitation of affected parties? • Tax holidays/exemptions? • Real estate development rights? • Advertising and marketing rights? • Interest rate/cost of debt subventions? • Other subsidies and subventions?	 NA[e] NA[f] ✓ ✓ ✓ UA UA

continued on next page

Table *continued*

Parameter	
Can the other forms of government support be availed over and above the government financial support through various instruments listed above?	UA

✓ = Yes, ✗ = No, NA = Not Applicable, UA = Unavailable

a   These are adequately covered in the contractual provisions available in the (model) concession agreements for reliefs during events of force majeure and change in law. Penalties are payable by authorities for delays in payments (such as annuities), unless there are specific programs that are announced to assist the distressed assets, as was done in the roads sector.

b   The viability gap funding (VGF) scheme states that it will apply only if the contract/concession is awarded in favor of a private sector company in which 51% or more of the subscribed and paid-up equity is owned and controlled by a private entity.

c   The VGF scheme guidelines state that the 100% equity expended by the concessionaire is a prerequisite for the government to disburse the VGF amount.

d   A private sector company shall be eligible for VGF only if it is selected based on open competitive bidding and is responsible for financing, construction, maintenance, and operation of the project during the concession period.

e   Land is usually provided free of cost.

f   Funding support for resettlement and rehabilitation of affected parties is undertaken by the government.

Source: Asian Development Bank. 2019. *Public–Private Partnership Monitor.* Second Edition.

The government supports the PPP projects in the country through direct and indirect ways, starting from project conceptualization to project funding and closure. Table 10 describes the various government support mechanisms that are available for PPP projects in the country.

Table 10: Government Support Facilities for Public–Private Partnership Projects

Government Support Type	Comments
Project Development Facility	For details, see table on Project Development Funding below and the text following it.
Land Acquisition and Resettlement	The Government of India has supported the acquisition of land for the development of projects under the PPP framework by the public entity prior to commencement of the bidding process. One of the key factors that determine the approval of the PPPAC for the development of the PPP project includes the extent of land availability (usually must not be less than 60%) with the public entity for the purpose of project development. The land acquisition process includes an assessment of the land required for a project, notification, and eventual acquisition, and the ability of the government or the line department in fulfilling the obligation to provide land without any encumbrance or encroachments. Shifting of utilities from the project site and the acquisition of right-of-way for the project development are also part of the process. Right to Fair Compensation and Transparency in Land Acquisition, Rehabilitation and Resettlement Act, 2013 provides for the acquisition of land for public purpose under a humane participation and informed and transparent process, to provide just and fair compensation to affected families. The Act clearly sets out the procedure to be adopted for the acquisition of land with respect to development of projects under the PPP framework.

continued on next page

Table 10 *continued*

Government Support Type	Comments
Viability Gap Funding	The CCEA, in its meeting on 25 July 2005, approved a scheme to support PPPs in infrastructure. The Scheme for Financial Support to PPPs in Infrastructure (VGF scheme) of the Government of India is administered by the Ministry of Finance. The VGF scheme provides financial support in the form of grants, one time or deferred, to infrastructure projects undertaken through PPPs with a view to make them commercially viable. The Government of India provides VGF of up to 20% of the total project cost, normally in the form of a capital grant at the stage of project construction. The state government or statutory entity that owns the project may, if it so decides, provide additional grants out of its budget, of up to 20% of the total project cost, capping the total grant by various entities to 40% of total project cost. The scheme requires the project authorities to seek in-principle approval of the Empowered Institution/Empowered Committee prior to seeking bids and to obtain the final approval after the selection of the bidder. Approvals to projects are given prior to invitation of bids, and actual disbursement takes place once the private entity has expended its portion of the equity. • VGF of up to ₹2 billion for each project may be sanctioned by the Empowered Committee, subject to the budgetary ceilings indicated by the Ministry of Finance.[a] • Amounts exceeding ₹2 billion may be sanctioned by the Empowered Committee with the approval of the Finance Minister.[b] **Eligible Sectors.** The sectors eligible under the VGF scheme are • roads and bridges, railways, seaports, airports, and inland waterways; • power; • urban transport, water supply, sewerage, solid waste management, and other physical infrastructure in urban areas; • infrastructure projects in special economic zones and internal infrastructure in national investment and manufacturing zones; • international convention centers and other tourism infrastructure projects; • capital investment in the creation of modern storage capacity, including cold chains and post-harvest storage; • education, health, and skills development, without annuity provision; • oil, gas, and liquefied natural gas storage facility (includes city gas distribution network); • oil and gas pipelines (includes city gas distribution network); • irrigation (dams, channels, embankments); • telecommunication (fixed network) (includes optic fiber, wire, and cable networks that provide broadband/internet); • telecommunication towers; • terminal markets; • common infrastructure in agriculture markets; and • soil testing laboratories. In November 2020, the central government approved the continuation and revamp of the scheme for financial support to Public Private Partnerships in Infrastructure Viability Gap Funding Scheme until 2024–2025 with a total outlay of ₹81 billion ($0.98 billion).[c]

continued on next page

Table 10 *continued*

Government Support Type	Comments

Government Guarantees	The key elements related to government guarantees are as follows:
	• The sovereign guarantee is normally extended to
	  – improve the viability of projects undertaken by government entities with significant social and economic benefits,
	  – enable public sector companies to raise resources on more favorable terms, and
	  – fulfill the requirement in cases where sovereign guarantee is a precondition for concessional loans from bilateral and multilateral agencies to sub-sovereign borrowers.
	• The Fiscal Responsibility and Budget Management Act, 2003 prescribes a limit of 0.5% of GDP for guarantees to be given in any financial year beginning with FY2004–2005.
	• The Ministry of Finance is the guarantee approving authority. After approval, guarantees are monitored by the concerned administrative ministries.
	• Under a "deductible" arrangement, in case of default of guarantee, the government would pay 70%–90% of the amount in default, and the balance 10%–30% would be paid by the borrowing institution.

Tax Subsidies	The government has provided several incentives such as tax exemption and duty-free imports of road building equipment and machinery to encourage private sector participation. Also, 100% exemption on income tax is available to eligible infrastructure projects for a period of 10 years. PPP projects may also qualify for various tax incentives offered by the government, such as • exemption from registration tax on acquisition of real estate for BOT projects; • application of, or exemption from, a lower rate of value-added tax for infrastructure facilities or construction of those facilities supplied to the state or local governments as BTO and BOT projects; • reduction of, or exemption from, various appropriation charges; • recognition of a certain percentage of the investment as a reserve to be treated as an expense for computing corporate taxes; • allowing the project company to issue infrastructure bonds at a concessional tax rate on interest earned; and • protection against reduction of tariffs or shortening of the concession period.
Dedicated Institutions for Facilitating Long-Term Funds for Infrastructure Projects	**India Infrastructure Finance Company Limited.** The IIFCL is wholly owned by the Government of India. The company was set up in 2006 to provide long-term financial assistance to viable infrastructure projects through the Scheme for Financing Viable Infrastructure Projects under a special purpose vehicle called the IIFCL. The sectors eligible for financial assistance from the IIFCL include transportation, energy, water, sanitation, communication, and social and commercial infrastructure. For greenfield projects, the IIFCL offers direct lending by way of senior debt and subordinate debt. For brownfield projects, the IIFCL provides financial support using two key instruments: takeout finance and credit enhancement scheme (partial credit guarantee). The IIFCL also provides refinancing to banks and other eligible financial institutions.

continued on next page

Table 10 *continued*

Government Support Type	Comments
	National Investment and Infrastructure Fund. The NIIF is India's first sovereign wealth fund set up by the government in February 2015. The government has 49% shareholding of the fund. The NIIF is a fund manager that invests in infrastructure and related sectors in India. The NIIF manages more than $4 billion of capital commitments across three funds: Master Fund, Fund of Funds, and Strategic Fund. The funds were set up to create infrastructure investments in India by raising capital from domestic and international institutions.
	Infrastructure Nonbanking Financial Companies. Infrastructure NBFCs, such as the Power Finance Corporation Ltd and the REC Ltd (acquired by the Power Finance Corporation in 2019), have diversified portfolios across the power sector value chain (generation, distribution, and transmission). On the other hand, the Housing and Urban Development Corporation Ltd, by virtue of its urban infrastructure mandate, has a wide sector presence. Urban infrastructure includes multiple sectors, such as water supply, sewerage, and housing.
	National Bank for Financing Infrastructure and Development. The government has formed this institution to support the development of long-term, nonrecourse infrastructure financing in India.[d] The shareholding of the bank will be held by the central government and a set of other entities including multilateral banks, pension funds, insurance companies, banks, and financial institutions. Functions of the NBFID include (i) extending loans and advances for infrastructure projects, (ii) taking over or refinancing such existing loans, (iii) attracting investment from private sector investors and institutional investors for infrastructure projects, (iv) organizing and facilitating foreign participation in infrastructure projects, (v) facilitating negotiations with various government authorities for dispute resolution in the field of infrastructure financing, and (vi) providing consultancy services in infrastructure financing.

BOT = build–operate–transfer, BTO = build–transfer–operate, CCEA = Cabinet Committee on Economic Affairs, FY = fiscal year, GDP = gross domestic product, IIFCL = India Infrastructure Finance Company Limited, NBFC = nonbanking financial company, NBFID = National Bank for Financing Infrastructure and Development, NIIF = National Investment and Infrastructure Fund,
PPP = public–private partnership, PPPAC = Public Private Partnership Approval Committee, VGF = viability gap funding.
[a] The Empowered Committee comprises Secretaries of Economic Affairs, NITI Aayog (formerly Planning Commission), Expenditure department, and the line ministry dealing with the subject.
[b] In March 2015, the Department of Economic Affairs issued a memorandum modifying the delegation of powers for formulation, appraisal, and approval of PPP National Highway projects. Under the memorandum, the threshold project cost for approval of projects by the CCEA based on PPPAC's recommendations has been increased from ₹5 billion to ₹10 billion. Based on the memorandum, the appraisal of projects below ₹250 million shall be done by the Ministry of Road Transport and Highways and approved by the Secretary of Road Transport and Highways; those between ₹250 million and ₹10 billion shall be appraised by the Standing Finance Committee chaired by the Secretary of Road Transport and Highways and approved by the Minister of Road Transport and Highways; and those above ₹10 billion shall be appraised by the PPPAC and approved by the CCEA.
[c] In November 2020, the Government of India issued a revamped scheme in the form of VGF, called the Guidelines for Financial Support of Public–Private Partnerships in Infrastructure. The scheme has been extended until 2024–2025 with a total outlay of ₹81 billion ($0.98 billion). The revamped scheme has introduced two sub-schemes for mainstreaming private participation in social infrastructure:
  (i) Sub-scheme 1 shall cater to social sectors such as wastewater treatment, water supply, solid waste management, health, and education sectors. Projects in these sectors face bankability issues and poor revenue streams to cater fully to capital costs. Projects eligible under this category should have at least 100% operational cost recovery. The central government will provide a maximum of 30% of total project cost (TPC) via VGF and the state government, sponsoring central ministry, or statutory entity may provide additional support of up to 30% of TPC.
  (ii) Sub-scheme 2 shall support demonstration and pilot social sector projects. The projects may be from health and education sectors where there is at least 50% operational cost recovery. In such projects, the central government and state governments together shall provide up to 80% of capital expenditure and up to 50% of operation and maintenance costs for the first 5 years. The central government shall provide a maximum of 40% of TPC and may provide a maximum of 25% of operational costs of the project in the first 5 years of commercial operations.

These sub-schemes are in addition to the ongoing VGF scheme for all other eligible sector projects that have been continuing since the inception of the scheme in 2006. The approval process has been modified to indicate that (i) a VGF of up to ₹2 billion for each project may be sanctioned by the Empowered Committee, subject to the budgetary ceilings indicated by the Ministry of Finance; and (ii) the amounts exceeding ₹2 billion may be sanctioned by the Empowered Committee with approval of the Finance Minister.

d In March 2021, the Government of India issued a gazette notification regarding the establishment of the NBFID through the National Bank for Financing Infrastructure and Development Act. The objective of the entity is to support the development of long-term, nonrecourse infrastructure financing in India, including developing bonds and derivative markets necessary for infrastructure financing, and to carry on the business of financing infrastructure and matters connected therewith or incidental thereto. The Act defines the development and financial objectives of the institution:

"The developmental objective of the Institution shall be to coordinate with the Central and State Governments, regulators, financial institutions, institutional investors, and such other relevant stakeholders, in India or outside India, to facilitate building and improving the relevant institutions to support the development of long-term nonrecourse infrastructure financing in India including the domestic bonds and derivatives markets. The financial objective of the Institution shall be to lend or invest, directly or indirectly, and seek to attract investment from private sector investors and institutional investors, in infrastructure projects located in India, or partly in India and partly outside India, with a view to foster sustainable economic development in India."

The Act also defines the legal form, functions, powers, and activities of the institution. Chapter IV, Article 17 of the Act defines in detail the 25 powers and functions mandated to the institution, in addition to their 10 subfunctions.

Sources: Asian Development Bank. 2019. *Public–Private Partnership Monitor.* Second Edition; ASA Law Firm. 2021. *Newsletter Weekly*; Government of India, Ministry of Finance, Department of Economic Affairs. 2020. *Scheme for Financial Support to Public Private Partnerships in Infrastructure (Viability Gap Funding Scheme)*; Government of India, Ministry of Finance, Department of Economic Affairs. 2010. *Government Guarantee Policy*; and PRS Legislative Research. 2021. *The National Bank for Financing Infrastructure and Development (NBFID) Bill, 2021.*

Parameter (Project Development Funding)	
What are the various sources of funds for public–private partnership (PPP) project preparation? • Budgetary allocations? • Dedicated project preparation/project development fund? • Technical assistance from multilateral, bilateral, and donor agencies? • Recovery of project preparation funding from the preferred bidder?	 ✓ ✓ ✓ ✓
At what stage of the PPP project can the project preparation/development funding be availed by the government agency? • Prefeasibility stage? • Detailed feasibility stage? • Transaction stage?	 ✓ ✓ ✓
Is there a threshold size (investment) for a PPP project to avail project development funding?	x[a]
Is there a list of project preparation/project development activities toward which the project development funding can be utilized?	✓
Can the project development funding be utilized to appoint transaction advisors for PPP projects?	✓
Is there a specific process to be followed by government agencies to appoint transaction advisors?	✓
What are the payment mechanisms for making payments to transaction advisors?[b] • Timesheet-based? • Milestone-based?	 ✓[c] ✓

continued on next page

Table *continued*

Parameter (Project Development Funding)	
Are there standard agreements and documents to avail project development funding?	✓
Who are the signatories to the project development funding agreements?	Authorized signatories from the Department of Economic Affairs and the sponsoring/ contracting authority

✓ = Yes, ✗ = No, NA = Not Applicable, UA = Unavailable.

[a] While there is no threshold size indicated in the Scheme and Guidelines for the India Infrastructure Project Development Fund, 2013, the operational management of the fund indicates three kinds of projects that are generally eligible for project development funding:
   (i) Revenue-generating commercial projects (concession/build–own–operate–transfer or its variants/lease contracts). A project financial internal rate of return (FIRR) of 20% or more on the private sector investment should be demonstrated. If the FIRR is below 20%, even with a viability gap funding of up to 40%, then the project shall not ordinarily be presented before the Empowered Institution.
   (ii) Efficiency enhancement/cost-saving projects (management or service contracts or engineering, performance-based operation and maintenance contracts). Where there is either no or low private sector investment, the financial savings/enhanced revenues should ordinarily be able to recover payouts by government within 8–10 years after project completion. Annuity- based projects would also be covered under this category.
   (iii) Nonrevenue-generating projects with high economic returns (e.g., sewerage system). For projects undertaken in PPP schemes based on economic return considerations, the project eligibility will be based on sector preferences to be established by the Empowered Institution and would be based on annuity payments by the sponsoring authority.

[b] See Government of India, Ministry of Finance, Department of Economic Affairs. 2022. *Transaction Advisors for PPP Projects: Manual for the Use of Panel*; and Government of India, Ministry of Finance, Department of Expenditure. 2010. *Model Request for Proposal for Selection of Financial Consultants and Transaction Advisors*. Office Memorandum. 29 March.

[c] The payment mechanism depends on the terms of the contract.

The Department of Economic Affairs (DEA) has issued the Scheme and Guidelines for the India Infrastructure Project Development Fund (IIPDF) primarily to support project preparation for contracting agencies. The revolving fund of ₹1 billion ($12.19 million) was first announced in the union budget of 2007–2008 for supporting the development of credible and bankable PPP projects that can be offered to the private sector. The IIPDF aims to assist contracting agencies in supporting procurement costs of PPPs, including the appointment of transaction advisors, and other expenses incurred for conducting feasibility studies, environment impact studies, financial structuring, legal reviews, and development of project documentation such as concession agreement, commercial assessment studies (i.e., traffic studies, demand assessment, capacity to pay assessment), and grading of projects. The IIPDF will assist contracting agencies ordinarily with up to 75% of project development expenses, while the agencies themselves will have to commit to co-funding the remaining 25%. Upon successful completion of the bidding process, the project development expenditure will be recovered from the successful bidder.[32]

[32] Government of India, MOF, DEA, Infrastructure Finance Secretariat. 2022. *Scheme for Financial Support for Project Development Expenses of PPP Projects – India Infrastructure Project Development Fund Scheme*.

Sources of Funding for the India Infrastructure Project Development Fund

The IIPDF was funded with an initial budgetary outlay of ₹1 billion ($12.19 million) by the Ministry of Finance (MOF), Government of India (footnote 33). This would be supplemented, subject to necessity, through budgetary support by the MOF from time to time. The IIPDF has the following attributes:

- Contributions from multilateral and bilateral agencies are governed by the IIPDF schemes and guidelines of 2013.[33]
- As per the 2013 IIPDF scheme and guidelines, project development funding should be recovered from a successful developer. A project development funding is an interest-free financial assistance for meeting the project development expenses. This is expected to be recovered from the successful private sector partner upon award of the project. The sponsoring authority will reimburse the IIPDF—the project development expenses along with a fee of up to 40% of the funding.
- As per the 2013 IIPDF scheme guidelines, the IIPDF will be available to sponsoring authorities for PPP projects for the purpose of meeting the project development costs, which may include the expenses incurred by the sponsoring authority with respect to feasibility studies, environment impact studies, financial structuring, legal reviews, and development of project documentation, such as concession agreement, commercial assessment studies (i.e., traffic studies, demand assessment, capacity to pay assessment), and grading of projects. These are all required for achieving financial close of such projects on individual or turnkey basis.[34] The IIPDF will contribute up to 75% of the project development expenses to the sponsoring authority as an interest-free loan.
- The IIPDF will be available to finance an appropriate portion of the cost of consultants and transaction advisors on a PPP project, where such consultants and transaction advisors are appointed by the sponsoring authority either from among the transaction advisors empaneled by the DEA or through a transparent system of procurement under a contract for services. Accordingly, the features of the existing IIPDF are enhanced; the fund has been restructured as a central sector scheme with a total outlay of ₹1.50 billion from 2022–2023 to 2024–2025 (footnote 33).
- Funding under the IIPDF scheme can be for a maximum of ₹50 million ($0.6 million) for a single project. Any cost above this would be borne by the project sponsoring authority.
- To seek project development funding from the IIPDF, the sponsoring authority will apply to the DEA's PPP Cell through a memorandum for consideration, which is an application to be made by the sponsoring authority in seeking project development funding from the IIPDF set up by the DEA. A standard set of information needs to be filled in the memorandum for consideration for seeking funding approval.

---

[33] Government of India, MOF, DEA. 2013. *Schemes and Guidelines for India Infrastructure Project Development Fund.*
[34] Financial close refers to the end of the procurement phase when the PPP contract has been signed, when any conditions precedent for financing are met, and when financing is in place so that the project company can commence construction.

Maturity of the Public–Private Partnership Market

Parameter	
PPP project statistics	
Is there a national public–private partnership (PPP) database for the country?	✓
Is the distribution of PPP projects across infrastructure sectors available?	✓
Is the distribution of PPP projects across various stages of the PPP life cycle available?	✓

✓ = Yes, ✗ = No, NA = Not Applicable, UA = Unavailable.
Source: Asian Development Bank. 2019. *Public–Private Partnership Monitor.* Second Edition.

The government maintains a repository of information on infrastructure projects implemented by the government on a PPP basis across a predefined set of parameters.[35] The database provides information on infrastructure projects through the functionality of viewing various standardized and customized reports across sectors, states, implementation status, and year of award. It also contains information on projects that were either under preconstruction, construction, or operation and maintenance (O&M) stage as of 1 April 2011, or awarded thereafter, and that have a project cost greater than ₹50 million ($0.60 million).

Parameter	
Does the country publish a national public–private partnership (PPP) project pipeline?	✓ᵃ
At what frequency is the national PPP project pipeline published?	UA
Is the national PPP project pipeline based on the National Infrastructure Pipeline for the country?	✓ᵃ

✓ = Yes, ✗ = No, NA = Not Applicable, UA = Unavailable.
ᵃ The *National Infrastructure Pipeline (NIP) 2019*, released in 2020, was developed by the Department of Economic Affairs, Ministry of Finance, Government of India. The NIP comprises both PPP and non-PPP projects.

In 2020, the Government of India, for the first time, announced the National Infrastructure Pipeline (NIP), 2019–2025 (including those proposed to be financed by the central government, the state government, and the private sector). The pipeline indicates the proposed investments across all infrastructure sectors for a 5-year horizon. In preparing the NIP, the DEA has collated information from various stakeholders, including line ministries, departments, state governments, and private sector across infrastructure subsectors. The subsector information was identified in line with the Harmonized Master List of Infrastructure. The NIP comprises all projects, including greenfield and brownfield projects, and those at various stages of project preparation and have met the minimum project cost threshold of ₹1 billion ($12.19 million). Details of the projects are provided in the respective sectors.

---

[35] Government of India, MOF, DEA. List of All PPP Projects (accessed 26 December 2023).

Parameter	
Sources of public–private partnership (PPP) financing	
Who are the typical entities financing public–private partnership (PPP) projects in the country?	
• Private developers?	✓
• Construction contractors?	✓
• Institutional, financial, private equity investors?	✓
• Pension funds?	✓
• Insurance companies?	✓
• Banks?	✓
• Nonbanking financial companies/financial institutions?	✓
• Donor agencies?	✓
• Government agencies and state-owned enterprises?	✓
What is the distribution of financing among these entities financing PPP projects?	UA
Does the country have the history or track record of issuing bonds by infrastructure projects?	✓
How many infrastructure projects and/or private developers for infrastructure projects have raised funding through bond issuances?	UA
What is the value of funding raised through capital markets by PPPs?	UA
Does the country have a matured derivatives market to hedge certain risks associated with PPPs?	✗
Does the country have a national development bank?	✓[a]
Does the country have credit rating agencies to rate infrastructure projects?	✓
Typically, what are the credit ratings achieved/received by infrastructure projects?	UA
Is there a threshold credit rating for infrastructure PPPs below which institutional investors, pension funds, and insurance companies would not invest in infrastructure PPPs?	✓
What is the typical funding model for infrastructure PPPs—corporate finance or project finance?	Both
Are there regulatory limits/restrictions for the maximum exposure that can be taken by banks to infrastructure projects?	✓

✓ = Yes, ✗ = No, NA = Not Applicable, UA = Unavailable

[a] India has multiple development banks such as the Infrastructure Finance Corporation of India, Industrial Development Bank of India, National Bank for Agriculture and Rural Development, Rural Electrification Corporation, and Power Finance Corporation, which were created to finance infrastructure.

Source: Asian Development Bank. 2019. *Public–Private Partnership Monitor.* Second Edition.

Key Sources of Public–Private Partnership Financing

Most infrastructure PPP projects are financed locally by state-owned banks, resulting in heavy reliance on domestic bank funding. In recent years, the banking sector has experienced some degree of stress due to considerable levels of nonperforming assets. This has led to reduced credit availability from domestic banks.[36] A lack of adequate financing has been one of the key challenges; hence, there is still a need to develop alternate sources of funding to reduce overdependence on domestic banks for funding infrastructure projects.

- **Equity (domestic and foreign).** Private equity investors are more keen in funding specific operational assets rather than portfolio-level investments. Currently, 100% foreign direct investment (FDI) is allowed in almost all infrastructure sectors. Apart from the FDI route, foreign investors registered as foreign institutional investors or foreign portfolio investors may invest through the Portfolio Investment Scheme route. Gaps in infrastructure financing due to a reduction of the capital available from traditional sources have also led to the creation of alternative sources of funding such as the Masala bonds, Infrastructure Investment Trusts, pension funds, and Infrastructure Debt Funds.[37]
- **Bond market.** The primary corporate debt market is dominated by the financial sector, and relatively small funds are raised by manufacturing and other sectors. The secondary market in corporate bonds has not picked up as much as for government securities. The primary market in corporate debt is basically a private placement market with most of the corporate bond issues privately placed among the wholesale investors (i.e., banks, mutual funds, provident funds, and other large investors such as the Life Insurance Corporation of India). The bond market, however, has been indirectly supporting infrastructure investments by investing in entities such as the NHAI, Power Finance Corporation, Rural Electrification Corporation, and most recently, the railways.
- **Rupee-denominated or Masala bonds.** These are plain vanilla bonds issued by an eligible Indian entity in foreign markets. The interest payments and principal reimbursements are denominated (expressed) in Indian rupees. Eligible resident entities are allowed to issue only plain vanilla Indian rupee-denominated bonds issued overseas in financial centers that are compliant to the Financial Action Task Force. The added benefit to Indian entities in relation to this form of funding is that their currency risk is obviated, which could possibly bring down the costs of domestic borrowing.
- **Infrastructure debt funds and infrastructure investment trusts.** The Reserve Bank of India has introduced these long-term funding options to address the banks' concerns related to asset liability management. Infrastructure debt funds (IDFs) are investment vehicles that can be set up as trusts or as nonbanking financial companies (NBFCs) and are used for investments in infrastructure projects. Foreign and domestic institutional investors, typically long-term investors, are permitted to invest in IDFs through units or bonds they issued. The IDFs, in turn, invest in infrastructure projects. Regulated by the Securities and Exchange Board of India, infrastructure investment trusts (InvITs) enable investments in the infrastructure sector by pooling small sums of money from multiple individual investors. InvITs may invest in projects directly or indirectly through a special purpose vehicle (SPV). Investment of PPP projects can

---

[36] Federation of Indian Chambers of Commerce and Industry. 2016. *Infrastructure Financing: Emerging Options in India*.
[37] A. Joshi and S. Talwar. 2017. *Infrastructure in India*. Economic Laws Practice.

only be through the SPV. There are two types of InvITs allowed: one is allowed to invest mainly in completed and revenue-generating infrastructure projects, and the other has the flexibility to invest in completed or under-construction projects. While the former must undertake a public offer of its units, the latter must opt for a private placement of its units. Both structures are required to be listed. Infrastructure companies have been slow to respond to IDFs and InvITs. Listing on the exchanges is mandatory for both publicly offered and privately placed InvITs.

- **National Investment and Infrastructure Fund.** This fund is India's first sovereign wealth fund set up by the Government of India in February 2015 (the government has 49% shareholding). The National Investment and Infrastructure Fund is a fund manager that invests in infrastructure and its related sectors in India. It manages more than $4 billion of capital commitments across three funds: Master Fund, Fund of Funds, and Strategic Fund.

- **National Bank for Financing Infrastructure and Development.** This is proposed under the National Bank for Financing Infrastructure and Development Bill, approved in March 2021 by the government. The National Bank for Financing Infrastructure and Development will be set up as a corporate body with authorized share capital of ₹1 trillion ($12.19 billion). The bank will have both financial and development objectives. Financial objectives will be to directly or indirectly lend, invest, or attract investments for infrastructure projects located entirely or partly in India. The central government will prescribe the sectors to be covered under the infrastructure domain. Development objectives include facilitating the development of the market for bonds, loans, and derivatives for infrastructure financing.[38]

- **External commercial borrowings.** These borrowings refer to commercial loans in the form of bank loans, securitized instrument buyers' credit, and suppliers' credit availed from nonresident lenders. Companies in the infrastructure sector, NBFC–infrastructure finance companies, NBFC-asset finance companies, holding companies, and core investment companies are now permitted to raise external commercial borrowings for an average maturity period of 5 years, thus allowing infrastructure companies to secure short- and long-term debt funding.

- **Pension funds.** CPP Investments (The Canada Pension Plan Investment Board), Norwegian State Pension Fund Global, Ontario Municipal Employees Retirement System, and Caisse de depot et placement du Quebec (CDPQ) have made various investments in India, exploring further opportunities in the country's financial services, telecoms, and digital and logistics sectors.

- **Partial credit guarantee scheme.** The partial credit guarantee scheme, developed jointly by the Asian Development Bank and the India Infrastructure Finance Company Limited, has been opted for by several borrowers in the infrastructure sector to refinance debt of operational projects, including conventional energy, renewables, and highways. This scheme provides an additional credit support in the form of a "first loss" guarantee, which escalates the credit rating of an operational project. The quantum of guarantee is limited to 50% of the total outstanding debt. The structure enables operational infrastructure projects to reach the required rating category for participation by insurance and pension funds.

---

[38]   PRS Legislative Research. 2021. *The National Bank for Financing Infrastructure and Development (NBFID) Bill, 2021.*

1. Key Sources of Public–Private Partnership Financing—Outlook

The Government of India released the Summary Report of the Task Force on the NIP for 2019–2025 on 31 December 2019. The NIP is a whole-of-government exercise and the first of its kind to provide world-class infrastructure across the country, with the goal of improving the quality of life for all citizens. It aims to improve project preparation and attract investments into infrastructure (both domestic and foreign). The NIP is crucial for India to achieve its target of becoming a $5 trillion economy by 2025 and its vision of becoming a $10 trillion economy by 2035.

The NIP estimates a total infrastructure investment and capital expenditure of ₹111 trillion ($1.556 trillion). Of the total pipeline, projects worth ₹44 trillion ($602.66 billion) (40% of NIP) are under implementation, projects worth ₹33 trillion ($451.99 billion) (30%) are at conceptual stage, and projects worth ₹22 trillion ($301.33 billion) (20%) are under development. Information regarding the stage of projects worth ₹11 trillion ($150.66 billion) (10% of NIP) is unavailable. The central government (39%) and state governments (40%) are expected to have almost equal share in implementing the NIP in India, followed by the private sector (21%). The breakdown of the investment estimates in terms of sponsoring bodies, according to the National Infrastructure Pipeline, is provided in Figure 9.

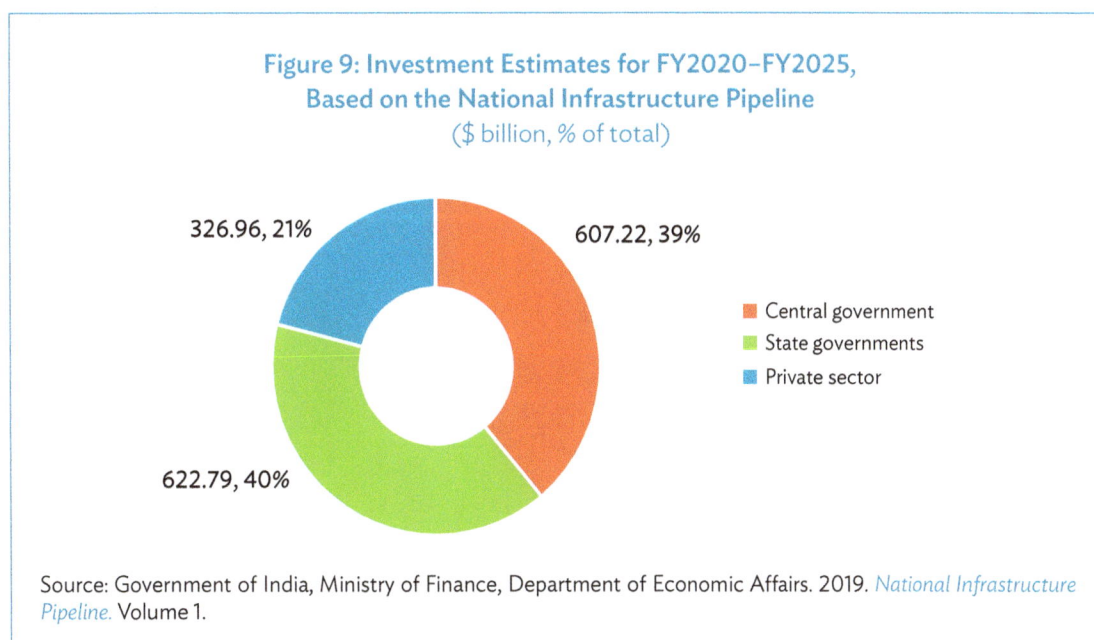

Figure 9: Investment Estimates for FY2020–FY2025, Based on the National Infrastructure Pipeline
($ billion, % of total)

- 326.96, 21%
- 607.22, 39%
- 622.79, 40%

Legend:
- Central government
- State governments
- Private sector

Source: Government of India, Ministry of Finance, Department of Economic Affairs. 2019. *National Infrastructure Pipeline.* Volume 1.

From a sector-focus perspective, the transport, energy and urban sectors have the highest proposed investment under the NIP, with 73% of the capital expenditure expected in these three sectors alone. A breakdown of the sector-wise expected investments till 2025 is presented in Figure 10.

Figure 10: Sector-wise Breakdown of Investments Proposed Under the National Infrastructure Pipeline, 2020–2025

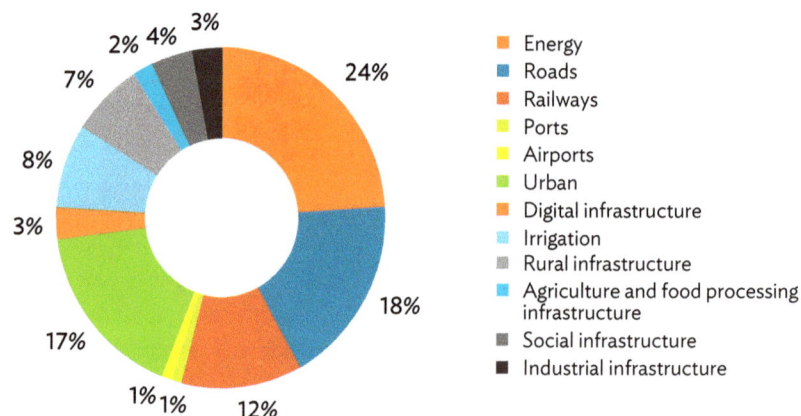

- Energy — 24%
- Roads — 18%
- Railways — 12%
- Ports — 1%
- Airports — 1%
- Urban — 17%
- Digital infrastructure — 3%
- Irrigation — 8%
- Rural infrastructure — 7%
- Agriculture and food processing infrastructure — 2%
- Social infrastructure — 4%
- Industrial infrastructure — 3%

Source: Government of India, Ministry of Finance, Department of Economic Affairs. 2019. *National Infrastructure Pipeline.* Volume 1.

2. Typical Contours of Infrastructure Financing

Equity sponsors play an important role in project development. Table 11 shows the most active project sponsors between July 2021 and August 2022 in India.

Table 11: Active Project Sponsors in India, July 2021 to August 2022

Name	Total Project Financing ($ million)	Total Project Financing (₹ billion)	No. of Projects
Adani Group	1,909.8	156.6	2
IRB Infrastructure Developers Ltd	220.6	18.1	2
Dilip Buildcon Limited	394.3	32.3	4
Zurich Airports	1,390.0	1,14.0	1
Ashoka Buildcon	182.6	15.0	1
Renew Power Limited	213.4	17.5	2
Mitsui	157.0	12.9	1
Torrent Group	73.4	6.0	1
KNR Construction	60.0	4.9	2
Enel SpA	50.0	4.1	1

Source: World Bank. Infrastructure Finance, PPPs and Guarantees. Custom Query (accessed 15 July 2023).

Credit Rating Agencies in India

There are six credit rating agencies in India.[39] Credit rating agencies are regulated by the Securities and Exchange Board of India.

- **CRISIL Limited.** CRISIL Limited, formerly Credit Rating Information Services of India Limited, pioneered credit rating in India in 1987. CRISIL Ratings is a business division of CRISIL Limited, majority of which is owned by S&P Global Inc., a leading provider of transparent and independent ratings, benchmarks, analytics, and data to capital and commodity markets worldwide. CRISIL is a full-service rating agency. In the context of emerging options for infrastructure financing, CRISIL has developed specific criteria for rating Real Estate Investment Trusts and Infrastructure Investment Trusts. In consultation with the MOF and other stakeholders, CRISIL developed a new credit rating framework for operational infrastructure projects based on "expected loss methodology." The ratings assigned under this framework are an opinion on the expected loss to be incurred over the life of the debt instrument and take into account not only the probability of default, but also post-default recoveries. In February 2017, CRISIL assigned the first infrastructure expected loss rating in India to Purulia and Kharagpur Transmission Co., an SPV owned by Sterlite Power Transmission.[40]
- **ICRA Limited.** ICRA Limited, formerly Investment Information and Credit Rating Agency of India Limited, is a public limited company set up in 1991 in Gurugram. Moody's Investors Service, an international credit rating agency, is ICRA's largest shareholder. ICRA is also a full-service rating agency, and its product portfolio includes rating for corporate debt, financial rating, structured finance, infrastructure, insurance, mutual funds, project and public finance, small and medium-sized enterprises, and market-linked debentures, among others.[41]
- **CARE Ratings Limited.** CARE Ratings Limited (or CareEdge Ratings) commenced operations in April 1993. It covers the full spectrum of credit rating, including manufacturing, infrastructure, financial sector and banks, and nonfinancial services, among others. The company has launched a new international credit rating agency called the ARC Ratings by teaming up with four partners from Brazil, Malaysia, Portugal, and South Africa. ARC Ratings has commenced operations and completed sovereign ratings of countries, including India.[42]
- **India Ratings and Research Private Limited.** India Ratings is a wholly owned subsidiary of the Fitch Group. It offers credit ratings for insurance companies, banks, corporate issuers, project finance, financial institutions, finance and leasing companies, managed funds, and urban local bodies.[43]

---

[39] Securities and Exchange Board of India. Name and Registered Addresses of Credit Rating Agencies.
[40] CRISIL Ratings Limited. CRISIL Ratings.
[41] ICRA Limited. Our Profile.
[42] CARE Ratings Limited. About Us.
[43] India Ratings and Research. Overview.

- **Acuite Ratings & Research Limited.** Established in 2005, Acuite is a joint initiative of the Small Industries Development Bank of India, Dun & Bradstreet India, and leading banks in India. It is also a full-service rating agency. Some of its products include bond ratings, commercial paper ratings, bank loan ratings, small and medium-sized enterprises ratings, and various grading services.[44]
- **Infomerics Valuation and Rating Private Limited** is a credit rating agency registered with the Securities and Exchange Board of India and accredited by the Reserve Bank of India. It was conceived and instituted by a team of professionals with experience in finance, banking, and administrative service.

---

[44]   Acuite Ratings & Research. Credit Ratings.

III. Sector-Specific Public–Private Partnership Landscape

A. Roads

Parameter	Value	Unit
Length of the total road network	6,331,791	kilometers
Quality of road infrastructure	4.5	1(low) – 7(high)

Source: Government of India, Ministry of Road Transport and Highways. 2022. *Year End Review* (accessed 9 September 2023).

1. Contracting Agencies in the Road Sector

The Ministry of Road Transport and Highways (MORTH) is the responsible federal government entity for the road and highway sector. The key agencies responsible for developing highways are the National Highways Authority of India (NHAI) and the National Highways and Infrastructure Development Corporation Limited (NHIDCL).

- NHAI, which is under the MORTH, is responsible for planning and procurement of national highways in the country. The NHAI is mandated to implement by phase the National Highways Development Project (NHDP), which is India's largest ever highway project. Its main mandate is to develop the arterial roads of the country for interstate movements of goods and passengers. These roads would traverse the length and width of the country, connecting the national and state capitals, major ports, and rail junctions. The NHAI is the lead agency for managing public–private partnership (PPP) contracts. It has also formed a special purpose vehicle (SPV) for funding road projects.[45]
- The NHIDCL is a fully owned company of the MORTH. The company promotes, surveys, establishes, designs, builds, operates, maintains, and upgrades national highways and strategic roads, including interconnecting roads that share international boundaries with neighboring countries.[46]
- The Border Roads Organization develops and maintains the road networks in India's border areas and friendly neighboring countries.

---

[45] Government of India, National Highways Authority of India. About NHAI.
[46] Government of India, MORTH, National Highways and Infrastructure Development Corporation Limited. Welcome to NHIDCL.

The Ministry of Rural Development is responsible for rural roads along with the following agencies:

- The Public Works Department and other road corporations govern and manage state highways and major district roads.
- Rural roads are developed, maintained, and monitored by the Ministry of Rural Development.
- Project roads for irrigation, power, and mines are governed and managed by state public works departments and project organizations.
- Urban roads for intracity networking are governed by municipal corporations.
- Village roads are being governed by the respective *zila-parishads* (district councils) and state governments.

2. Road Sector Laws and Regulations

The main regulations governing the roads and highways sector in India are summarized in Table 12.

Table 12: Key Regulations for the Road Sector in India

Act	Description
The National Highways Act, 1956	Provides for the declaration of certain highways to be national highways and for matters connected therewith.
The Motor Vehicles Act, 1988	Consolidates and amends laws relating to motor vehicles.
The National Highways Authority of India Act, 1988	Provides for the constitution of an authority for the development, maintenance, and management of national highways and for matters connected therewith or incidental thereto.
The Central Road and Infrastructure Fund Act, 2000	Gives statutory status to the Central Road Fund, governed by the Resolution of Parliament passed in 1988, for the development and maintenance of national highways and improvement of safety at railway crossings and, for these purposes, to levy and collect by way of cess (tax or levy), a duty of excise and duty of customs on motor spirit commonly known as petrol, high-speed diesel oil, and for other matters connected therewith.
The Control of National Highways (Land and Traffic) Act, 2002	Provides for control of land within the national highways, right-of-way, and traffic moving on the national highways, and for removal of unauthorized occupation thereon.
The Carriage by Road Act, 2007	Provides for the regulation of common carriers, limiting their liability and declaration of value of goods delivered to them to determine their liability for loss of, or damage to, such goods occasioned by the negligence or criminal acts of themselves, their servants or agents, and for matters connected therewith or incidental thereto.
National Highways Fee (Determination of Rates and Collection) Rules, 2008 and subsequent amendments of 2008, 2010, 2011, 2013, 2014, 2015, 2016, 2017, 2018, 2019, and 2022.	Defines and regulates the toll tariff framework for use of any section of national highway, permanent bridge, bypass or tunnel forming part of the national highway, as the case may be, in accordance with the provisions of the rules.

Sources: Government of India, Ministry of Road Transport and Highways (MORTH). Acts / Rules; Government of India, MORTH. 2000. *Central Road and Infrastructure Fund Act*; and Government of India, MORTH. 2008. *National Highways Fee Rules, 2008;* and Government of India. National Highways Authority of India.

The commonly applied regulations for developing national highways are as follows:

- A list of operational standards for road design;
- The National Road Safety Policy, which outlines the policy initiatives to be implemented by the government at all levels to improve the road safety activities in the country;
- Notifications and rules of the MORTH and the NHAI; and
- The Indian Road Congress, which was set up by the Government of India in December 1934, in consultation with state governments, to provide a regular national forum for pooling experience and ideas on all matters concerned with planning, design construction, and maintenance of highways.

Foreign Investment Restrictions in the Road Sector

The maximum equity investment allowed for foreign investors in greenfield projects is 100% through the automatic route.

Parameter	2021	2022	2023
Maximum allowed foreign ownership of equity in greenfield projects	100%	100%	100%

Standard Contracts in the Road Sector

Type of Contract	Availability
Public–private partnership/concession agreement	✓
Performance-based operation and maintenance contract	✓
Engineering, procurement, and construction contract	✓

✓ = Yes, ✗ = No, NA = Not Applicable, UA = Unavailable.

In addition to traditional models, the MORTH initiated two new models in recent years: (i) hybrid annuity model (HAM), a variant to the annuity or government pay model with a 40% upfront capital support and annuity; and (ii) toll–operate–transfer (TOT), intended to monetize public-funded national highway projects that are operational and are generating toll revenues for at least 2 years (modified to 1 year for select preapproved projects, after the commercial operation date).

Under the HAM mode, the government provides 40% of the project cost as construction support to the private developer during the construction period, and the balance of 60% as annuity payments over the concession period along with interest on the outstanding amount to the concessionaire. There is a separate provision for operation and maintenance (O&M) payments by the government to the concessionaire. The private party does not have to bear the traffic risk. All payments have been inflation indexed by a price multiple index, which is a weighted average of the wholesale price index and consumer price index for industrial workers in the ratio of 70:30. This mitigates the inflation risk for the developer.[47]

---

[47]   Government of India, MORTH. Standard Documents (accessed 15 July 2023).

In the TOT model, the right of collection and appropriation of fees for selected operational national highway projects constructed through public funding shall be assigned for a predetermined concession period to concessionaires (developers or investors) against upfront payment of a lumpsum amount to the NHAI. Such assignment of rights shall be based on the toll revenue potential of the identified national highway projects. O&M obligations of such projects shall be with the concessionaire until the completion of the concession period. The concessionaires for such projects shall be appointed through a transparent and uniform procurement process within the ambit of a predefined and approved implementation framework.

3. Road Sector Master Plan

While each state has its own plan for developing state roads, at the central level, the national government has plans for national highways. The Government of India has launched major initiatives to upgrade and strengthen national highways through various phases of the NHDP. The overall vision and progress under the NHDP are shown in Table 13.

Table 13: Phases and Progress of Projects Under the National Highways Development Project

NHDP Phase	Total Length (km)	Length Completed up to 31 Mar 2022	Length Completed During 1 Apr 2022 to 31 Dec 2022	Length Completed up to 31 Dec 2022	Length to Be Completed
SARDP-NE (Phase A)	6,418	4,212	261	4,473	1,945
LWE (including Vijayawada Ranchi Route)	6,085	5,797	31	5,818	267
EAP (WB, JICA, ADB)	2,855	1,521	243	1,764	1,091
Bharatmala Pariyojana Phase – I	34,800	8,942	2,847	11,789	23,011
Bharatmala Pariyojana (I+II+III+IV); port connection and upgradation with 2-, 4-, and 6-laning; development of North–South, and East–West Corridor	46,278	37,579	1,106	38,685	7,593
Phase V, 6-laning of Golden Quadrilateral and high-density corridor	6,500	3,799	289	4,088	2,412
Phase VI: Expressways	1,000	209	10	219	781

continued on next page

Table 13 *continued*

NHDP Phase	Total Length (km)	Length Completed up to 31 Mar 2022	Length Completed During 1 Apr 2022 to 31 Dec 2022	Length Completed up to 31 Dec 2022	Length to Be Completed
Phase VII: Ring roads, bypasses, flyovers, and other structures	700	150	31	181	519

ADB = Asian Development Bank, EAP = externally aided projects, JICA = Japan International Cooperation Agency, km = kilometer, LWE = left wing extremism affected area, SARDP-NE = Special Accelerated Road Development Program for North Eastern India region, WB = World Bank.

Sources: Government of India, Ministry of Road Transport and Highways. 2021. *Annual Report 2020-21*; and Government of India, Ministry of Road Transport and Highways. 2023. *Annual Report 2022–2023*.

The MORTH has initiated several programs on highway development in the country with specific goals for the medium and long term.

Bharatmala Pariyojana

In October 2017, the Cabinet Committee on Economic Affairs approved the implementation of an umbrella program for national highways, the Bharatmala Pariyojana (Phase I). The program aimed to construct and upgrade the national highways (34,800 kilometers [km] long) over 5 years (2017–2018 through 2021– 2022) at an estimated outlay of ₹5,350 billion ($73.28 billion). The program sought to optimize the efficiency of freight and passenger movement across the country by bridging critical infrastructure gaps. Also envisaged are effective interventions, such as the development of economic corridors, inter-corridors and feeder routes, and national corridor. As of March 2023, about 38% of the length had been completed. The plan under the program is shown in Table 14.[48]

Under the Bharatmala program, up to 60%–70% of roads are proposed to be taken up under the HAM; 10% under the BOT (toll); and the rest under engineering, procurement, and construction (EPC). Bharatmala I faced delays on account of the coronavirus disease (COVID-19) pandemic, and certain projects are still being executed. Bharatmala II is being considered for the construction of road projects totaling 5,000 km combined.

---

[48]   Government of India, MORTH. 2023. *Report of the Comptroller and Auditor General of India on Implementation of Phase 1 of Bharatmala Pariyojana.* No. 19 of 2023 (Performance Audit).

Table 14: Project Progress Under the Bharatmala Pariyojana Project
(as of 31 March 2023)

Components of BPP–I	CCEA Approved Length (km)	CCEA Approved Estimates (₹ billion)	Total Sanctioned Cost of BPP–I Projects (₹ million)	National Highways Length Completed (km)	National Highways Length Completed (%)
Economic corridors	9,000	1,200	2,856	3,807	42.3
Inter-corridors and feeder roads	6,000	800	1,040	1,614	26.9
National corridor efficiency improvement	5,000	1,000	1,050	1,638	32.7
Border and international connectivity roads	2,000	250	140	1,256	62.8
Coastal and port connectivity roads	2,000	200	75	104	5.2
Expressways	800	400	1,581	958	119.7
Subtotal	**24,800**	**3,850**	**6,743**	**9,377**	**37.8**
Ongoing projects, including NHDP	10,000	1,500	1,722	4,122	41.2
Total	**34,800**	**5,350**	**8,465**	**13,499**	**38.7**

BPP-I = Bharatmala Pariyojana Phase I, CCEA = Cabinet Committee on Economic Affairs, km = kilometer, NHDP = National Highways Development Project.

Note: Numbers may not sum precisely because of rounding.

Source: Government of India, Ministry of Road Transport and Highways. 2023. *Report of the Comptroller and Auditor General of India on Implementation of Phase I of Bharatmala Pariyojana*. No. 19 of 2023 (Performance Audit).

Setu Bharatam

To ensure safe and smooth flow of traffic, the MORTH has envisaged a plan to replace level crossings on national highways with road over bridge (ROB) or road under bridge (RUB) under a scheme known as the Setu Bharatam. Under this program, out of 174 ROBs or RUBs to be constructed, 91 have been sanctioned with an estimated cost of ₹71.05 billion ($0.97 billion). Out of the 91 sanctioned, 59 ROBs or RUBs have been awarded and are in various stages of progress.[49]

Highway Projects in North-East India

Projects worth ₹1,900 billion ($26.02 billion) have been sanctioned for the construction of roads for more than 12,000 km in the North-East region. The projects being executed by the NHIDCL in 2022 cost around ₹1.66 trillion ($22.74 billion), covering 10,892 km of roads in all the North-East states. According to the latest information from the Ministry of Development of North-East Region, the total length of national highways in the state of Assam in 2013 was 2,771 km, and in July 2023, it was 3,651 km.[50]

---

49   Government of India, MORTH. Setu Bharatam (accessed 15 July 2023).
50   Government of India, Ministry of Development of North-East Region, Press Information Bureau. 2023. Infrastructure Projects in Assam. Press release. 3 August.

Logistics Parks

A network of 35 multimodal logistics parks has been identified for development under Phase 1 of Bharatmala Pariyojana. The availability of the land parcels needed to develop multimodal logistics parks has been confirmed at seven locations, and detailed project reports have been initiated in all the nodes (footnote 46).

According to the Summary Report of the Task Force on National Infrastructure Pipeline, a total capital expenditure of ₹20.34 trillion ($278.59 billion) by both central and state governments will be made between FY2020 and FY2025. About 1,820 projects have been identified to be implemented in 2020–2025. The central government's total capital expenditure for these projects is estimated at ₹13.8 trillion ($189.02 billion) over FY2020 to FY2025.

Projects Under Conceptualization and Development in the Road Sector

Figure 11 provides the number of PPP projects that are under conceptualization and development in the road sector of India.

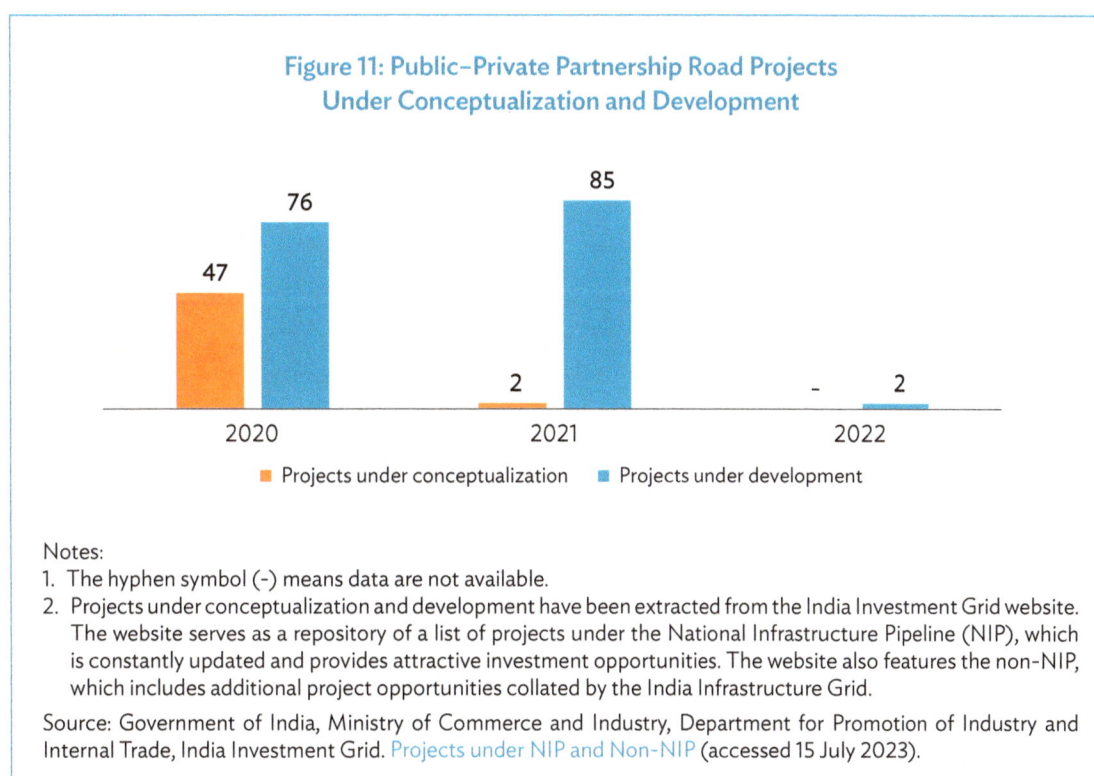

Figure 11: Public–Private Partnership Road Projects Under Conceptualization and Development

Notes:
1. The hyphen symbol (-) means data are not available.
2. Projects under conceptualization and development have been extracted from the India Investment Grid website. The website serves as a repository of a list of projects under the National Infrastructure Pipeline (NIP), which is constantly updated and provides attractive investment opportunities. The website also features the non-NIP, which includes additional project opportunities collated by the India Infrastructure Grid.

Source: Government of India, Ministry of Commerce and Industry, Department for Promotion of Industry and Internal Trade, India Investment Grid. Projects under NIP and Non-NIP (accessed 15 July 2023).

4. Features of Past Public–Private Partnership Projects in the Road Sector

The World Bank Private Participation in Infrastructure (PPI) database has been the basis for evaluating past PPP projects in each sector. The World Bank database is used for consistency across the 15 countries covered as part of the PPP Monitor and to enable cross-country and cross-sector comparisons. Figures 12 to 16 are an elaboration of the data from the World Bank PPI database.

However, in India, the Department of Economic Affairs (DEA) maintains a comprehensive database of awarded PPP projects until 2019 (footnote 36). Beyond 2019, data is available on the National Infrastructure Pipeline (NIP) website. The DEA's database is also used as basis for evaluating PPP projects, and it supplements the data provided by the World Bank PPI database.

Figure 12 provides the number of PPP projects procured through various modes, including direct appointment and competitive bids, in the road sector of India.

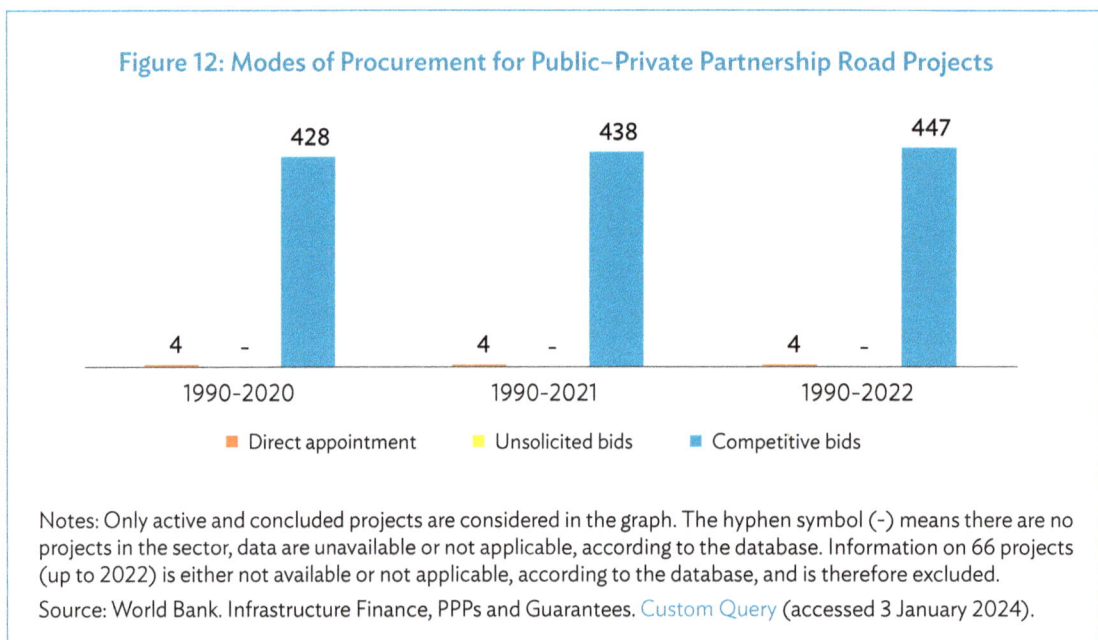

Figure 12: Modes of Procurement for Public–Private Partnership Road Projects

Notes: Only active and concluded projects are considered in the graph. The hyphen symbol (–) means there are no projects in the sector, data are unavailable or not applicable, according to the database. Information on 66 projects (up to 2022) is either not available or not applicable, according to the database, and is therefore excluded.
Source: World Bank. Infrastructure Finance, PPPs and Guarantees. Custom Query (accessed 3 January 2024).

Figure 13 shows the number of PPP projects that reached financial close and the total value of those projects in the road sector of India.

Figure 13: Public–Private Partnership Road Projects Reaching Financial Close

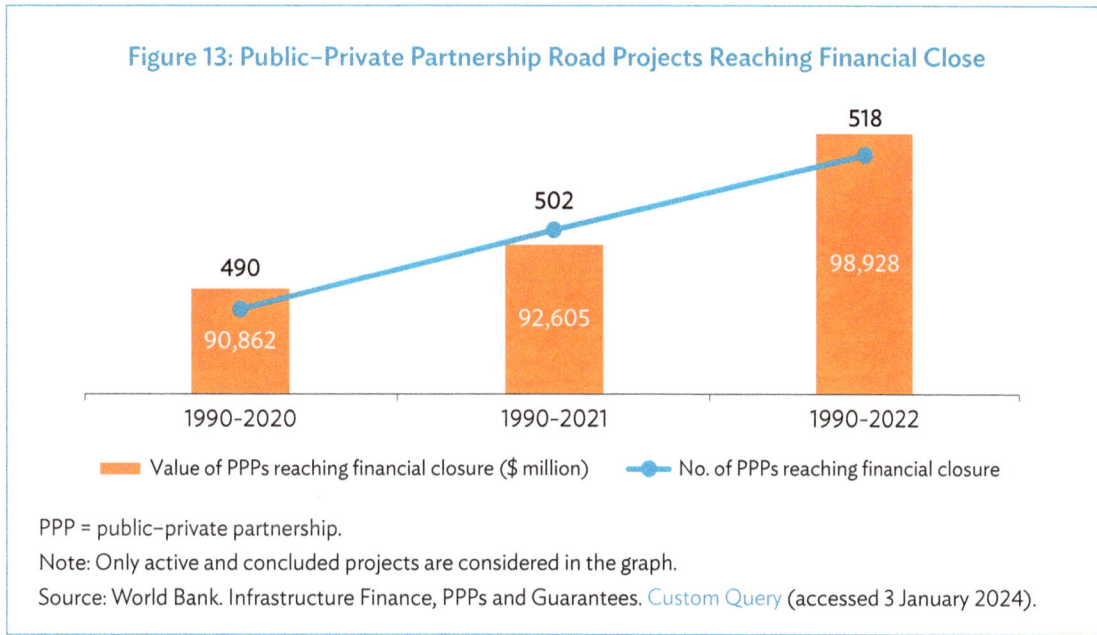

PPP = public–private partnership.
Note: Only active and concluded projects are considered in the graph.
Source: World Bank. Infrastructure Finance, PPPs and Guarantees. Custom Query (accessed 3 January 2024).

Figure 14 shows the number of PPP projects with foreign sponsor participation in the road sector of India.

Figure 14: Public–Private Partnership Road Projects with Foreign Sponsor Participation

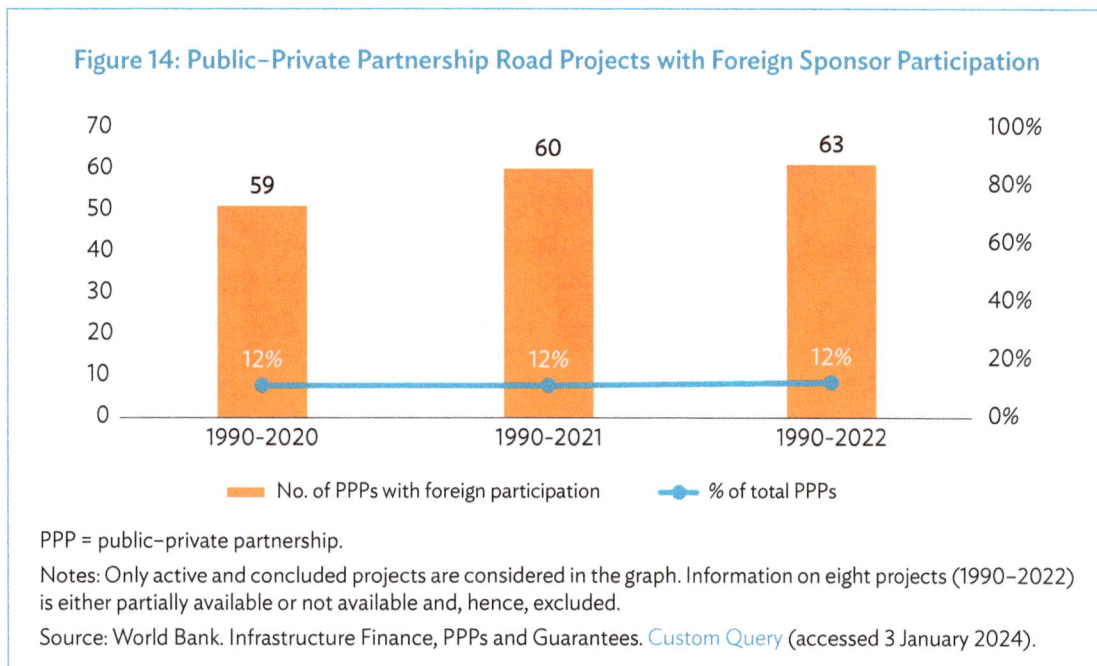

PPP = public–private partnership.
Notes: Only active and concluded projects are considered in the graph. Information on eight projects (1990–2022) is either partially available or not available and, hence, excluded.
Source: World Bank. Infrastructure Finance, PPPs and Guarantees. Custom Query (accessed 3 January 2024).

Figure 15 shows the number of PPP projects that received government support, including viability gap funding (VGF) and government guarantees, in the road sector of India.

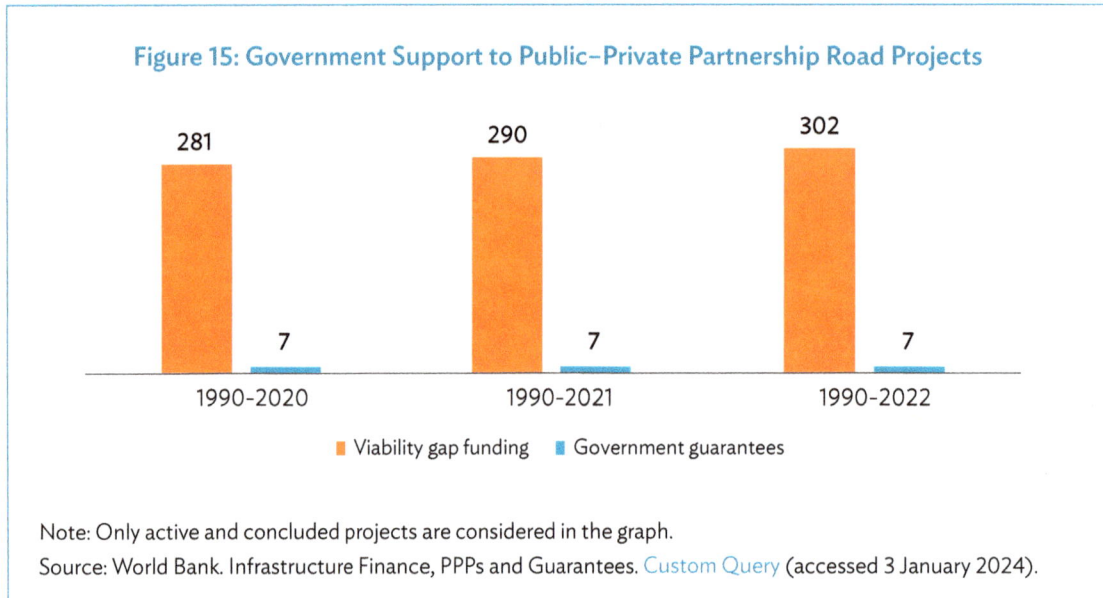

Figure 15: Government Support to Public–Private Partnership Road Projects

Period	Viability gap funding	Government guarantees
1990–2020	281	7
1990–2021	290	7
1990–2022	302	7

Note: Only active and concluded projects are considered in the graph.
Source: World Bank. Infrastructure Finance, PPPs and Guarantees. Custom Query (accessed 3 January 2024).

Figure 16 shows the number of PPP projects that received payment in the form of user charges and government pay (offtake) in the road sector of India.

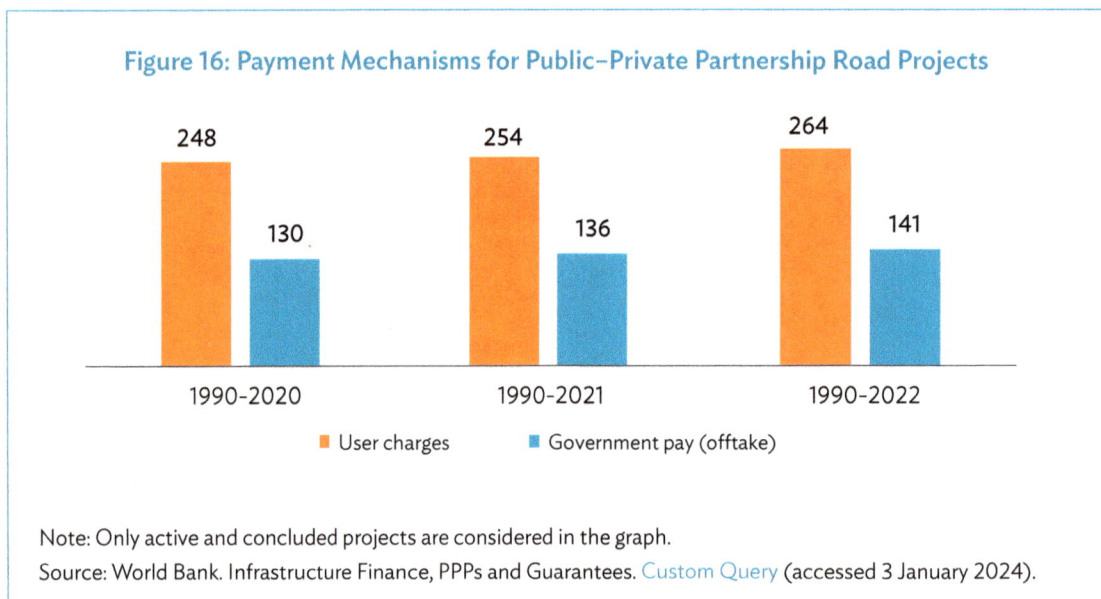

Figure 16: Payment Mechanisms for Public–Private Partnership Road Projects

Period	User charges	Government pay (offtake)
1990–2020	248	130
1990–2021	254	136
1990–2022	264	141

Note: Only active and concluded projects are considered in the graph.
Source: World Bank. Infrastructure Finance, PPPs and Guarantees. Custom Query (accessed 3 January 2024).

Past PPP projects in the road sector classified in terms of PPP variant or scheme, based on the DEA database, are presented in Table 15.

Table 15: Number of Road and Bridge Projects Across Public–Private Partnership Variants

Public–Private Partnership Variant	No. of Projects
Build–operate–transfer	305
Build–operate–transfer (toll + annuity)	29
Build–operate–transfer (annuity)	117
Build–operate–transfer (toll)	85
Build–own–operate–transfer	3
Design–build–finance–operate	2
Design–build–finance–operate–maintain–transfer (annuity)	8
Design–build–finance–operate–transfer	79
Design–build–finance–operate–transfer (annuity)	12
Design–build–finance–operate–transfer (toll)	53
Design–build–operate–transfer	1
Design–build–operate–transfer (annuity)	11
Hybrid annuity model	50
Management contract (operation and maintenance)	31
Not available	38
Total	**824**

Note: Data was last updated on 5 December 2019.
Source: Government of India, Ministry of Finance, Department of Economic Affairs. List of All PPP Projects (accessed 15 July 2023).

Tariffs in the Road Sector

Tariffs for PPP projects in the country are regulated by the NHAI by way of toll notifications issued with an annual indexation factor. The central government may, via an Official Gazette notification, levy fees at such rates as may be laid down by rules made for services or benefits rendered in relation to the use of ferries, permanent bridges, temporary bridges, and tunnels on national highways, and the use of sections of national highways. For projects supported by public funds, annuities, or SPVs, the government collects a user fee (toll) by engaging the contractors through competitive e-bidding. For projects with private investment and/or under an operate–maintain–transfer scheme, the concessionaire collects the user fee (toll). In India, tolling is generally under an open system, whereby the fee payable is a fixed amount based on the length of stretch under one project, which is normally 60 km. If a stretch is shorter, then the user fee collected is based only on the actual length.[51]

Annual revision takes effect from 1 April, and the fee is rounded to the nearest ₹5 in accordance with the new user fee rules. However, some roads built before 2008 are governed by the old rules, wherein the fee is rounded to ₹1 only. According to the rule, a concessionaire has the right to collect a user fee until the completion of the concession period under the agreement. Once a highway is built, a fee is collected to recover the cost. Once the cost is recovered, the fee is collected at a reduced rate of 40% as the road is to be maintained in good condition for the users.

The levy of user fees is governed by the

- National Highways Fee (Determination of Rates and Collection) Rules, 2008; and
- National Highways Rules, 1997, permitting collection of fees for (i) the use of sections of national highways, and permanent and temporary bridges on national highways; and (ii) the use of sections of national highways and permanent bridges delivered as a public-funded project.

According to National Highways Fee (Determination of Rates and Collection) Rules, 2008, the base fees per kilometer are established for the base year 2007–2008 for various types of vehicles for highways of four lanes or above. For two-lane highways, the rate was fixed at 60% of base fees indicated above. The base fee increase was also linked to the additional capital expenditure that may be incurred beyond the average cost computed by the NHAI. From the base year onward, the annual increase was provided by indexing it to the wholesale price index of the country and considering 40% of the wholesale price index as the increase for the subsequent year. The toll for public- and private-funded projects are the same.

Typical Risk Allocation for Public–Private Partnership Projects in the Road Sector

The NHAI has issued model agreements for different PPP variants. The risk allocation model for roads differs for each model. A typical risk allocation for road projects on build–operate–transfer (BOT) (toll) model of the NHAI is shown in the following table:

Type of Risk	Private	Public	Shared	Comment
Financing risk	✓			
Construction risk	✓			
Traffic risk	✓			
Collection risk	✓			
Tariff risk	✓			

continued on next page

---

[51] Government of India, MORTH. NH User Fee (Toll). Gazette Notifications.

Table *continued*

Type of Risk	Private	Public	Shared	Comment
Competition risk		✓		The model agreement provides exclusivity for 10 years or until the project achieves 90% utilization.
Government payment risk	NA			
Environmental and social risks		✓		
Land acquisition risk		✓		
Permits			✓	
Geotechnical risk			✓	
Brownfield risk: inventories, studies, property boundaries, project scope		✓		
Political risk		✓		
Force majeure			✓	
Foreign exchange risk	✓			

NA = not applicable.

Table 16 provides a snapshot of risk sharing across various models.

Table 16: Generic Risk-Sharing Matrix Across Variants of Public–Private Partnerships in the Road Sector

Model	Financing Risk	Construction Risk	Traffic Risk	O&M Risk	Typical Concession Period
BOT (toll)	Concessionaire	Concessionaire	Concessionaire	Concessionaire	30 years
BOT (annuity)	Concessionaire	Concessionaire	Authority	Concessionaire	15 years
HAM	Concessionaire	Concessionaire	Authority	Concessionaire	15 years
TOT	Concessionaire	Not Relevant	Concessionaire	Concessionaire	30 years
OMT	Authority	Not Relevant	Authority	Concessionaire	UA

BOT = build–operate–transfer, HAM = hybrid annuity model, O&M = operation and maintenance, OMT = operate–maintain–transfer, TOT = toll–operate–transfer, UA = unavailable.

Source: Government of India, Ministry of Finance, Department of Economic Affairs. Online PPP Structuring Toolkit.

Financing Details for Public–Private Partnership Projects in the Road Sector

Parameter	1990–2020	1990–2021	1990–2022
PPP projects with foreign lending participation	7	8	8
PPP projects that received export credit agency/international financing institution support	1	1	1
Typical debt-to-equity ratio	(60–80) : (40–20)		
Time for financial close	Typically, 6 months (extendable)		
Typical concession period	15–20 years		
Typical financial internal rate of return	UA		

PPP = public–private partnership, UA = unavailable.
Source: World Bank. Infrastructure Finance, PPPs and Guarantees. Custom Query (accessed 3 January 2024).

5. Challenges in the Road Sector

While the road sector is the most mature sector for PPPs in India and has seen innovative models and many successes, it nonetheless faces financing and operational issues. Some of these issues are as follows:

- Increased costs, stressed assets, and financing constraints
  - > Land acquisition costs have increased in recent years because of the higher compensation required under the Right to Fair Compensation and Transparency in Land Acquisition, Rehabilitation and Resettlement Act, in addition to the general surge in market rates.
  - > As per a 2016 report by the Standing Committee on Transport, Tourism and Culture, numerous road assets have turned into nonperforming assets.[52] The Committee attributes this to project bids being prepared without proper study and projects being awarded in a hurry, resulting in stalling of projects. This has placed significant strain on lenders, creating reluctance in new lending. Additionally, many banks are approaching or reaching the sector lending limits set by the Reserve Bank of India, adding to the challenges.
- During construction stage, delays in receiving approvals, including environmental clearance and forest clearance, and delays in achieving financial closures continue to affect investor confidence. However, the NHAI has been taking several initiatives to address these issues.
- Aggressive bidding continues to affect the sector in models where traffic risk is assumed by the private sector, or in models where HAM is implemented. Although the number of projects relying solely on tolls has decreased compared to the previous decade, the challenge lies in resolving the operational projects that have been stalled because of aggressive bidding.
- Several project developers are facing disputes with the NHAI for operational and financial reasons, which occasionally require significant time for resolution or have the potential to evolve into legal disputes.[53]

---

[52] PRS Legislative Research. 2016. *Summary of Report Prepared by Standing Committee on Transport, Tourism and Culture.*
[53] *Deccan Herald.* 2022. *Contractors Claims ₹88,000 Crore in Highway Project Disputes.* 20 March.

The MORTH has been taking several policy and technology initiatives to address these issues, including special steps to assist languishing projects, faster and affordable dispute resolution mechanisms such as establishing the Society for Affordable Redressal of Disputes, and implementation of automatic toll pay system in a competitive manner. In 2022, the MORTH made a few changes in model concession agreements (MCAs) of various procurement modes, a summary of which follows:

- Changes in MCA of build–operate–transfer (toll) projects
  - Changes have been made to the relevant clauses of the MCA of BOT (toll) project, permitting the change of ownership from the existing 2 years to 1 year after the commercial operation date (COD). This move will free the equity or funds of construction companies to take up other projects.[54]
- Changes in MCA of hybrid annuity model
  - the MORTH has amended the standard request for proposal document of the HAM mode project to incorporate provisions relating to threshold technical capacity prescribed for similar work experience for EPC works related to major bridges and tunnels. This enables the NHAI to procure concessionaires that have appropriate experience in major bridges and tunnels for projects being executed under HAM mode. Changes have been made to the relevant clauses of the model request for proposal and MCA of the HAM project to allow the lowest quoted bid project cost as the basis for awarding the HAM project and O&M cost to be fixed as in EPC projects.

B. Railways

Parameter	Value	Unit
Length of total railway network (FY2021–2022)	128,305	total track (km)
Total number of passengers carried	231,126	million passenger-km
Total volume of freight carried	719,762	million ton-km
Quality of railways infrastructure	4.40	1(low) – 7(high)

FY = fiscal year, km = kilometer.
Sources: Government of India, Ministry of Railways. 2022. *Indian Railways Yearbook, 2021–2022*; and The Global Economy. 2019. *Railroad Infrastructure Quality—Country Rankings, 2009–2019* (accessed 15 July 2023).

1. Contracting Agencies in the Railway Sector

The Indian Railways, or entities under it, assume the role of contracting agencies depending on the nature of the railway project. For example, for land development tenders, the Rail Land Development Authority is the contracting agency; for railway station development, it is the Indian Railway Stations Development Corporation. The Ministry of Railways (Railway Board) is the contracting agency

---

[54]   Government of India, Ministry of Road Transport and Highways. 2022. *Annual Report 2022–23.*

for railway system development and zonal railways when projects are limited to specific zones. Table 17 shows the key agencies that engage with private sector players across various projects in the railway sector.

Table 17: Key Entities Responsible for the Railway Sector in India

Agency	Function (Indicative List)
Rail Land Development Authority (RLDA)	The RLDA is a statutory authority under the Ministry of Railways, set up by an amendment to the Railways Act, 1989 for developing vacant railway land for commercial use and for the purpose of generating revenue through nontariff measures.
Dedicated Freight Corridor Corporation of India Limited (DFCCIL)	Set up in 2006 by the Ministry of Railways, the DFCCIL is a special purpose vehicle for the construction and operation and maintenance of dedicated freight corridors. The DFCCIL is responsible for planning and development, mobilization of financial resources and construction, and operation and maintenance of dedicated freight corridors.
Indian Railway Stations Development Corporation Limited (IRSDC)	The IRSDC is a special purpose vehicle formed through a joint venture of the RLDA and Ircon International Limited, an initiative by the Ministry of Railways. The joint venture aims to develop and/or redevelop new and existing railway stations and develop real estate on railway and/or government land. The company's mandate is to carry on any railway infrastructure work including development of railway stations under schemes such as build–operate–transfer, build–own–operate–transfer, build–lease–transfer, or any projects found suitable and related to railway station infrastructure projects and other ancillary fields.

Sources: Dedicated Freight Corridor Corporation of India Limited. About Us; Indian Railway Stations Development Corporation Limited. About IRSDC; and Rail Land Development Authority. About Us.

The Ministry of Railways, through the Railway Board, has directly awarded projects related to passenger train operations. In 2019, the Railway Board, on nomination, awarded the first passenger train for private operations to the Indian Railways Catering and Tourism Corporation (IRCTC), a quasi-government agency involved traditionally in catering services and special train operations. The IRCTC signed concession agreements with private service providers, wherein operators will share their profits with the IRCTC, which in turn will pay haulage charges to the railways. Similarly, in 2020, the Railway Board came up with a procurement process to allow private participation in operating passenger train services over 12 clusters comprising more than 150 origin–destination pair of routes through introduction of 151 modern trains. The Ministry of Railways, through the Railway Board, is the direct contracting agency for these projects.

2. Railway Sector Laws and Regulations

The following are the basic regulations that apply to government-financed railway projects on government infrastructure:

- Railways Act, 1989;
- Railway Protection Force (Amendment) Act, 2003;
- Railways (Amendment) Act, 2005;
- Railways (Amendment) Act, 2008;
- Participative Model for Rail Connectivity and Capacity Augmentation Projects, 2012; and
- Metro Rail Policy, 2017.

The Participative Model for Rail Connectivity and Capacity Augmentation Projects (2012) aims to fast-track Indian Railways by attracting private investment through public–private partnership (PPP). The policy provides five models for last-mile connectivity and capacity augmentation projects.[55]

The Metro Rail Policy (2017) boosts private investment in various ways, such as by providing viability gap funding (VGF) for projects undertaken through a PPP. The policy mandates that at least one of the project components adopt the PPP scheme to avail a grant of up to 10% of the project cost. Equity participation is also provided for project development wherein the Government of India will give financial support to metro rail projects in the form of equity and subordinate debt (equivalent of central government taxes)—subject to an overall ceiling of 20% of the project cost, excluding private investment and cost of land, rehabilitation, and resettlement—and contribute an equivalent share as that of the state government (subject to 20% upper cap).[56]

Sector Regulator
The Railway Board is the apex regulating authority designated to control the functions of the Indian Railways at present. Policies and pieces of legislation under different functions are being developed, amended, and regulated by the Indian Railways under the guidelines set by the different directorates falling under it. For instance, the National Transport Development Policy Committee aims to provide an integrated and sustainable transport system. Similarly, the directorate of Research Design and Standards Organization sets the technical standards of the industry (footnote 13).

Foreign Investment Restrictions in the Railway Sector

The following table indicates the maximum foreign ownership allowance in the railway sector.

Parameter	2021	2022	2023
Maximum allowed foreign ownership of equity in greenfield projects	100%	100%	100%

Source: Invest India. National Investment Promotion and Facilitation Agency. FDI Policy of India (accessed 15 July 2023).

---

[55]   Government of India, Ministry of Railways. 2012. *Participative Model for Rail Connectivity and Capacity Augmentation Projects.*
[56]   Government of India, Ministry of Housing and Urban Affairs. 2017. *Metro Rail Policy, 2017.*

In the railway infrastructure segment, the Indian Railways has, in the recent past, allowed 100% foreign ownership.[57]

Foreign direct investment (FDI) is allowed in the construction and O&M of the following (footnote 13):

- suburban corridor projects through PPP;
- high-speed train projects;
- dedicated freight lines;
- rolling stock including train sets, and locomotives or coaches manufacturing and maintenance facilities;
- railway electrification;
- signaling systems;
- freight terminals;
- passenger terminals;
- infrastructure in industrial park pertaining to railway lines or sidings, including electrified railway lines and connectivity to main railway line; and
- mass rapid transport systems.

This has opened opportunities for private sector participation in the projects of the Indian Railways. One hundred percent FDI is also permitted in metro rail projects. However, these projects fall under the mass rapid transit system and are not typically considered a part of the Indian Railways—thus they are not extensively covered in this section (footnote 13).

Standard Contracts in the Railway Sector

Type of Contract	Availability
Public–private partnership/concession agreement	✓
Performance-based operation and maintenance contract	✓
Engineering, procurement, and construction contract	✓

✓ = Yes, ✗ = No, NA = Not Applicable, UA = Unavailable.
Source: Model Concession Agreement for the Railway Sector.

Although the railway sector opened for private sector participation more than 20 years ago (through a policy on development of goods sheds or sidings by private investment in railway premises, dated 23 October 1997), it has remained primarily in the non-passenger category. In 2006, the government issued a policy document and an MCA for private container train operations, giving private sector operators a nonexclusive right to haul the concessionaire's trains carrying export–import traffic and/or domestic traffic on identified routes. The Private Freight Terminal scheme was launched in 2012 and was later revised in January 2015. This policy aims to attract private investment in setting up freight terminals through revenue-sharing principles.

---

57   Invest India. National Investment Promotion and Facilitation Agency. Policy in India (accessed 15 July 2023).

The government introduced multiple railways policies and schemes on rolling stock for freight trains at various times:[58]

- **Wagon Leasing Scheme.** Launched in 2008 and revised in 2014, this scheme aims to develop strong leasing market by encouraging third-party leasing of wagons (35-year term after signing).
- **Liberalized Wagon Investment Scheme.** Launched in 2008 and revised in 2018, the policy seeks to provide investors with the benefit of owning and running the wagons with a special rebate in the freight (20-year term after signing).
- **General-Purpose Wagon Investment Scheme.** This scheme is the latest policy addition established in 2018 to encourage private investment in general-purpose wagons, such as BOX or BOXN (high-sided bogie open wagons with side discharge arrangement for loading of coal and other bulk traffic) and bogie compressed pneumatic or BCN (a special type of bogie-covered wagon with a higher carrying capacity and air brake). The scheme does not include special purpose wagons that are designed to carry a specific commodity. A rebate of 10% shall be given on the base freight on each loaded wagon. Such rebate, however, shall ordinarily be for a period of 15 years subject to a cap to the extent of the lease charges payable by the Indian Railways to the Indian Railway Finance Corporation for procurement of rolling stock. If the investment has been recovered in a period of less than 15 years, the freight rebate shall cease from the date of such full recovery. To increase private sector interest, the Indian Railways, in November 2019, liberalized the scheme, under which (i) end users (other than logistics service providers) also have been granted permission to load third-party cargo in their rakes in empty direction, which would not only reduce the empty run of the General-Purpose Wagon Investment Scheme rakes but will also entail additional revenue to end user investors in the form of freight rebate; and (ii) the design loan charges on general-purpose wagons have been reduced from 5% to 1%, which will help minimize the initial investment required for procuring wagons.
- **Automobile Freight Train Operator Scheme.** The policy, launched in 2021, aims to provide an opportunity to logistics service providers and road transporters to invest in wagons and use rail transport to tie up with end users.
- **Master Circular on Gati Shakti Multi-Modal Cargo Terminal.** Launched in 2021 and modified in 2022, the policy seeks to promote the growth of new cargo terminals and improve existing ones.

Further, there were policies in the operations of freight trains in specific categories:

- **Liberalized Special Freight Train Operator Scheme issued in 2013 and revised in 2018 and 2020.** The policy provides opportunity for logistics service providers or manufacturers to invest in wagons and take advantage of rail transport in tying up with end users and in marketing the train services they own for rail transportation of select commodities, which would be beneficial for railways and private players themselves (valid for a period of 20 years from the date of commercial operations of trains by the Special Freight Train Operator, extendable to 20 years).

---

[58]   Government of India, Indian Railways. Master Circulars (accessed 15 July 2023).

- **Automobile Freight Train Operator Scheme issued in 2013 and revised in 2015 and 2021.** The policy provides opportunity for private logistics companies or transporters to run freight trains catering to the automobile sector with a flexibility to induct new higher capacity wagons, provided they meet the conditions set by the Research Design and Standards Organization (valid for a period of 20 years from the date of commercial operations of trains by the Automobile Freight Train Operator, extendable until expiry of the life of the wagons) (footnote 60).

The above items fall within the classification of licenses. The Indian Railways formulated participative models in the construction of fixed rail infrastructure. Five of these models were developed to cater to state governments, local bodies, ports, companies, and foreign direct investors. The five models are nongovernment railway model; joint venture model; BOT through competitive bidding model; customer funded model; and capacity augmentation, annuity model. Of these five, the nongovernment railway model and joint venture model have seen some success.

The Station Redevelopment Program by Zonal Railways was launched on 8 February 2017, and 23 stations were taken up for bidding during the first stage. The modified Swiss challenge method was selected for the redevelopment of the first 23 stations.[59]

In 2020, the Indian Railways issued a draft MCA for public consultation in the areas of railway station development and operations of passenger trains. This is the first instance where the private sector is being invited for train operations. The Ministry of Railways also prepared an indicative list of 100 origin–destination pairs to introduce train services by private entities, divided into clusters such that each cluster would require operation of a minimum of 12 rakes.[60]

In 2019, India's first privately run train, Lucknow–Delhi Tejas Express, by the IRCTC, a public sector unit under Indian Railways, began operations. With the Tejas Express being managed by the IRCTC, the physical infrastructure of the train, including locomotives, coaches, loco pilots, guards, and security personnel, are owned by Indian Railways. However, the services provided, such as ticketing and refunds, parcels, catering, and housekeeping will be contracted to private players through the IRCTC under the PPP model. The IRCTC has signed concession agreements with private service providers, under which operators will share their profits with the IRCTC, which in turn will pay haulage charges to the railways.[61]

The government plans to open passenger train operations for more private sector players. However, tender for passenger train operations launched in October 2020 with the Ministry of Railways had to be withdrawn in November. The scope of the project broadly included designing, engineering, procurement, financing, and O&M of passenger trains, either with distributed power or through powerheads, comprising a minimum of 16 coaches. Train services will be provided for more than 109 origin-destination pair of routes grouped in 12 clusters through introduction of 151 modern trains. The 109 origin–destination pairs have been formed into 12 clusters (projects) across the Indian Railways network. The railways have identified about 100 destinations where passenger trains will be run by companies that win these private contracts.

---

[59] Indian Railway Stations Development Corporation Limited (accessed 15 July 2023).
[60] Government of India, Ministry of Railways. 2020. *Draft Model Concession Agreement for Discussion on Re-development of Railway Station.* 20 January.
[61] I. Mufti and R. Sampal. 2019. Why Tejas is '1st Private Train' — Railways Owns It, Outside Vendors Provide Food and Clean It. *The Print.* 6 October.

3. Railway Sector Master Plan

In early 2021, the Ministry of Railways issued a draft National Rail Plan (NRP), articulating the long-term objectives and targets for the railway sector.[62] The NRP aims to augment capacity of the railways and target higher modal share in transporting both freight and passengers. It will serve as a common platform for all future infrastructure, business, and financial planning for railways. The key objective of the NRP is to establish capacity that exceeds demand by 2030, effectively accommodating the anticipated growth in demand until 2050. This initiative aims to elevate the modal share of railways in freight from the current 27% to 45% by 2030. This commitment aligns with the national objective to reduce carbon emissions and achieve net-zero carbon emissions by 2030 (footnote 63). In addition to other objectives, the NRP seeks to significantly decrease the transit time for freight by raising the average speed of freight trains from the current 22 km per hour to 50 km per hour. Simultaneously, the initiative aims to slash the overall cost of rail transportation by almost 30%, with the intention of passing on these cost savings to customers.

As part of the NRP, Vision 2024 has been launched to accelerate implementation of critical projects by 2024 such as 100% electrification, multitracking of congested routes, upgrading of speed to 160 km per hour on the Delhi–Howrah and Delhi–Mumbai routes, upgrading of speed to 130 km per hour on all other Golden Quadrilateral–Golden Diagonal routes, and elimination of all level crossings on all Golden Quadrilateral–Golden Diagonal routes. Three additional dedicated freight corridors (namely East Coast, East-West, and North-South), along with several high-speed rail corridors, are identified in the plan. The NRP clearly identifies the role of the private sector in achieving its objectives and indicates the sustained involvement of the private sector in areas such as operations and ownership of rolling stock, development of freight and passenger terminals, and development and operations of track infrastructure.[63]

The National Infrastructure Pipeline (NIP) also indicates specific targets for the railway sector including higher private participation. The NIP seeks to privatize 30% of net cargo volumes and 500 passenger trains, along with 30% of 750 stations. The initiative also aims to secure rolling stock through procurement from the private sector.

The government launched the Amrit Bharat Station Scheme on 6 August 2023 to revitalize 1,309 railway stations across the nation. The scheme plans to upgrade 76 railway stations across the central railway network. The foundation stone for the redevelopment of 508 railway stations—spread across 27 states and union territories and costing more than ₹244.7 billion—was laid on 6 August 2023.[64]

The overall capital expenditure plan for the sector is shown in Table 18.

---

[62]   Government of India, Ministry of Railways. 2020. *National Rail Plan*.
[63]   Government of India, Ministry of Railways, Press Information Bureau. 2020. Indian Railways Issues Draft National Rail Plan. Press release. 18 December.
[64]   Government of India, Prime Minister's Office, Press Information Bureau. 2023. PM Lays Foundation Stone for Redevelopment of 508 Railway Stations across the Country. Press release. 6 August.

**Table 18: Capital Expenditure Plan for Projects in the Railway Sector
Under the National Infrastructure Pipeline**

Project Category	No. of Projects	Capital Expenditure, FY2020–FY2025	
		($ billion)	(₹ trillion)
Railway track	695	199.91	16.39
Railway rolling stock	61	44.66	3.66
Railway terminal infrastructure	37	2.39	0.20
Total	**793**	**246.96**	**20.25**

FY = fiscal year.
Source: Government of India, Ministry of Commerce and Industry, Department for Promotion of Industry and Internal Trade. India Investment Grid (accessed January 2024).

The passenger train operations indicated above comprise one of the key initiatives of the Ministry of Railways to induct the private sector into the train operations in India. The Ministry of Railways has identified more than 150 pairs of train services to introduce 151 modern train sets or rakes through private sector participation. These services have been formed into 12 clusters across the Indian Railways network. Each train shall have a minimum length of 384 meters (equal to 16 cars of the Indian Railways' trains). The project is proposed to be developed under a PPP model, in which the private entity shall be responsible for financing, procuring, and operating and maintaining the trains. The private entity can procure trains through ownership model or leasing model. The Indian Railways shall provide fixed infrastructure, including access to tracks, stations, overhead catenary for traction, train control system, and watering and cleaning lines. The private entity will be required to pay the Indian Railways fixed haulage charges, energy charges, and a share in gross revenue.[65]

Projects Under Conceptualization and Development in the Railway Sector

Currently, there are various projects that are being procured through PPP, including modernization of railway stations and operation of passenger trains. Upgrading or modernization of railway stations has been ongoing for the last few years under various schemes. Presently, railway stations are upgraded and/or modernized under the Adarsh Station Scheme based on identified needs for providing better passenger amenities at stations. Under the scheme, 1,253 stations have been identified for development, out of which 1,215 stations so far have been developed. The remaining 38 stations are planned to be developed under the Adarsh Station Scheme by 2022–2023. The expenditure on beautification or upgradation of stations under the Adarsh Station Scheme is generally funded under Plan Head–53 "Customer Amenities." In FY2022–2023, a total of ₹27.00 billion had been allocated under Plan Head–53.[66]

---

[65] Government of India, Press Information Bureau. 2021. Ministry of Railways: Modernisation of Railway Stations. Press release. 10 March.
[66] Government of India, Ministry of Railways, Press Information Bureau. 2022. Beautification of Railway Stations. Press release. 5 August.

Figure 17 shows the number of PPP projects that are under conceptualization and development in the railway sector of India.

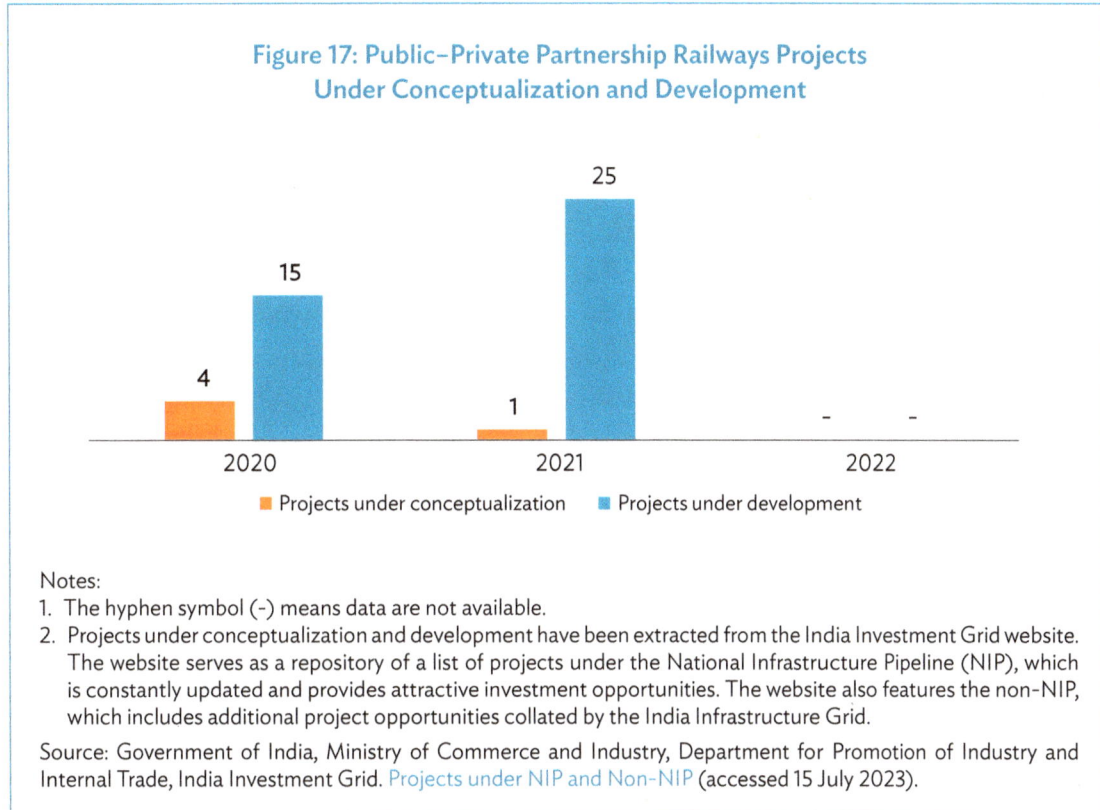

Figure 17: Public–Private Partnership Railways Projects Under Conceptualization and Development

Notes:
1. The hyphen symbol (-) means data are not available.
2. Projects under conceptualization and development have been extracted from the India Investment Grid website. The website serves as a repository of a list of projects under the National Infrastructure Pipeline (NIP), which is constantly updated and provides attractive investment opportunities. The website also features the non-NIP, which includes additional project opportunities collated by the India Infrastructure Grid.

Source: Government of India, Ministry of Commerce and Industry, Department for Promotion of Industry and Internal Trade, India Investment Grid. Projects under NIP and Non-NIP (accessed 15 July 2023).

4. Features of Past Public–Private Partnership Projects in the Railway Sector

Figure 18 shows the number of PPP projects procured through various modes, including direct appointment and competitive bids, in the railway sector of India.

Figure 18: Modes of Procurement for Public–Private Partnership Railway Projects

Notes: Only active and concluded projects are considered in the graph. Information on one project (up to 2022) is either not available or not applicable, according to the database, and is therefore excluded.

Source: World Bank. Infrastructure Finance, PPPs and Guarantees. Custom Query (accessed 3 January 2024).

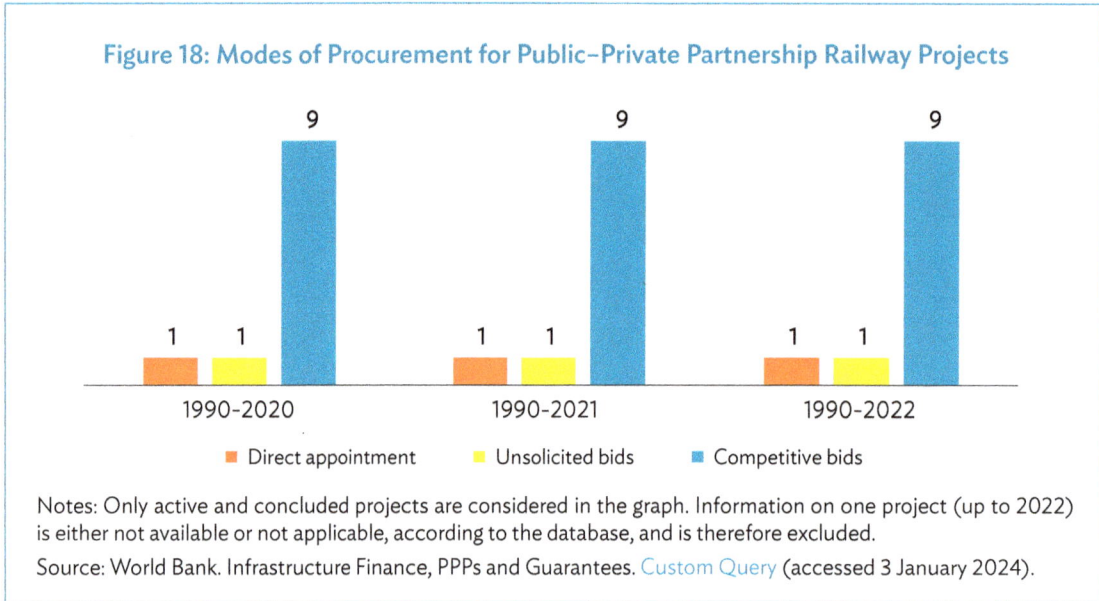

Figure 19 shows the number of PPP projects that reached financial close and the total value of those projects in the railway sector of India.

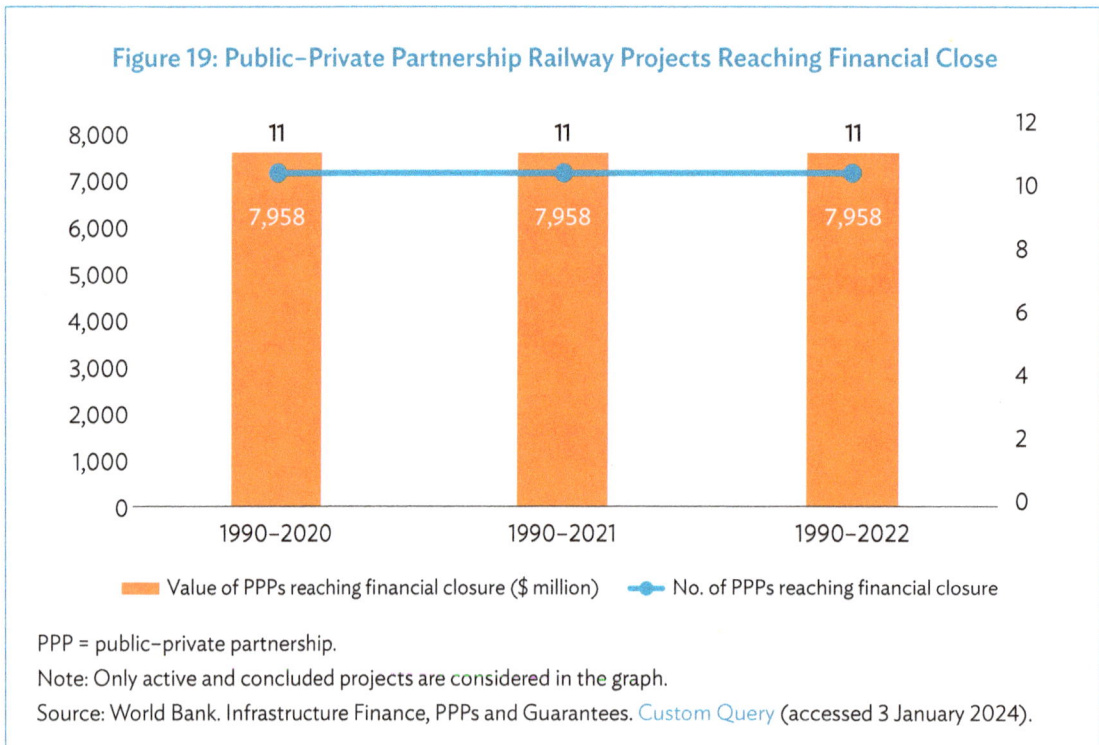

Figure 19: Public–Private Partnership Railway Projects Reaching Financial Close

PPP = public–private partnership.

Note: Only active and concluded projects are considered in the graph.

Source: World Bank. Infrastructure Finance, PPPs and Guarantees. Custom Query (accessed 3 January 2024).

Over the past 3 fiscal years, there has been no change in the number and distribution of PPP projects in the sector that have foreign sponsors or received government support. Additionally, there has been no change in the manner of their payment mechanisms. It is expected that in the coming years, this number can increase as the Ministry of Railways is likely to explore PPPs for the redevelopment of railway stations in the country.

Figure 20 shows the number of PPP projects with foreign sponsor participation in the railway sector of India.

Figure 20: Public–Private Partnership Railway Projects with Foreign Sponsor Participation

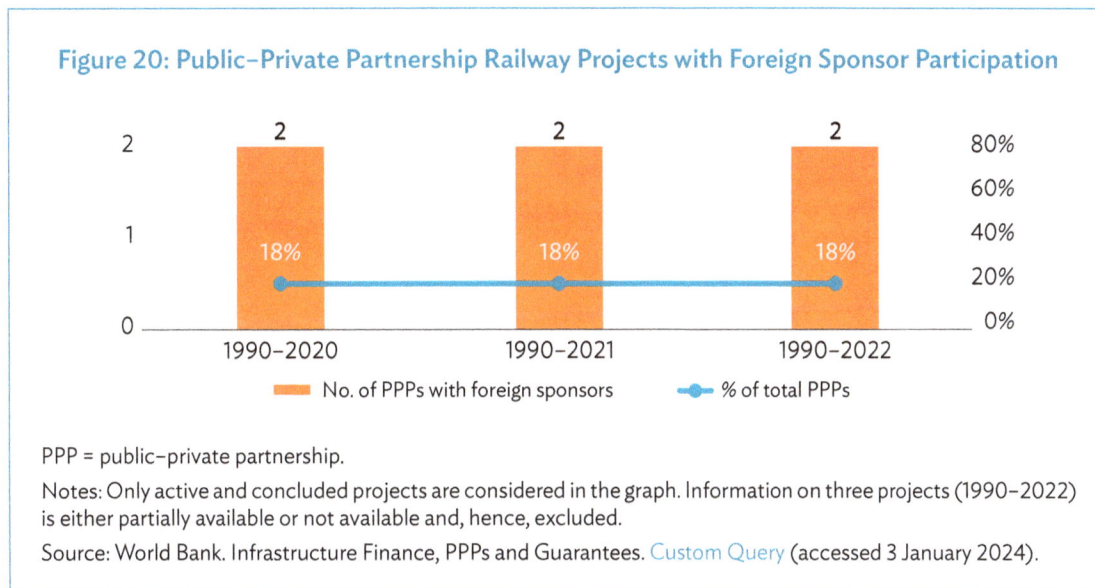

PPP = public–private partnership.

Notes: Only active and concluded projects are considered in the graph. Information on three projects (1990–2022) is either partially available or not available and, hence, excluded.

Source: World Bank. Infrastructure Finance, PPPs and Guarantees. Custom Query (accessed 3 January 2024).

The number of PPP projects that received government support in the railway sector of India is shown in Figure 21.

Figure 21: Government Support to Public–Private Partnership Railway Projects

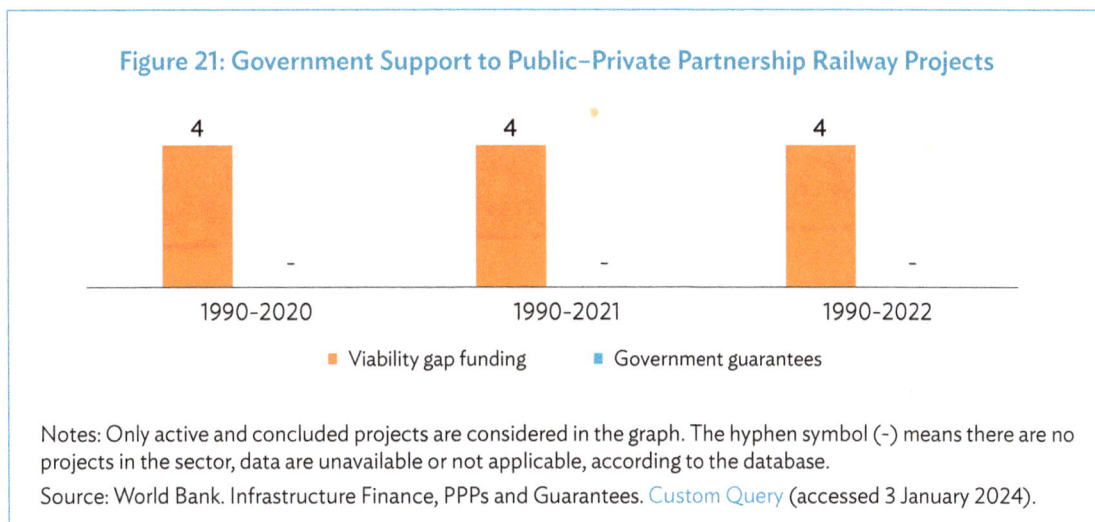

Notes: Only active and concluded projects are considered in the graph. The hyphen symbol (-) means there are no projects in the sector, data are unavailable or not applicable, according to the database.

Source: World Bank. Infrastructure Finance, PPPs and Guarantees. Custom Query (accessed 3 January 2024).

Figure 22 shows the number of railway PPP projects that received payment in the form of user charges and government pay.

Figure 22: Payment Mechanisms for Public–Private Partnership Railway Projects

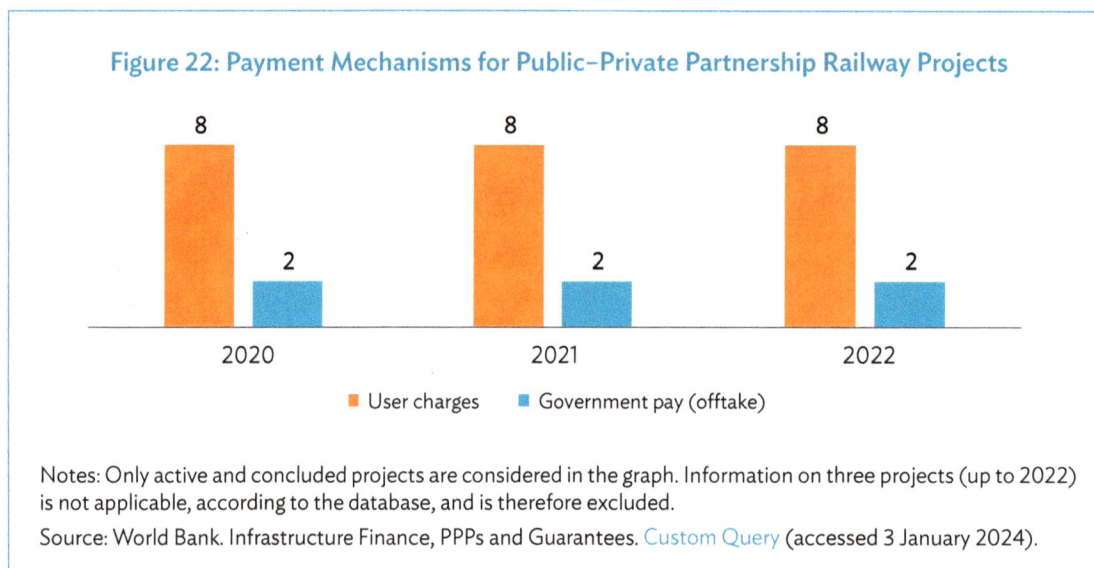

Notes: Only active and concluded projects are considered in the graph. Information on three projects (up to 2022) is not applicable, according to the database, and is therefore excluded.

Source: World Bank. Infrastructure Finance, PPPs and Guarantees. Custom Query (accessed 3 January 2024).

Past PPP projects in the railway sector classified in terms of PPP variant or scheme, according to the Department of Economic Affairs (DEA) database, are shown in Table 19.

Table 19: Number of Railway Projects Across Public–Private Partnership Variants

Public–Private Partnership Variant	No. of Projects
Build–operate–transfer	4
Build–operate–transfer (annuity)	1
Build–own–operate–transfer	2
Design–build–finance–operate	1
Design–build–finance–operate–transfer	1
Total	**9**

Note: Data was last updated on 5 December 2019.

Source: Government of India, Ministry of Finance, Department of Economic Affairs. List of All PPP Projects (accessed 15 July 2023).

Tariffs in the Railway Sector

All tariffs are set by the Railway Board (Ministry of Railways) through railway notifications for passenger and freight trains. Since the responsibility of operations of all trains lies with the Indian Railways, and private sector operators are not involved in the railway operations yet, the tariffs applicable for trains run by the Indian Railways shall also apply to the railways developed in a joint venture model.

For passenger train operations, according to the draft bidding documents issued by the Ministry of Railways, the selection of bidders shall be based on the highest share of gross revenues offered by the qualified bidder (in addition to the actual haulage charges), whereby revenues for concessionaire are defined to comprise market-linked user fare and charges or fees for other related services. This signifies that the tariff for PPP passenger trains shall not be regulated and will be determined by the private sector based on market conditions.

Typical Risk Allocation for Public–Private Partnership Projects in the Railway Sector

The following table shows the typical risk allocation for the design–build–finance–operate–transfer model agreement. There are no projects currently operational under this model.

Type of Risk	Private	Public	Shared
Traffic			✓
Collection risk		✓	
Tariff risk	✓		
Competition risk	✓		
Government payment risk	✓		
Environmental and social risks		✓	
Land acquisition risk		✓	
Permits			✓
Geotechnical risk			✓
Brownfield risk: inventories, studies, property boundaries, project scope		✓	
Political risk		✓	
Force majeure			✓
Foreign exchange risk	✓		

Financing Details of Public–Private Partnership Projects in the Railway Sector

Parameter	1990–2020	1990–2021	1990–2022
Public–private partnership (PPP) projects with foreign lending participation	UA	UA	UA
PPP projects that received export credit agency/international financing institution support	UA	UA	UA
Typical debt-to-equity ratio	(65–75) : (35–25)		
Time for financial close	UA		
Typical concession period	15–20 years		
Typical financial internal rate of return	UA		

UA = Unavailable.
Source: World Bank. Infrastructure Finance, PPPs and Guarantees. Custom Query (accessed 3 January 2024).

5. Challenges in the Railway Sector

- **Return rate conflicts.** The Ministry of Finance has benchmarked the return on investment at 14% for a railway project to be economically viable. However, two of the six projects audited by the Comptroller and Auditor General have been approved by the Ministry of Railways despite having a projected internal rate of return of 10.5% and 11.8%. On the contrary, projects with an internal rate of return as high as 22% have not progressed.[67] As of July 2023, all railway projects should aim for at least a 12% rate of return on investment, according to the Indian Railway Financial Code. Signaling works, which are integral to rail safety, do not require a financial viability assessment.[68]

- **Absence of set timetables for freight trains.** Railway lines are shared by both freight and passenger trains. Considering the sensitivities, passenger trains are always given preference resulting in significant time delays and congestion on lines, making it unviable for using freight rails. As a result, most zonal railways have higher than optimal utilization of line capacity. The Dedicated Freight Corridor projects are expected to improve rail share in carrying freight traffic. There is also a lack of infrastructure facilities for the smooth running of terminals and sidings. Institutionalizing timetables for freight rails will facilitate the efficient operations of railway lines.

- **Railways use the revenue earned from freight to cross-subsidize revenue from passenger traffic.** This is also one of the major reasons for the higher share of roads in freight transport. Recent improvements in road infrastructure and faster transit with initiatives like FASTag are expected to pose significant challenges to freight transport by rail in the future.

---

[67]   Comptroller and Auditor General of India. 2014. *Selection of Private Partners.*
[68]   A. Dastidar. 2023. Signalling Now Part of Rail Safety, Won't Need Financial Viability Test. *The Indian Express.* 14 July.

C. Ports

Parameter	Value	Unit
Total number of major ports	13	number
Total number of nonmajor ports	200	number
Total freight capacity of all ports (FY2021)	1560.61	MTPA
Total container traffic at ports (2021)	19,940,000	TEU
Quality of port infrastructure (2019)	4.5	1(low) – 7(high)

FY= fiscal year, MTPA = million tons per annum, TEU = twenty-foot equivalent unit.
Sources: Economist Intelligence Unit. The Infrascope Archives 2009–19: India; Press Information Bureau. 2022. Cargo Handling Capacity of Ports. 11 February; The Global Economy. Port Infrastructure Quality - Country Rankings (accessed 15 July 2023); The Global Economy. Port Traffic—Country Rankings (accessed 15 July 2023); World Bank.Container Port Traffic: India (accessed 15 July 2023); Government of India; Ministry of Ports, Shipping and Waterways; and Government of India; Ministry of Ports, Shipping and Waterways. Ports Wing.

1. Contracting Agencies in the Port Sector

The Ministry of Ports, Shipping and Waterways oversees the ports, shipping, and waterways sector in the country. Port development is a concurrent responsibility of both the central and state governments, according to the Constitution of India. The center-run ports (called major ports by law) are controlled by the central government while the state-run ports (called minor or nonmajor ports) are within the jurisdiction of the respective states that have coastlines.

Port Trusts are the contracting agencies for the 12 major ports. Overall, there are 13 major ports; however, one major port is a corporatized port, with two-thirds of the shares owned by the Government of India and one third by the Chennai Port Trust. The major ports were regulated by the Major Port Trusts Act, 1963, which has been replaced by the Major Port Authorities Act, 2021.

The maritime states of Andhra Pradesh, Gujarat, Karnataka, Kerala, Maharashtra, Odisha, Tamil Nadu, and West Bengal operate either through exclusively set-up Maritime Boards (authorities) or as a department under the provincial government. They have rights to plan for and develop the port sector, and enter into concessions with private sector players. Nonmajor ports are regulated by the Indian Ports Act, 1908. The Ministry of Ports, Shipping and Waterways has proposed to repeal and replace the Indian Ports Act, 1908.

For inland waterways, the Inland Waterways Authority of India (IWAI) is the overseeing authority that reports to the Ministry of Ports, Shipping and Waterways. The IWAI was set up in 1986 to develop and regulate inland waterways for shipping and navigation. It primarily undertakes projects for development and maintenance of inland waterways transport infrastructure on national waterways through a grant received from the Ministry of Ports, Shipping and Waterways. The IWAI has its head office at Noida; regional offices at Bhubaneswar, Guwahati, Kochi, Kolkata, and Patna; and suboffices at Badarpur, Dhubri, Dibrugarh, Farakka, Goa, Hemnagar, Kollam, Prayagraj, Sahibganj, Varanasi, and Vijayawada.[69]

---

[69]   Government of India; Ministry of Ports, Shipping and Waterways. Inland Waterways Authority of India.

2. Port Sector Laws and Regulations

All major ports fall under the jurisdiction of the government, and thus are governed by policy directives stipulated under the Major Port Trusts Act, 1963—except the Ennore Port, which is governed under the Companies Act, 1956. The Ministry of Ports, Shipping and Waterways promulgated a new regulation, the Major Port Authorities Bill, 2020, which provides for the regulation, operation, and planning of major ports in India and provides greater autonomy to these ports. The Parliament approved the Major Port Authorities Bill, 2020 giving way to the Major Port Authorities Act, 2021, which looks to reorient the governance model in central ports to the landlord model, wherein port infrastructure is leased to private operators. The Major Port Authorities Act, 2021 was notified in the gazette by the government in February 2021. The Act aims "to provide for the regulation, operation, and planning of Major Ports in India and to vest the administration, control, and management of such ports upon the Boards of Major Port Authorities and for matters connected therewith or incidental thereto."

The Act replaces the Major Port Trusts Act of 1963, which has been restrictive in many ways in the current market conditions. It aims to decentralize decision-making at major ports. The new Act defines public–private partnership (PPP) projects as projects taken up through a concession contract by the Board. For such projects, the Board may fix the tariff for initial bidding purposes. The appointed concessionaire will be free to fix the actual tariffs based on market conditions and other conditions as may be notified. The revenue share in such projects will be based on a specific concession agreement. Tariff issues have been a major hindrance in promoting PPPs in major ports in recent years. The Act also provides for the constitution of an Adjudicatory Board by the central government. This Board will replace the existing Tariff Authority for Major Ports constituted under the 1963 Act.

The Inland Waterways Authorities Act, 1985 was enacted to create the IWAI and its powers, functions, and activities. The government has also enacted the National Waterways Act, 2016, which provides for existing national waterways, the declaration of certain inland waterways as national waterways, and the regulation and development of these waterways for the purposes of shipping and navigation and related matters. The Act was instrumental in declaring the National Waterways 6 through 111, along with their limits as national waterways for the purposes of shipping and navigation.

Regulators in the Port Sector

The reform process for major ports was initiated in the 1990s as part of the broader strategy for infrastructure development, which called for private sector participation. The Tariff Authority for Major Ports (TAMP) was established in 1997 to regulate the tariffs for major ports. All major economic functions were directly under the ambit of the TAMP until January 2008 when the model concession agreement (MCA) was approved, allowing private sector participation, which led to improving the terminal efficiencies and investment by the private sector into port development. The government approved the revised MCA for PPP projects in major ports on 3 January 2018, and the update was released on 11 November 2021 to provide clarity on the responsibilities and obligations of parties and remedial measures in case of change in law. The Major Port Authorities Act, 2021 proposed to create an Adjudicatory Board to carry out the residual function of the TAMP, look into disputes between ports and PPP concessionaires, review stressed PPP projects and suggest measures to revive such projects, and look into complaints regarding the services rendered by the ports and private operators within the ports.[70]

The Ministry of Ports, Shipping and Waterways finalized the guidelines for dealing with stressed PPP projects at the major ports on 10 May 2022.[71] These guidelines have been framed for the following:

(i)   Projects that became stressed during construction stage—i.e., pre-commercial operation date (COD) stage where the work was halted because of the concessionaire's inability to proceed with project execution. This was often attributed to factors such as aggressive bidding, overly optimistic projections related to volumes and charges, and unforeseen dynamic changes in their business environment.

(ii)   Projects at pre-COD and post-COD stages, where work has stopped because of the inability of the concessionaire to continue with the execution of the project because of the borrowings of the concessionaire being categorized by lenders as a nonperforming asset and/or proceedings initiated against it before the National Company Law Tribunal under the Insolvency and Bankruptcy Code 2016 or under Section 241(2) of the Companies Act 2013.

The State Maritime Boards regulate ports development in their respective states. However, tariffs at minor ports, unlike major ports, are not regulated.

The key agencies responsible for major ports and inland waterways are shown in Table 20.

Table 20: Key Entities Responsible for the Port Sector in India

Agency	Function (Indicative List)
Ministry of Ports, Shipping and Waterways (MOPSW)	• The MOPSW oversees the shipping and port sectors, which include shipbuilding and ship repair, major ports, national waterways, and inland water transport.
Indian Ports Association (IPA)	• The IPA was constituted in 1966 under the Societies Registration Act to foster growth and development of all major ports that are under the supervisory control of the MOPSW. Over the years, the IPA has consolidated its activities and has strengthened its institutional capacity. It is considered as the think tank for major ports and has the goal of integrating the maritime sector.
Major Ports Adjudicatory Board (former Tariff Authority for Major Ports [TAMP])	• The Major Ports Adjudicatory Board replaced TAMP in 2023 as the nodal body for tariff setting and public–private partnership (PPP) dispute resolution for all 12 major ports in India. It will be governed by the Major Port Authorities Act, 2021. The Adjudicatory Board shall consist of a presiding officer and two members. The presiding officer shall be a retired Judge of the Supreme Court of India or a retired Chief Justice of a High Court. The two members shall either be a retired Chief Secretary of a state government or equivalent, or a retired Secretary of the Government of India or equivalent.

continued on next page

---

[70]   Government of India; Ministry of Ports, Shipping and Waterways. Tariff Authority for Major Ports.
[71]   Government of India; Ministry of Ports, Shipping and Waterways; Press Information Bureau. 2022. Guidelines for Early Resolution of Stuck Public Private Partnership (PPP) Projects at Major Ports. Press release. 11 May.

Table 20 *continued*

Agency	Function (Indicative List)
Sagarmala Development Company Limited (SDCL)	• Incorporated in August 2016, the SDCL has been set up under the Companies Act, 2013 and under the administrative control of the MOPSW. Implementation of the projects identified under the Sagarmala program will be taken up by the relevant ports, state governments, maritime boards, and central ministries mainly through private or public–private partnership mode. The SDCL will provide equity support for these projects via special purpose vehicles set up by the ports, states, and central ministries, as well as through a funding window. It will implement only those residual projects that cannot be funded by any other means or mode.
Inland Waterways Authority of India (IWAI)	• IWAI came into existence on 27 October 1986 to develop and regulate inland waterways for shipping and navigation. It primarily undertakes projects for development and maintenance of inland waterways transport infrastructure on national waterways through a grant received from the MOPSW.
Indian Port Rail Corporation Limited (IPRCL)	• The IPRCL is incorporated under the Companies Act, 2013 under the administrative control of the MOPSW, with stake by the 11 major ports and 10% by Rail Vikas Nigam Limited. It is also proposed that the IPRCL may raise funding from multilateral and bilateral agencies and other financial institutions. It aims to execute the last-mile connectivity, rail connectivity, and internal rail projects of the major ports more effectively and efficiently using a special purpose vehicle.

Sources: Government of India; Ministry of Ports, Shipping and Waterways. Sagarmala; Government of India; Ministry of Ports, Shipping and Waterways. About Us; Government of India; Ministry of Ports, Shipping and Waterways. IPRCL; Indian Ports Association; and Inland Waterways Authority of India. About Us.

Foreign Investment Restrictions in the Port Sector

Parameter	2021	2022	2023
Maximum allowed foreign ownership of equity in greenfield projects	100%	100%	100%

Standard Contracts in the Port Sector

The centrally controlled ports (major ports) are guided by the model documents approved by the DEA. On the other hand, the states and provinces have freedom to choose their own standard bidding documents and are not required to abide by the standard contracts issued by the central government. For example, the state of Gujarat (Gujarat Maritime Board), the largest maritime state in terms of throughput, has developed its own model agreements.

Type of Contract	Availability
Public–private partnership/concession agreement	✓
Performance-based operation and maintenance contract	✓
Engineering, procurement, and construction contract	✓

✓ = Yes, ✗ = No, NA = Not Applicable, UA = Unavailable.

The MCA in 2021 recommended the following modifications over the existing MCA suggested in 2018:[72]

- A provision on "Change in Cargo due to change in law or unforeseen Events" has been introduced for the first time. It gives the flexibility to undertake change in cargo in situations where traffic for a particular commodity has dropped during the concession period because of external and unforeseen factors.
- The new MCA provides flexibility to the concessionaires to fix their tariff based on market conditions.
- The minimum guaranteed throughput will be linked to royalty payment and a new bidding parameter has been proposed in line with changes in tariff levying mechanism.
- A provision of compensation for the termination of the concession agreement due to the concessionaire's default before the commencement of operations has been added.
- A provision has also been included for the of the terminal's draft through extra dredging during the concession period, with the cost and risk of dredging being shared.
- Key performance indicators for the concessioning authority have been established.
- The start date for license fee payments has been specified.
- Performance security has been assumed for the entire concession duration, consistent with the other sectors.

3. Port Sector Master Plan

The master plan for the ports and waterways sector is covered under the Sagarmala Program. The concept of the Sagarmala Program was approved in March 2015. As part of the program, the National Perspective Plan for the comprehensive development of India's maritime sector, including 7,500 km of coastline and 14,500 km of potentially navigable waterways, was prepared in April 2016.

The Sagarmala Program includes more than 800 projects (with an estimated total cost of ₹5.48 trillion or $66.8 billion) that have been identified for implementation over 2015–2035 across the areas of port modernization and new port development, port connectivity enhancement, port-linked industrialization, and coastal community development. According to the 2022–2023 Annual Report by the Ministry of Ports, Shipping and Waterways, 220 projects with a total cost of ₹1,122 billion ($13.69 billion) had been completed and 231 projects (with an estimated total cost of ₹2,208 billion or $26.93 billion) were under Implementation.[73] Table 21 indicates the project plan and status of the projects across various focus areas.

---

[72]   Government of India; Ministry of Ports, Shipping and Waterways. 2021. Model Concession Agreement 2021 for Public–Private Partnership (PPP) in Major Ports. 12 November.
[73]   Government of India; Ministry of Ports, Shipping and Waterways. 2023. Annual Report 2022–23.

Table 21: Estimated Expenditure of Initiatives in the Port Sector Under the Sagarmala Program of the Ministry of Ports, Shipping and Waterways

Pillar	Completed		Under Implementation		Under Development		Total Cost	
	Number	Value (₹ billion)	Number	Value (₹ billion)	Number	Value (₹ billion)	Number	Value (₹ billion)
Port modernization	89	312	63	640	89	1,543	241	2,496
Port connectivity	69	320	67	762	73	339	209	1,422
Port-led industrialization	9	458	21	727	3	12	33	1,198
Coastal community development	20	14	19	25	43	73	82	113
Coastal shipping and IWT	33	17	61	52	143	102	237	172
Grand Total	**220**	**1,122**	**231**	**2,208**	**351**	**2,071**	**802**	**5,401**

IWT = inland waterways transport.

Note: Numbers may not sum precisely because of rounding.

Source: Government of India; Ministry of Ports, Shipping and Waterways. 2023. Annual Report 2022–23.

Projects Under Conceptualization and Development in the Port Sector

Figure 23 shows the number of PPP projects that are under conceptualization and development in the port sector of India.

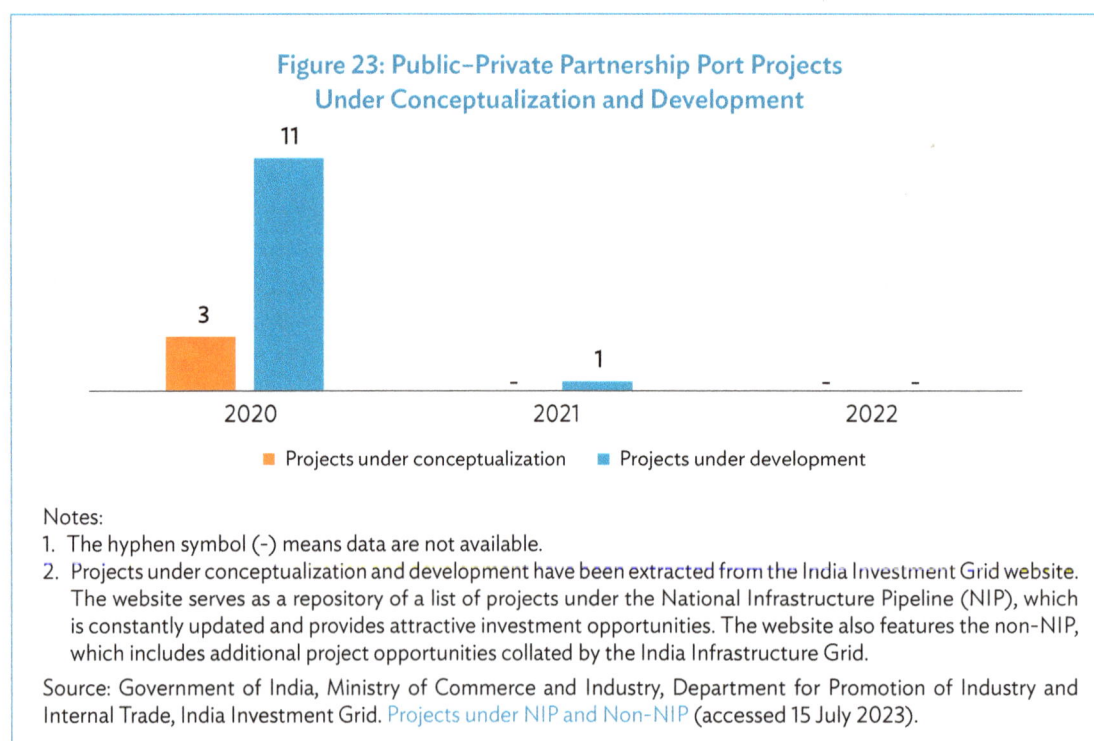

Figure 23: Public–Private Partnership Port Projects Under Conceptualization and Development

■ Projects under conceptualization   ■ Projects under development

Notes:
1. The hyphen symbol (-) means data are not available.
2. Projects under conceptualization and development have been extracted from the India Investment Grid website. The website serves as a repository of a list of projects under the National Infrastructure Pipeline (NIP), which is constantly updated and provides attractive investment opportunities. The website also features the non-NIP, which includes additional project opportunities collated by the India Infrastructure Grid.

Source: Government of India, Ministry of Commerce and Industry, Department for Promotion of Industry and Internal Trade, India Investment Grid. Projects under NIP and Non-NIP (accessed 15 July 2023).

4. Features of Past Public–Private Partnership Projects in the Port Sector

Figure 24 shows the number of PPP projects procured through various modes, including direct appointment and competitive bids, in the port sector of India.

Figure 24: Modes of Procurement for Public–Private Partnership Port Projects

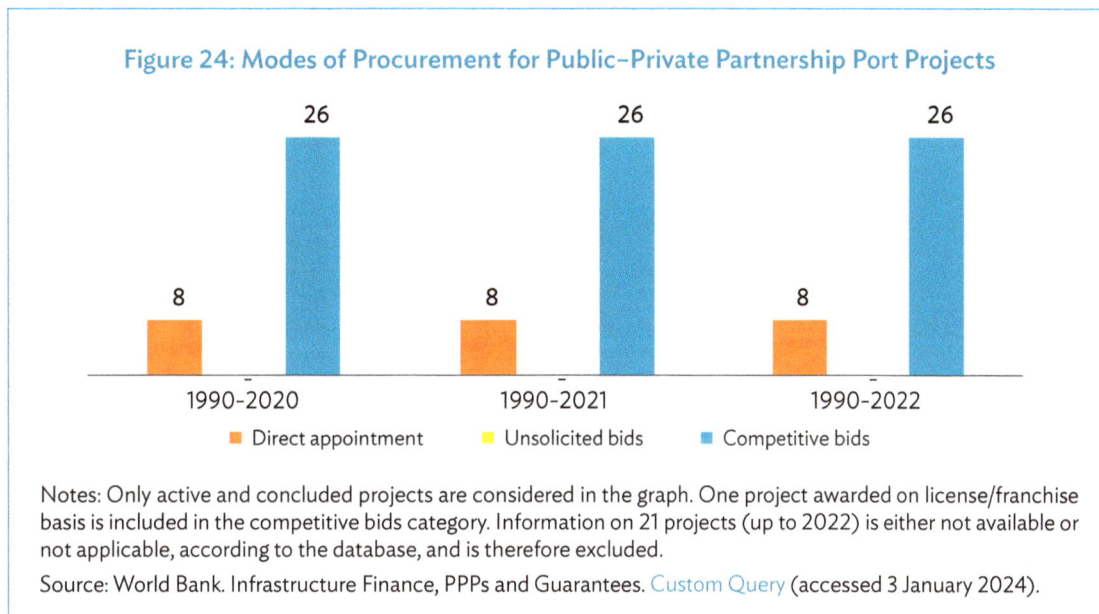

Notes: Only active and concluded projects are considered in the graph. One project awarded on license/franchise basis is included in the competitive bids category. Information on 21 projects (up to 2022) is either not available or not applicable, according to the database, and is therefore excluded.
Source: World Bank. Infrastructure Finance, PPPs and Guarantees. Custom Query (accessed 3 January 2024).

Figure 25 shows the number of PPP projects that reached financial close and the total value of those projects in the port sector of India.

Figure 25: Public–Private Partnership Port Projects Reaching Financial Close

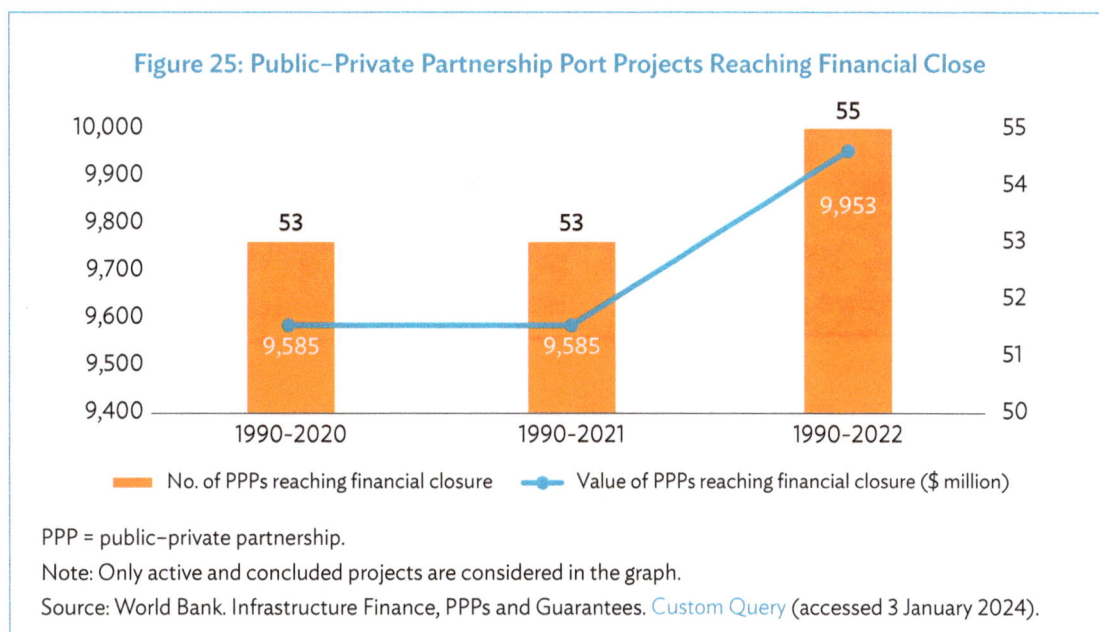

PPP = public–private partnership.
Note: Only active and concluded projects are considered in the graph.
Source: World Bank. Infrastructure Finance, PPPs and Guarantees. Custom Query (accessed 3 January 2024).

Figure 26 shows the number of PPP projects with foreign sponsor participation in the port sector of India.

Figure 26: Public–Private Partnership Port Projects with Foreign Sponsor Participation

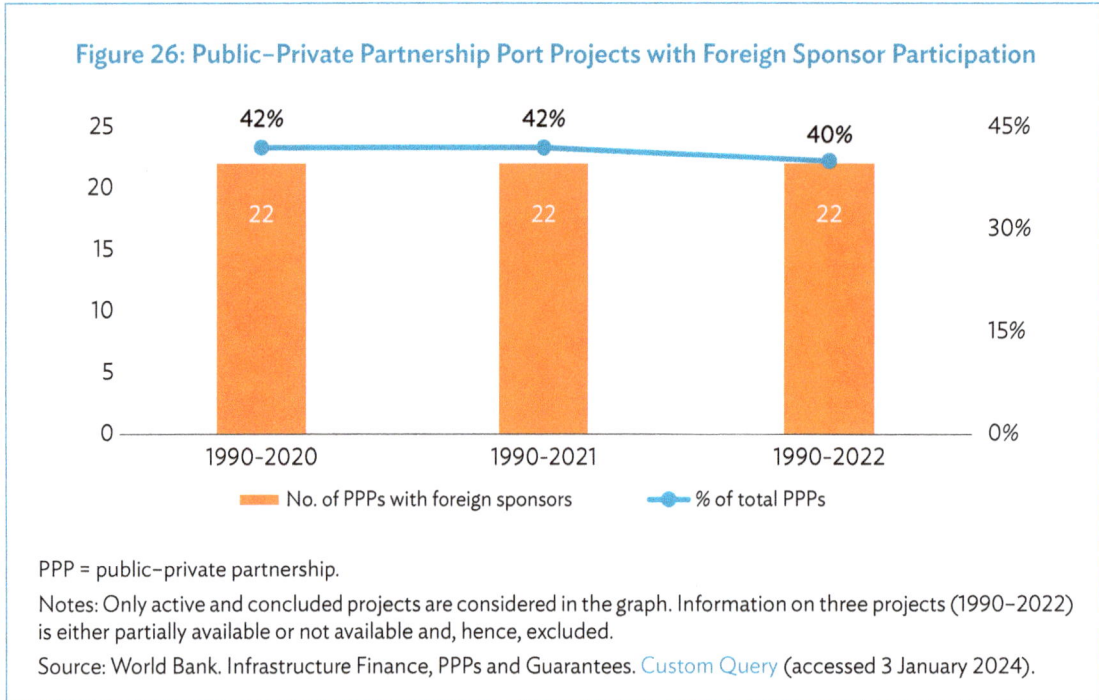

PPP = public–private partnership.

Notes: Only active and concluded projects are considered in the graph. Information on three projects (1990–2022) is either partially available or not available and, hence, excluded.

Source: World Bank. Infrastructure Finance, PPPs and Guarantees. Custom Query (accessed 3 January 2024).

Figure 27 shows the number of PPP projects that received government support including viability gap funding and government guarantees in the port sector of India.

Figure 27: Government Support to Public–Private Partnership Port Projects

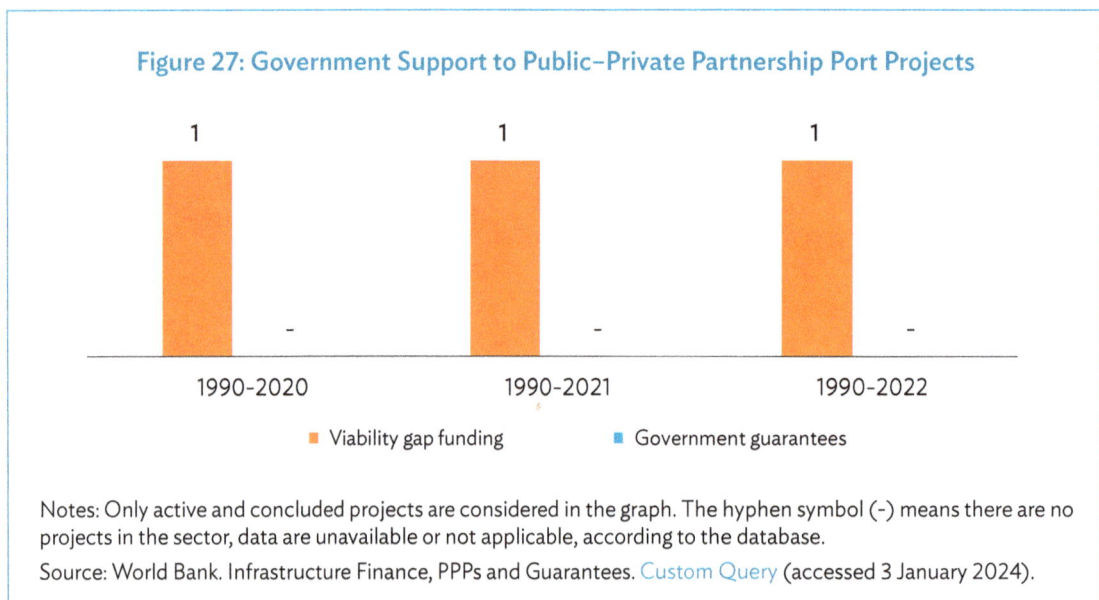

Notes: Only active and concluded projects are considered in the graph. The hyphen symbol (-) means there are no projects in the sector, data are unavailable or not applicable, according to the database.

Source: World Bank. Infrastructure Finance, PPPs and Guarantees. Custom Query (accessed 3 January 2024).

Figure 28 shows the number of PPP projects that received revenue in the form of user charges in the port sector of India. Other port sector projects in India have not received revenues in any other form.

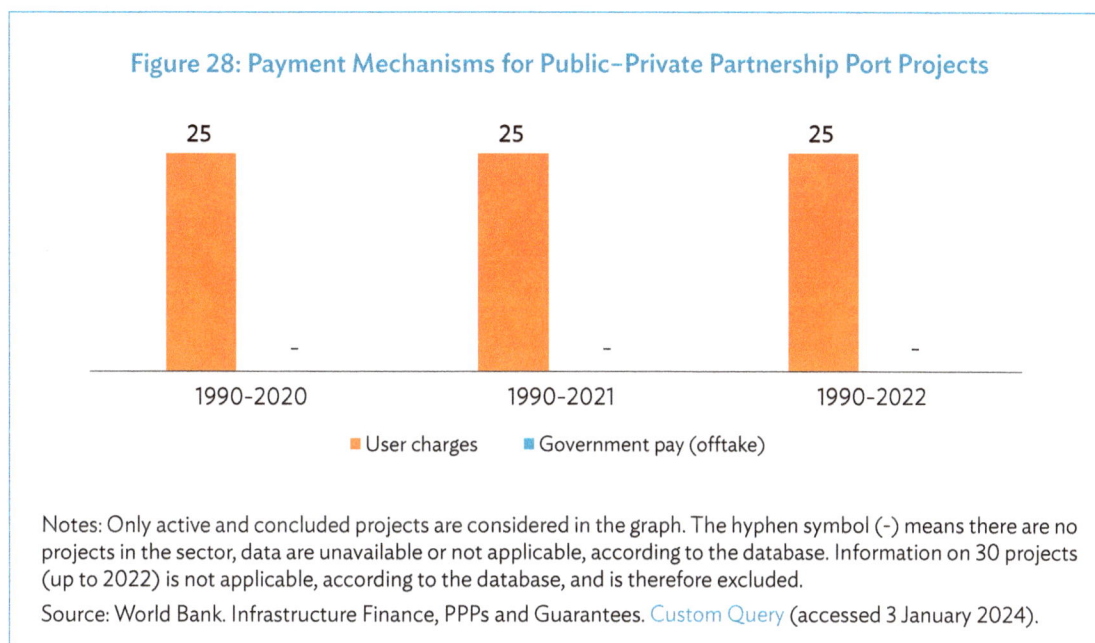

Figure 28: Payment Mechanisms for Public–Private Partnership Port Projects

Notes: Only active and concluded projects are considered in the graph. The hyphen symbol (-) means there are no projects in the sector, data are unavailable or not applicable, according to the database. Information on 30 projects (up to 2022) is not applicable, according to the database, and is therefore excluded.
Source: World Bank. Infrastructure Finance, PPPs and Guarantees. Custom Query (accessed 3 January 2024).

The payment mechanisms for the port sector (major ports) are in the form of revenue share or royalty per ton or twenty-foot equivalent unit, in addition to land lease and license fees.

Past PPP projects in the port sector classified in terms of PPP variant or scheme, according to the Department of Economic Affairs (DEA) database, are shown in Table 22.

Table 22: Number of Port Projects Across Public–Private Partnership Variants

Public–Private Partnership Variant	No. of Projects
Build–operate–transfer	29
Build–operate–transfer (annuity)	1
Build–own–lease–transfer	1
Build–own–operate	1
Build–own–operate–manage	5
Build–own–operate–share–transfer	12
Build–own–operate–transfer	17

continued on next page

Table 22 *continued*

Public–Private Partnership Variant	No. of Projects
Design–build–finance–operate	1
Design–build–finance–operate–transfer	24
Lease	1
Management contract (operation and maintenance)	1
Operate–maintain–share–transfer	1
Not available	5
Total	**99**

Note: The list includes nonmajor ports and terminals awarded within major ports. Data was last updated on 5 December 2019.

Source: Government of India, Ministry of Finance, Department of Economic Affairs. List of All PPP Projects (accessed 15 July 2023).

Tariffs in the Port Sector

Private sector operators in the major port sector are under a regulated tariff regime. There were multiple tariff regimes that were enacted for major ports over time including Tariff Guidelines 2005, Upfront Tariff Guidelines 2008, Reference Tariff Guidelines 2013, Tariff Guidelines 2019, Tariff Policy for Major Port Authorities 2021, and Tariff Guidelines 2021 for future PPP concessionaire.[74]

The tariff has been typically fixed based on cost-plus model and restricting the returns of the private sector player on return of net capital employed. Changing tariff guidelines, which restricted tariff flexibility to port operators, had led to financial distress. Consequently, the sector had become unattractive to private sector players in major ports until the guidelines of 2013 provided some flexibility. The 2021 guidelines allow the concessionaires at major ports to set tariffs based on market dynamics. The Major Port Authority Act, 2021 also gives the port authority the power to fix tariffs, which will serve as a reference tariff for purposes of bidding for major PPP projects, facilitating greater flexibility in the governance of major ports.

State governments, however, provide full flexibility to the port operators at the minor ports and select them based on either royalty per ton or twenty-foot equivalent unit or on highest revenue share basis.

---

[74]   Government of India; Ministry of Ports, Shipping, and Waterways. 2021. *Tariff Policy for Major Port Authorities 2021.* *3 November; and* Government of India; Ministry of Ports, Shipping and Waterways. 2021. *Tariff Guidelines 2021 for Future PPP Concessionaire. 21 December.*

Typical Risk Allocation for Public–Private Partnership Projects in the Port Sector

Typical risk allocation arrangements in port PPP contracts, most of which are in build–operate–transfer (BOT) scheme, are presented in the following table.

Type of Risk	Private	Public	Shared
Demand risk	✓		
Competition risk (exclusivity)	✓		
Tariff implementation or escalation risk	✓		
Environmental and social risks		✓	
Land acquisition risk		✓	
Permits			✓
Geotechnical risk	✓		
Foreign exchange risk	✓		
Force majeure risk			✓
Political risk		✓	

Financing Details of Public–Private Partnership Projects in the Port Sector

Parameter	1990–2020	1990–2021	1990–2022
Public–private partnership (PPP) projects with foreign lending participation	2	2	4
PPP projects that received export credit agency/international financing institution support	3	3	4
Typical debt-to-equity ratio	(75–70) : (25–30)		
Time for financial close	Typically, 6 months		
Typical concession period	30 years		
Typical financial internal rate of return	UA		

UA = Unavailable.
Source: World Bank. Infrastructure Finance, PPPs and Guarantees. Custom Query (accessed 3 January 2024).

5. Challenges in the Port Sector

- The existence of multiple tariff regimes and inflexible contracts has highlighted the need for more adaptable and collaborative partnerships. This situation presents an opportunity for private operators to advocate for more flexibility and responsiveness in addressing challenges beyond those classified as force majeure.
- The experience of losses due to delayed decision-making and resolutions by major port trusts underscores the importance of empowering these trusts and clarifying ownership.

This situation could lead to the development of more precise contractual clauses, reducing ambiguity and fostering a higher level of confidence among private sector players regarding fair contractual enforcement.

- The intense competition with minor ports, which have greater flexibility in tariff setting and providing value-added facilities, can motivate major ports to innovate and improve their competitiveness.
- The current state of road and rail networks, cargo handling equipment, navigational aids, information technology systems, dredging capacity, and technical expertise highlights areas for improvement. Addressing these areas could significantly enhance the efficiency of Indian ports and make them more attractive to private sector players.

The competitiveness and efficiency of both major and nonmajor ports are likely to improve in the short term through developments under the Major Ports Authority Bill—revising the model concession agreements (MCAs) to make them balanced and increasing investments in technology and connectivity—and through the initiatives of Sagarmala. With the aim to reduce litigations in the port sector, the Ministry of Ports, Shipping and Waterways has launched the new MCA, 2021. In addition, new tariff guidelines have been issued to provide flexibility for the private firm to fix tariffs based on the existing market dynamics, and introduce differential royalty rates to promote coastal shipping and transshipment.

D. Airports

Parameter	Value	Unit
No. of airports (2022)	147.0	number
Total passenger capacity (2022)	123.2	million passengers
Quality of air transport infrastructure (2019)	4.9	1(low) – 7(high)

Sources: Airports Authority of India. List of Airports (accessed 15 July 2023); Government of India, Ministry of Civil Aviation. 2023. Annual Report 2022; and The Global Economy. Compare Countries with Annual Data from Official Resources (accessed 15 July 2023).

1. Contracting Agencies in the Airport Sector

The Ministry of Civil Aviation is responsible for the formulation of national policies and programs for developing and regulating the civil aviation sector in India. The ministry exercises administrative control over attached and autonomous organizations such as the Airports Authority of India (AAI), the Directorate General of Civil Aviation, and the Bureau of Civil Aviation Security. Key pieces of legislation and policies governing the airport sector include the AAI Act, 1994; Policy on Airport Infrastructure; Domestic Air Transport Policy; Aircraft Act, 1934; and Airport Rules and the Open Sky Policy.

2. Airport Sector Laws and Regulations

- The AAI Act, 1994 established the Airports Authority of India.
- The National Civil Aviation Policy, 2016, issued by the Ministry of Civil Aviation, focuses on strengthening air connectivity nationwide and rationalizing fares to be affordable to masses. Accordingly, the policy encourages the development of airports through public–private partnership (PPP) mode, with the AAI and the state governments contributing as public enterprises. In October 2016, the Ministry of Civil Aviation launched the "Ude Deshka Aam Naagrik" (UDAN) Regional Connectivity Scheme, which is a key component of the policy, to provide air connectivity to currently underserved and unserved airports, make air travel accessible to citizens, and stimulate regional connectivity through a market-based mechanism.
- The Airports Economic Regulatory Authority Act 2008 established a regulatory authority for major airports in India.

Table 23 indicates the key agencies in the airport sector, along with a brief description of their functions.

Table 23: Key Entities Responsible for the Airport Sector in India

Agency	Functions (Indicative List)
Ministry of Civil Aviation	• The MOCA is the apex entity for planning and development of the aviation sector. • Site clearance for all greenfield airports is granted by the MOCA, based on the reports submitted by the AAI and the DGCA.
Airports Economic Regulatory Authority	• Formed by Airports Economic Regulatory Authority Act, 2008, AERA is the regulatory authority for major airports in India. • In 2019, the criterion for classifying a "major airport" was amended from the present. • The minimum threshold to classify an airport as a "major airport" has increased from 1.5 million passengers per annum to 3.5 million passengers per annum. This came into force by amending the Airports Economic Regulatory Authority Act, 2008 into Airports Economic Regulatory Authority of India (Amendment) Act, 2019. • AERA determines and regulates the tariff for aeronautical services and passenger service fees, airport security fees, user development fees, and other charges to monitor performance standards relating to quality, continuity, and reliability of services at major airports.
Airports Authority of India	• The AAI was formed on 1 April 1995 by merging the International Airports Authority of India and the National Airports Authority to accelerate the integrated development, expansion, and the modernization of operational, terminal, and cargo facilities at the country's airports, and make them conform to international standards. • In accordance with the guidelines prescribed by the International Civil Aviation Organization, the MOCA publishes regulations for airport and airline operators to ensure safety and security of operations. The AAI is responsible for implementing the guidelines and monitoring compliance. • The AAI is responsible for developing, financing, operating, and maintaining all public sector airports.

continued on next page

Table 23 *continued*

Agency	Functions (Indicative List)
	• The AAI acts as operator and regulator of airports and is the only body (except the Indian Air Force) empowered to provide air traffic services over the Indian airspace and adjoining oceanic areas, in accordance with the International Civil Aviation Organization standards. • Communication, navigation, surveillance and air traffic management, and other allied infrastructure required for a greenfield airport will be mandatorily provided by the AAI.
Directorate General of Civil Aviation	• The DGCA is the regulatory body primarily dealing with safety issues. It is responsible for regulating air transport services to, from, and within India and for enforcement of civil air regulations, air safety, and airworthiness standards. The DGCA also coordinates all regulatory functions with the International Civil Aviation Organization. • The aerodrome licenses are granted by the DGCA.
Bureau of Civil Aviation Security (BCAS)	• The BCAS is responsible for laying down standards and measures with respect to security of civil flights at international and domestic airports.
Aircraft Accident Investigation Bureau	• The AAIB has been mandated for immediate and unrestricted access to all relevant evidence related to investigation of accidents from any agency or organization without seeking prior consent from judicial bodies or other government authorities.
Ministry of Home Affairs and Ministry of Finance	• Customs regulations are administered by the MOF, and immigration regulations are administered by the MHA. • Clearance for customs-related services is issued by the MOF. • The MHA issues licenses regarding the location of the airport, acquisition and installation of security equipment, and verification of developers' credentials. • Clearances for immigration-related services is issued by the MHA.

AAI = Airports Authority of India, AAIB = Aircraft Accident Investigation Bureau, AERA = Airports Economic Regulatory Authority, BCAS = Bureau of Civil Aviation Security, DGCA = Directorate General of Civil Aviation, MHA = Ministry of Home Affairs, MOCA = Ministry of Civil Aviation, MOF = Ministry of Finance.

Sources: Government of India, Ministry of Civil Aviation. Organizational Set Up; Government of India. Airports Economic Regulatory Authority of India; Government of India, Airports Economic Regulatory Authority of India. *Airports Economic Regulatory Authority of India (Amendment) Act, 2019*; Government of India. Airports Authority of India; and Government of India. Directorate General of Civil Aviation.

Foreign Investment Restrictions in the Airport Sector

Parameter	2021	2022	2023
Maximum allowed foreign ownership of equity in greenfield projects	100%	100%	100%

Table 24 shows a snapshot of foreign direct investment allowed across various services.

Table 24: Foreign Direct Investment Allowed in the Airport and Aviation Sector

Sector and Activity	Percentage of Equity and FDI Cap
Airports Sector	
• Greenfield projects	100% (Automatic route)
• Brownfield projects	100% (Automatic route)
Air Transport Services	
• Scheduled air transport services and scheduled domestic passenger airlines	Automatic up to 49% (Automatic up to 100% for NRIs), Government route beyond 49%
• Regional air transport services	
• Nonscheduled air transport services	100% (Automatic route)
• Helicopter services and seaplane services requiring DGCA approval	
Other Services in Aviation Sector	
• Ground handling services subject to sector regulations and security clearance	100% (Automatic route)
• Maintenance and repair organizations, flying training institutes, and technical training institutes	100% (Automatic route)

DGCA = Directorate General of Civil Aviation, FDI = foreign direct investment, NRI = nonresident Indian.

Source: Government of India, Ministry of Commerce and Industry, Department for Promotion of Industry and Internal Trade. 2020. *Consolidated FDI Policy.*

Standard Contracts in the Airport Sector

Type of Contract	Availability
Public–private partnership/concession agreement	✓
Performance-based operation and maintenance contract	✓
Engineering, procurement, and construction contract	✓

✓ = Yes, ✗ = No, NA = Not Applicable, UA = Unavailable.

The two largest airports given for private sector participation were the brownfield airports of Mumbai and New Delhi, while the next largest airports were greenfield projects of Bengaluru and Hyderabad. All of these airports had their concession agreements signed. All the four airports were either awarded purely on revenue share model or upfront fees plus revenue share model. The tariff was regulated and reviewed at periodic intervals.

In 2018, the Ministry of Civil Aviation shifted away from revenue share as a bid parameter and proposed the following model for the selection of developers for greenfield airports in the country:

- The maximum blended aeronautical yield in terms of Indian rupee per passenger shall be predetermined by the Concession Authority at the beginning of the concession period. It shall undergo minor adjustments to account for inflation and certain eventualities over the concession period.

- The maximum blended aeronautical yield for greenfield airports for FY2019 was proposed to be ₹400 per passenger. The number has been arrived at based on projected cash flow analysis for greenfield airports of different capacities and a review of aeronautical yields at Indian and global airports in the past.
- The bid parameter is proposed to be the "concession fee per passenger" payable to the Concession Authority in terms of Indian rupee per passenger. The bids will differ for each airport in line with its projected traffic, financial returns, and risk profile.
- The concession period was proposed to be 40 years.[75]

3. Airport Sector Master Plan

The AAI has earmarked 25 airports for leasing. It has already leased out eight of its airports through the PPP model. The AAI Board recommended leasing out six airports (Amritsar, Bhubaneswar, Indore, Raipur, Trichy, and Varanasi) for operation, management, and development under PPP. These facilities are managed by the state-owned AAI and witnessed traffic between 1.04 million and 2.52 million passengers in FY2022–2023.

In February 2019, the Ministry of Civil Aviation bid out six profit-making airports (Ahmedabad, Guwahati, Jaipur, Lucknow, Mangalore, and Thiruvananthapuram) based on highest per-passenger fee offered to the AAI. One of the leading private developers in the country won the rights to operate, manage, and develop these airports for a period of 50 years.

Table 25 shows the expected investments over the next 5 years, based on the National Infrastructure Pipeline.

Table 25: Estimated Capital Expenditure Plan for the Airport Sector Under the National Infrastructure Pipeline

Project Category	No. of Projects	Capital Expenditure, FY2020–FY2025	
		($ billion)	(₹ billion)
Greenfield airports	8	4.41	361.47
Expansion and modernization of existing airports	50	6.47	530.20
Total	**58**	**10.88**	**891.67**

FY = fiscal year.
Source: Government of India, Ministry of Finance, Department of Economic Affairs. 2019. *National Infrastructure Pipeline.* Volume 2.

---

[75]   Government of India, Press Information Bureau. 2018. *Ministry of Civil Aviation: New Transaction Structure for Future Greenfield Airports Proposed Under Nabh Nirmaan 2018.* Press release. 14 August.

Projects Under Conceptualization and Development in the Airport Sector

Figure 29 shows the number of PPP projects that are under conceptualization and development in the airport sector of India.

Figure 29: Public–Private Partnership Airport Projects Under Conceptualization and Development

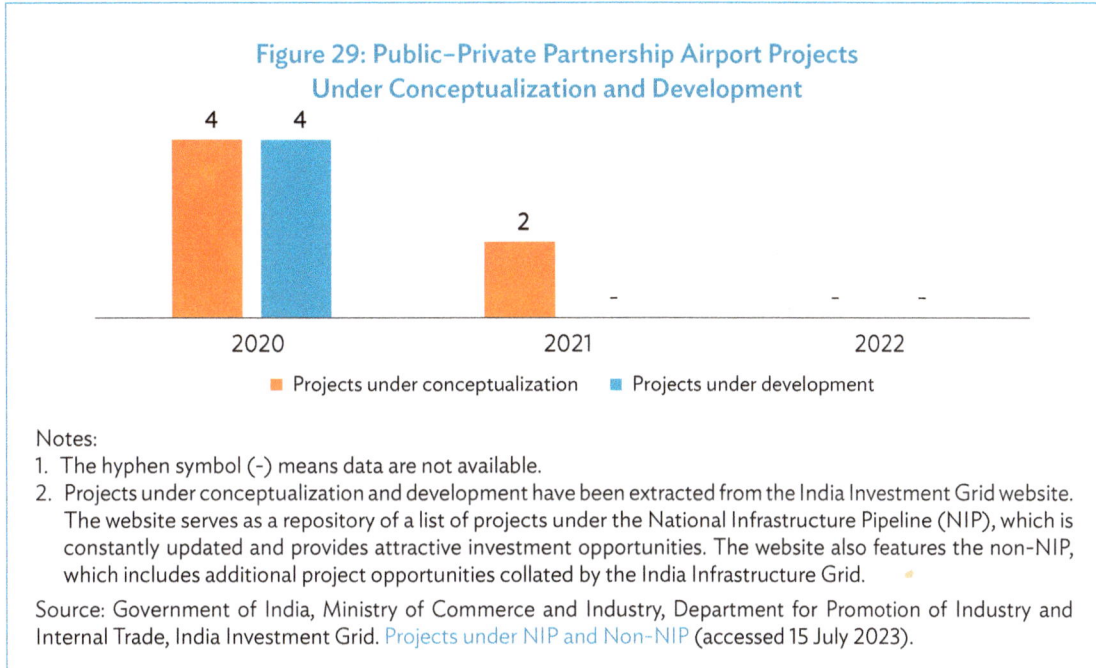

Notes:
1. The hyphen symbol (-) means data are not available.
2. Projects under conceptualization and development have been extracted from the India Investment Grid website. The website serves as a repository of a list of projects under the National Infrastructure Pipeline (NIP), which is constantly updated and provides attractive investment opportunities. The website also features the non-NIP, which includes additional project opportunities collated by the India Infrastructure Grid.

Source: Government of India, Ministry of Commerce and Industry, Department for Promotion of Industry and Internal Trade, India Investment Grid. Projects under NIP and Non-NIP (accessed 15 July 2023).

4. Features of Past Public–Private Partnership Projects in the Airport Sector

Figure 30 shows the number of PPP projects procured through various modes, including direct appointment and competitive bids, in the airport sector of India.

Figure 30: Modes of Procurement for Public–Private Partnership Airport Projects

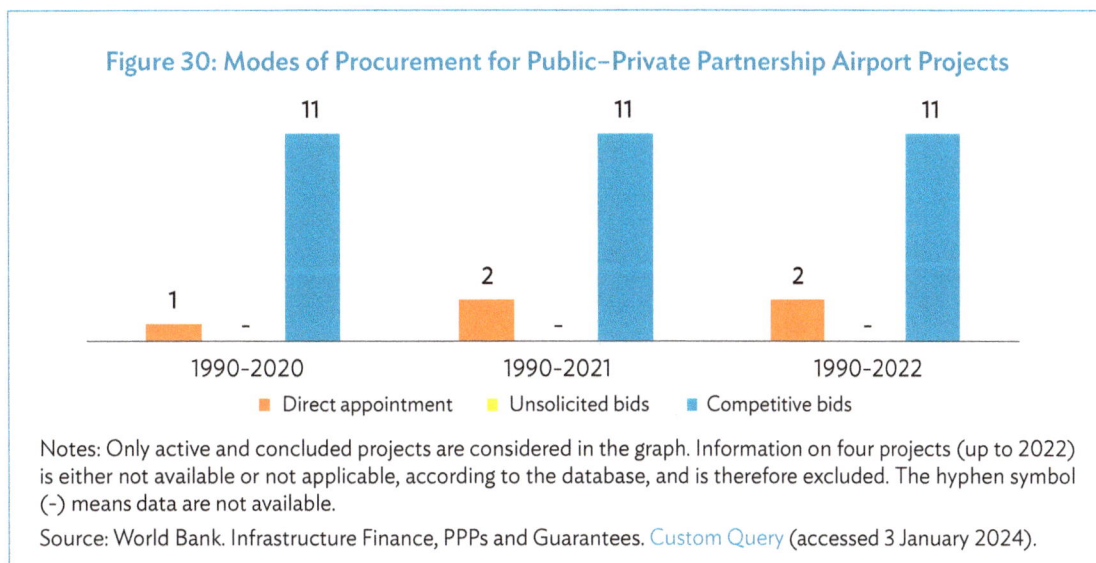

Notes: Only active and concluded projects are considered in the graph. Information on four projects (up to 2022) is either not available or not applicable, according to the database, and is therefore excluded. The hyphen symbol (-) means data are not available.

Source: World Bank. Infrastructure Finance, PPPs and Guarantees. Custom Query (accessed 3 January 2024).

Figure 31 shows the number of PPP projects that reached financial close and the total value of those projects in the airport sector of India.

Figure 31: Public–Private Partnership Airport Projects Reaching Financial Close

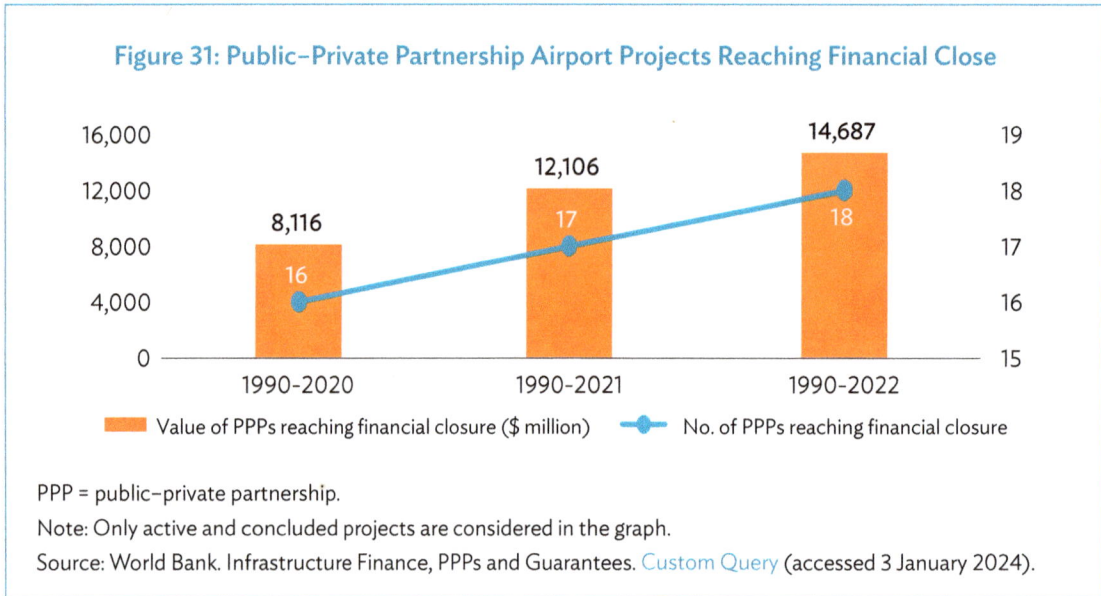

PPP = public–private partnership.

Note: Only active and concluded projects are considered in the graph.

Source: World Bank. Infrastructure Finance, PPPs and Guarantees. Custom Query (accessed 3 January 2024).

Figure 32 shows the number of PPP projects with foreign sponsor participation in the airport sector of India.

Figure 32: Public–Private Partnership Airport Projects with Foreign Sponsor Participation

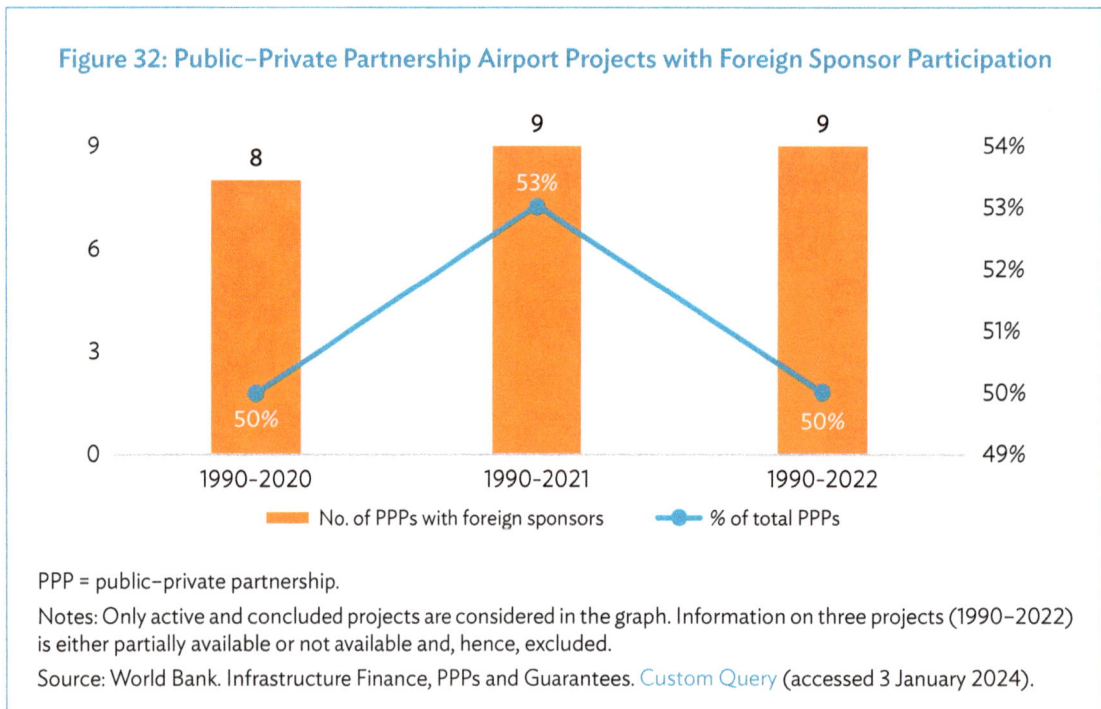

PPP = public–private partnership.

Notes: Only active and concluded projects are considered in the graph. Information on three projects (1990–2022) is either partially available or not available and, hence, excluded.

Source: World Bank. Infrastructure Finance, PPPs and Guarantees. Custom Query (accessed 3 January 2024).

Figure 33 shows the number of PPP projects that received government support including viability gap funding and government guarantees in the airport sector.

Figure 33: Government Support to Public–Private Partnership Airport Projects

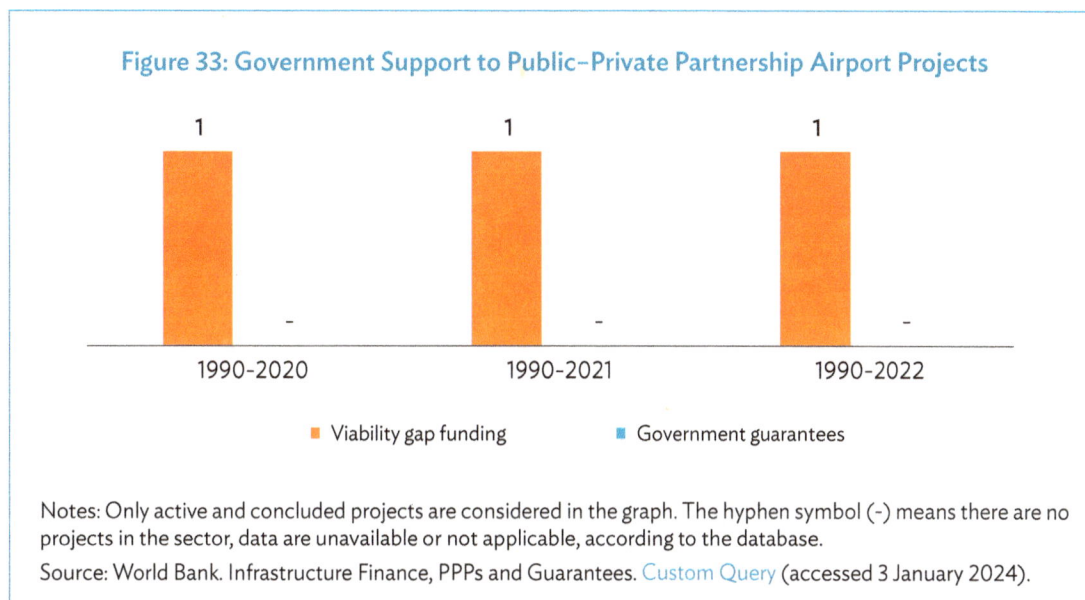

Notes: Only active and concluded projects are considered in the graph. The hyphen symbol (-) means there are no projects in the sector, data are unavailable or not applicable, according to the database.

Source: World Bank. Infrastructure Finance, PPPs and Guarantees. Custom Query (accessed 3 January 2024).

Figure 34 shows the number of PPP projects that received payment in the form of user charges and government pay (offtake) in the airport sector of India.

Figure 34: Payment Mechanisms for Public–Private Partnership Airport Projects

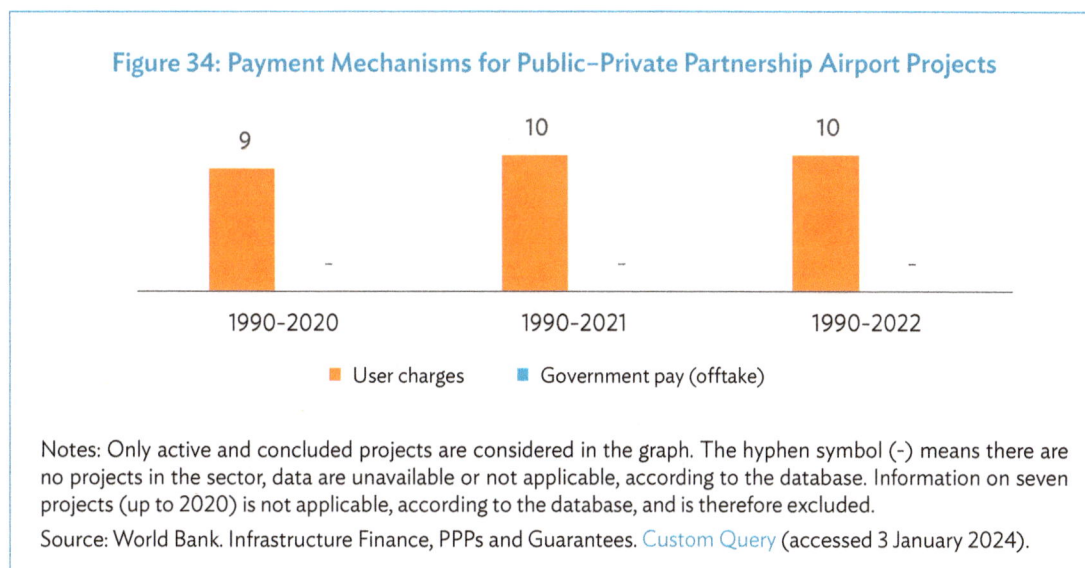

Notes: Only active and concluded projects are considered in the graph. The hyphen symbol (-) means there are no projects in the sector, data are unavailable or not applicable, according to the database. Information on seven projects (up to 2020) is not applicable, according to the database, and is therefore excluded.

Source: World Bank. Infrastructure Finance, PPPs and Guarantees. Custom Query (accessed 3 January 2024).

Table 26 shows the past PPP projects in the airport sector classified in terms of PPP variant or scheme, based on the Department of Economic Affairs (DEA) database.

Table 26: Number of Airport Projects Across Public–Private Partnership Variants

Public–Private Partnership Variant	No. of Projects
Build–own–operate	1
Build–own–operate–transfer	4
Design–build–finance–operate	1
Design–build–finance–operate–transfer	1
Not available	2
Operation, management, and development agreement	2
Total	**11**

Note: Data was last updated on 5 December 2019.

Source: Government of India, Ministry of Finance, Department of Economic Affairs. List of All PPP Projects (accessed 15 July 2023).

Tariffs in the Airport Sector

In 2011, the regulator for major airports issued directions to determine the tariff for airport operators and service providers. These included

- Airports Economic Regulatory Authority of India (Terms and Conditions for Determination of Tariff for Airport Operators) Guidelines, 2011; and
- Airports Economic Regulatory Authority of India (Terms and Conditions for Determination of Tariff for Services Provided for Cargo Facility, Ground Handling, and Supply of Fuel to the Aircraft) Guidelines, 2011.

The user charges levied by the major airports for aeronautical services are determined based on the provisions of the Government Support Agreement and are periodically reviewed by the Airports Economic Regulatory Authority based on the return of capital employed earned by the concessionaire or special purpose vehicle (SPV) for each control period, and the multiyear tariff proposal submitted by the concessionaire or the SPV. The major airports must submit to the regulator a schedule of charges and investments in their Regulated Asset Base. The regulator then determines the charges based on a guaranteed return on the Regulator Asset Base factoring in the cost of capital, depreciation, operation and maintenance (O&M), and taxes.[76]

---

[76]   Government of India, Airports Economic Regulatory Authority of India. Directions/Guidelines.

However, the Airports Economic Regulatory Authority of India (Amendment) Act, 2019 (an amendment to the Airports Economic Regulatory Authority of India Act, 2008) has added a clause indicating that in case tariffs are pre-incorporated into the bidding documents, after approval by Airports Economic Regulatory Authority, the Authority shall not determine any tariffs for such projects during the operations period. The amendment in the Act states:

> Notwithstanding anything contained in subsections (1) and (2), the Authority shall not determine the tariff or tariff structures or the amount of development fees in respect of all airport or part thereof, if such tariff or tariff structures or the amount of development fees has been incorporated in the bidding document, which is the basis for award of operatorship of that airport;
>
> Provided that the Authority shall be consulted in advance regarding the tariff, tariff structures, or the amount of development fees proposed to be incorporated in the said bidding document and such tariff, tariff structures, or the amount of development fees shall be notified in the Official Gazette.[77]

The Joint Venture Committee or the SPV is free to fix the charges for non-aeronautical services, subject to the applicable law and provisions in the development and maintenance contracts.

The Airports Economic Regulatory Authority of India (Amendment) Act, 2021 allows tariff determination of a "group of airports" by way of amending the definition of "major airport." The bill amends the provisions of the law in relation to tariffs for single airports.[78]

Typical Risk Allocation for Public–Private Partnership Projects in the Airport Sector

The typical risk allocation arrangements in airport PPP contracts based on the development, construction, operation, and maintenance agreement signed for greenfield airports are presented in the following table.

Type of Risk	Private	Public	Shared	Comment
Demand risk	✓			
Financing risk	✓			
Construction risk	✓			
Competition risk (exclusivity)		✓		No new airport permission within 150 kilometers of aerial distance for 25 years from start of operations
Tariff implementation or escalation risk				Tariff is regulated.
Environmental and social risks		✓		

continued on next page

---

[77] Government of India. 2019, The Airports Economic Regulatory Authority of India (Amendment) Act, 2019. *The Gazette of India.* 24 September.
[78] Government of India. 2021. *The Airports Economic Regulatory Authority of India (Amendment) Bill, 2021.*

Table *continued*

Type of Risk	Private	Public	Shared	Comment
Land acquisition risk		✓		
Permits			✓	
Foreign exchange risk	✓			
Force majeure risk			✓	
Political risk		✓		

Financing Details of Public–Private Partnership Projects in the Airport Sector

Parameter	1990–2021	1990–2022	1990–2023
PPP projects with foreign lending participation	UA	UA	UA
PPP projects that received export credit agency/international financing institution support	UA	UA	UA
Typical debt-to-equity ratio	(70–80) : (30–20)		
Time for financial close	3 months extendable by mutual consent		
Typical concession period	30 years		
Typical financial internal rate of return	UA		

PPP = public–private partnership, UA = unavailable.

Source: World Bank. Infrastructure Finance, PPPs and Guarantees. Custom Query (accessed 3 January 2024).

5. Challenges in the Airport Sector

- While the cost of land acquisition for greenfield projects can be a challenge, it also presents an opportunity for innovative solutions and partnerships. The implementation of newer laws on compensation in land acquisition, although making projects seem unaffordable, ensures fair compensation and could lead to better growth and development.
- Airport companies have the potential to generate substantial returns over the concession period. This potential has motivated them to invest significantly in creating airport megastructures. While these costs have raised concerns when passed on to airport users, they also highlight the importance of strategic planning and proportionate spending. Addressing these concerns could lead to more efficient capital expenditure and improved user satisfaction.
- Delays in securing necessary clearances and approvals can lead to project delays and cost overruns. However, these challenges underscore the importance of efficient project management and the potential benefits of streamlining the approval process. Overcoming these obstacles could result in timely project completion and cost efficiency.

E. Energy

Parameter	Value	Unit
Electric power consumption (2023)	1,327	kilowatt-hour per capita
Share of renewable energy (2022)	43	% of installed electricity capacity
Access to electricity (2021)	99.6	% of population
Getting electricity (score out of 100)	89.4	number
Investment in energy with private participation	1,620	current $ million

Sources: Government of India, Ministry of Power, Central Electricity Authority. 2023. *Growth of Electricity Sector in India from 1947 to 2023;* Government of India, Press Information Bureau. 2022. *Renewable Energy in India.* 9 September; World Bank. Access to Electricity: India (accessed 15 July 2023); Invest India. Renewable Energy (accessed 15 July 2023); The Global Economy. Share of Clean Energy—Country Rankings (accessed 15 July 2023); and United Nations, Department of Economic and Social Affairs. 2019. *Energy Statistics Pocketbook.*

1. Contracting Agencies in the Energy Sector

In India, there are different authorities for the power sector and for the oil and gas sector.

Power
The Ministry of Power is an apex organization under the central government, which formulates and administers the energy sector program in consultation with other central ministries and departments. The Ministry of Power is a holding body for generation (tariff regulation), scheduling and dispatching, transmission, and distribution (footnote 13).

Oil and Gas
The Ministry of Petroleum and Natural Gas is an apex organization under the central government. Its major functions include (i) exploration, production, refining, distribution and marketing, and import and export of oil and natural gas; and (ii) conservation of petroleum products and liquefied natural gas (footnote 13).

2. Energy Sector Laws and Regulations

Power
The power sector in India is mainly governed by the Electricity Act, 2003 (amended in 2007), which seeks to create a liberal framework for developing this sector. Some of its salient features include the following:

- De-licensing of generation and free permission for captive generation;
- Open access in transmission to be provided to distribution licensees and generation companies;
- Open access in distribution to be allowed by state electricity regulatory commissions (SERCs) in phases;

- Trading to be recognized as a distinct activity and the regulatory commissions as the authority in safeguarding it by fixing ceiling on trading margins; and
- The follow-on policy to include the National Tariff Policy 2006, which assures customers of electricity at reasonable rates and competitive price—this policy was amended into the Revised Tariff Policy, 2016 to ensure the financial viability of the sector, attract investments, and minimize regulatory risks.

The Ministry of Power amended the Electricity Act, 2003 through the Electricity (Amendment) Bill, 2022. The Electricity Bill (4th proof says Act), 2022 specifies the following:[79]

- Provide for the constitution of the Electricity Contract Enforcement Authority, which will have the sole authority to adjudicate upon specified contract-related disputes in the electricity sector.
- Constitute a common selection committee to select the chairperson and members of the Appellate Tribunal, the central and state regulatory commissions, and the Electricity Contract Enforcement Authority.
- Increase the number of members (including the chairperson) in SERCs from three to four. Further, at least one member in both the Central Electricity Regulatory Commission (CERC) and SERCs must have background in law.
- Authorize the State Commission to determine the floor and ceiling tariffs for retail supply, if there is more than one discom in an area.
- Set up a cross-subsidy balancing fund by the state government to deposit surplus of cross-subsidy from one discom, and to provide for any deficit of another discom in the same or any other area.
- Empower the CERC and SERCs to adjudicate disputes related to the performance of contracts. These refer to contracts related to the sale, purchase, or transmission of electricity.

The Ministry of Power issued a notification dated 30 June 2023 introducing the Electricity (Amendment) Rules, 2023 (Amendment Rules), which has changed the provisions relating to captive generating power plants.[80] The Amendment Rules provide that if a captive generating plant is established by an affiliate company, then the captive user must hold no less than 51% of ownership in that affiliate company, instead of the earlier 26%.

Renewable Energy

The Ministry of New and Renewable Energy (MNRE) is the nodal ministry of the Government of India for all matters relating to new and renewable energy. The MNRE aims to develop and deploy new and renewable energy to supplement the energy requirements of the country. Its main function is to facilitate research, design, development, manufacturing, and deployment of new and renewable energy systems and/or devices for transportation, as well as portable and stationary applications in rural, urban, industrial, and commercial sectors. It focuses on solar, wind, small hydro, and biofuel projects.

The MNRE leads the country's efforts toward achieving 40% of installed power generation capacity from non-fossil fuel sources and reducing emission intensity of greenhouse gases by 33% to 35% from the 2005 level by 2030.

---

[79]   PRS Legislative Research. 2022. Electricity (Amendment) Bill, 2022.
[80]   Government of India. 2023. The Electricity Act, 2003 (Act 36 of 2003). *The Gazette of India.* 30 June.

In 2018, the ministry provided a notification on the National Wind-Solar Hybrid Policy, which aims to "provide a framework for promotion of large grid connected wind-solar photovoltaic (PV) hybrid system for efficient and optimal utilization of wind and solar resources, land and transmission infrastructure." The policy encourages "new technologies, methods and wayouts involving combined operation of wind and solar PV plants and seeks to promote new hybrid projects as well as hybridization of existing wind and solar projects."[81]

The Government of India revised the Solar Mission in 2014. It targets 100-gigawatt (GW) installed capacity of solar electricity by 2022. As of March 2023, India generated 16.1% of its total energy through solar power.[82]

In 2023, the Government of India launched the National Green Hydrogen Mission, with an outlay of ₹197.44 billion up to FY 2029-2030. It will contribute to India's goal to become Aatma Nirbhar (self-reliant) through clean energy as well as toward for the global clean energy transition. The Mission will lead to significant decarbonization of the economy, reduced dependence on fossil fuel imports, and enable India to assume technology and market leadership in green hydrogen.[83]

Oil and Gas

The oil and gas sector is governed by the Petroleum and Natural Gas Regulatory Board Act, 2006, which regulates the refining, storage, transportation, distribution, and marketing of petroleum products, excluding the production of crude oil and natural gas. The sector has the following key elements (footnote 13):

- The open acreage policy enables private participants to come up with proposals for exploration and development of fields not identified by the government.
- Other policies include New Hydrocarbon Exploration and Licensing Policy and Small Fields Policy (March 2016) for monetization of 67 discoveries through international competitive bidding. New gas pricing formula linked to the global market was made effective from November 2014.
- The Petroleum and Minerals Pipeline Act, 1962 governs the laying of pipelines for transport of petroleum and minerals. The Petroleum Act, 1934 governs the importation, transportation, storage, production, refining, and blending of petroleum, and deals substantially with midstream activities of petroleum. The Oil Fields Act, 1948 is the basic statute for licensing and leasing of petroleum and gas blocks by the Government of India, empowering the government with the broad authority to make rules providing for the basic regulation of oil fields and for the development of mineral oil resources. Along with the Petroleum Rules, 2002, the Oilfields (Regulation and Development) Act, 1948 governs the grant of production exploration licenses and mining leases.
- The Policy on Shale Gas and Oil, 2013 allows companies to apply for shale gas and oil rights with their petroleum exploration licenses and petroleum mining leases.

---

[81] Government of India, Ministry of New and Renewable Energy. 2018. *National Wind-Solar Hybrid Policy, 2018*.
[82] Government of India, Ministry of Power. 2023. Power Sector at a Glance.
[83] Government of India, Ministry of New and Renewable Energy, Press Information Bureau. 2024. Government Issues Scheme Guidelines for Pilot Projects on Use of Green Hydrogen in the Transport Sector. Press release. 14 February.

State initiatives for renewable energy include the following (footnote 13):

- SERCs in Andhra Pradesh, Gujarat, Haryana, Kerala, Madhya Pradesh, Maharashtra, Odisha, Punjab, Rajasthan, Tamil Nadu, and West Bengal have announced preferential tariffs for purchase of power from wind power projects;
- New Solar Policy (2016) for Delhi, Haryana, and Himachal Pradesh; and
- New Solar Policy (2015) for Andhra Pradesh, Gujarat, Jharkhand, and Telangana.

Table 27 describes the functions of regulatory authorities in the energy sector.

Table 27: Regulatory Entities in the Energy Sector in India

Agency	Functions (Indicative List)
Central Electricity Regulatory Commission (CERC)	Handles regulation at the central power market level under the mandates of the Electricity Act of 2003. The CERC determines the tariffs for generators owned by the central government and for those supplying electricity to more than one state. It sets the tariffs for transmission and is also in charge of licensing interstate transmission and trading by generators, grid discipline and grid security, market development and market monitoring, and promotion of renewable energy and energy efficiency by regulating renewable energy certificates and energy saving certificates. The CERC also has oversight over the two power exchanges—the Indian Energy Exchange and the Power Exchange India. The Central Advisory Committee is in place to advise the CERC on policy questions, compliance of power market licensees, and standards of performance by utilities; however, it has no direct policy or regulatory control.
Petroleum and Natural Gas Regulatory Board	Assists the Ministry of Petroleum and Natural Gas in storing, transporting, distributing, and marketing petroleum, petroleum products, and natural gas, excluding the production of crude oil and natural gas.
Directorate General of Hydrocarbons (DGH)	Promotes sound management of the oil and natural gas resources with a balanced regard for the environment, safety, and technological and economic aspects of the petroleum industry—under the Ministry of Petroleum and Natural Gas. The DGH also regulates the exploration and optimal exploitation of hydrocarbons.
State Electricity Regulatory Commissions (SERCs)	Regulates the electricity generated by individual state's generators and sold within a single state. SERCs grant licenses for intrastate transmission, trading, and distribution. The Government of India is planning a national-level selection committee for appointing chairpersons and members in all SERCs to set the bodies free from political intervention and improve decision-making at the central level.
Forum of Regulators of India	Brings together the CERC and the SERCs in a forum to discuss and exchange views around model guidelines or regulations (model guidelines on rooftop solar and net metering rules, tariff rationalization, and tariff guidelines).

Sources: Government of India. Central Electricity Regulatory Commission; Government of India. Petroleum and Natural Gas Regulatory Board; and Government of India, Ministry of Petroleum and Natural Gas. Directorate General of Hydrocarbons.

Foreign Investment Restrictions in the Energy Sector

Parameter	2021	2022	2023
Maximum allowed foreign ownership of equity in greenfield projects			
• Power generation	100%	100%	100%
• Power transmission	100%	100%	100%
• Power distribution	100%	100%	100%
• Oil and gas	100%	100%	100%

A foreign direct investment of up to 49% is allowed in the following:

- power exchanges and automatic routes under the Central Electricity Regulatory Commission, and
- petroleum and natural gas refining sector (for public sector undertakings without involving any disinvestment or dilution of domestic equity).

Standard Contracts in the Energy Sector

Type of Contract Availability	
Power sector	
Public–private partnership/concession agreement	✓
Power purchase agreement	✓
Capacity take-or-pay contract	✓
Fuel supply agreement	✓
Transmission and use of system agreement	✓
Performance-based operation and maintenance contract	✗
Engineering, procurement, and construction contract	✓

✓ = Yes, ✗ = No, NA = Not Applicable, UA = Unavailable.
Source: Asian Development Bank. 2019. *Public–Private Partnership Monitor.* Second Edition.

3. Energy Sector Master Plan

The *Make in India* campaign, launched in September 2014, has proposed a massive infrastructure development program for the energy sector. The program comprises the following (footnote 13):

- Setting up of ultra-mega power projects of 4,000-megawatt capacity each. The Power Finance Corporation has been identified as the nodal agency for ultra-mega power projects with likely investment of $27.39 billion (₹2 trillion).

- Investing $114.87 billion (₹8.2 trillion) for thermal power projects and $2.64 billion (₹193 billion) for hydropower projects. Investment in the transmission line sector is proposed at $8.01 billion (₹584.5 billion) and includes Green Corridor I ($1.28 trillion or ₹93.2 trillion), Green Corridor II ($0.55 billion or ₹40.3 billion), tariff-based competitive bidding ($1.58 billion or ₹115.2 billion), and a scheme totaling $4.60 billion (₹335.8 billion) to be awarded by the power grid.
- Adding 175 GW of renewable energy generation capacity by 2022. As of February 2023, the total installed renewable energy capacity reached 168.96 GW.[84]
- Attracting investments, such as expansion plans for 23 refineries, and tapping foreign investment in export-oriented infrastructure, including product pipelines and export terminals.

An overall total capital expenditure of ₹1.95 trillion ($26.71 billion) by the central and state governments would be made over FY2020 through FY2025 on 163 projects in petroleum and natural gas sectors, identified for implementation during the period. Of these, only two projects with an estimated expenditure of ₹107.51 billion ($1.47 billion) have been earmarked for public–private partnership (PPP) while the remaining would be on engineering, procurement, and construction (EPC) model.

Tables 28 and 29 show the planned investments in the power sector, according to the NIP. In the power sector, an estimated total capital expenditure of ₹14.10 trillion ($172.05 billion) by both the central and state governments would be incurred over FY2020–FY2025. Table 28 shows the breakdown of the total estimated expenditure of ₹9.54 trillion ($116.37 billion) for the identified projects to be executed by central public sector units and private players.

Table 28: Capital Expenditure Plan for the Energy Sector by Segment, Based on the National Infrastructure Pipeline

Project Category	Capital Expenditure, FY2020–FY2025	
	($ billion)	(₹ billion)
Generation	39.86	3,268.11
NTPC	14.64	1,199.99
NHPC	5.37	440.49
THDC	1.27	103.85
SJVN	1.26	103.34
DVC	0.35	28.48
State (Hydro)	9.19	753.75
Private (Hydro)	7.79	638.29
Distribution	39.40	3,230.34
DDUGJY, IPDS, Proposed New Scheme	39.40	3,230.34

continued on next page

84   *The Economic Times.* 2023. *India's Renewable Energy Capacity Reaches 168.96 GW till Feb 2023: Minister R K Singh.* 21 March.

Table 28 *continued*

Project Category	Capital Expenditure, FY2020–FY2025	
	($ billion)	(₹ billion)
Transmission	37.09	3,040.50
PGCIL	7.99	655.00
DVC	0.07	5.49
State	23.18	1,900.01
Private	5.86	480.00
Subtotal	**116.36**	**9,538.95**
States	**55.69**	**4,565.33**
Total	**172.05**	**14,104.28**

DDUGJY = Deen Dayal Upadhyaya Gram Jyoti Yojana, DVC = Damodar Valley Corporation, FY = fiscal year, IPDS = Integrated Power Development Scheme, NHPC = National Hydroelectric Power Corporation, NTPC = National Thermal Power Corporation Limited, PGCIL = Power Grid Corporation of India Limited, SJVN = Satluj Jal Vidut Nigam, THDC = Tehri Hydro Development Corporation.

Note: Numbers may not sum precisely because of rounding.

Source: Government of India, Ministry of Finance, Department of Economic Affairs. 2019. *National Infrastructure Pipeline.* Volume 2.

Table 29 shows the year-wise estimated capital expenditure for FY2019 through FY2025 in the power sector.

Table 29: Estimated Year-on-Year Capital Expenditure Plan in the Energy Sector, Based on the National Infrastructure Pipeline

Project Category		FY2020	FY2021	FY2022	FY2023	FY2024	FY2025	Total
Generation	₹ billion	300.56	538.19	637.89	634.74	649.82	506.90	3,268.11
	$ billion	3.67	6.56	7.78	7.74	7.93	6.18	39.86
Distribution	₹ billion	211.27	420.00	442.07	600.00	700.00	857.00	3,230.34
	$ billion	2.58	5.12	5.39	7.32	8.54	10.45	39.40
Transmission	₹ billion	548.75	538.97	507.12	515.22	515.22	415.22	3,040.50
	$ billion	6.69	6.57	6.19	6.28	6.28	5.06	37.09
Subtotal	**₹ billion**	**1,060.58**	**1,497.16**	**1,587.08**	**1,749.96**	**1,865.04**	**1,779.12**	**9,538.95**
	$ billion	**12.94**	**18.26**	**19.36**	**21.35**	**22.75**	**21.70**	**116.36**

continued on next page

Table 29 *continued*

Project Category		FY2020	FY2021	FY2022	FY2023	FY2024	FY2025	Total
States	₹ billion	580.81	758.34	630.27	484.91	387.32	330.90	4,565.33
	$ billion	7.08	9.25	7.69	5.91	4.72	4.04	55.69
Total	**₹ billion**	**1,641.40**	**2,255.51**	**2,217.34**	**2,234.87**	**2,252.36**	**2,110.02**	**1,4104.28**
	$ billion	**20.02**	**27.51**	**27.05**	**27.26**	**27.47**	**25.74**	**172.05**

FY = fiscal year.

Note: Numbers may not sum precisely because of rounding.

Source: Government of India, Ministry of Finance, Department of Economic Affairs. 2019. *National Infrastructure Pipeline.* Volume 1.

Renewable Power Plans

The project categories included are solar, wind, small hydro, and biopower. The capital expenditure for these projects is estimated at ₹9.3 trillion ($113.38 billion). A summary of the projects is highlighted in Table 30.

Table 30: Capital Expenditure Plan for the Renewable Energy Sector, Based on the National Infrastructure Pipeline

Project Category	Target by Dec 2025 (GW)	Actual Achievement Until Mar 2023 (GW)	Capacity to Be Added by FY2025 (GW)	Capital Expenditure, FY2020–FY2025 ($ billion)	Capital Expenditure, FY2020–FY2025 (₹ billion)
Solar power	149.70	66.78	118.00	57.58	4,720.00
Wind power	96.99	42.63	59.90	51.15	4,193.00
Small hydropower	7.00	4.94	2.35	2.87	235.00
Biopower	12.04	10.24	2.10	1.79	147.00
Total renewables	**265.73**	**124.59**	**182.35**	**113.38**	**9,295.00**

Year-wise Capital Expenditure	FY2020	FY2021	FY2022	FY2023	FY2024	FY2025	Total
₹ billion	305.0	1,510.0	1,440.0	1,700.0	2,170.0	2,170.0	9,295.0
$ billion	3.72	18.42	17.57	20.74	26.47	26.47	113.38

FY= fiscal year, GW = gigawatt.

Note: Numbers may not sum precisely because of rounding.

Sources: Government of India, Ministry of Finance, Department of Economic Affairs. 2019. *National Infrastructure Pipeline.* Volume 2; and Government of India, Ministry of Power, Central Electricity Authority, Renewable Project Monitoring Division. 2023. *Monthly Renewable Energy Generation Report.*

Table 31 summarizes the total energy sector capital expenditure to be incurred from FY2020 to FY2025.

Table 31: Total Year-on-Year Capital Expenditure Plan for the Energy Sector in India

Project Category		FY2020	FY2021	FY2022	FY2023	FY2024	FY2025	Phasing Not Provided[a]	Total
Power	₹ billion	1,641.40	2,255.51	2,217.34	2,234.87	2,252.36	2,110.02	14,104.28	1,641.40
	$ billion	20.02	27.51	27.05	27.26	27.47	25.74	172.05	20.02
Renewable energy	₹ billion	305.00	1,510.00	1,440.00	1,700.00	2,170.00	2,170.00	9,295.00	305.00
	$ billion	3.72	18.42	17.57	20.74	26.47	26.47	113.38	3.72
Atomic energy	₹ billion	116.35	214.62	283.24	331.24	326.74	282.84	1,555.03	116.35
	$ billion	1.42	2.62	3.45	4.04	3.99	3.45	18.97	1.42
PNG	₹ billion	273.32	435.10	483.14	415.23	228.58	105.35	1,945.72	273.32
	$ billion	3.33	5.31	5.89	5.07	2.79	1.29	23.73	3.33
Total	**₹ billion**	**2,336.07**	**4,415.22**	**4,423.72**	**4,681.34**	**4,977.68**	**4,668.21**	**26,900.03**	**2,336.07**
	$ billion	**28.50**	**53.86**	**53.96**	**57.10**	**60.72**	**56.94**	**328.13**	**28.50**

FY = fiscal year, PNG = petroleum and natural gas.

Note: Numbers may not sum precisely because of rounding.

[a] Expenditure plan for which phasing details are not defined.

Source: Government of India, Ministry of Finance, Department of Economic Affairs. 2019. *National Infrastructure Pipeline.* Volume 2.

Projects Under Conceptualization and Development in the Energy Sector

Figure 35 shows the number of PPP projects that are under conceptualization and development in the energy sector of India.

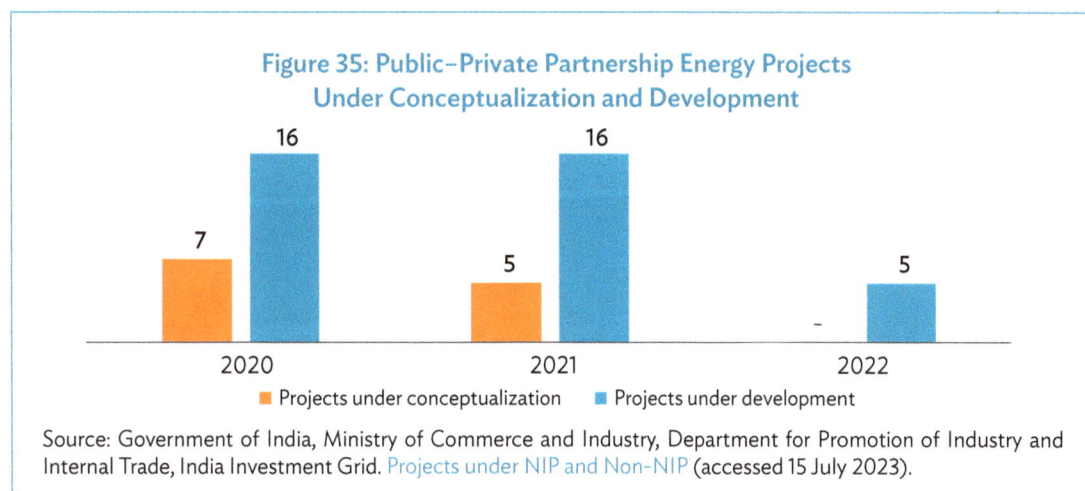

Figure 35: Public–Private Partnership Energy Projects Under Conceptualization and Development

Source: Government of India, Ministry of Commerce and Industry, Department for Promotion of Industry and Internal Trade, India Investment Grid. Projects under NIP and Non-NIP (accessed 15 July 2023).

4. Features of Past Public–Private Partnership Projects in the Energy Sector

Figure 36 shows the number of PPP projects procured through various modes, including direct appointment and competitive bids, in the energy sector of India.

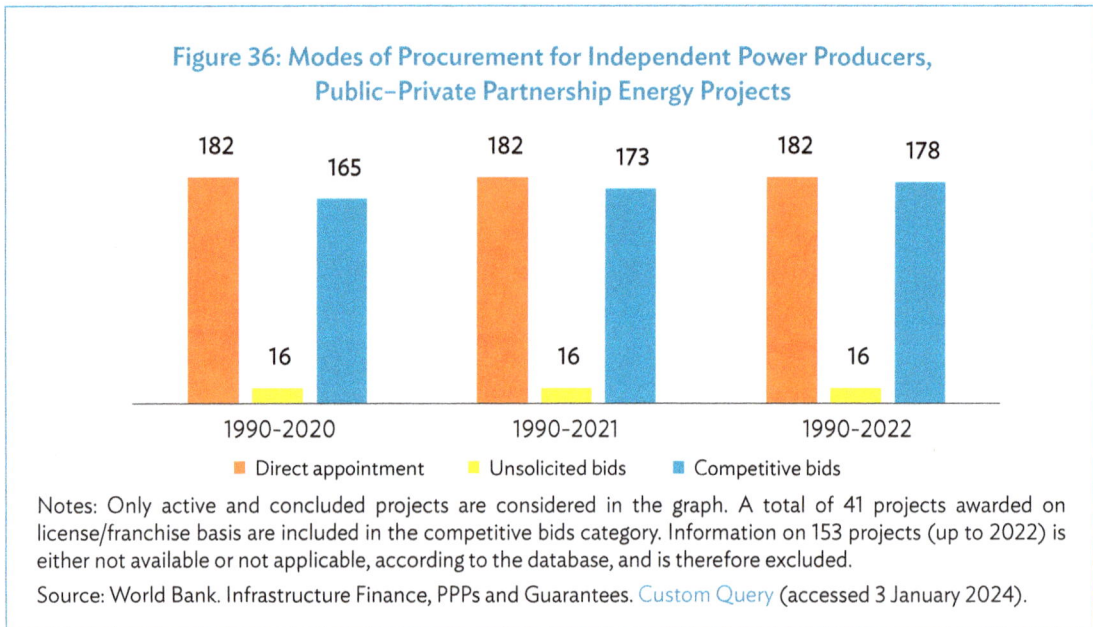

Figure 36: Modes of Procurement for Independent Power Producers, Public–Private Partnership Energy Projects

Notes: Only active and concluded projects are considered in the graph. A total of 41 projects awarded on license/franchise basis are included in the competitive bids category. Information on 153 projects (up to 2022) is either not available or not applicable, according to the database, and is therefore excluded.

Source: World Bank. Infrastructure Finance, PPPs and Guarantees. Custom Query (accessed 3 January 2024).

Figure 37 shows the number of PPP projects that reached financial close and the total value of those projects in the energy sector of India.

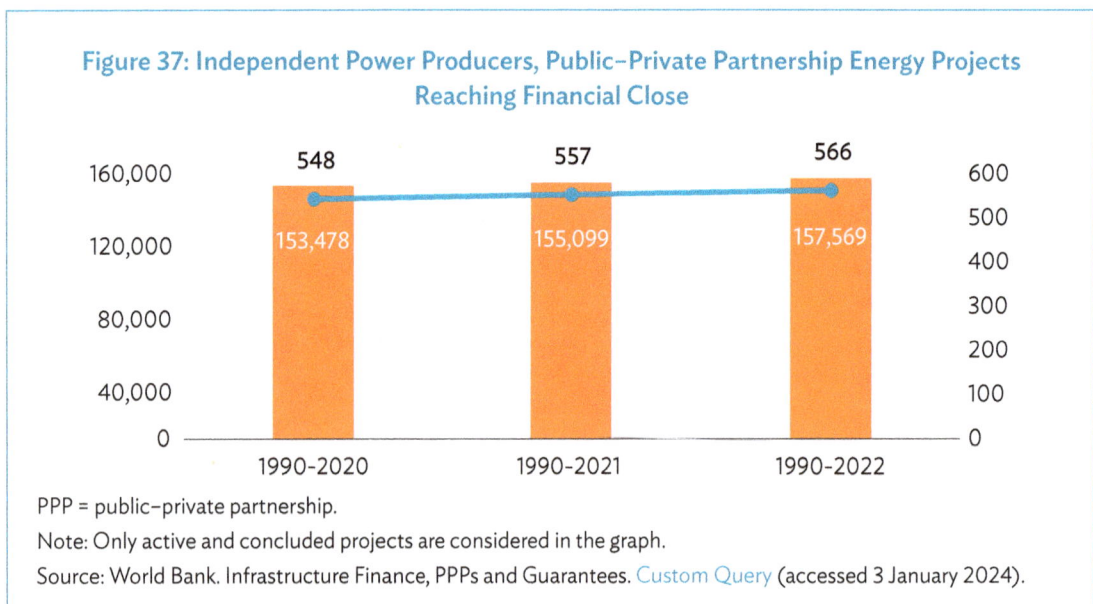

Figure 37: Independent Power Producers, Public–Private Partnership Energy Projects Reaching Financial Close

PPP = public–private partnership.

Note: Only active and concluded projects are considered in the graph.

Source: World Bank. Infrastructure Finance, PPPs and Guarantees. Custom Query (accessed 3 January 2024).

Figure 38 shows the number of PPP projects with foreign sponsor participation in the energy sector of India.

Figure 38: Independent Power Producers, Public–Private Partnership Energy Projects with Foreign Sponsor Participation

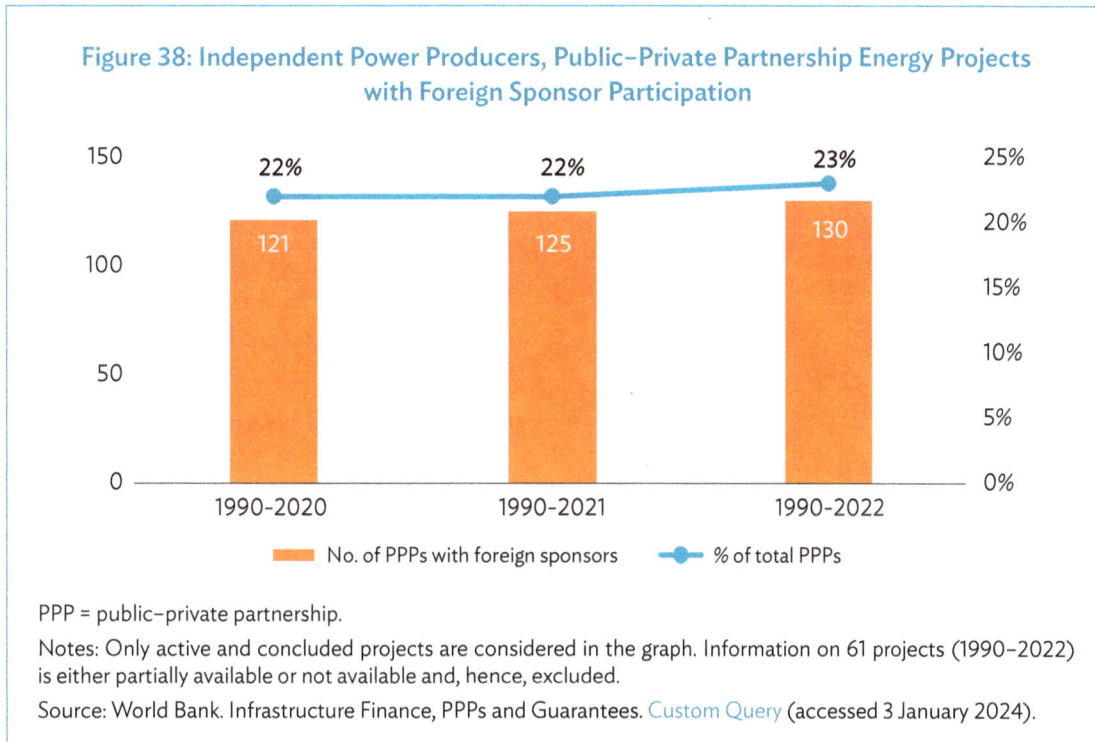

PPP = public–private partnership.

Notes: Only active and concluded projects are considered in the graph. Information on 61 projects (1990–2022) is either partially available or not available and, hence, excluded.

Source: World Bank. Infrastructure Finance, PPPs and Guarantees. Custom Query (accessed 3 January 2024).

The number of PPP projects that received government support in the energy sector of India is shown in Figure 39.

Figure 39: Government Support to Independent Power Producers, Public–Private Partnership Energy Projects

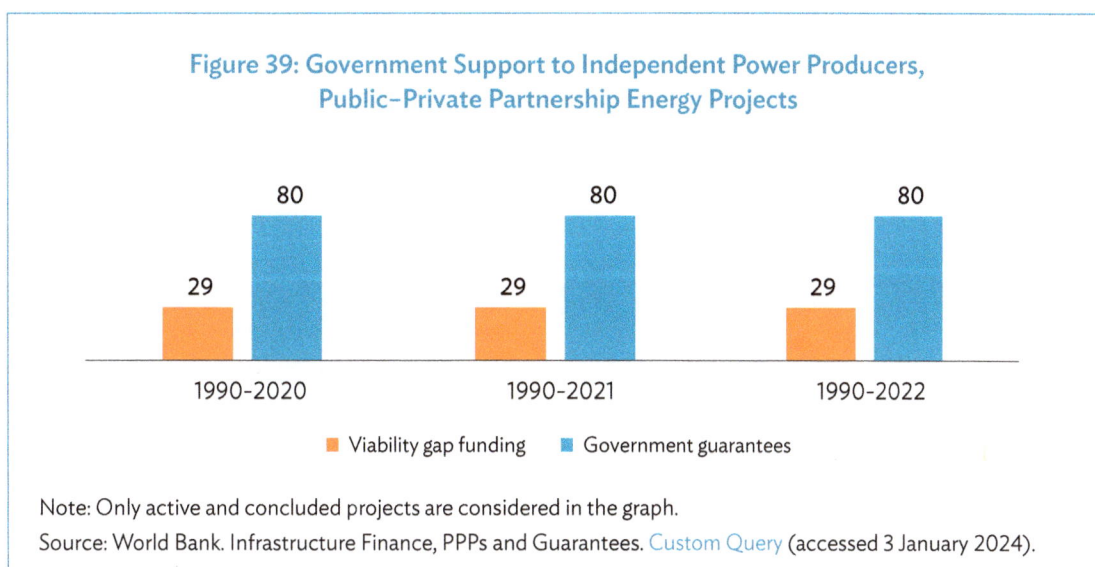

Note: Only active and concluded projects are considered in the graph.

Source: World Bank. Infrastructure Finance, PPPs and Guarantees. Custom Query (accessed 3 January 2024).

Figure 40 shows the number of PPP projects that received payment in the form of user charges and government pay (offtake) in the energy sector of India.

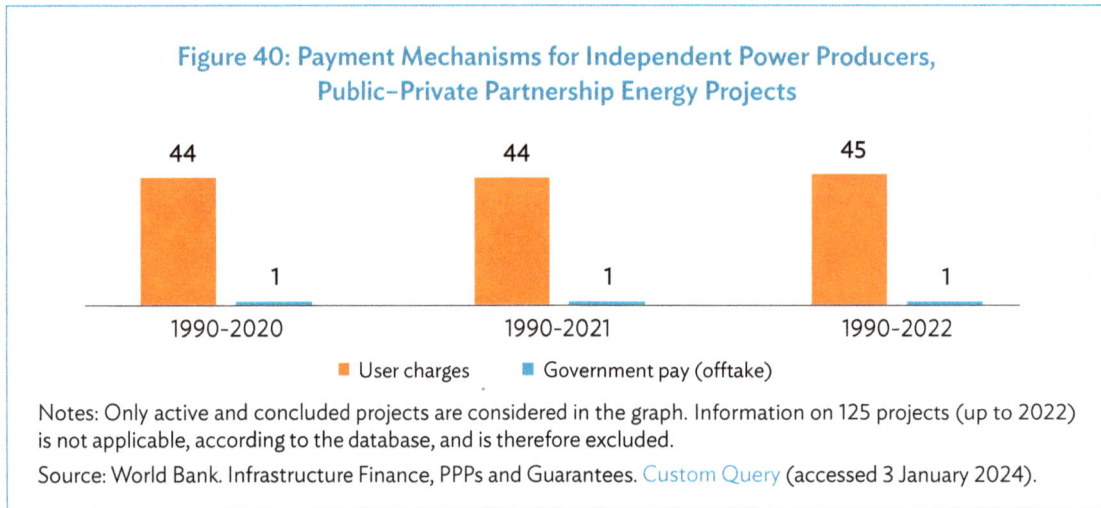

Figure 40: Payment Mechanisms for Independent Power Producers, Public–Private Partnership Energy Projects

Period	User charges	Government pay (offtake)
1990–2020	44	1
1990–2021	44	1
1990–2022	45	1

■ User charges   ■ Government pay (offtake)

Notes: Only active and concluded projects are considered in the graph. Information on 125 projects (up to 2022) is not applicable, according to the database, and is therefore excluded.

Source: World Bank. Infrastructure Finance, PPPs and Guarantees. Custom Query (accessed 3 January 2024).

Table 32 shows the past PPP projects in the energy sector classified in terms of PPP variant or scheme, based on the Department of Economic Affairs (DEA) database.

Table 32: Number of Energy Projects Across Public–Private Partnership Variants

Public–Private Partnership Variant	No. of Projects
Build–operate–transfer	58
Build–own–operate	126
Build–own–operate–manage	44
Build–own–operate–transfer	205
Design–build–finance–operate–transfer	9
Design–build–finance–operate–transfer (toll)	1
DTR secondary side maintenance and RPU-based franchisee	1
Input-based distribution franchisee	5
Licensee model	6
Management contract (O&M)	1
Not available	11
Rehabilitate–operate–maintain–transfer	2
Total	**469**

DTR = distribution transformer, O&M = operation and maintenance, RPU = revenue realization per unit.

Note: Data was last updated on 5 December 2019.

Source: Government of India, Ministry of Finance, Department of Economic Affairs. List of All PPP Projects (accessed 15 July 2023).

Table 33 indicates the number of projects across various energy subsectors, according to the DEA database.

Table 33: Number of Energy Projects Based on Subsectors

Subsector	No. of Projects
Electricity distribution	16
Electricity generation (grid)	79
Electricity transmission	34
Oil, gas, liquefied natural gas storage	1
Renewable energy (grid)	339
Total	**469**

Note: Data was last updated on 5 December 2019.

Source: Government of India, Ministry of Finance, Department of Economic Affairs. List of All PPP Projects (accessed 15 July 2023).

Tariffs in the Energy Sector

The implementing and regulating agency, the Central Regulatory Electricity Commission, will carry out the regulatory functions for PPP power projects. The Tariff Policy, 2006 sets directives for the various aspects of power project development, such as the requirements for competitive bidding, rates of return for power projects, financing limits in relation to debt-to-equity ratios, and depreciation rates for power assets.

For renewable energy, the policy requires that each state electricity regulator specify a time-bound renewable purchase obligation with distribution companies and establish preferential tariffs for the purchase of electricity from nonconventional technologies. In January 2016, the central government approved amendments to the tariff policy to increase statewide renewable purchase obligation targets to 17% by 2022, including a minimum of 8% provision for solar energy (from the previous target of 3%). In June 2023, the Government of India introduced two changes to the prevailing power tariff system through an amendment to the Electricity (Rights of Consumers) Rules, 2020. These changes are the introduction of a Time of Day Tariff, and the rationalization of smart metering provisions.

The Petroleum Planning and Analysis Cell, along with the Ministry of Petroleum and Natural Gas, regulates the tariff for petroleum and petroleum products, including hydrocarbon.

The applicable tariffs for power plants based on the "Determination of levelized generic tariff for FY2022–FY2023 under Regulation 8 of the Central Electricity Regulatory Commission (Terms and Conditions for Tariff Determination from Renewable Energy Sources) Regulations, 2020" are listed in Table 34. The Central Electricity Regulatory Commission uses a normative approach for arriving at the tariff and provides the necessary variations required to differentiate the norms or factors used for determining the tariff from state to state.

**Table 34: Tariffs Set Up by the Central Electricity Regulatory Commission
for Energy Projects in India**

IPP Type	Nature of Facility	Levelized Total Tariff, FY2022–FY2023	
		(₹/kWh)	($ cent/kWh)
Solar thermal		Project-specific	Project-specific
Solar PV		Project-specific	Project- specific
Wind		Project- specific	Project- specific
Small hydropower	Himachal Pradesh, Uttarakhand, West Bengal, and Northeastern States (below 5 MW)	5.23	6.28
	Himachal Pradesh, Uttarakhand, West Bengal, and Northeastern States (5 MW to 25 MW)	4.76	5.71
	Other states (below 5 MW)	5.84	7.01
	Other states (5 MW to 25 MW)	5.76	6.72
Biomass[a]	Biomass power projects (other than rice straw and *juliflora* [plantation]-based project) with water-cooled condenser and travelling grate boiler	8.10	9.72
	Biomass power projects (other than rice straw and *juliflora* [plantation]-based project) with air-cooled condenser and travelling grate boiler	8.36	10.03
	Biomass power projects (rice straw and *juliflora* [plantation]-based project) with water-cooled condenser and travelling grate boiler	8.20	10.00
	Biomass power projects (rice straw and *juliflora* [plantation]-based project) with air-cooled condenser and travelling grate boiler	8.46	10.32
	Biomass power projects (other than rice straw and *juliflora* [plantation]-based project) with water-cooled condenser and AFBC boiler	8.00	9.76
	Biomass power projects (other than rice straw and *juliflora* [plantation]-based project) with air-cooled condenser and AFBC boiler	8.25	10.06
	Biomass power projects (rice straw and *juliflora* [plantation]-based project) with water-cooled condenser and AFBC boiler	8.09	9.87
	Biomass power projects (rice straw and *juliflora* [plantation]-based project) with air-cooled condenser and AFBC boiler	8.35	10.19
	Bagasse based co-generation project	6.43	7.84
	Biomass gasifier power project	7.76	9.36
	Biogas	8.59	10.48

AFBC = atmospheric fluidized bed combustion, FY = fiscal year, IPP = independent power producer, kWh = kilowatt-hour, MW = megawatt, PV = photovoltaic.

[a] Net levelized tariff (upon adjusting for accelerated depreciation benefit, if availed); tariff for all modes other than small hydropower is indicated for the state of Andhra Pradesh.

Source: Central Electricity Regulatory Commission. 2022. *Generic Tariff for RE Technologies for FY 2022–23.*

In accordance with Regulation 7 of the Renewable Energy Tariff Regulations, the Central Electricity Regulatory Commission shall determine project-specific tariff for the following renewable energy technologies:

- solar PV and solar thermal;
- wind energy (including onshore and offshore);
- biomass-gasifier-based projects, when a project developer opts for project-specific tariff;
- biogas-based projects, when a project developer opts for project-specific tariff;
- municipal solid waste and refuse-derived-fuel-based projects with Rankine cycle technology;
- hybrid solar thermal power projects;
- other hybrid projects, including renewable or renewable-conventional sources, for which renewable technology is approved by the Ministry of New and Renewable Energy; and
- any other new renewable energy technologies approved by the Ministry of New and Renewable Energy.

Typical Risk Allocation for Public–Private Partnership Projects in the Energy Sector

Typical risk allocation arrangements in energy PPP contracts are presented in the following table.

Type of Risk	Private	Public	Shared	Comments
Demand risk		✓		
Revenue collection risk		✓		
Tariff risk	✓			
Government payment risk		✓		
Environmental and social risks	✓			
Land acquisition risk			✓	
Permits	✓			
Handover risk	✓			
Political risk		✓		
Regulatory risk		✓		
Interconnection risk			✓	
Brownfield risk: asset condition			No data	
Grid performance risk	✓			
Hydrology risk	✓			
Exploration and drilling risk			No data	

Source: Asian Development Bank. 2019. *Public–Private Partnership Monitor.* Second Edition.

Financing Details for Public–Private Partnership Projects in the Energy Sector

Parameter	1990–2020	1990–2021	1990–2022
Public–private partnership (PPP) projects with foreign lending participation	48	54	58
PPP projects that received export credit agency/international financing institution support	64	66	68
Typical debt-to-equity ratio	70:30		
Time for financial close	UA		
Typical concession period	25 years		
Typical financial internal rate of return	UA		

✓ = Yes, ✗ = No, NA = Not Applicable, UA = Unavailable.

5. Challenges in the Energy Sector

Some of the key opportunities for growth in the energy sector are the following:

- The industrial and commercial sectors present a significant opportunity for demand growth. Enhancing the contracting capacity of distribution companies could help utilize the existing thermal capacity surplus. Establishing power purchase agreements (PPAs) could alleviate financial distress and technical constraints, preventing load shedding and promoting demand and capacity offtake.
- Ensuring that state government utilities honor PPAs could boost investor confidence. Addressing concerns about higher tariffs of signed wind and solar power PPAs could alleviate the financial challenges of state distribution companies. Upholding the sanctity of contracts and ensuring timely dispute resolution could attract private sector participation and safeguard existing investments.
- Improving gas pipeline infrastructure could propel the growth of the industry. Addressing domestic production difficulties, pricing and allocation of gas, and enhancing infrastructure could also stimulate gas demand and consumption.

F. Water and Wastewater

Parameter	Value	Unit
Improved drinking water access (2022)	93.0	% of population with access
Improved sanitation facilities access (2022)	78.0	% of population with access
Investment in water and sanitation with private participation (2021)	278.2	current $ million

Sources: United Nations Children's Fund (UNICEF). Drinking Water, Sanitation and Hygiene (WASH) Estimates; and World Bank. *Investment in Water and Sanitation with Private Participation* (accessed 15 July 2023).

1. Contracting Agencies in the Water and Wastewater Sectors

In the water sector, the Ministry of Jal Shakti, Department of Water Resources, River Development and Ganga Rejuvenation is responsible for laying down policy guidelines and programs for the development and regulation of the country's water resources.

In the wastewater sector, under the Constitution of India, sanitation is a state government responsibility, and the delivery of related programs depends on urban local bodies (ULBs), which are backed by their respective state governments in terms of policy and fiscal support. The central government is mainly involved in delineating policies, providing funding for various programs of national importance such as the Jawaharlal Nehru National Urban Renewal Mission (JNNURM), and formulating national service level benchmarks.

The Ministry of Housing and Urban Affairs (MOHUA) has also conceived many schemes for supporting ULBs in improving water infrastructure and sewage treatment.

2. Water and Wastewater Sectors Laws and Regulations

The following are the laws and regulations that govern the water and wastewater sectors in India.[85]

Water
- The National Water Policy, 2012 serves as a policy guideline for developing and managing water resources in the country. The policy prioritizes water use in the following order: drinking, irrigation, hydropower, ecology, agricultural and nonagricultural industries, navigation, and other uses. These priorities may be modified or added if warranted by area- and region-specific considerations. The policy also encourages private participation in planning and operation of water systems.
- The Draft National Water Framework Bill, 2016 has been prepared and submitted to states and union territories to obtain their views and comments. The bill has been drafted to address the need for a national framework law as an umbrella statement of general principles governing legislative and/or executive powers by the central government, states, and local bodies.
- Comprehensive Mission Document for National Water Mission, Volume 1, 2011
- Comprehensive Mission Document for National Water Mission, Volume 2, 2008
- Hydro-Meteorological Data Dissemination Policy, 2018.

Wastewater
- The National Faecal Sludge and Septage Management Policy, 2017 aims to achieve 100% access to safe sanitation, integrated urban sanitation, and safe disposal of faecal waste. It sets environmental discharge norms and advocates a suitable, cost-effective, and phased strategy to meet these standards.
- The Water (Prevention and Control of Pollution) Act, 1974 and the subsequent Water (Prevention and Control of Pollution) Cess Act, 1977 were enacted to prevent water pollution

---

[85] Government of India; Ministry of Jal Shakti; Department of Water Resources, River Development and Ganga Rejuvenation. *Policy/Schemes – Policies* (accessed 15 July 2023).

caused by the discharge of untreated or inadequately treated domestic sewage in urban areas and untreated industrial effluents. The Central and State Pollution Control Boards, set up under these Acts, have been given the authority to regulate pollution of water bodies. The Boards are responsible for establishing standards for acceptable qualities of treated municipal sewage that can be discharged into water bodies, and monitoring and controlling pollution levels through various interventions.

- The Environment Protection Act, 1986 was formulated to cover various areas of the environment, including water pollution.
- At the state level, many states have promulgated municipal acts and other acts relating to the creation of separate boards or entities for providing water supply and sewerage services.

Parameter	2021	2022	2023
Can the private sector be given water abstraction rights?	✓	✓	✓
Are there regulations in place on raw water extraction?	✓	✓	✓
Are there regulations in place on the release of treated effluents?	✓	✓	✓

Table 35 describes the functions of key agencies responsible for the water and wastewater sectors in India.

Table 35: Key Entities Responsible for the Water and Wastewater Sectors in India

Agency	Function (Indicative List)
Ministry of Jal Shakti	• In 2019, the former Ministry of Water Resources, River Development and Ganga Rejuvenation was reorganized into the Ministry of Jal Shakti. The Ministry works with two departments—(i) Department of Water Resources, River Development and Ganga Rejuvenation (Jal Sansadhan, Nadi Vikas Aur Ganga Sanrakshan Vibhag); and (ii) Department of Drinking Water and Sanitation (Peya Jal Aur Swachhata Vibhag). The Ministry is responsible for the development, conservation, and management of water as a national resource; overall national perspective of water planning and coordination in relation to the diverse uses of water and interlinking of rivers; overall policy issues; water resources, and major, medium, and minor irrigation works; and regulation and development of interstate rivers and water laws and legislation, among others.
Ministry of Drinking Water and Sanitation	• Responsible for rural drinking water and related activities
Ministry of Housing and Urban Affairs (MOHUA)	• Responsible for urban drinking water • Responsible for formulating policies, such as the National Urban Sanitation Policy, and funding programs (e.g., Jawaharlal Nehru Urban Renewal Mission and Urban Infrastructure Development Scheme for Small and Medium Towns) • MOHUA's Central Public Health and Environmental Engineering Organisation formulates technical standards for the sewerage sector and approves detailed project reports for projects in the sewerage sector, which are provided with funding under various MOHUA schemes.
Ministry of Commerce and Industry	• Responsible for industrial water and related policies and issues

continued on next page

Table 35 *continued*

Agency	Function (Indicative List)
Ministry of Power	• Responsible for hydropower development and related policies and issues
Ministry of Ports, Shipping and Waterways	• Responsible for inland navigation and related policies and issues
Ministry of Environment, Forest and Climate Change (MOEFCC)	• The MOEFCC acts as the regulatory and monitoring body for environment-related outcomes and impacts of sewerage projects. The MOEFCC's Central Pollution Control Board, a national regulatory authority constituted under the Water (Prevention and Control of Pollution) Act of 1974, defines performance standards for the sewerage sector in terms of treated wastewater quality.
Ministry of Agriculture and Farmers Welfare	• Responsible for water planning for agriculture, micro-irrigation, and management of water-related disaster such as drought
Ministry of Home Affairs	• Manages water-related disasters such as floods
National Water Resource Council	• Responsible for all policy decisions taken in the country
Central Ground Water Board	• Conducts scientific studies; exploration aided by drilling; monitoring of groundwater regime; and assessment, augmentation, management, and regulation of the country's groundwater sources.
National Water Development Agency	• Carries out detailed studies (e.g., feasibility studies), surveys, and investigations with respect to peninsular components of the national perspective for water resources development
Central Pollution Control Board	• Responsible for monitoring water quality
Municipal Corporations (Urban Local Bodies)	• Locally, these corporations provide services like water supply, sanitation, health, drainage, and solid waste management.

Sources: Asian Development Bank. 2019. *Public–Private Partnership Monitor.* Second Edition; Government of India. Ministry of Jal Shakti. *Department of Water Resources, River Development and Ganga Rejuvenation*; and Government of India, Ministry of Jal Shakti, Department of Water Resources, River Development and Ganga Rejuvenation. 2011. *Comprehensive Mission Document for National Water Mission.* Volume 1.

Wastewater

The Ministry of Water Resources recently formulated a policy for public–private partnership (PPP) projects in the wastewater sector through an innovative hybrid annuity model (HAM) under the Namami Gange Programme. This approach seeks to ensure performance, efficiency, and sustainability of the proposed wastewater investments by using long-term PPP contracts, wherein the private sector will be responsible for technological innovation, construction, and operation and maintenance (O&M) of assets. Under the hybrid annuity program, up to 40% of the capital investment will be paid by the central government for milestones linked to construction progress, with the balance paid through annuities over the remaining life of the concession extending up to 20 years. The Government of India plans to establish a special purpose vehicle (SPV) to develop and structure projects, identify private sector partners, and create capacity to effectively monitor performance during the concession period. The SPV will enter into tripartite agreements with respective states and ULBs to support individual projects.[86]

---

[86]   Federation of Indian Chambers of Commerce and Industry, and 2030 Water Resources Group. 2016. Urban Wastewater Public–Private Partnerships. White Paper.

PPPs in the sewerage sector are typically in the form of build–operate–transfer (BOT), end-user PPP, annuity, user charge, and design–build–operate. Of these, the most successful variants have been the BOT, end-user PPP, and the design–build–operate model.

At the national level, the Ministry of Jal Shakti, through the Department of Water Resources, River Development and Ganga Rejuvenation, has taken up a flagship program under the National Mission for Clean Ganga called the Namami Gange Programme. The Namami Gange Programme is an integrated conservation mission, approved as the flagship program by the Union Government in June 2014, with a budget outlay of ₹200 billion, to effectively abate pollution and conserve and rejuvenate the National River Ganga. Creating sewage treatment capacity is one of the key objectives of the program.

As of July 2023, 259 out of 442 sanctioned projects have been completed—a 58.6% project completion rate. A total of 132 projects are under progress, 42 are under tendering, and 12 have Administration Approval and Expenditure Sanction issued. About 45.1% of the sanctioned cost of ₹3,736 billion ($45.6 billion) has already been incurred.[87]

Foreign Investment Restrictions in the Water and Wastewater Sectors

Parameter	2021	2022	2023
Maximum allowed foreign ownership of equity in greenfield projects			
• Bulk water supply and treatment	100%	100%	100%
• Water distribution	100%	100%	100%
• Wastewater treatment	100%	100%	100%
• Wastewater collection	100%	100%	100%

Standard Contracts in the Water and Wastewater Sectors

The standard contracts in the water and wastewater sectors are shown below.

Type of Contract	
Public–private partnership/concession agreement	✓
Bulk water supply agreement	✓
Performance-based operation and maintenance contract	✓
Engineering, procurement, and construction contract	✓

✓ = Yes, ✗ = No, NA = Not Applicable, UA = Unavailable.
Source: Asian Development Bank. 2019. *Public–Private Partnership Monitor.* Second Edition.

---

[87]   Government of India, Ministry of Jal Shakti, National Mission for Clean Ganga. 2023. *Monthly Project Progress Report.* July.

3. Water and Wastewater Sectors Master Plan

As explained earlier, water supply and wastewater planning, procurement, and execution are done at the level of ULBs, with approvals from respective state governments. For example, the state of Telangana in Southern India has conceived a program named Mission Bhagiratha, a massive project with an outlay of ₹450.28 billion ($5.5 billion).[88] The program aims to

- ensure safe and sustainable piped drinking water supply from surface water sources at (i) 100 liters per capita per day (LPCD) for rural areas, (ii) 135 LPCD for municipalities, and (iii) 150 LPCD for municipal corporations, with 10% quantity allocated to industrial requirements; and
- provide each household with a tap connection.

The project scope includes the following:[89]

- 26 segments in 32 districts;
- the entire water supply chain;
- sourcing water from major rivers or reservoirs fed by these rivers;
- purifying the raw water in the nearby water treatment plant;
- pumping treated water to major overhead service reservoirs and sumps at the highest points;
- transmitting from the highest point through a secondary pipeline network to all habitations by gravity;
- providing tap connections to each household through a modern, rationalized intravillage network; and
- an estimated total pipeline network of 146,000 km.

The Mission Bhagiratha is under construction. It is funded by the government but is expected to involve private sector players in the O&M contracts. Similarly, the master plans will be prepared at various levels of local governments for provision of water supply and wastewater treatment.

In addition to specific initiatives being taken at the respective ULBs in each state, under the MOHUA, the Government of India has launched the Atal Mission for Rejuvenation and Urban Transformation (AMRUT).[90] The Mission aims to provide basic civic amenities like water supply, sewerage, urban transport, and parks to improve the quality of life for all, especially for poor people and disadvantaged groups. It covers 500 cities, including all cities and towns with a population of more than 100,000 with notified municipalities. The total outlay for AMRUT is ₹500 billion for 5 years from FY2015–FY2016 to FY2019–FY2020. AMRUT was implemented as a central sponsored scheme, wherein the project fund is divided among states and union territories in an equitable formula—50:50 weightage is given to the urban population of each state or union territory and several statutory towns.

---

[88] Mission Bhagiratha (accessed 15 July 2023).
[89] Government of India; Ministry of Jal Shakti; Department of Water Resources, River Development and Ganga Rejuvenation. Namami Gange Programme.
[90] Government of India, Ministry of Housing and Urban Affairs. Atal Mission for Rejuvenation and Urban Transformation (accessed 15 July 2023).

Universal coverage of water supply is a priority under the Mission. At the inception of AMRUT, the water supply coverage was 64%; the target is to cover all households by the end of the Mission. AMRUT also aims to provide 13.9 million water tap connections to achieve universal coverage against 2.29 million tap connections that have been provided so far. Against the total plan size of ₹776.40 billion ($9.47 billion), ₹390.11 billion ($4.76 billion or 50%) has been allocated to water supply. A substantial coverage of sewerage and septage management is the second top priority under the Mission. At the inception of AMRUT, sewerage coverage was 31% of households, which is aimed to be doubled to 62% by the end of the Mission.

Sewerage and septage sector projects include decentralized or networked underground sewerage systems, sewage treatment plants, rehabilitation of old sewerage system and treatment plants, and recycling and reuse of water for beneficial purposes. Projects related to fecal sludge management and mechanical and biological cleaning of sewers are also eligible for funding. Against the total plan size of ₹776.40 billion ($9.47 billion), ₹324.56 billion ($3.96 billion or 42%) has been allocated to sewerage and septage management.

Following this, the AMRUT 2.0 scheme was launched on 1 October 2021, to be implemented for a period of 5 years (i.e., from FY2021–FY2022 to FY2025–FY2026). The second phase is designed to provide universal coverage of water supply through functional taps to all households in all the statutory towns in the country and coverage of sewerage/septage management in 500 cities covered in the first phase of the AMRUT scheme. AMRUT 2.0 will promote circular economy of water through development of the City Water Balance Plan for each city, focusing on recycle and reuse of treated sewage, rejuvenation of water bodies, and water conservation.[91]

As of March 2023, 80% of projects under AMRUT 2.0 have been completed, with 40% of the total allocated project costs having been incurred. Additionally, as of March 2023, 13.7 million water tap connections (against the targeted 13.9 million) and 10.5 million sewer connections (against the targeted 14.5 million)—including households covered through Faecal Sludge and Septage Management—have been provided through AMRUT. A total sewage treatment capacity of 6,347 million liters per day (MLD) is being developed through the AMRUT projects, of which, 2,840 MLD sewage treatment capacity has been created and 1,437 MLD capacity has been developed for recycle and reuse. Against the central government's share of ₹359.90 billion ($4.4 billion) for projects, ₹317.84 billion ($3.88 billion) has been released so far.[92]

Another scheme has been conceived under the Ministry of Jal Sakthi, called the Jal Jeevan Mission. It aims to establish functional household tap connections by 2024 to every rural household with a service level at the rate of 55 LPCD.[93]

Table 36 shows the estimated investments in the water sector until 2025, based on the National Infrastructure Pipeline of the Government of India.

[91]   Government of India, Ministry of Housing and Urban Affairs, Press Information Bureau. 2022. AMRUT Scheme. Press release. 22 December.
[92]   Government of India, Ministry of Housing and Urban Affairs, Press Information Bureau. 2023. Success of AMRUT. Press release. 20 March.
[93]   Government of India, Ministry of Jal Shakti, Department of Drinking Water and Sanitation. Jal Jeevan Mission.

Table 36: Capital Expenditure Plan for the Water Sector, Based on the National Infrastructure Pipeline

Project Category	No. of Projects	Capital Expenditure, FY2020–FY2025 ($ billion)	(₹ billion)
Water supply and sanitation, green parks, sewage treatment plant (AMRUT)	405	5.78	473.82
Water supply, rejuvenation of water bodies, wastewater collection and treatment (Jal Jeevan Mission)	0	34.09	2,794.92

AMRUT = Atal Mission for Rejuvenation and Urban Transformation, FY = fiscal year.

Source: Government of India, Ministry of Finance, Department of Economic Affairs. 2019. *National Infrastructure Pipeline.* Volume 2.

Projects Under Conceptualization and Development in the Water and Wastewater Sectors

Figure 41 shows the number of PPP projects that are under conceptualization and development in the water and wastewater sectors of India.

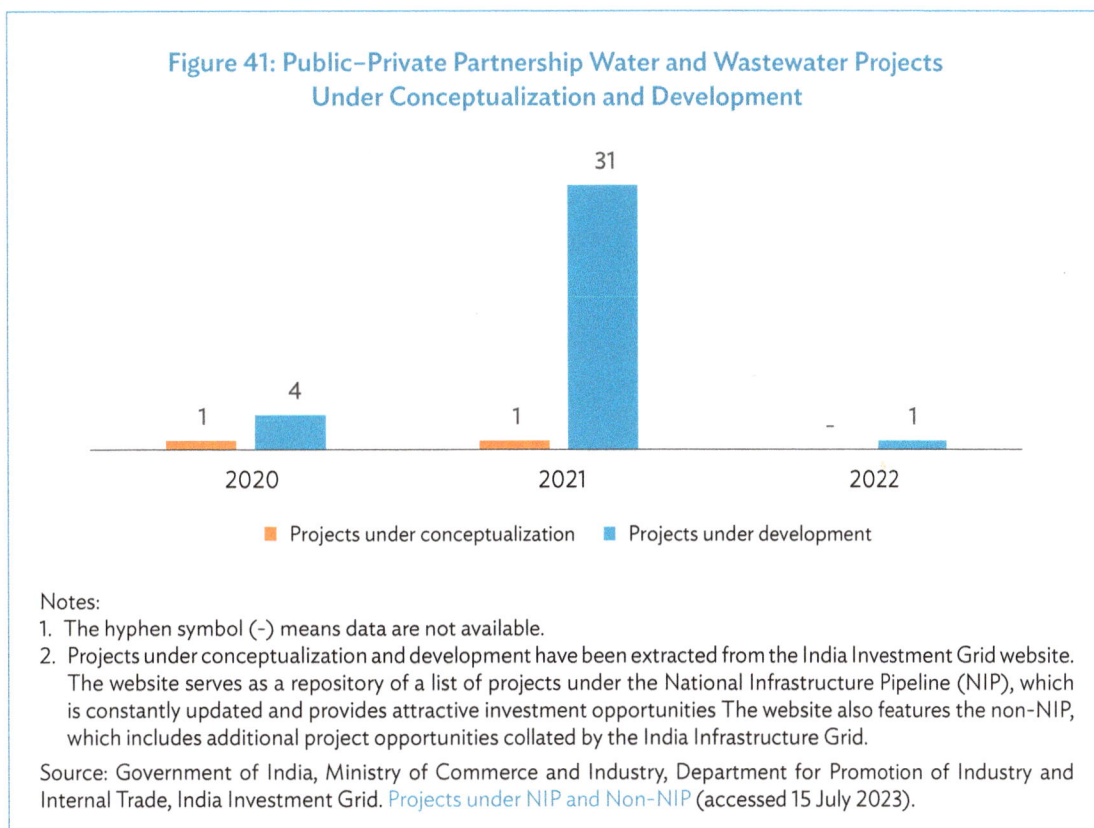

Figure 41: Public–Private Partnership Water and Wastewater Projects Under Conceptualization and Development

Notes:
1. The hyphen symbol (-) means data are not available.
2. Projects under conceptualization and development have been extracted from the India Investment Grid website. The website serves as a repository of a list of projects under the National Infrastructure Pipeline (NIP), which is constantly updated and provides attractive investment opportunities The website also features the non-NIP, which includes additional project opportunities collated by the India Infrastructure Grid.

Source: Government of India, Ministry of Commerce and Industry, Department for Promotion of Industry and Internal Trade, India Investment Grid. Projects under NIP and Non-NIP (accessed 15 July 2023).

4. Features of Past Public–Private Partnership Projects in the Water and Wastewater Sectors

Figure 42 shows the number of PPP projects procured through various modes, including direct appointment and competitive bids, in the water and wastewater sectors of India.

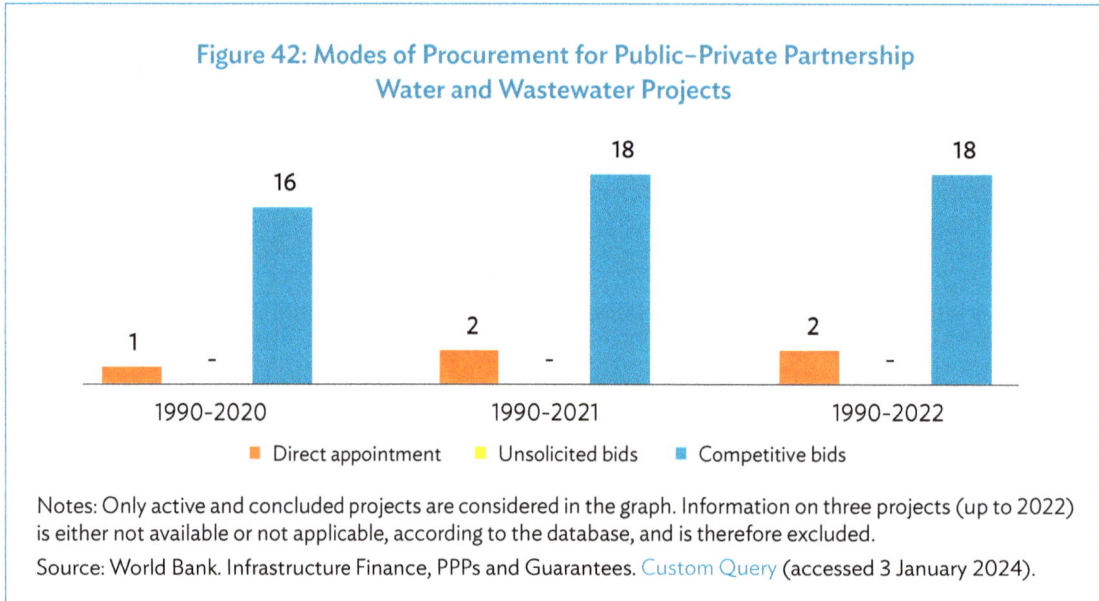

Figure 42: Modes of Procurement for Public–Private Partnership Water and Wastewater Projects

Notes: Only active and concluded projects are considered in the graph. Information on three projects (up to 2022) is either not available or not applicable, according to the database, and is therefore excluded.
Source: World Bank. Infrastructure Finance, PPPs and Guarantees. Custom Query (accessed 3 January 2024).

Figure 43 shows the number of PPP projects that reached financial close and the total value of those projects in the water and wastewater sectors of India.

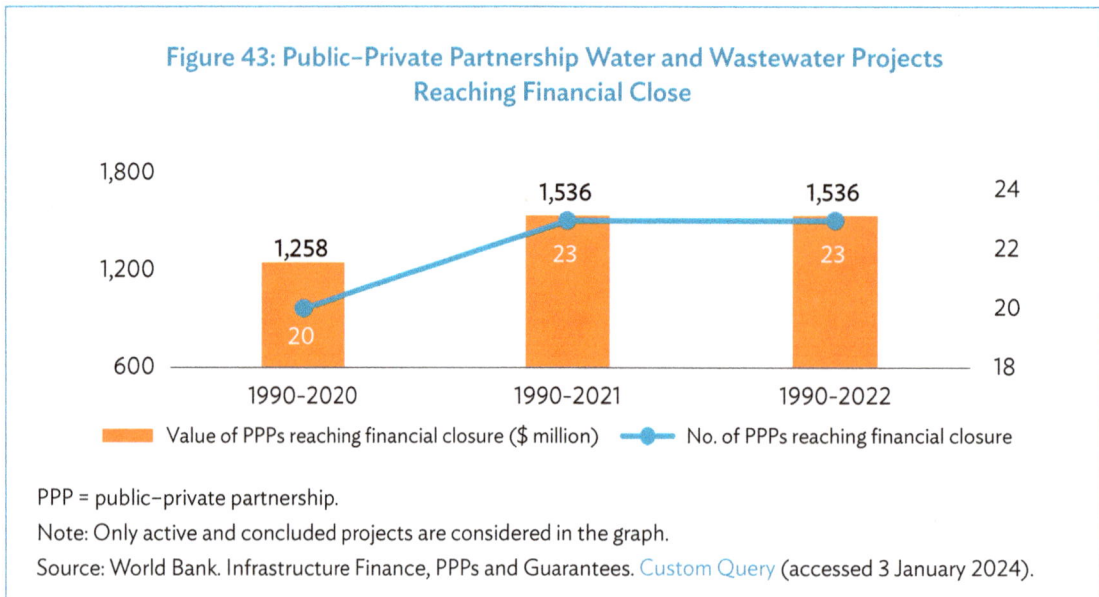

Figure 43: Public–Private Partnership Water and Wastewater Projects Reaching Financial Close

PPP = public–private partnership.
Note: Only active and concluded projects are considered in the graph.
Source: World Bank. Infrastructure Finance, PPPs and Guarantees. Custom Query (accessed 3 January 2024).

Figure 44 shows the number of PPP projects with foreign sponsor participation in the water and wastewater sectors of India.

Figure 44: Public–Private Partnership Water and Wastewater Projects with Foreign Sponsor Participation

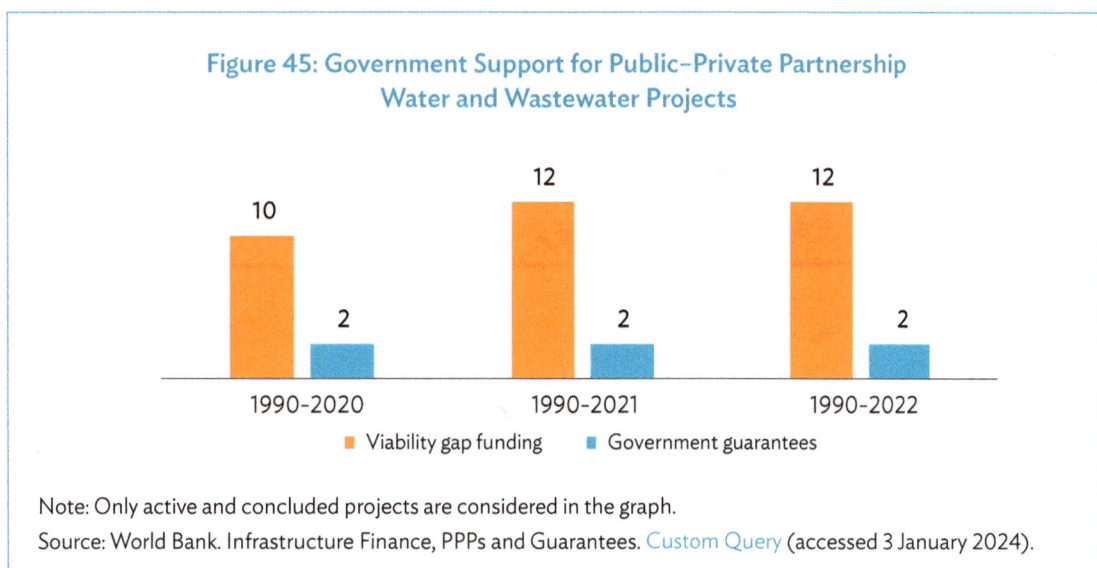

No. of PPPs with foreign sponsors   % of total PPPs

PPP = public–private partnership.

Notes: Only active and concluded projects are considered in the graph. Information on one project (1990–2022) is either partially available or not available and, hence, excluded.

Source: World Bank. Infrastructure Finance, PPPs and Guarantees. Custom Query (accessed 3 January 2024).

The number of PPP projects that received government support, including viability gap funding, government guarantees, and availability or performance payment, in the water and wastewater sectors of India is shown in Figure 45.

Figure 45: Government Support for Public–Private Partnership Water and Wastewater Projects

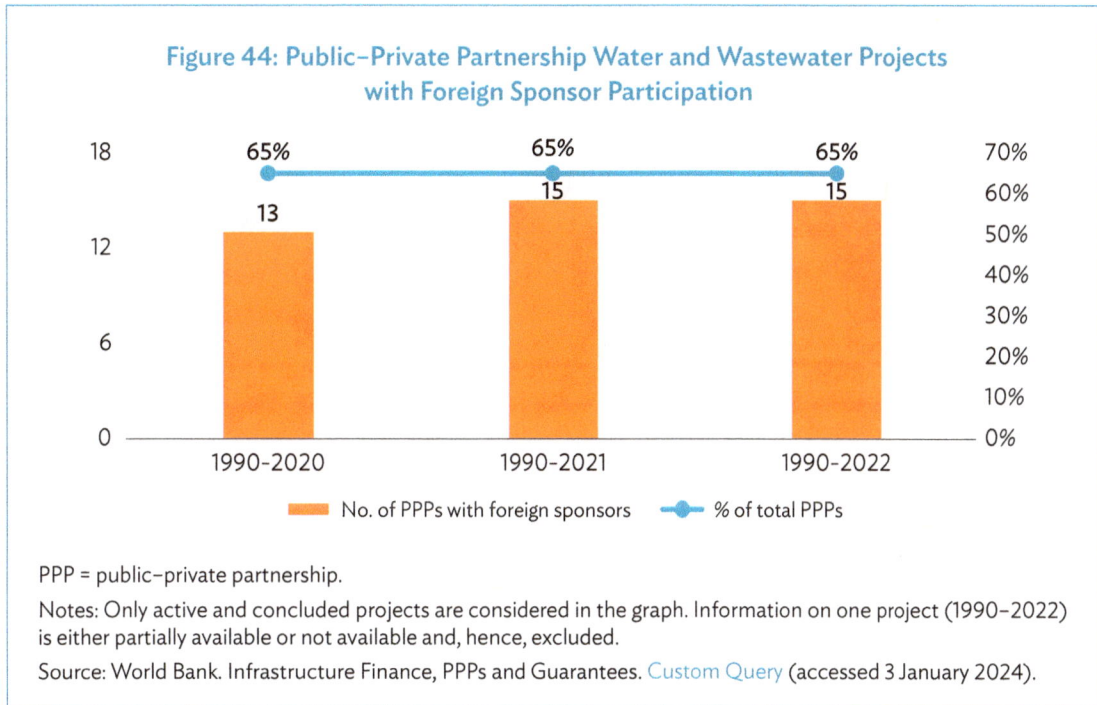

Viability gap funding   Government guarantees

Note: Only active and concluded projects are considered in the graph.

Source: World Bank. Infrastructure Finance, PPPs and Guarantees. Custom Query (accessed 3 January 2024).

Figure 46 shows the number of PPP projects that received payment in the form of user charges and government pay (offtake) in the water and wastewater sectors of India.

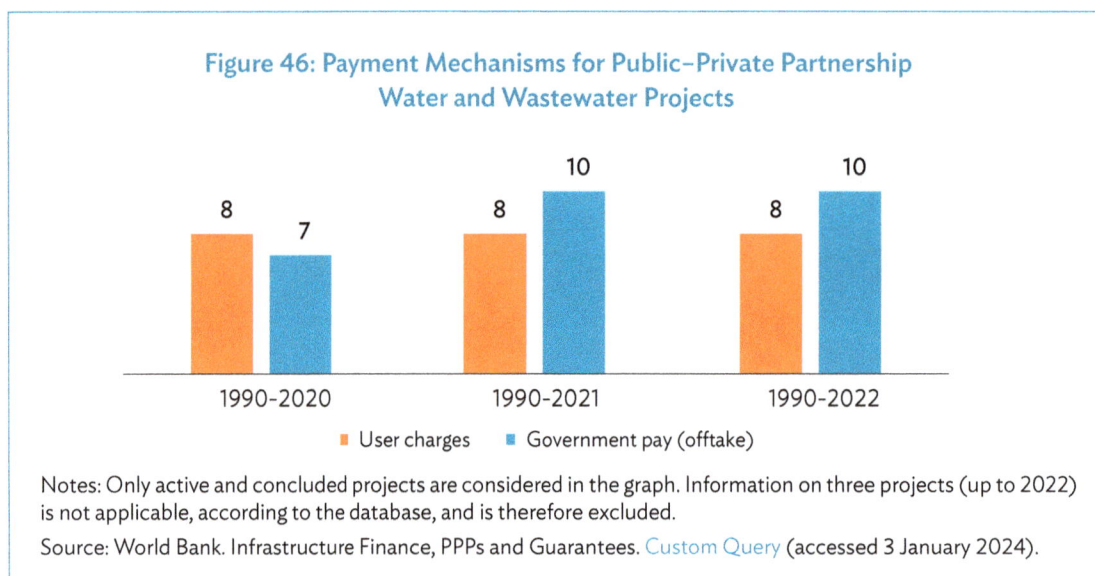

Figure 46: Payment Mechanisms for Public–Private Partnership Water and Wastewater Projects

Notes: Only active and concluded projects are considered in the graph. Information on three projects (up to 2022) is not applicable, according to the database, and is therefore excluded.

Source: World Bank. Infrastructure Finance, PPPs and Guarantees. Custom Query (accessed 3 January 2024).

Past PPP projects in the water and wastewater sectors in terms of PPP variant or scheme, based on the Department of Economic Affairs (DEA) database, are shown in Table 37.

Table 37: Number of Water and Wastewater Projects Across Public–Private Partnership Variants

Public–Private Partnership Variant	No. of Projects
Build–operate–transfer	10
Build–operate–transfer (annuity)	3
Build–own–operate	2
Build–own–operate–transfer	8
Design–build–finance–operate–transfer	7
Design–build–operate–transfer	2
Design–build–own–operate–transfer	3
Management contract (operation and maintenance)	3
Not available	10
Total	**48**

Note: Data was last updated on 5 December 2019.

Source: Government of India, Ministry of Finance, Department of Economic Affairs. List of All PPP Projects (accessed 15 July 2023).

Table 38 indicates the number of water and wastewater projects across various subsectors, based on the DEA database.

Table 38: Number of Water and Wastewater Projects Based on Subsectors

Subsector	No. of Projects
Sewage collection, treatment, and disposal system	21
Water supply pipeline	20
Water treatment plants	7
Total	**48**

Note: Data was last updated on 5 December 2019.

Source: Government of India, Ministry of Finance, Department of Economic Affairs. List of All PPP Projects (accessed 15 July 2023).

Tariffs in the Water and Wastewater Sectors

The tariff for the water and wastewater sectors is a local government responsibility and is determined by the respective local government authorities, such as cities and municipalities. Tables 39 to 45 show sample tariffs for two large cities in India.

Water tariffs and tariff grids in the two major cities of Hyderabad and Bengaluru are extracted from secondary sources. Tables 39 and 40 reflect the water tariff and tariff grid for the city of Hyderabad, while Table 41 reflects its tariff for wastewater. Similarly, Tables 42 and 43 reflect the water tariff and tariff grid for the city of Bengaluru, while Tables 44 and 45 reflect the tariff and tariff grid for its wastewater.

Table 39: Water Tariff for the Hyderabad Metropolitan Water Supply and Sewerage Board

	Consumption per Month (rate/cubic meter)					
	15 cubic meters		50 cubic meters		100 cubic meters	
Water	$	₹	$	₹	$	₹
Tariff	0.53	43.40	0.23	18.83	0.37	30.30
• Fixed charge	0.53	43.40	0.16	13.10	0.08	6.55
• Variable charge	0.00	0.00	0.07	5.73	0.29	23.75
• Other charges						
• Value-added tax						
Tariff reference date: 1 December 2011						

Source: International Benchmarking Network of the World Bank (IBNET) Tariff Database. Tariffs for Hyderabad Metropolitan Water Supply & Sewerage Board, HMWS&SB (India) (accessed 15 July 2023).

Table 40: Tariff Grid for the Hyderabad Metropolitan Water Supply and Sewerage Board

Water	Consumption (cubic meter per month)	Tariff (rate/cubic meter) $	₹
1st Block	0 to 41.8	0.00	0.00
2nd Block	41.81 to 50	0.42	34.43
3rd Block	50.01 to 100	0.52	42.63
4th Block	100.01 to 200	0.67	54.93
5th Block	200.01 and more	0.77	63.12
Other charges		0.00	0.00
Fixed charges ($/month)		8.00	655.84

Source: International Benchmarking Network of the World Bank (IBNET) Tariff Database. Tariffs for Hyderabad Metropolitan Water Supply & Sewerage Board, HMWS&SB (India) (accessed 15 July 2023).

Table 41: Tariff for Wastewater for the Hyderabad Metropolitan Water Supply and Sewerage Board

Wastewater	15 cubic meters $	₹	50 cubic meters $	₹	100 cubic meters $	₹
Tariff	0.19	15.56	0.10	8.19	0.14	11.46
• Fixed charge	0.00	0.00	0.00	0.00	0.00	0.00
• Variable charge	0.19	15.56	0.10	8.19	0.14	11.46
• Other charges	0.00	0.00	0.00	0.00	0.00	0.00
• Value-added tax	0.00	0.00	0.00	0.00	0.00	0.00
Tariff reference date: 1 December 2011						

Source: International Benchmarking Network of the World Bank (IBNET) Tariff Database. Tariffs for Hyderabad Metropolitan Water Supply & Sewerage Board, HMWS&SB (India) (accessed 15 July 2023).

Table 42: Water Tariff for the Bangalore Water Supply and Sewerage Board

Water	Consumption per Month (rate/cubic meter)					
	15 cubic meters		50 cubic meters		100 cubic meters	
	$	₹	$	₹	$	₹
Tariff	0.20	16.38	0.32	26.20	0.54	44.22
• Fixed charge	0.05	4.09	0.02	1.64	0.02	1.64
• Variable charge	0.08	6.55	0.27	22.11	0.50	40.95
• Other charges	0.06	4.91	0.02	1.64	0.01	0.82
• Value-added tax	0.00	0.00	0.00	0.00	0.00	0.00
Tariff reference date: 2 November 2014						

Source: International Benchmarking Network of the World Bank (IBNET) Tariff Database. Tariffs for Bangalore Water Supply and Sewerage Board (India) (accessed 15 July 2023).

Table 43: Tariff Grid for the Bangalore Water Supply and Sewerage Board

Water	Consumption (cubic meter per month)	Price after October 2013 (rate/cubic meter)	
		$	₹
1st Block	0 to 8	0.00	0.00
2nd Block	8.01 to 25	0.18	14.74
3rd Block	25.01 to 50	0.42	34.39
4th Block	50.01 and more	0.73	59.78
Other charges		0.00	0.00
Other fixed charges ($/month)		0.91	74.52
Fixed charge 1st block ($/cubic meter)		0.49	40.13
Fixed charge 2nd block ($/cubic meter)		0.82	67.15
Fixed charge 3rd block ($/cubic meter)		1.22	99.91
Fixed charge 4th block ($/cubic meter)		2.45	200.63

Source: International Benchmarking Network of the World Bank (IBNET) Tariff Database. Tariffs for Bangalore Water Supply and Sewerage Board (India) (accessed 15 July 2023).

Table 44: Tariff for Wastewater for the Bangalore Water Supply and Sewerage Board

Wastewater	Consumption per Month (rate/cubic meter)					
	15 cubic meters		50 cubic meters		100 cubic meters	
	$	₹	$	₹	$	₹
Tariff	0.04	3.28	0.07	5.73	0.13	10.65
• Fixed charge	0.02	1.64	0.00	0.00	0.00	0.00
• Variable charge	0.02	1.64	0.07	5.73	0.13	10.65
• Other charges	0.00	0.00	0.00	0.00	0.00	0.00
• Value-added tax	0.00	0.00	0.00	0.00	0.00	0.00
Tariff reference date: 2 November 2014						

Source: International Benchmarking Network of the World Bank (IBNET) Tariff Database. Tariffs for Bangalore Water Supply and Sewerage Board (India) (accessed 15 July 2023).

Table 45: Tariff Grid for Wastewater for the Bangalore Water Supply and Sewerage Board

Wastewater	Consumption (cubic meter per month)	Price after October 2013 (rate/cubic meter)	
		$	₹
1st Block	0 to 8	0.00	0.00
2nd Block	8.01 to 25	0.04	3.28
3rd Block	25.01 to 50	0.11	9.01
4th Block	50.01 and more	0.18	14.74
Other charges		0.00	0.00
Fixed charges ($/month)		0.23	18.83

Source: International Benchmarking Network of the World Bank (IBNET) Tariff Database. Tariffs for Bangalore Water Supply and Sewerage Board (India) (accessed 15 July 2023).

Typical Risk Allocation for Public–Private Partnership Projects in the Water and Wastewater Sectors

The typical risk allocation for water contracts is indicated below:

Type of Risk	Private	Public	Shared
Demand risk	✓		
Revenue collection risk			✓
Tariff risk		✓	
Government payment risk		✓	
Environmental and social risks	✓		
Land acquisition risk		✓	
Interface risk			✓
Handover risk	✓		
Political risk		✓	
Foreign exchange risk		✓	

Source: Asian Development Bank. 2019. *Public–Private Partnership Monitor.* Second Edition.

The risk allocation framework under various PPP variants is articulated in the tool kit on water and sanitation prepared by the DEA. Table 46 presents the risk allocation matrix based on the tool kit.

Table 46: Typical Risk Allocation Matrix for Variants of Public–Private Partnership Projects in the Water and Wastewater Sectors in India

Type of Risk	BOT (with fixed payment)	BOT (with user charges)	Concession (for brownfield assets)	Performance-Based Management Contracts	Service Maintenance Contracts
Pre-Operative Task Risks					
Delays in land acquisition	Public sector	Public sector	Public sector	Not relevant	Not relevant
External linkages	Public sector	Public sector	Public sector	Not relevant	Not relevant
Financing risks	Private sector	Private sector	Private sector	Not relevant	Not relevant
Planning	Private sector	Private sector	Private sector	Not relevant	Not relevant
Construction Phase Risks					
Design risk	Private sector	Private sector	Private sector	Not relevant	Not relevant
Construction risk	Private sector	Private sector	Private sector	Not relevant	Not relevant
Approvals	Private sector	Private sector	Private sector	Not relevant	Not relevant
Operations Phase Risks					
Operation and maintenance risk	Private sector	Private sector	Private sector	Private sector	Private sector

continued on next page

Table 46 *continued*

Type of Risk	BOT (with fixed payment)	BOT (with user charges)	Concession (for brownfield assets)	Performance-Based Management Contracts	Service Maintenance Contracts
Volume risk	Public sector	Private sector	Private sector	Public sector	Public sector
Payment risk	Public sector	Private sector	Private sector	Public sector	Public sector
Financial risk	Private sector	Private sector	Private sector	Private sector	Not relevant
Performance risk	Private sector	Private sector	Private sector	Private sector	Private sector
Environmental risk	Private sector	Private sector	Private sector	Private sector	Private sector
Handover Risk Events					
Handover risk	Private sector	Private sector	Private sector	Private sector	Not relevant
Terminal value risk	Private sector	Private sector	Private sector	Private sector	Not relevant
Other Risks					
Change in law	Public sector	Public sector	Public sector	Public sector	Public sector
Force majeure	Shared	Shared	Shared	Shared	Shared
Concessionaire risk	Public sector	Public sector	Public sector	Public sector	Public sector
Sponsor risk	Private sector	Private sector	Private sector	Private sector	Private sector
Concessionaire's event of default	Private sector	Private sector	Private sector	Private sector	Private sector
Government's event of default	Public sector	Public sector	Public sector	Public sector	Public sector

BOT = build–operate–transfer.
Sources: Asian Development Bank. 2019. Public–Private Partnership Monitor. Second Edition; and Government of India, Ministry of Finance, Department of Economic Affairs. 2010. *PPP Toolkit for Improving PPP Decision-Making Processes*.

Financing Details for Public–Private Partnership Projects in the Water and Wastewater Sectors

Parameter	1990–2020	1990–2021	1990–2022
Public–private partnership (PPP) projects with foreign lending participation	UA	1	1
PPP projects that received export credit agency/international financing institution support	1	2	2
Typical debt-to-equity ratio	45:55		
Time for financial close	UA		
Typical concession period	15–20 years		
Typical financial internal rate of return	UA		

✓ = Yes, ✗ = No, NA = Not Applicable, UA = Unavailable
Source: World Bank. Infrastructure Finance, PPPs and Guarantees. Custom Query (accessed 3 January 2024).

5. Challenges in the Water and Wastewater Sectors

- Enhancing the institutional capacity of urban local bodies (ULBs) can lead to better planning, preparation, and execution of PPPs. This includes improving governance and project management, which can increase the number and quality of PPPs undertaken. Additionally, increasing budget allocations for ULBs can help manage project preparatory expenses and fulfill annuity obligations.
- Establishing robust guarantee frameworks can protect the private sector in the event of default by ULBs. This can increase the interest of the private sector in PPP projects. Addressing politically sensitive issues such as tariff revisions can ensure appropriate tariffs for cost recovery, enhancing the sustainability of PPP projects.
- Improving the accuracy of data on connections, infrastructure, and metering can make it easier for private players to enter into contracts with ULBs.
- Enhancing the creditworthiness of ULBs can boost private sector confidence in the ULBs' ability to fulfill their obligations.

The centrally sponsored programs, such as Atal Mission for Rejuvenation and Urban Transformation (AMRUT), AMRUT 2.0, Jal Jeevan Mission, Namami Gange Programme, and the Jawaharlal Nehru National Urban Renewal Mission (JNNURM), have been leading to substantial reforms in the way ULBs function. Also, there is a gradual acceptability from the public at all levels of private sector involvement in infrastructure development.

G. Information and Communication Technology

Parameter	Value	Unit
Telephone subscribers	1.62	per 100 inhabitants
Cellular phone subscribers	81.99	per 100 inhabitants
Cellular network coverage	93.50	% of population covered
Internet subscribers (fixed broadband)	1.96	per 100 inhabitants
Internet bandwidth per internet user	5.68	kbps

ICT = information and communication technology, kbps = kilobits per second.
Sources: The Global Economy. Internet Bandwidth - Country Rankings (accessed 15 July 2023); The Global Economy. Internet Subscribers, per 100 people - Country Rankings (accessed 15 July 2023); The Global Economy. Mobile Network Coverage - Country Rankings (accessed 15 July 2023); The Global Economy. Mobile Phone Subscribers, per 100 people - Country Rankings (accessed 15 July 2023); and World Bank. Fixed Telephone Subscriptions (per 100 people) (accessed 15 July 2023).

The information and communication technology (ICT) industry in India comprises

- information technology (IT), consisting of software, IT services, and IT-enabled services and/or business process outsourcing, and contributing to around 7.9% of the country's GDP; and
- telecom industry, consisting of wireless, wireline, and other telecommunication services such as internet, broadband, and satellite, and contributing to around 6.5% of the country's GDP.

1. Contracting Agencies and Players in the Information and Communication Technology Sector

Key Agencies in the Information and Communication Technology Sector

- The Department of Telecommunications, under the Ministry of Communications, is responsible for formulating development policies, granting licenses for various telecom services, and enforcing wireless regulatory measures.
- The Ministry of Electronics and Information Technology is the competent authority to enter into contracts for IT sector projects.
- The Telecom Regulatory Authority of India (TRAI) was established in 1997 through an Act of Parliament to regulate telecom services and fix or revise tariffs for telecom services, which used to be the responsibility of the central government. The TRAI Act was amended by an ordinance in January 2000 to establish the Telecommunications Dispute Settlement and Appellate Tribunal, which was intended to take over the adjudicatory and disputes functions from the TRAI. The Telecommunications Dispute Settlement and Appellate Tribunal was set up to adjudicate any dispute between a licensor and a licensee, between two or more service providers, and between a service provider and a group of consumers, and to hear and dispose appeals against any direction, decision, or order of the TRAI. The TRAI is responsible for the regular review and issuance of tariff orders for telecom and broadcasting services in the country, in addition to licensing, regulation of activities, and consumer protection, among others.

Information and Communication Technology Players

The major IT players in India are Tata Consultancy Services (generates roughly 70% of the revenue for Tata Sons, and is one of the global leaders in the IT sector), Infosys, HCL Technologies Limited, Wipro, Tech Mahindra, and Mindtree. The major telecom players in the country are Reliance Jio, Bharti Airtel, Vodafone Idea, and Bharat Sanchar Nigam Limited.

2. Information and Communication Technology Sector Laws and Regulations

The key policies and acts under the Ministry of Electronics and Information Technology are listed below:[94]

- Information Technology Act, 2000;
- National Policy on Software Products, 2019;
- National Policy on Electronics, 2019;
- National Cyber Security Policy, 2013;
- Internet of Things Policy, 2016; and
- Right to Information Act.

---

[94] Government of India, Ministry of Electronics and Information Technology. Acts and Rules, Policies and Guidelines (accessed 15 July 2023).

The key policies and acts under the Ministry of Communications include the following:[95]

- National Telecom Policy, 2012;
- Broadband Policy, 2004;
- Amendment to Broadband Policy, 2004;
- National Digital Communications Policy, 2018;
- Indian Telegraph Act; and
- National Broadband Mission, 2019.

Standard Contracts and Licenses in the Information and Communication Technology Sector

Parameter	Availability
What standardized contracts are available and used in the market?	
• Public–private partnership/concession agreement?	✓
• Performance-based operation and maintenance contract?	✓
• Engineering, procurement, and construction contract?	UA
• License agreement?	UA

✓ = Yes, ✗ = No, NA = Not Applicable, UA = Unavailable.
Source: Government of India, Ministry of Electronics and Information Technology. 2017. *Guidance Notes for IT PPP Projects.*

Foreign Investment Restrictions in the Information and Communication Technology Sector

Parameter	2021	2022	2023
Maximum allowed foreign ownership of equity in greenfield projects			
• Fixed line infrastructure	100%	100%	100%
• Fixed line services	100%	100%	100%
• Wireless/mobile infrastructure	100%	100%	100%
• Wireless/mobile services	100%	100%	100%

For the telecom sector, a foreign direct investment (FDI) of up to 49% is allowed under an automatic route. An FDI beyond 49% will go through the approval of the Department of Telecommunication and Foreign Investment Promotion Board.[96]

---

[95] Government of India. Department of Telecommunications.
[96] Government of India, Department of Telecommunications. FDI Policy in Telecom.

3. Information and Communication Technology Sector Master Plan

The Ministry of Communications, through key documents including the National Broadband Mission and National Digital Communications Policy of 2018, articulates the sector's goals and objectives to be achieved by 2022. Some of these key goals are the following:

* Provide universal broadband connectivity at 50 megabits per second (Mbps) to every citizen.
* Provide all villages in India access to broadband under the BharatNet project. In August 2020, the Government of India announced extending broadband to all villages in India over a 1,000-day period. The Bharat Broadband Network Limited has implemented the BharatNet project, which aims to connect 250,000 *gram panchayats* (village councils) in India via a broadband using an optimal mix of underground fiber, fiber over power lines, and radio and satellite media network, and to provide 100 Mbps of speed to all *gram panchayats*. The project totaled ₹171.45 billion ($2.35 billion) and was expected to be completed by FY2022. A capital expenditure of ₹130 billion ($1.78 billion) was expected to be incurred over FY2020–FY2022 for this project. It was also expected to provide 1 gigabit per second connectivity to all *Gram Panchayats* of India by 2020 and 10 gigabits per second by 2022. To fast track the project implementation, the government, in June 2021, decided to revise the implementation strategy of BharatNet by adopting a public–private partnership (PPP) mode in 16 states of the country. The revised strategy also includes creation, upgrading, O&M, and utilization of BharatNet by the concessionaire who will be selected through a competitive international bidding process, with an estimated maximum viability gap funding of up to ₹190.4 billion approved. About 361,000 villages including the *gram panchayats* will be covered. The PPP model will leverage private sector efficiency for operation, maintenance, utilization, and revenue generation, and is expected to result in faster rollout of BharatNet. The selected concessionaire (private sector partner) is expected to provide reliable, high-speed broadband services based on a predefined Services Level Agreement.[97] As of August 2023, 194,000 villages have received connectivity under the project.[98]
* Accelerate fiberization by increasing the route length of the optical fiber cable from the current 2.2 million km to 5.0 million km.
* Enable 100 Mbps broadband on demand to all key development institutions, including all educational institutions.
* Enable fixed line broadband access to 50% of households.
* Achieve a unique mobile subscriber density of 55 by 2020 and 65 by 2022.
* Enable deployment of public Wi-Fi hotspots to reach 5 million by 2020 and 10 million by 2022.
* Ensure connectivity to all uncovered areas.
* Attract investments of $100 billion in the digital communications sector.
* Train 1 million personnel on "new age skills."
* Expand Internet of Things ecosystem to 5 billion connected devices.

---

97   Government of India, Press Information Bureau. 2021. Cabinet Approves BharatNet Implementation through Public Private Partnership Model in 16 States with Optical Fibre Connectivity to All Inhabited Villages. Press release. 30 June.
98   S. R. Singh. 2023. Cabinet Approves ₹1.39 trillion for BharatNet Project. *The Hindu Business Line*. 5 August.

- Increase tower density from the current 0.42 towers per thousand population to 1.0 per thousand population by setting up an additional 1 million towers.
- Facilitate the rollout of 5G network and strengthen the 4G network.
- Increase by around two and a half times the number of fiberized telecom towers in the country.
- Make available government services in real time via mobile technology.
- Improve India's ranking in the ICT Development Index of the International Telecommunications Union from 134 in 2017 into the top 25 nations.[99]

In terms of India's progress in attaining the goals set by the ICT Master Plan by 2022, the results are mixed.

- About 52% of India's population had internet access in 2022 against the target of 100%.[100]
- Broadband connectivity reached 93% of villages in 2022 against the target of 100%. [101]
- To add to the ICT master plan, the Prime Minister launched 5G services on 1 October 2022 for India to attain 350 million 5G subscriptions by 2026, accounting for 27% of all mobile subscriptions.
- Additionally, the Union Cabinet approved a $1.65 billion production-linked incentive scheme for telecom and networking products under the Department of Telecom.
- On December 2022, 42 companies committed an investment of $502.95 million, comprising 28 micro, small, and medium-sized enterprises (MSMEs) and 14 non-MSMEs.
- To drive the development of 6G technology, the Department of Telecom has developed a 6G innovation group.[102]
- In the IT sector, the government introduced the Software Technology Parks Scheme, which is a 100% export-oriented scheme for the development and export of computer software, including the export of professional services.[103]

Data centers have been listed in the Harmonized Master List of Infrastructure Sub-sectors in October 2022, thereby making it easier for banks to finance this sub-sector and broaden the scope of private participation.

The estimated capital expenditure planned for the sector, based on the National Infrastructure Pipeline, is summarized in Table 47.

---

[99] Government of India, Ministry of Communications, Department of Telecommunications. 2019. *National Broadband Mission*; and Government of India, Department of Telecommunications. 2018. *National Digital Communications Policy, 2018*.

[100] R. Majumdar. 2023. 52% of Indian Population Had Internet Access in 2022, Says Report. *The Economic Times*. 3 May.

[101] T. S. Thakur. 2022. Broadband Connectivity Reaches 93.21% Villages of India. *TelecomTalk*. 11 July.

[102] India Brand Equity Foundation (IBEF). Telecom Industry in India.

[103] IBEF. IT and BPM Industry in India.

Table 47: Capital Expenditure Plan for the Information and Communication Technology Sector in India

Project Category	No. of Projects	Capital Expenditure, FY2020–FY2025 ($ billion)	(₹ billion)
4G project of BSNL and MTNL	2	4.55	372.84
Network for spectrum	1	1.80	147.68
BharatNet	1	1.59	130.00
Private player capex	2	27.81	2,280.00
Others	8	1.42	116.40
Total	**14**	**37.17**	**3,046.92**

BSNL = Bharat Sanchar Nigam Limited, FY = fiscal year, MTNL = Mahanagar Telephone Nigam Limited.

Source: Government of India, Ministry of Finance, Department of Economic Affairs. 2019. *National Infrastructure Pipeline.* Volume 2.

Projects Under Conceptualization and Development in the Information and Communication Technology Sector

Figure 47 provides the number of PPP projects that are under conceptualization and development in the ICT sector of India.

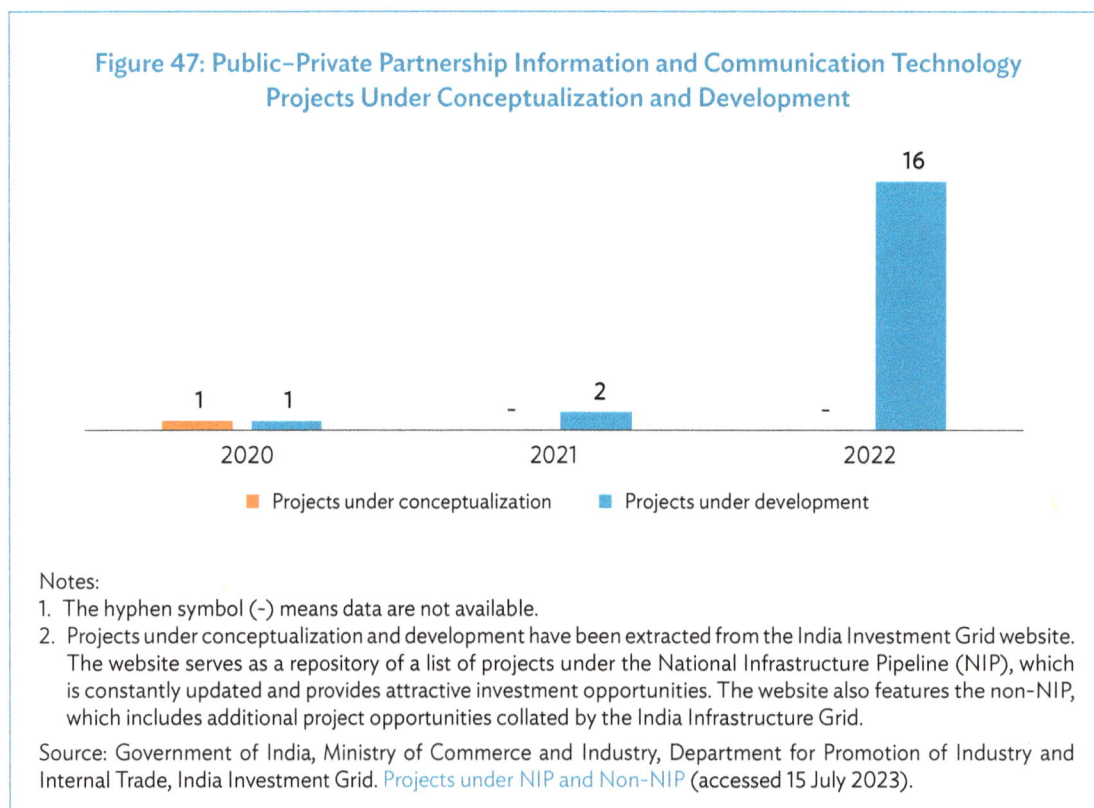

Figure 47: Public–Private Partnership Information and Communication Technology Projects Under Conceptualization and Development

Notes:
1. The hyphen symbol (-) means data are not available.
2. Projects under conceptualization and development have been extracted from the India Investment Grid website. The website serves as a repository of a list of projects under the National Infrastructure Pipeline (NIP), which is constantly updated and provides attractive investment opportunities. The website also features the non-NIP, which includes additional project opportunities collated by the India Infrastructure Grid.

Source: Government of India, Ministry of Commerce and Industry, Department for Promotion of Industry and Internal Trade, India Investment Grid. Projects under NIP and Non-NIP (accessed 15 July 2023).

4. Features of Past Public–Private Partnership Projects in the Information and Communication Technology Sector

Figure 48 shows the number of PPP projects procured through various modes, including direct appointment and competitive bids, in the ICT sector of India.

Figure 48: Modes of Procurement for Public–Private Partnership Information and Communication Technology Projects

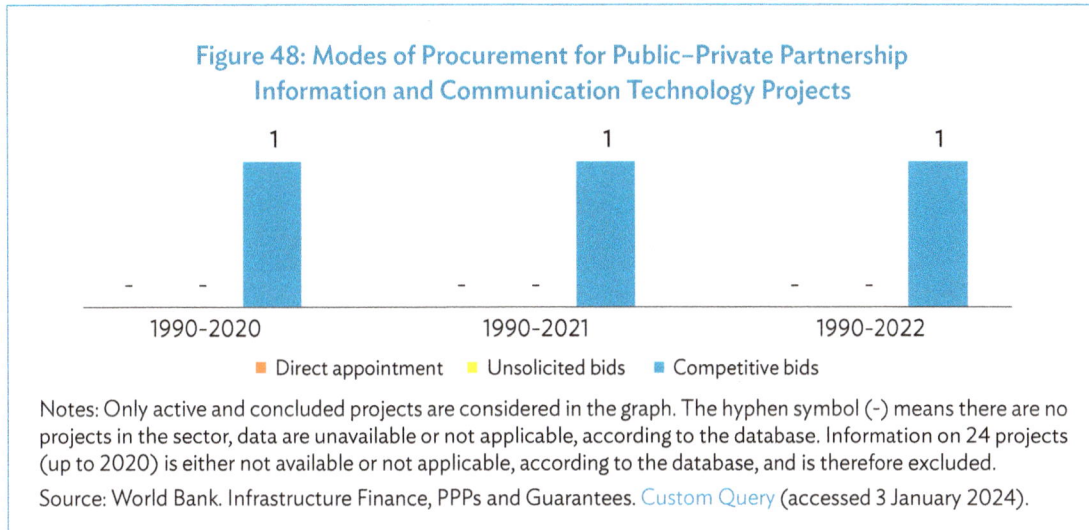

Notes: Only active and concluded projects are considered in the graph. The hyphen symbol (-) means there are no projects in the sector, data are unavailable or not applicable, according to the database. Information on 24 projects (up to 2020) is either not available or not applicable, according to the database, and is therefore excluded.

Source: World Bank. Infrastructure Finance, PPPs and Guarantees. Custom Query (accessed 3 January 2024).

Figure 49 shows the number of PPP projects that reached financial close and the total value of those projects in the ICT sector of India.

Figure 49: Public–Private Partnership Information and Communication Technology Projects Reaching Financial Close

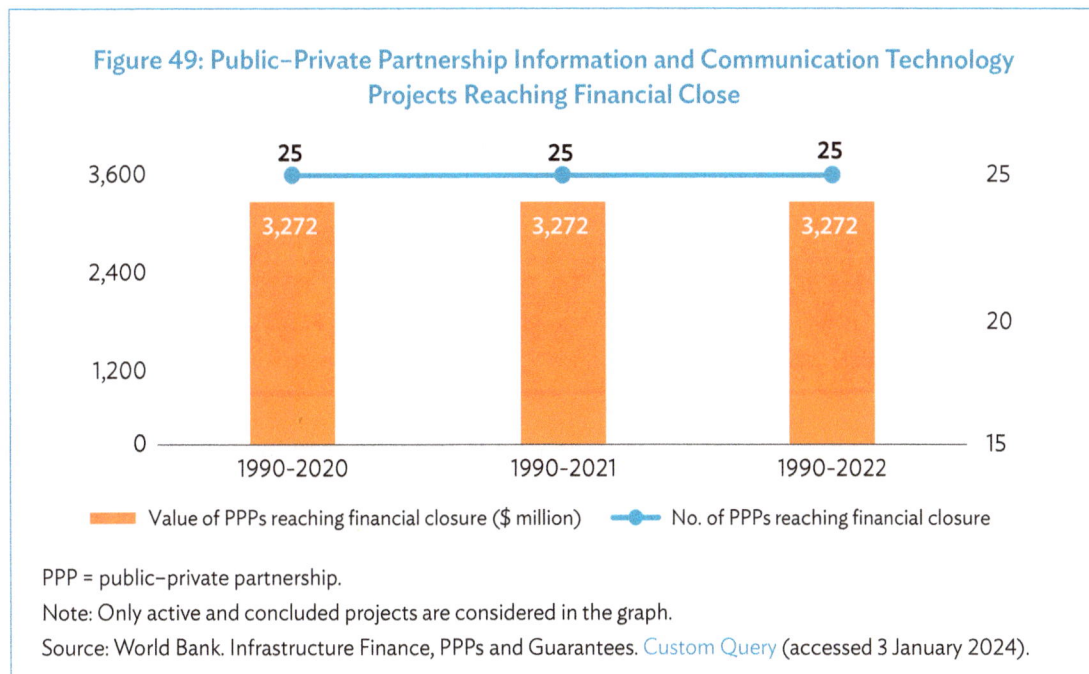

PPP = public–private partnership.

Note: Only active and concluded projects are considered in the graph.

Source: World Bank. Infrastructure Finance, PPPs and Guarantees. Custom Query (accessed 3 January 2024).

Figure 50 shows the number of PPP projects with foreign sponsor participation in the ICT sector of India.

Figure 50: Public–Private Partnership Information and Communication Technology Projects with Foreign Sponsor Participation

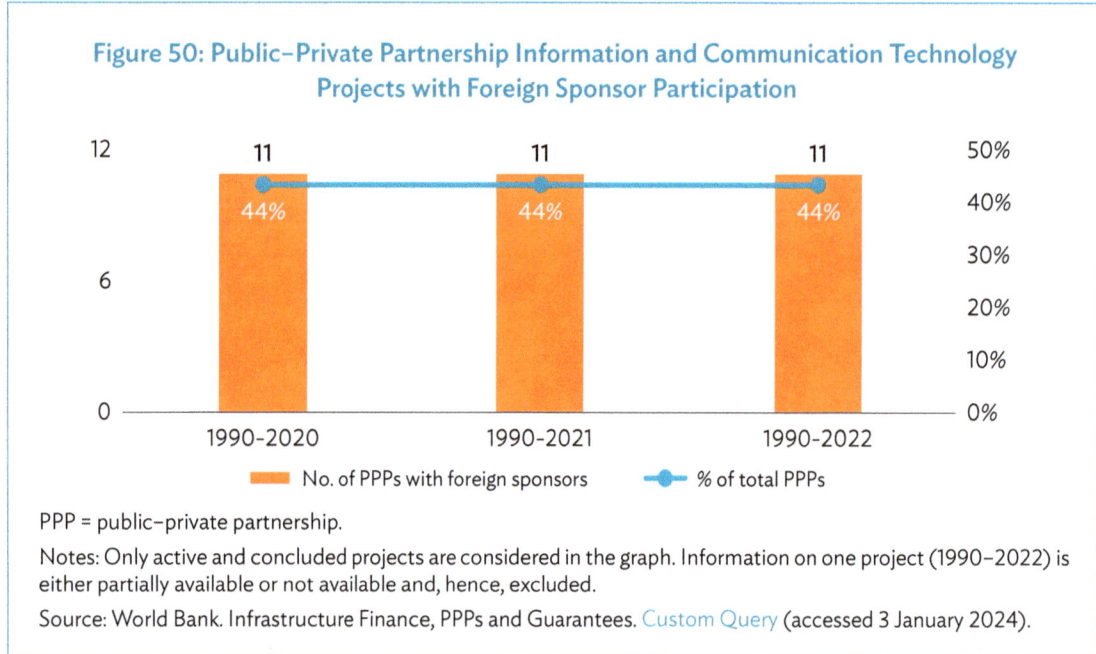

PPP = public–private partnership.

Notes: Only active and concluded projects are considered in the graph. Information on one project (1990–2022) is either partially available or not available and, hence, excluded.

Source: World Bank. Infrastructure Finance, PPPs and Guarantees. Custom Query (accessed 3 January 2024).

According to the World Bank Private Participation in Infrastructure (PPI) database, no projects in the ICT sector in India received government support.

Figure 51 shows the number of PPP projects that received payment in the form of user charges and government pay (offtake) in the ICT sector of India.

Figure 51: Payment Mechanisms for Public–Private Partnership Information and Communication Technology Projects

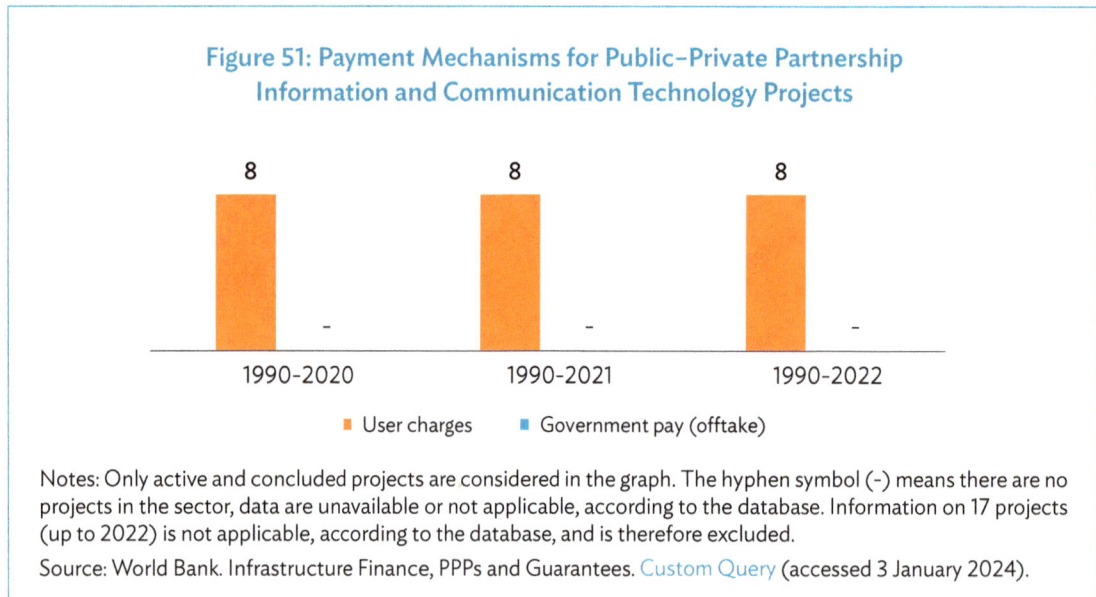

Notes: Only active and concluded projects are considered in the graph. The hyphen symbol (-) means there are no projects in the sector, data are unavailable or not applicable, according to the database. Information on 17 projects (up to 2022) is not applicable, according to the database, and is therefore excluded.

Source: World Bank. Infrastructure Finance, PPPs and Guarantees. Custom Query (accessed 3 January 2024).

Past PPP projects in the ICT sector, based on the Department of Economic Affairs (DEA) database, are shown in Table 48.

Table 48: Number of Information and Communication Technology Projects

Subsector	No. of Projects
Telecommunication network and services	60
Total	**60**

Note: Data was last updated on 5 December 2019.

Source: Government of India, Ministry of Finance, Department of Economic Affairs. List of all PPP Projects (accessed 15 July 2023).

Tariffs in the Information and Communication Technology Sector

The Telecom Regulatory Authority of India (TRAI) has been mandated to regulate tariff for the telecommunication sector in India under the TRAI Act. The TRAI initiated tariff regulation for telecommunication services in India with the notification of the Telecommunication Tariff Order (TTO), 1999. The TTO has been amended from time to time considering the changes in the sector landscape. The TTO provided for three types of tariffs at a broader level: (i) tariffs specified in the TTO, (ii) tariffs subjected to tariff ceiling specified in the TTO, and (iii) tariffs under forbearance.

The TRAI has expanded the scope of forbearance regime over the years and has given service providers the freedom to design the tariffs suited to the prevailing market conditions. However, the forbearance is subject to reporting requirements and adherence to specified principles of tariff assessments (i.e., transparency, nondiscrimination, and nonpredation). Over the years, the TRAI has moved from the "fixation of tariff rates" stage to the "forbearance with prior approval" stage, and finally to a stage of "forbearance regime with post-facto reporting obligation" with regulatory oversight. Accordingly, at present, except for a small list of regulated tariff products, tariffs for all other telecommunication services are under forbearance.[104] This freedom has led to the emergence of a multiple number of tariff plans and offers by telecom service providers both in the prepaid and postpaid segments.

Typical Risk Allocation for Public–Private Partnership Projects in the Information and Communication Technology Sector

The typical risk allocation for ICT sector contracts is indicated in Table 49. This is based on the build–own–operate–transfer model for projects implemented in India (e.g., central processing center for income tax and passport). The typical contract period is 7–10 years. Table 49 indicates the typical risk allocation for PPP projects in the ICT sector.

---

[104] Government of India, Telecom Regulatory Authority of India. 2021. *Consultation Paper on Validity Period of Tariff Offers.* *13 May.*

Table 49: Typical Risk Allocation for Public–Private Partnership Projects in the Information and Communication Technology Sector (Build-Own-Operate-Transfer Model)

Type of Risk	Private	Public	Shared	Comments
Pre-Go Live risks			✓	
Technology risk		✓		Largely by the public sector, as the private partner did not define the bill-of-material. However, the private partner is responsible for technology update.
Latent defect risk	✓	✓		If the private party (or any of its subcontractors) designs and constructs the facilities, the risk is allocated to the private party; otherwise, the risk is allocated to the nodal agency.
Completion risk	✓			
Design risk	✓			
Cost overrun risk			✓	Shared depending on the nature of the cost overrun. In case the cost overrun is due to the private party, then the risk is allocated to the private party.
Planning risk			✓	In relation to any nondesign and construction of the solution, the risk is allocated to the nodal agency. In relation to any design, the risk is allocated to the private party.
Availability risk	✓			
Market, demand, or volume risk	✓		✓	In case the demand varies within a particular band, the risk is allocated to the private sector; for anything else, the risk is shared.
Utilities supply risk	✓			This risk is allocated to the private party, unless the utilities are supplied by the nodal agency and such supplies are not covered by a special insurance.
Insolvency and outside creditor risk	✓			
Subcontractor risk	✓			
Operating risk (technology, environment, cost, and management)	✓			
Maintenance risk	✓			
Force majeure risk			✓	If risks are insurable, risk is allocated to the private party. If risks are not insurable, then risk is shared as the nodal agency may pay some compensation.

continued on next page

Table 49 *continued*

Type of Risk	Private	Public	Shared	Comments
Political risk			✓	In relation to discriminatory changes in law and expropriating actions, the risk is allocated to the nodal agency. In relation to general changes in law, the risk is allocated to the private party.
Regulatory risk			✓	
Tax rate change risk		✓		
Inflation risk		✓		
Residual value risk	✓			

Source: Government of India, Ministry of Electronics and Information Technology. 2017. Guidance Notes for IT PPP Projects.

Financing Details for Public–Private Partnership Projects in the Information and Communication Technology Sector

Parameter	1990–2020	1990–2021	1990–2022
Public–private partnership (PPP) projects with foreign lending participation	UA	UA	UA
PPP projects that received export credit agency/international financing institution support	3	3	3
Typical debt-to-equity ratio	UA		
Time for financial close	UA		
Typical concession period	10 years		
Typical financial internal rate of return	UA		

UA = Unavailable.
Source: World Bank. Infrastructure Finance, PPPs and Guarantees. Custom Query (accessed 3 January 2024).

5. Challenges in the Information and Communication Technology Sector

Opportunities for growth in the ICT sector include the following:

- **Broadband connectivity.** Investments in infrastructure need to be enhanced and universal last-mile broadband connectivity needs to be promoted. Regardless of the trunk infrastructure, the quality and speed of service provisioning is highly dependent upon the last-mile connectivity infrastructure.
- **Coordination among stakeholders and agencies.** Creation of the digital communications infrastructure requires coordination and alignment of work among multiple stakeholders and agencies—central ministries and departments, state governments, local and municipal authorities, industries, and user communities—to achieve the intended objectives.

- **Implementation of Indian Telegraph Right-of-Way Rules, 2016.** Addressing the complexities and uncertainties of right-of-way policies across the country can reduce the cost of fiber rollouts, making it more affordable and accessible.
- **Debt stress in the telecom services sector.** The presence of hyper-competitive pricing in the industry, while challenging, also presents an opportunity for innovative financial strategies to alleviate debt stress and reduce nonperforming assets in the sector.

H. Social Infrastructure

The social infrastructure sector in India includes healthcare (primary, secondary, and tertiary), education (primary, secondary, higher secondary, higher), and public housing. India's distinct demographic advantage of having a large working population can be maximized by providing adequate social infrastructure in sectors like education, healthcare, water supply, sanitation, and housing.

Parameter	Value	Unit
Government expenditure on education (2020)	4.5	% of GDP
Education spending as % of government spending	16.5	%
Primary school gross enrollment (2021)	102.00	%
Adult literacy rate (2022)	76.32	%
Total health expenditure (2020)	2.96	% of GDP
Health spending per capita (current, US$, 2020)	56.63	$
Maternal mortality ratio (modeled estimates per 100,000 live births) (2018–2020)	97	per 100,000 live births
Infant mortality rate (2020)	28	below 1 year per 1,000 live births
Life expectancy at birth (2020)	70	year
Child malnutrition (2020)	32.1	% below 5 years old
Number of existing affordable housing units	UA	number
Affordable housing gap	UA	%

GDP = gross domestic product, UA = unavailable.

Sources: World Bank. Total Adult Literacy Rate (% of people ages 15 and above) (accessed 15 July 2023); World Bank. Total Government Expenditure on Education (% of GDP) - India (accessed 15 July 2023); World Bank. Current Health Expenditure (% of GDP) - India (accessed 15 July 2023); World Bank. Primary School Enrollment (% gross) – India (accessed 15 July 2023); and Government of India, Ministry of Health and Family Welfare, Press Information Bureau. 2022. Significant Decline in the Maternal Mortality Ratio (MMR) from 130 in 2014-16 to 97 per lakh live births in 2018-20. Press release. 30 November.

1. Contracting Agencies in the Social Infrastructure Sector

Healthcare Services

The Ministry of Health and Family Welfare is the contracting agency for the healthcare sector. The regulatory role of the ministry includes regulation of clinical establishments, professional and technical education, food safety, medical technologies, medical products, clinical trials, research, and implementation of health-related laws.[105]

At the local level, the Department of Health and Family Welfare acts as the contracting agency for public–private partnership (PPP) projects in the healthcare sector.

Education Services

At the central level, the Ministry of Human Resource Development is the government contracting agency for PPP projects in the education sector.

At the local level, the Department of School Education and Literacy and the Department of Higher Education of various state governments also act as the contracting agency.

Public Housing

The Ministry of Housing and Urban Affairs is the contracting agency for public housing projects.

Government Buildings

The Ministry of Housing and Urban Affairs is the contracting agency for government building projects.

2. Social Infrastructure Sector Laws and Regulations

Healthcare Sector Regulations

The National Health Policy, 2017 is the pertinent policy for the healthcare sector.

Education Sector Regulations

The National Education Policy, 2020 is the policy for the education sector.

The Right to Education Act, 2009 is the overarching act for the education sector.

Public Housing Regulations

The key regulations for housing and development are articulated in the National Urban Housing and Habitat Policy of 2007.[106] The following are the major objectives of the policy:

---

[105] Government of India, Ministry of Health and Family Welfare. 2017. *National Health Policy, 2017.*
[106] Government of India, Ministry of Housing and Urban Poverty Alleviation. 2007. *National Urban Housing and Habitat Policy, 2007.*

- facilitating accessibility to serviced land and housing for economically weaker sections and lower income groups;
- encouraging land assembly, development, and disposal by both private and public sectors;
- forging strong partnerships between public, private, and cooperative sectors;
- creating adequate housing stock, both on rental and ownership basis; and
- using technology to modernize and enhance energy and cost efficiency, productivity, and quality.

Government Building Regulations

No centrally available data.

Other Social Infrastructure Regulation—Prisons and Correction Centers

No centrally available data.

Standard Contracts in the Social Infrastructure Sector

Healthcare

Parameter	Availability
What standardized contracts are available and used in the market?	
• Public–private partnership/concession agreement?[a]	✓
• Performance-based operation and maintenance contract?	✗
• Engineering, procurement, and construction contract	✗

✓ = Yes, ✗ = No, NA = Not Applicable, UA = Unavailable.
[a] Government of India, NITI Aayog. Model Agreements.

Education Services

Parameter	Availability
What standardized contracts are available and used in the market?	
• Public–private partnership/concession agreement?[a]	✓
• Performance-based operation and maintenance contract?	✗
• Engineering, procurement, and construction contract	✗

✓ = Yes, ✗ = No, NA = Not Applicable, UA = Unavailable.
[a] Government of India, NITI Aayog. Framework of Model Concession Agreements.

Public Housing

Parameter	Availability
What standardized contracts are available and used in the market?	
• Public–private partnership/concession agreement?	✗
• Performance-based operation and maintenance contract?	✗
• Engineering, procurement, and construction contract?	✗

✓ = Yes, ✗ = No, NA = Not Applicable, UA = Unavailable.

Government Buildings

Parameter	Availability
What standardized contracts are available and used in the market?	
• Public–private partnership/concession agreement?	✗
• Performance-based operation and maintenance contract?	✗
• Engineering, procurement, and construction contract?	✗

✓ = Yes, ✗ = No, NA = Not Applicable, UA = Unavailable.

Foreign Investment Restrictions in the Social Infrastructure Sector

Parameter	2021	2022	2023
Maximum allowed foreign ownership of equity in greenfield projects[a]			
• Construction of healthcare facilities	100%	100%	100%
• Services, including hospital management, specialist hospital/clinic, mental hospital, dental clinic, and laboratory and medical check-up services	100%	100%	100%
• Private maternity hospital, general medical services clinic, public hospital, public medical clinic, residential health services, and basic healthcare services facility	100%	100%	100%
• Construction of education facilities[b]	100%	100%	100%
• Nonformal education services (vocational training, computer education, and language education)	100%	100%	100%
• Formal education services	100%	100%	100%
• Government buildings	100%	100%	100%
• Prisons and correction centers	NA	NA	NA
• Public housing	100%	100%	100%

NA = not applicable.

[a] Invest India. National Investment Promotion and Facilitation Agency. FDI Policy of India (accessed 15 July 2023).
[b] Construction and development projects (i.e., development of townships, construction of residential and commercial premises, roads or bridges, hotels, resorts, hospitals, educational institutions, recreational facilities, city and regional level infrastructure, townships).

3. Social Infrastructure Sector Master Plan

Healthcare

India's Ministry of Health and Family Welfare introduced the National Health Policy in 2017 to progressively achieve universal health coverage, reinforce trust in the public healthcare system, and align the growth of the private healthcare sector with public health goals (footnote 106).

The policy also highlights quantitative objectives. The indicative, quantitative goals and objectives are outlined under three broad components: (i) health status and program impact, (ii) health systems performance, and (iii) health system strengthening. Some of the specific quantitative goals and objectives of the National Health Policy, 2017 are to

- increase life expectancy at birth from 67.5 years to 70 years by 2025 (in progress);
- reduce infant mortality rate to 28 by 2019 (achieved in 2020);
- increase utilization of public health facilities by 50% from current levels by 2025 (in progress);
- meet the need of family planning above 90% at national and subnational levels by 2025 (in progress);
- provide access to safe water and sanitation to all by 2020 (Swachh Bharat Mission) (in progress, India was declared open defecation free in 2019);
- increase the government's health expenditure as a percentage of GDP from the existing 1.15% to 2.50% by 2025 (in progress);
- increase states' healthcare sector spending to more than 8% of their budget by 2020 (in progress);
- establish primary and secondary care facility according to the norms in high-priority districts (selected based on population and time to reach norms) by 2025 (in progress);
- ensure district-level electronic database of information on health system components by 2020;
- strengthen the health surveillance system and establish registries for diseases of public health importance by 2020; and
- establish federated integrated health information architecture, health information exchanges, and national health information network by 2025 (in progress).

The policy proposed a potentially achievable target of raising public health expenditure to 2.5% of the GDP in a time-bound manner. The policy has a holistic coverage to ensure universal coverage and improve healthcare infrastructure and services, including those in rural and urban areas. Programs have been conceived to improve child and adolescent health and address malnutrition and micronutrient deficiencies through various initiatives, such as universal immunization and control of communicable diseases. The policy also articulates the need for mainstreaming the potential of Ayurveda, Yoga, Naturopathy, Unani, Siddha, Sowa-Rigpa, and Homoeopathy in providing holistic healthcare. The policy discusses human resources at various levels of medical education (footnote 110).

Education

The new National Education Policy was approved in July 2020, replacing the National Policy on Education of 1986.[107] The new policy aims to bring transformational reforms in school and in higher

---

[107] Government of India, Ministry of Human Resource Development. 2020. *National Education Policy, 2020.*

education, such as modification of the curricular structure and improvement of enrollment ratios. Some of the key objectives of the policy are as follows:

- An autonomous body, the National Educational Technology Forum, will be created to provide a platform for the free exchange of ideas on the use of technology to enhance learning, assessment, planning, and administration.
- The National Education Policy, 2020 emphasizes setting up of a Gender Inclusion Fund and Special Education Zones for disadvantaged regions and groups.
- Central and state governments will work together to increase public investment in the education sector to reach 6% of GDP.

School Education
- The new National Education Policy aims to universalize education from preschool to secondary level, targeting 100% gross enrollment ratio in school education by 2030.
- The current 10+2 system will be replaced by a new 5+3+3+4 curricular structure corresponding to ages 3 to 8, 8 to 11, 11 to 14, and 14 to 18, respectively.
- A new and comprehensive framework, the National Curriculum Framework for Teacher Education 2021, was formulated by the National Council for Technical Education in consultation with the National Council of Educational Research and Training. The overarching objective of this National Curriculum Framework is to transform the school education system of India as envisioned in the National Education Policy 2020 through corresponding positive changes in the curriculum, including pedagogy. By 2030, the minimum degree qualification for teaching will be an integrated 4-year degree on Bachelor of Education (footnote 108).

Higher Education
- Gross enrollment ratio in higher education will be raised to 50% by 2035; a total of 35 million seats will be added in higher education.
- Models of exemplary multidisciplinary education at a global standard will be established in the country, comparable to the Indian Institute of Technology and the Indian Institute of Management. The National Research Foundation will be created as an apex body for fostering a strong research culture and building research capacity in higher education.
- The Higher Education Commission of India will be set up as a single overarching umbrella body for the entire higher education, excluding medical and legal education. The Higher Education Commission of India will have four independent verticals: (i) National Higher Education Regulatory Council for regulation, (ii) General Education Council for standard setting, (iii) Higher Education Grants Council for funding, and (iv) National Accreditation Council for accreditation. Public and private higher education institutions will be governed by the same set of norms for regulation, accreditation, and academic standards (footnote 108).

Public Housing
The Pradhan Mantri Awas Yojana – Urban Mission was launched as a centrally sponsored scheme in 2015. It seeks to meet the gap in urban housing units by 2022 through increased private sector participation and active involvement of the states. The Mission initially covered 500 Class I cities and

was to be implemented in three phases between 2015 and 2022.[108] It has four broad components or verticals, out of which a credit-linked subsidy will be implemented as a central sector scheme:

- slum rehabilitation of slum dwellers with participation of private developers using land as a resource;
- promotion of affordable housing for weaker sections through credit-linked subsidy—to encompass all 4,041 statutory census towns from the outset;
- affordable housing in partnership with public and private sectors—central assistance of ₹150,000 per house for economically weaker sections will be provided; and
- subsidy for beneficiary-led individual house construction or enhancement—central assistance of ₹150,000 per house for economically weaker sections will be provided.

Under the Pradhan Mantri Awas Yojana – Urban Mission, as of August 2023, 7.66 million houses have been completed, and a financial outlay of ₹1,424.94 billion has been incurred.[109]

In 2017, the Ministry of Housing and Urban Affairs (MOHUA) released the report on *Public–Private Partnership Models for Affordable Housing*. The report comprehensively describes the basic strategies for PPPs in affordable housing, implementation models along with the associated risk allocation frameworks, and the incentives and schemes available.[110]

Table 50 shows the expected investments in the social infrastructure sector, according to estimates based on the *National Infrastructure Pipeline, 2019*.

Table 50: Year-on-Year Capital Expenditure Plan for the Social Infrastructure Sector, Based on the National Infrastructure Pipeline

Social Infrastructure		FY2020	FY2021	FY2022	FY2023	FY2024	FY2025	Total
Higher Education	₹ billion	52.87	54.99	119.53	130.43	128.48	-	486.30
	$ billion	0.64	0.67	1.46	1.59	1.57	-	5.93
School Education	₹ billion	50.53	71.32	70.77	63.98	65.69	55.62	377.91
	$ billion	0.62	0.87	0.86	0.78	0.80	0.68	4.61
Health and Family Welfare	₹ billion	287.19	401.32	399.14	160.96	97.56	65.44	1,411.61
	$ billion	3.50	4.90	4.87	1.96	1.19	0.80	17.21
Sports	₹ billion	13.2	15.47	14.24	13.89	12.2	8.4	77.40
	$ billion	0.16	0.19	0.17	0.17	0.15	0.10	0.94

continued on next page

[108] Jones Lang LaSalle. 2016. *Affordable Housing in India: Key Initiatives for Inclusive Housing for All.*
[109] Government of India, Ministry of Housing Affairs. 2023. *PMAY-U PMAY-U E-Newsletter. Issue No. 79.* 31 August.
[110] Government of India, Ministry of Housing and Urban Affairs. 2017. *Public–Private Partnership Models for Affordable Housing.*

Table 50 *continued*

Social Infrastructure		FY2020	FY2021	FY2022	FY2023	FY2024	FY2025	Total
Tourism	₹ billion	11.04	15.81	20.59	18.63	11.96	7.15	85.18
	$ billion	0.13	0.19	0.25	0.23	0.15	0.09	1.03
Total	₹ billion	**414.83**	**558.91**	**389.85**	**387.89**	**315.89**	**136.61**	**2,203.98**
	$ billion	**5.06**	**6.82**	**4.76**	**4.73**	**3.85**	**1.67**	**26.88**

– = data unavailable, FY = fiscal year.

Note: Numbers may not sum precisely because of rounding.

Source: Government of India, Ministry of Finance, Department of Economic Affairs. 2019. *National Infrastructure Pipeline.* Volume 2.

Projects Under Conceptualization and Development in the Social Infrastructure Sector

Figure 52 shows the number of PPP projects that are under conceptualization and development in the social infrastructure sector of India.

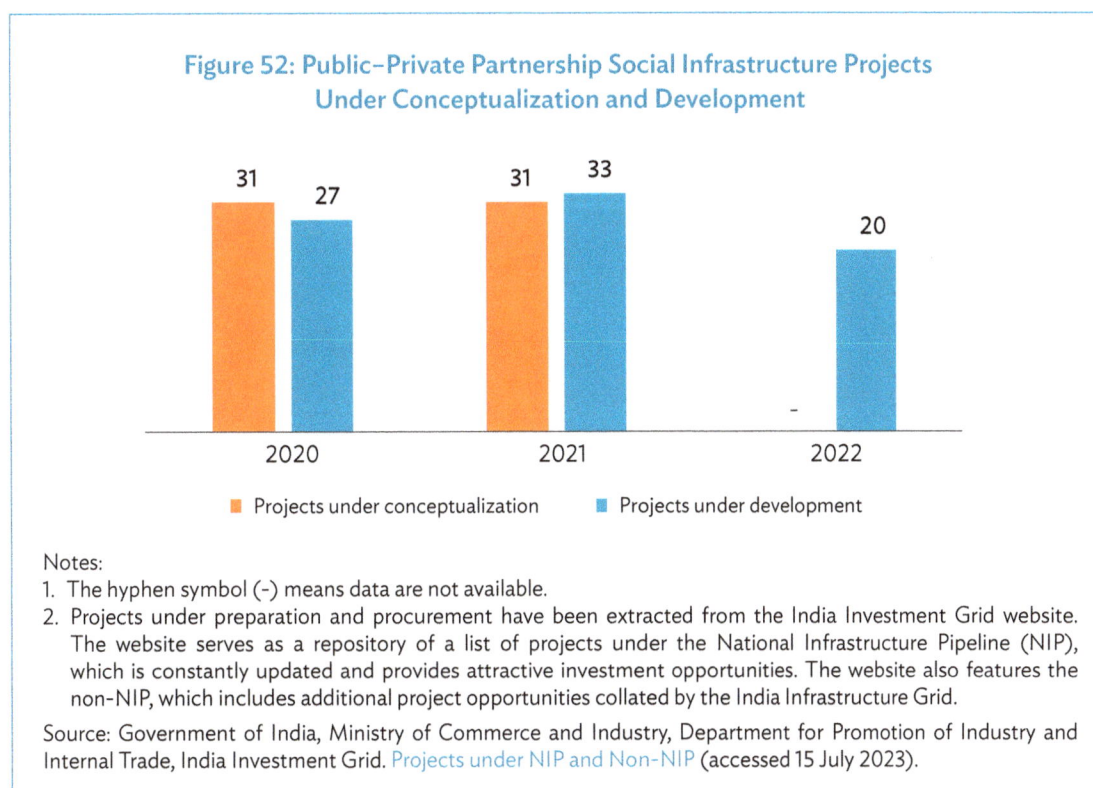

Figure 52: Public–Private Partnership Social Infrastructure Projects Under Conceptualization and Development

Notes:
1. The hyphen symbol (-) means data are not available.
2. Projects under preparation and procurement have been extracted from the India Investment Grid website. The website serves as a repository of a list of projects under the National Infrastructure Pipeline (NIP), which is constantly updated and provides attractive investment opportunities. The website also features the non-NIP, which includes additional project opportunities collated by the India Infrastructure Grid.

Source: Government of India, Ministry of Commerce and Industry, Department for Promotion of Industry and Internal Trade, India Investment Grid. Projects under NIP and Non-NIP (accessed 15 July 2023).

4. Features of Past Public–Private Partnership Projects in the Social Infrastructure Sector

The PPP Monitor defines social infrastructure sector as covering healthcare, education, public housing, and government building infrastructure. This definition has been adopted across all countries for consistency. The World Bank Private Participation in Infrastructure (PPI) database does not comprehensively cover all projects and/or subsectors in the social sector category. To showcase a more comprehensive list, projects from the Department of Economic Affairs (DEA) database have been considered (Table 51).

The DEA's classification of sectors is different from the classification done for this PPP Monitor. The database maintained by the DEA, however, classifies the sector as "social and commercial infrastructure" and covers six subsectors: (i) cold chain, (ii) common infrastructure for industrial parks and special economic zones, (iii) education, (iv) healthcare, (v) post-harvest storage infrastructure for agriculture and horticulture produce including cold storage, and (vi) tourism. However, to align with the PPP Monitor's definition of social infrastructure sector, only projects under the education and healthcare sectors are taken into consideration. The PPP database does not have any information on affordable housing nor on government building projects. Past PPP projects in the social infrastructure sector classified in terms of PPP variant or scheme, based on the DEA database, are shown in Table 51.

Table 51: Number of Social Infrastructure Projects Across Public–Private Partnership Variants

Public–Private Partnership Variant	No. of Projects
Build–operate–transfer	37
Build–own–operate–manage	2
Build–own–operate–transfer	2
Design–build–finance–operate–transfer	2
Design–build–operate–transfer	2
Design–build–own–operate–transfer	2
Lease	2
Management contract (O&M with rehabilitation/expansion)	1
Management contract (O&M)	1
Total	**51**

O&M = operation and maintenance.

Note: Data was last updated on 5 December 2019.

Source: Government of India, Ministry of Finance, Department of Economic Affairs. List of Infrastructure Projects (accessed 15 July 2023).

Table 52 indicates the number projects across various subsectors based on the DEA database.

Table 52: Number of Social Infrastructure Projects Based on Subsectors

Subsector	No. of Projects
Education	37
Healthcare	14
Total	**51**

Note: Data was last updated on 5 December 2019.
Source: Government of India, Ministry of Finance, Department of Economic Affairs.
List of Infrastructure Projects (accessed 15 July 2023).

Tariffs in the Social Infrastructure Sector

No centrally available data.

Typical Risk Allocation for Public–Private Partnership Projects in the Social Infrastructure Sector

The Ministry of Housing and Urban Affairs has released a list of typical generic PPP models in the affordable housing space (footnote 111). The risk allocation for the Government Land-Based Subsidized Housing Model is as follows:

Type of Risk	Private	Public	Shared	Comments
Land risk	✓			
Design risk	✓	✓		
Construction risk		✓		
Financing risk		✓		
Cost recovery risk	✓			
Offtake risk	✓	✓		
Trunk infrastructure risk	✓			

Financing Details for Public–Private Partnership Projects in the Social Infrastructure Sector

Parameter	1990–2020	1990–2021	1990–2022
PPP projects with foreign lending participation	NA	NA	NA
PPP projects that received export credit agency/international financing institution support	NA	NA	NA
Typical debt-to-equity ratio	NA		
Time for financial close	NA		
Typical concession period	NA		
Typical financial internal rate of return	NA		

NA = not applicable, PPP = public–private partnership.

5. Challenges in the Social Infrastructure Sector

Public Housing
The development of affordable housing presents several opportunities for improvement (footnote 111):

- The high cost of land is a key consideration. By ensuring more affordable land costs, value can be effectively transferred to the end users.
- Developers and builders often face challenges in financing land. Developing innovative financing solutions could greatly aid in the delivery of affordable housing. .
- The absence of well-defined titles can limit the involvement of financial institutions and real estate developers in new and redevelopment projects. By improving title clarity, land can be better utilized, potentially easing land shortages and reducing land prices .

Education
Some of the opportunities for growth and development in India's higher education sector are as follows:[111]

- The gross enrollment ratio of India in higher education is currently at 27.3%, which presents a significant opportunity to expand access to higher education.
- There is vast potential to improve the quality of education infrastructure facilities such as real estate, classrooms, libraries, hostels, furniture, sports facilities, transport, and commercial buildings. Private sector participation is critical for establishing colleges and in providing quality physical infrastructure.
- While faculty shortages have been a challenge, this opens opportunities to attract and retain well-qualified teachers, thereby enhancing the quality of education.
- The adoption of more rigorous quality standards in accreditation and branding activities can significantly elevate the reputation and credibility of India's higher education institutions.

---

[111]   Y. A. Sheikh. 2017. Higher Education in India: Challenges and Opportunities. *Journal of Education and Practice.* 8 (1). pp. 39–42.

I. Other Infrastructure—Municipal Solid Waste

1. Contracting Agencies in the Municipal Solid Waste Sector

The Ministry of Housing and Urban Affairs (MOHUA) is entrusted with the responsibility of broad policy formulation and monitoring of programs regarding urban housing and urban development. The MOHUA formulates the policies and strategies pertaining to various aspects of the water supply, sanitation, and solid waste management or municipal solid waste (MSW) sectors and provides technical and financial assistance to the states. The Central Public Health and Environmental Engineering Organisation is the MOHUA's technical wing. It deals with matters related to urban water supply and sanitation, including solid waste management.

Local governments and urban local bodies (ULBs) are the executing and contracting agencies for MSW projects and are responsible for solid waste management at the local level. The Government of India, through programs such as the Swachh Bharat Mission, provides financial support so that MSW programs and projects are implemented in an efficient and timely manner.

Besides the ULBs, states have specific responsibilities in solid waste management. These are summarized as follows:[112]

- The Secretary-in-Charge of the Urban Development Department (UDD) of the concerned state or union territory has the overall responsibility in implementing municipal solid waste management (MSWM) systems in cities and towns in line with MSW rules.
- The UDD is required to prepare a state policy and strategy for MSWM in the state.
- The UDD has to report to the Ministry of Urban Development on service-level benchmarks for MSW service provision in the ULBs.
- The UDD is also responsible for approval of land transfer from the state to the ULBs (for all projects).
- States have the power to regulate the creation of staff positions (technical and nontechnical) in the ULBs.
- The State Pollution Control Board is responsible for monitoring compliance with the MSWM plan and the MSW rules. It is also authorized to give environmental clearance to facilities listed in the Environmental Impact Assessment Notification, 2006.
- The power to authorize municipal authorities or operators to set up treatment and disposal facilities also lies with the State Pollution Control Board.

2. Municipal Solid Waste Sector Laws and Regulations

Sector Regulations

- The sector is mainly governed by the Solid Waste Management Rules, 2016 (notified in 2018). These rules, notified by the Ministry of Environment, Forests and Climate Change,

---

[112] Government of India, Ministry of Housing and Urban Affairs. 2016. *Municipal Solid Waste Management Manual.*

have replaced the Municipal Solid Wastes (Management and Handling) Rules, 2000, which had been in place for 16 years.
- The important regulations for the sector are provided in Table 53.

Table 53: Applicable Regulations for the Municipal Solid Waste Sector in India

Regulation	Description
Manual on MSWM, 2016	• Guidelines published by the MOHUA through the CPHEEO in 2016 for implementing all aspects of MSWM, including segregation, collection, transportation, treatment, and disposal.
Swachh Bharat Mission, 2014	• The SBM guidelines cover household toilets, community and public toilets, and solid waste management. Subsequently, SBM 2.0 was launched in 2021 to carry forward the progress from SBM 1.0 and go from ODF to ODF+ and ODF++ status. Cities and towns that are working toward ensuring sustainability of the ODF status to ensure proper maintenance of toilet facilities is called SBM ODF+. Safe collection, conveyance, treatment, and disposal of all fecal sludge and sewage is called SBM ODF++.
National Urban Sanitation Policy, 2008	• Broadly covers aspects of urban sanitation, with a specific focus on eliminating open defecation in cities and reorienting institutions for developing citywide approach to sanitation, covering all sanitation aspects including solid waste management.
Rules for special waste	• Plastic Waste Management Rules, 2011 (revised in 2016 and amended in 2022) • Bio-Medical Waste (Management and Handling) Rules, 1998 (amended in 2003 and 2011) and Bio-Medical Waste Management Rules, 2016 • E-Waste Management Rules, 2011 (revised in 2016) • Battery (Management and Handling) Rules, 2001
Other relevant rules and task force reports	• Interministerial Task Force on Integrated Plant and Nutrient Management Using City Compost, 2005 • Fertilizer Control Order, 2009; Phosphate Rich Organic Manure, 2013 by the Ministry of Agriculture • Report of the Task Force on Waste to Energy, Planning Commission, 2014
Other relevant acts	• Environment Protection Act, 1986 • Hazardous and Other Wastes (Management and Transboundary Movement Rules, 2016)—for the control of hazardous waste • Construction and Demolition Waste Management Rules, 2016—for waste generated from construction, remodeling, and repair and demolition of any civil structure

CPHEEO = Central Public Health and Environmental Engineering Organisation, MOHUA = Ministry of Housing and Urban Affairs, MSWM = municipal solid waste management, ODF = open defecation free, SBM = Swachh Bharat Mission.

Source: Government of India, Ministry of Housing and Urban Affairs. 2016. *Municipal Solid Waste Management Manual.*

Table 54 describes the roles of the key agencies responsible for the municipal solid waste sector.

Table 54: Key Entities Responsible for the Municipal Solid Waste Sector in India

Agency	Function (Indicative List)
Central Public Health and Environmental Engineering Organisation, Ministry of Housing and Urban Affairs	Assists the Ministry of Housing and Urban Affairs in urban water supply and sanitation, including solid waste management. It plays a vital role in processing schemes for external funding agencies, including the World Bank, Japan Bank for International Cooperation, Asian Development Bank, other bilateral and multilateral funding agencies, and institutional financing such as the Life Insurance Corporation of India.
Ministry of Environment, Forests and Climate Change	Involved in framing the rules for managing and handling solid waste under the following acts: (i) Environment (Protection) Act, (ii) Water (Prevention and Control of Pollution) Act, (iii) Air (Prevention and Control of Pollution) Act, and (iv) Central Pollution Control Board.
Ministry of New and Renewable Energy	The Ministry of New and Renewable Energy supports municipal solid-waste-based power generation projects.

Source: Asian Development Bank. 2019. *Public–Private Partnership Monitor.* Second Edition.

Standard Contracts and Licenses

Parameter	Availability
What standardized contracts are available and used in the market?	
• Public–private partnership/concession agreement?	✓
• Power purchase agreement?	✓
• Long-term waste supply contract?	✓
• Capacity take or pay contract?	✓
• Transmission and use of system agreement?	✓
• Performance-based operation and maintenance contract?	✓
• Engineering, procurement, and construction contract?	✓

✓ = Yes, ✗ = No, NA = Not Applicable, UA = Unavailable.
Source: Asian Development Bank. 2019. *Public–Private Partnership Monitor.* Second Edition.

Foreign Investment Restrictions

Parameter	2021	2022	2023
Maximum allowed foreign ownership of equity in greenfield projects	100%	100%	100%

Note: 100% foreign direct investment is allowed in urban infrastructure projects.

3. Municipal Solid Waste Sector Master Plan

Solid waste management is essentially a municipal function. Accordingly, the ULBs develop their MSWM systems and carefully access their requirements of tools, equipment, vehicles, and processing and disposal facilities in a way and at a pace that is locally doable, meets the long-term needs of the ULB, and is also financially sustainable. It is imperative to take stock of the situation and develop an MSWM plan. This plan should be in consonance with the MSW Rules, 2016, the state policy and strategy on MSWM, and the state sanitation strategy developed under the National Urban Sanitation Policy.

From a national perspective, the points below indicate the solid waste management sector's potential:[113]

*   India has the potential to generate approximately 3 GW of electricity from waste by 2050.
*   The government allows 100% FDI under the automatic route for urban infrastructure areas, including waste management, subject to relevant rules and regulations.
*   The central government has been implementing the Swachh Bharat Abhiyan, emphasizing waste management at different stages of generation, collection, and disposal.
*   The MSW sector in India is projected to see a capital expenditure and an O&M requirement of about $65 billion (₹4.75 trillion) by 2030.
*   India has the potential to generate approximately 90 million tons of waste per year by 2030–2032.
*   High population growth because of changing lifestyles will increase the waste volumes in India.

Projects Under Conceptualization and Development in the Municipal Solid Waste Sector

Figure 53 shows the number of public–private partnership (PPP) projects that are under conceptualization and development in the municipal solid waste sector of India.

Figure 53: Public–Private Partnership Municipal Solid Waste Projects Under Conceptualization and Development

Notes:
1. The hyphen symbol (-) means data are not available.
2. Projects under conceptualization and development have been extracted from the India Investment Grid website. The website serves as a repository of a list of projects under the National Infrastructure Pipeline (NIP), which is constantly updated and provides attractive investment opportunities in projects. The website also features the non-NIP which includes additional project opportunities collated by the India Infrastructure Grid.

Source: Government of India, Ministry of Commerce and Industry, Department for Promotion of Industry and Internal Trade, India Investment Grid. Projects under NIP and Non-NIP (accessed 15 July 2023).

---

[113] *PR Newswire, Research and Markets.* 2019. The Waste to Energy (WtE) and Waste Management Market in India, 2019–2025: High Population Growth and Changing Lifestyles to Increase Waste Volumes in India. 28 November.

4. Features of Past Public–Private Partnership Projects in the Municipal Solid Waste Sector

Figure 54 shows the number of PPP projects procured through various modes, including direct appointment and competitive bids, in the MSW sector of India.

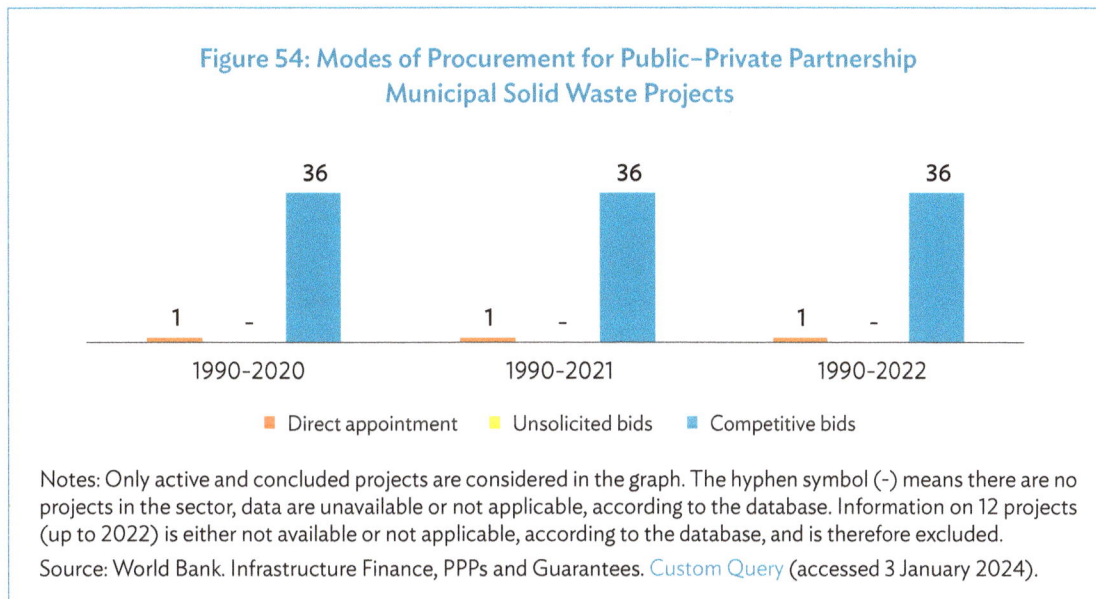

Figure 54: Modes of Procurement for Public–Private Partnership Municipal Solid Waste Projects

Notes: Only active and concluded projects are considered in the graph. The hyphen symbol (-) means there are no projects in the sector, data are unavailable or not applicable, according to the database. Information on 12 projects (up to 2022) is either not available or not applicable, according to the database, and is therefore excluded.

Source: World Bank. Infrastructure Finance, PPPs and Guarantees. Custom Query (accessed 3 January 2024).

Figure 55 shows the number of PPP projects that reached financial close and the total value of those projects in the MSW sector of India.

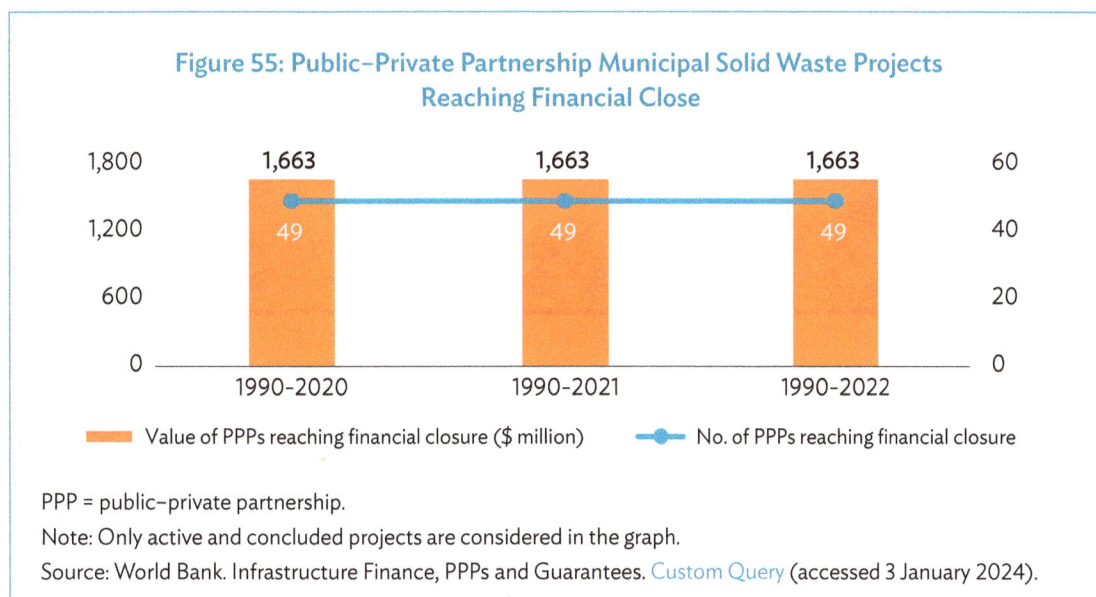

Figure 55: Public–Private Partnership Municipal Solid Waste Projects Reaching Financial Close

PPP = public–private partnership.

Note: Only active and concluded projects are considered in the graph.

Source: World Bank. Infrastructure Finance, PPPs and Guarantees. Custom Query (accessed 3 January 2024).

Figure 56 shows the number of PPP projects with foreign sponsor participation in the MSW sector of India.

Figure 56: Public–Private Partnership Municipal Solid Waste Projects with Foreign Sponsor Participation

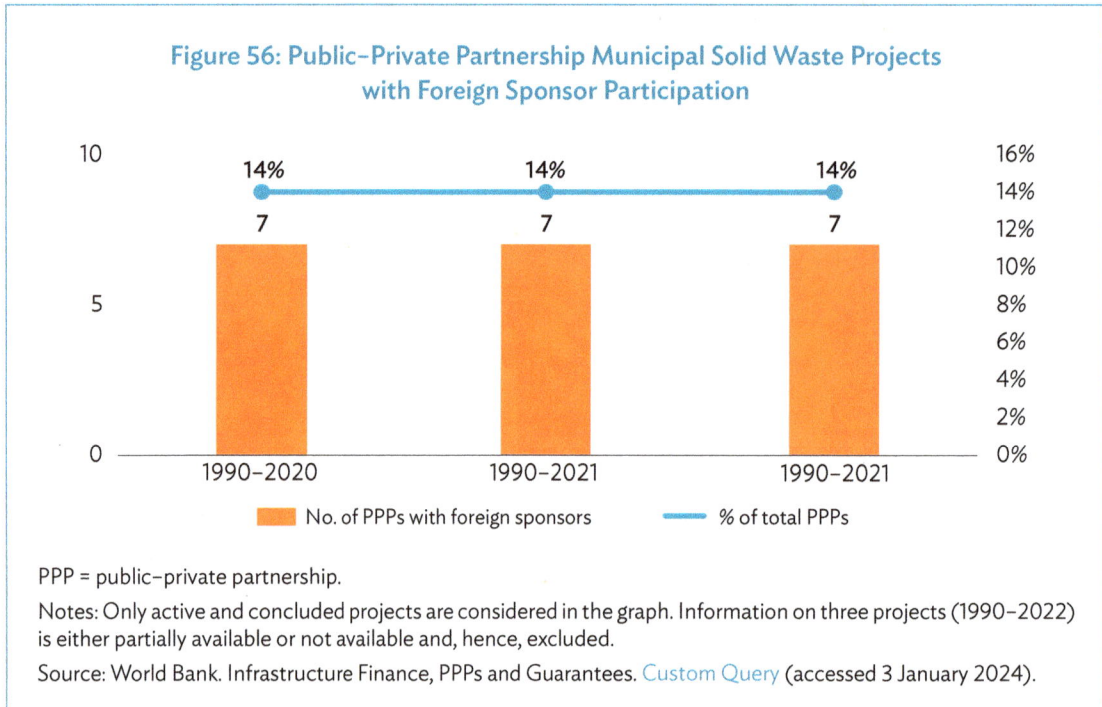

PPP = public–private partnership.

Notes: Only active and concluded projects are considered in the graph. Information on three projects (1990–2022) is either partially available or not available and, hence, excluded.

Source: World Bank. Infrastructure Finance, PPPs and Guarantees. Custom Query (accessed 3 January 2024).

The number of PPP projects that received government support, including viability gap funding, government guarantees, and availability or performance payment, in the MSW sector of India is shown in Figure 57.

Figure 57: Government Support to Public–Private Partnership Municipal Solid Waste Projects

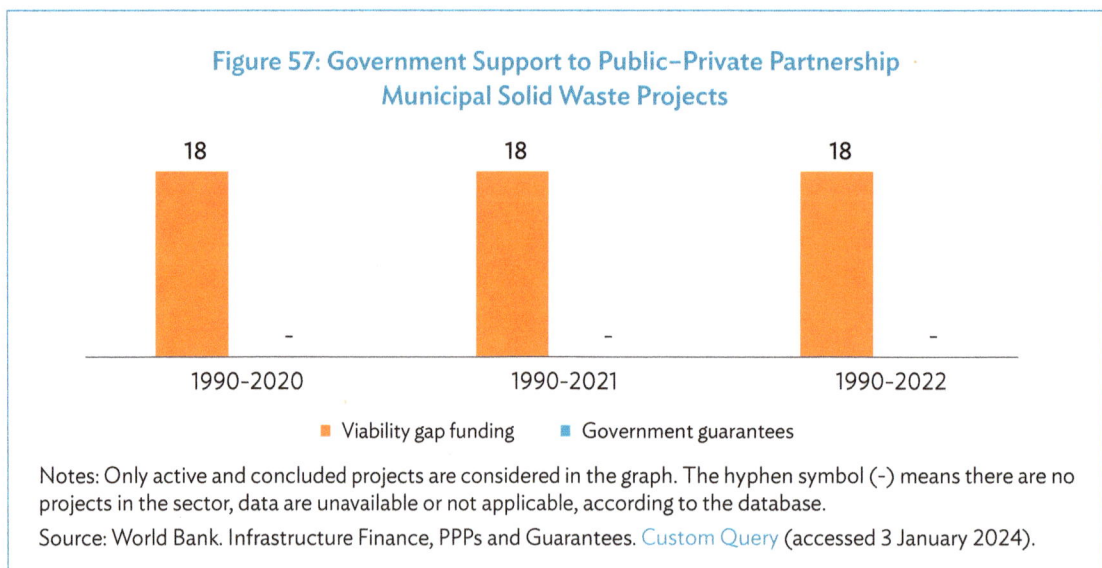

Notes: Only active and concluded projects are considered in the graph. The hyphen symbol (-) means there are no projects in the sector, data are unavailable or not applicable, according to the database.

Source: World Bank. Infrastructure Finance, PPPs and Guarantees. Custom Query (accessed 3 January 2024).

Figure 58 shows the number of PPP projects that received payment in the form of user charges and government pay (offtake) in the MSW sector of India.

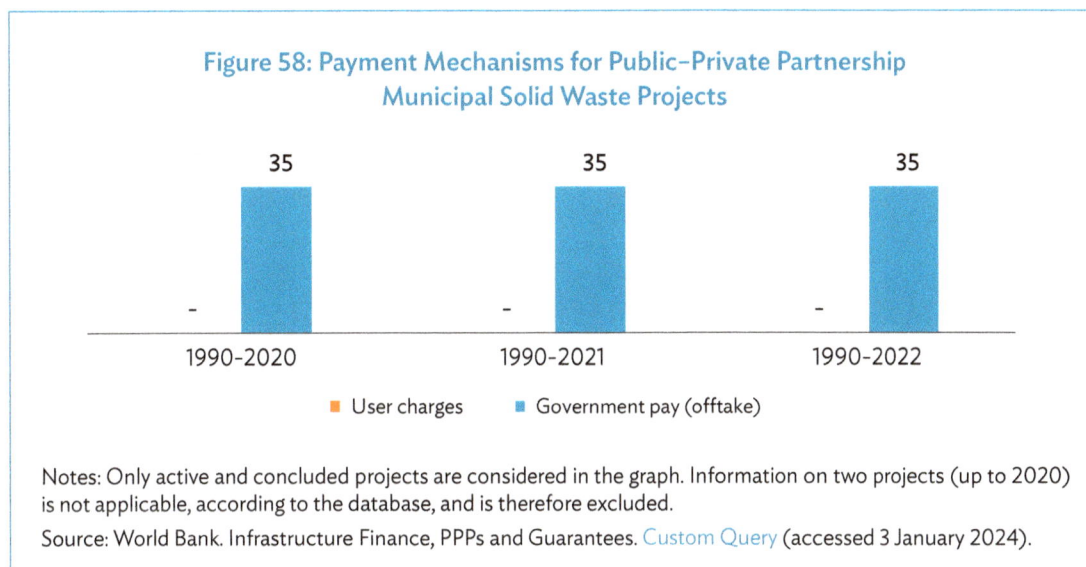

Figure 58: Payment Mechanisms for Public–Private Partnership Municipal Solid Waste Projects

	1990-2020	1990-2021	1990-2022
	35	35	35

■ User charges   ■ Government pay (offtake)

Notes: Only active and concluded projects are considered in the graph. Information on two projects (up to 2020) is not applicable, according to the database, and is therefore excluded.
Source: World Bank. Infrastructure Finance, PPPs and Guarantees. Custom Query (accessed 3 January 2024).

Past PPP projects in the municipal solid waste sector classified in terms of PPP variant or scheme, based on the DEA database, are shown in Table 55.

Table 55: Number of Municipal Solid Waste Projects Across Public–Private Partnership Variants

Public–Private Partnership Variant	No. of Projects
Build–operate–transfer	7
Build–operate–transfer (annuity)	2
Build–own–operate–transfer	23
Design–build–finance–operate	2
Design–build–finance–operate–transfer	10
Design–build–finance–operate–transfer (toll)	1
Design–build–operate–transfer	4
Design–build–own–operate–transfer	6
Not available	11
Service contract	4
Total	**70**

Note: Data was last updated on 5 December 2019.
Source: Government of India, Ministry of Finance, Department of Economic Affairs. List of all PPP Projects (accessed 15 July 2023).

Tariffs in Other Infrastructure Sectors (Solid Waste Management)

Data unavailable.

Typical Risk Allocation for Past Public–Private Partnership Projects in the Municipal Solid Waste Sector

Typical risk allocation arrangements in MSW PPP contracts for a build-own-operate-transfer project are given below.

Type of Risk	Public	Private	Shared
Delay in land acquisition	✓		
Financing risk		✓	
Approvals		✓	
Design risk		✓	
Construction risk		✓	
Operation and maintenance risk		✓	
Volume risk	✓		
Payment risk	✓		
Environmental, health, and safety risks		✓	
Change in law risk	✓		
Force majeure risk			✓

Sources: Asian Development Bank. 2019. *Public–Private Partnership Monitor.* Second Edition; and Government of India, Ministry of Finance, Department of Economic Affairs. Public Private Partnership in India (accessed 15 July 2023).

The MOHUA, under the Swachh Bharat Mission, prepared a tool kit for contracting agencies and practitioners. It includes a risk allocation framework across various models for engaging private sector partners (Table 56).

**Table 56: Risk Allocation Matrix for Variants of Public–Private Partnerships
in the Municipal Solid Waste Sector**

Type of Risk	Risk Allocation		
	Service Contract	Management Contract	BOT/Concession
Design risk	ULB and/or state agency	Private developer	Private developer
Construction risk	To be borne by both parties in accordance with the provision	To be borne by the private developer other than the asset transfer delay	
Operation risk	To be borne by the private developer other than the change in scope of the project by the ULB and/ or state agency		
Revenue risk	ULB and/or state agency	Partly by ULB and the private player in accordance with the provision of the contract	
Financial risk	ULB and/or state agency	Private developer	Private developer
Environmental risk	ULB and/or state agency	Private developer other than the preexisting environmental liability to be taken care by ULB and/or state agency	
Force majeure risk	Additional cost to rectify resulting in increased cost of operation, time overrun, nonachievement of service levels	To be borne by the parties in accordance with the provisions of the contract	
Insurance risk	Financial loss	To be borne by the private developer in accordance with the provisions of the contract	

BOT = build–operate–transfer, ULB = urban local body.
Source: Government of India, Ministry of Housing and Urban Affairs. *Toolkit for Public Private Partnership Frameworks in Municipal Solid Waste Management* (accessed 30 August 2020).

Financing Details for Public–Private Partnership Projects in the Municipal Solid Waste Sector

Parameter	1990–2021	1990–2022	1990–2023
PPP projects with foreign lending participation	UA	UA	UA
PPP projects that received export credit agency/ international financing institution support	UA	UA	UA
Typical debt-to-equity ratio	60:40		
Time for financial close	UA		
Typical concession period	15–30 years		
Typical financial internal rate of return	UA		

PPP = public–private partnership, UA = unavailable.
Source: World Bank. Infrastructure Finance, PPPs and Guarantees. Custom Query (accessed 3 January 2024).

5. Challenges in the Municipal Solid Waste Sector

The successful execution of MSW projects could be enhanced by addressing the following areas:

- ULBs could benefit from increased knowledge and institutional abilities in managing solid waste, including recycling, reuse, and energy recovery. This would enable them to formulate more effective plans for solid waste management.
- There is potential for growth in the capacity to conceive and structure projects with suitable risk allocation, and to manage private sector operators more effectively.
- Greater cooperation from citizens in supporting solid waste management, such as proper waste segregation (wet and dry, recyclable), could reduce operational costs for the operator and enhance the effective use of the collected waste.
- Providing sufficient land in suitable locations would make it easier for the private operator to execute the project, enhancing the overall efficiency of MSW projects.

IV. Local Government Public–Private Partnership Landscape

To better appreciate the local government public–private partnership (PPP) landscape in India, Table 57 provides an overview of the spending, income, and debt profiles of the subnational governments.

Table 57: Structure and Financial Profile of India's Subnational Governments

Parameter	Value	Unit
Number of Subnational Governments (SNGs)		
• Municipal level	283,963	number
• Intermediate level	0	number
• Regional or state level	36	number
Total number of SNGs	283,999	number
Total SNG expenditure as % of gross domestic product (GDP)		
Total SNG expenditure as % of GDP	14.8	%
• SNG current expenditure as % of GDP	12.7	%
• SNG staff expenditure as % of GDP	0.0	%
• SNG investment as % of GDP	2.1	%
Total SNG expenditure as % of the total general government expenditure (% of total public expenditure)	53.9	%
• SNG current expenditure as % of total current expenditure of the general government	0.0	%
• SNG staff expenditure as % of total staff expenditure of the general government	0.0	%
• SNG investment as % of total investment of the general government	56.8	%
Current expenditure of SNG as % of total SNG expenditure	86.1	%
Staff expenditure of SNG as % of total SNG expenditure	0.0	%
Investments of SNG as % of total SNG expenditure	13.9	%
SNG Expenditure by Function		
• General public services	29.7	%
• Defense	NA	%
• Security and public order	4.4	%
• Economic affairs	26.6	%
• Environmental protection	NA	%
• Housing and community amenities	3.9	%

continued on next page

Table 57 *continued*

Parameter	Value	Unit
• Health	6.0	%
• Recreation, culture, and religion	1.0	%
• Education	17.5	%
• Social protection	10.9	%
SNG Revenue Profile		
Total SNG revenue as % of GDP	13.0	%
• SNG tax revenue as % of GDP	10.1	%
• SNG grants and subsidies as % of GDP	2.0	%
• SNG other revenues as % of GDP	0.9	%
Total SNG revenue as % of total general government revenue	64.5	%
• SNG tax revenue as % of total general government tax revenue	56.6	%
• SNG grants and subsidies as % of total general government grants and subsidies	0.0	%
• SNG other revenues as % of total other revenues	0.0	%
SNG tax revenue as % of total SNG revenue	77.9	%
SNG grants and subsidies as % of total SNG revenue	15.3	%
SNG other revenues as % of total SNG revenue	6.7	%
SNG Debt Profile		
Outstanding SNG debt as % of GDP	21.5	%
Outstanding SNG debt as % of total outstanding debt of general government	32.5	%
Parameters for Transfers to the SNGs from the National Government		
Score on transfers to SNGs	B+	
• Score on system for allocating transfers	B	
• Score on timeliness of information on transfers	B	
• Score on extent of collection and reporting of consolidated fiscal data for general government	A	
Value of central government transfers to SNGs	UA	% of GDP
Value of actual budgetary allocation to SNGs from the national government	UA	% of total expenditure
Value of deviation of actual against the budgeted transfers to SNGs	UA	% of budgeted transfers

✓ = Yes, × = No, NA = Not Applicable, UA = Unavailable.

Notes: The Public Financial Management and Accountability Assessment report, developed by the World Bank and other development partners, comprises scoring of various indicators and rates them from A to D. Ratings of A to D are based on the criteria stated in the Public Expenditure and Financial Accountability framework and are broadly interpreted as follows:
A = represents performance that meets good international practice—the criteria for the indicator are met in a complete, orderly, accurate, timely, and coordinated way.
B = typically represents a level of performance ranging from good to medium by international standards.
C = represents a level of performance ranging from medium to poor.
D = represents either that a process or procedure does not exist at all, or that it is not functioning effectively.

Sources: Government of India. Local Government Directory; National Institute of Public Finance and Policy. 2010. *India Public Expenditure and Financial Accountability: Public Financial Management Performance Assessment Report*; Organisation for Economic Co-operation and Development, and United Cities and Local Governments. 2016. *Subnational Governments Around the World: Structure and Finance—Country Profiles.* OECD Publishing; and EPWRF India Time Series.

Local Governance System in India

Local self-government in India refers to government jurisdictions below the level of the state. India is a federal republic with three spheres of government: central (union), state, and local. The 73rd and 74th amendments to the Constitution of India gave recognition and protection to local governments, and each state (province) has its own local government legislation. The ministries for housing and urban affairs, Panchayati Raj, and rural development all have oversight responsibility for local government at the national level and each state has its own enabling legislation. Urban local bodies (ULBs) include municipal corporations for cities, municipalities for larger towns, and town *panchayats* for smaller towns. Both urban and local governments are governed by state-level legislation, which determines local tax-raising powers.[114] The structure of India's local government is presented in Figure 59.

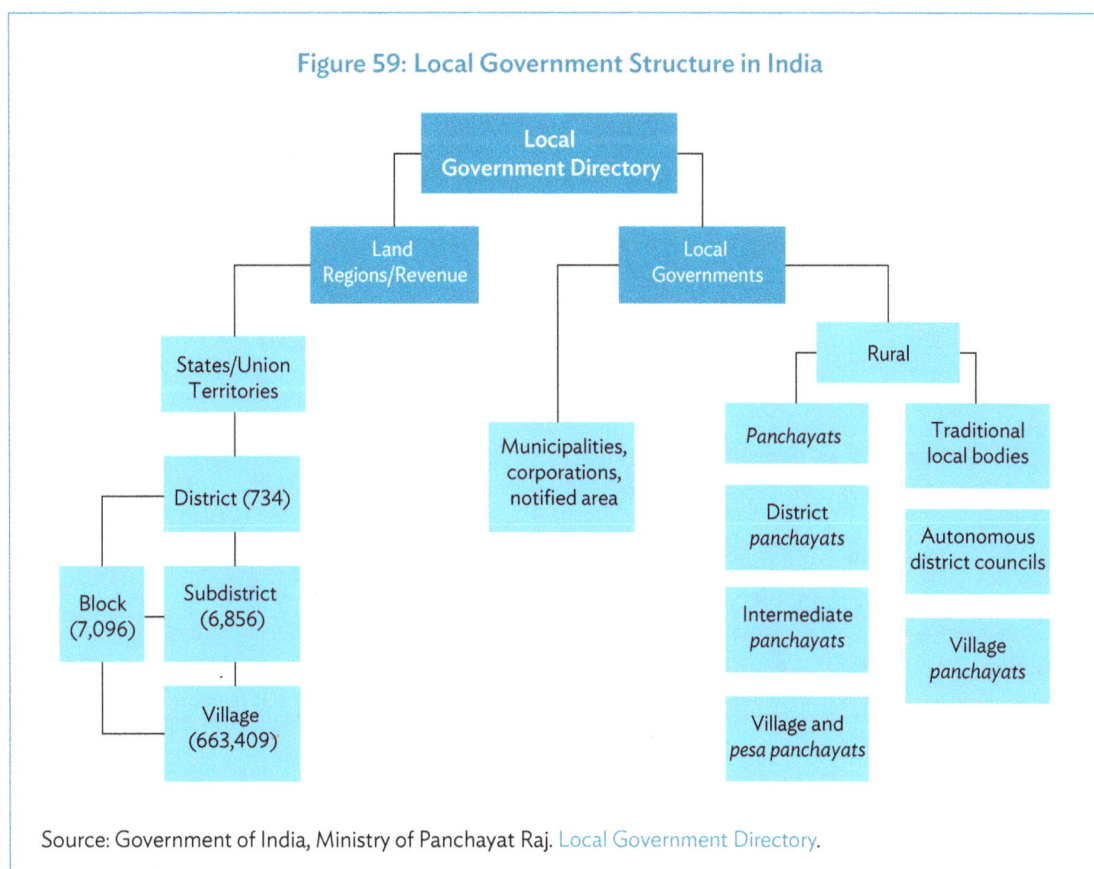

Figure 59: Local Government Structure in India

Source: Government of India, Ministry of Panchayat Raj. Local Government Directory.

---

114   Commonwealth Local Government Forum. 2019. *The Local Government System in India*. CLGF Regional Project Office.

In the case of rural areas, there are three nested bodies. At the apex is the district council or *zilla parishad*, which is made up of a cluster of block councils or *panchayat samitis*, which in turn, are made up of village councils or *gram panchayats*. Each village has a village assembly or *gram sabha* comprising all adults in the village, who have the power to directly elect members of the *panchayat*. States with a population of less than 2 million may also choose to have a two-tiered structure, without the intermediate block-level institution.[115]

In urban areas, there are three types of local bodies: (i) municipal corporations or *mahanagar palikas* for areas with a population of more than 1 million, (ii) municipal councils (municipalities) or *nagar palikas* for areas with less than one million people, and (iii) town councils or *nagar panchayats* for areas transitioning from rural to urban. For ease of administration, large municipal areas may be further subdivided into wards (footnote 115).

In line with their objectives of promoting local economic development and social justice, local government bodies have the power to prepare development plans for the areas they serve and implement a wide range of schemes relating to 29 core areas for rural local governments and 18 for ULBs. These include health, education, poverty alleviation, housing, and promotion of small-scale industries, among others.

However, since individual state governments are responsible for the functioning of their respective local governments (rather than the central government), the actual powers and functions of these institutions are highly dependent on the laws of the state in which they operate (footnote 115).

Infrastructure Development Plan of Local Governments

Municipal bodies are local self-governments whose mandate includes the provision of basic services such as healthcare, water supply, education, housing, transport, and waste management.

Various schemes have been announced by the central government to support the local governments in their investment plans for infrastructure development. These schemes aim to develop infrastructure in municipalities by investing in mobility, water supply, municipal waste management, and capacity development, among others. Some of the programs under the Ministry of Urban and Housing Affairs include the following:

- The Smart Cities Mission aims to transform 100 cities into smart cities over a short term (until June 2024).
- The Atal Mission for Rejuvenation and Urban Transformation (AMRUT) aims to provide basic services to households (e.g., water supply, sewerage, urban transport) and builds amenities in cities to improve the quality of life for all, especially for poor people and disadvantaged groups.
- The Swachh Bharat Mission aims to help efficiently manage municipal waste in the form of municipal collection, waste-to-energy, and waste-to-compost.

---

[115]   *India Development Review*. 2020. IDR Explains: Local Government in India. 28 January.

- The Jawaharlal Nehru National Urban Renewal Mission (JNNURM), launched in 2005, was implemented by the Ministry of Housing and Urban Poverty Alleviation. JNNURM has two components: (i) Basic Services for Urban Poor, and (ii) Integrated Housing and Slum Development Program (IHSDP). JNNURM aims to achieve integrated development of slums by providing shelter, basic services, and other related civic amenities, with a view to providing utilities to the urban poor. Under the Basic Services for Urban Poor component, the project cost is shared in the ratio of 50:50 for cities with a population of more than 1 million (based on Census 2001), 80:20 for other smaller mission cities, and 90:10 for the North Eastern and special category states. The full cost of construction of dwelling units and associated infrastructure was shared based on this sharing pattern without any limitation. Under the IHSDP, the project cost is shared in the ratio of 80:20 for the remaining smaller cities and 90:10 for the North Eastern and special category states. A cost ceiling of ₹100,000 per dwelling unit, including the cost of infrastructure, was applied to projects taken up under the IHSDP scheme.[116]
- The Capacity Building Scheme for Urban Local Bodies aims to identify the gaps in skilled labor across ULBs and undertake the necessary capacity-building programs to bridge those gaps.
- The Pradhan Mantri Awas Yojana aims at providing affordable housing to residents of the country, where interest subsidy is provided on housing loans availed by beneficiaries under a credit link subsidy scheme.

Sectors in Which Local Governments Can Implement Public–Private Partnership Projects

Local governments have the autonomy to induct private partners and undertake PPP projects across all the segments under their purview. There have been many local governments across the country that have taken up PPP projects across urban transportation, water supply, municipal solid waste management, housing, city parking facilities, and other general infrastructure.[117]

Revenues for Local Governments

The Constitution of India does not lay down the revenue base for municipalities. The power to determine their revenue base—be it the tax authority, tax base, tax rate setting, local tax autonomy, or even the grant-in-aid and other form of assistance—rests with the state government. Within this framework, state governments specify the taxes that municipalities can levy, which historically have comprised taxes on land and buildings; taxes on advertisements other than advertisements published in the newspapers; taxes on professions, trades, calling, and employment; and taxes on entertainment. In addition, there are charges, fees, and fines forming the nontax revenue base of municipalities. Transfers from the higher to lower tiers of government and revenue-sharing arrangements are perhaps the most important feature of public finance and have been instrumental in making local financial

[116] Indian Council for Research on International Economic Relations. 2019. *State of Municipal Finances in India: A Study Prepared for the Fifteenth Finance Commission.*
[117] Reserve Bank of India. 2022. *Report on Municipal Finances.*

adjustments. However, the states determine the choice of tax rates and exemption policy. An absence of autonomy in matters relating to tax rate setting is one of the key features of the functioning of municipal governments.[118]

With the introduction of the goods and services tax (GST) in 2017, this financial autonomy has been restricted. Several taxes have been subsumed under the GST. For example, in compliance with the new GST regime, the Municipal Corporation of Greater Mumbai has had to abolish octroi, which, on average, had contributed almost 35% of its annual total revenue. The Municipal Corporation of Greater Mumbai is one of the largest municipal corporations in India and is responsible for running Mumbai, the country's financial capital.[119]

Table 58 provides a snapshot of the revenues of the 4,259 ULBs in India based on the statistics published by the Indian Council for Research on International Economic Relations.

Table 58: Revenues of Urban Local Bodies in India

Revenue Item	FY2015–FY2016		FY2016–FY2017		FY2017–FY2018	
	₹ billion	$ billion	₹ billion	$ billion	₹ billion	$ billion
Total Tax Revenue	**411.69**	**5.02**	**434.44**	**5.30**	**429.54**	**5.24**
Tax revenue as % of total revenue	28.09%		26.82%		25.02%	
Property tax	201.66	2.46	216.60	2.64	255.52	3.12
Other tax	209.92	2.56	217.73	2.66	173.88	2.12
Total Nontax Revenue	**290.54**	**3.54**	**286.23**	**3.49**	**303.77**	**3.71**
Nontax revenue as % of total revenue	19.82%		17.67%		17.69%	
Total Central and State Transfers	**606.42**	**7.40**	**726.92**	**8.87**	**761.43**	**9.29**
Total transfers as % of total revenue	41.37%		44.88%		44.35%	
Central transfers	133.06	1.62	198.19	2.42	205.69	2.51
Central transfers: CFC grants	75.08	0.92	115.42	1.41	123.25	1.50
Other central transfers	57.98	0.71	82.77	1.01	82.45	1.00
State transfers	473.36	5.77	528.73	6.45	555.74	6.78
Market Borrowings	**41.79**	**0.51**	**44.21**	**0.54**	**37.94**	**0.46**

continued on next page

[118] O. P. Mathur. 2018. *The Financing of Urban Infrastructure Issues and Challenges*. Background note prepared for the Urban Development: Technological Solutions and Governance Challenges conference. 19–20 April.
[119] S. Mankikar. 2018. The Impact of GST on Municipal Finances in India: A Case Study of Mumbai. *ORF Issue Brief*. No. 257. Observer Research Foundation.

Table 58 *continued*

Revenue Item	FY2015–FY2016 ₹ billion	FY2015–FY2016 $ billion	FY2016–FY2017 ₹ billion	FY2016–FY2017 $ billion	FY2017–FY2018 ₹ billion	FY2017–FY2018 $ billion
Borrowings as % of total revenue	2.85%		2.73%		2.21%	
Other Sources of Finance	115.35	1.41	128.00	1.56	184.28	2.25
Other sources as % of total revenue	7.87%		7.90%		10.73%	
Total Revenues of Urban Local Bodies	1,465.79	17.88	1,619.79	19.76	1,716.97	20.94
Share of Total Municipal Revenue in GDP (%)	1.064		1.054		1.004	

CFC = Central Finance Commission, FY = fiscal year, GDP = gross domestic product.

Note: Numbers may not sum precisely because of rounding.

Source: Indian Council for Research on International Economic Relations. 2019. *State of Municipal Finances in India: A Study Prepared for the Fifteenth Finance Commission.*

The summary of expenditures of ULBs is presented in Table 59.

Table 59: Expenditures of Urban Local Bodies in India

Expenditure Item	FY2015–FY2016 ₹ billion	FY2015–FY2016 $ billion	FY2016–FY2017 ₹ billion	FY2016–FY2017 $ billion	FY2017–FY2018 ₹ billion	FY2017–FY2018 $ billion
Revenue Expenditure	669.24	8.16	745.47	9.09	781.96	9.54
Revenue expenditure as % of total expenditure	56.27%		60.12%		58.99%	
Capital Expenditure	520.13	6.34	494.60	6.03	543.57	6.63
Capital expenditure as % of total expenditure	43.73%		39.88%		41.01%	
Total Municipal Expenditure	1,189.38	14.51	1,240.07	15.13	1,325.53	16.17
Share of Total Municipal Expenditure in GDP (%)	0.864		0.807		0.775	

FY = fiscal year, GDP = gross domestic product.

Note: Numbers may not sum precisely because of rounding.

Source: Indian Council for Research on International Economic Relations. 2019. *State of Municipal Finances in India: A Study Prepared for the Fifteenth Finance Commission.*

Borrowings by Local Governments

Municipalities have several options for financing urban infrastructure facilities, which—besides own taxes, user charges, and grants-in-aid—include borrowings from the banks and financial intermediaries and mobilization of funds from the capital market. Yet, lending for urban infrastructure in India has been limited. While commercial banks' lending for infrastructure has risen, they have not considered urban infrastructure as one of their priority sectors. Even nonbanking companies, like nonbanking financial companies, barely lend for core urban infrastructure such as water, sanitation, and drainage (footnote 123).

Municipal Bonds

Although India's municipal financing has been dominated by budgetary outlays, cities have tapped into the capital markets through one-off bond issuances since as early as 1997, when the Bangalore Municipal Corporation issued a municipal bond of ₹1.25 billion with a state guarantee. The first nonguaranteed municipal bond was issued by Ahmedabad Municipal Corporation in 1998. Since then, there have been 29 municipal bond issuances in India, raising about ₹23.83 billion cumulatively since the issuance of the first bonds. However, issuances had dropped sharply after 2005, and 82% of the value of issuances were from ULBs and the rest through the pooled-finance mechanism in Tamil Nadu and Karnataka.

In 2015, a separate regulatory framework for municipal bond financing was put in place by the Securities and Exchange Board of India. The higher share of financing to be secured by the ULBs for projects under Smart Cities Mission and AMRUT is also expected to provide impetus, at least among the small pool of better-rated ULBs.

Following the issuance of a ₹2 billion bond by the Pune Municipal Corporation 2020, civic bodies of Indore and Hyderabad have raised issued bonds. The bond issues were supported by an escrow of own funds and assigned revenue including octroi grants, property tax, and water and sanitation charges. Some examples of issues of municipal bonds are presented in Table 60.

Table 60: Select Case of Municipal Bond Issues in India

Issuer (Year)	Pune Municipal Corporation (2016)	Indore Municipal Corporation (2018)	Greater Hyderabad Municipal Corporation (2018, in 2 tranches)	Vadodara Municipal Corporation (2022)
Loan size (₹ billion)	2.00	1.40	3.95 (2.00 in February and 1.95 in August)	1.00
Coupon	7.59%	9.25%	8.90% and 9.38%	7.15%
Tenor	10 years	10 years (call/put option in 7 years)	10 years	5 years

continued on next page

Table 60 *continued*

Issuer (Year)	Pune Municipal Corporation (2016)	Indore Municipal Corporation (2018)	Greater Hyderabad Municipal Corporation (2018, in 2 tranches)	Vadodara Municipal Corporation (2022)
Credit rating	AA+(SO) by India Ratings and CARE Ratings	AA (SO) by Brickwork and SMERA	AA by CARE Ratings and India Ratings	AA/Stable by CRISIL
Guarantee	No	No	No	No
Structured payments	Escrow of property tax, debt service reserve account, and sinking fund account	Escrow of property tax, debt service reserve account, and sinking fund account	Escrow and debt servicing	Trustee-administered escrow and payment, debt service reserve account
Issue of proceeds	24/7 water supply scheme	AMRUT	Strategic road development plan	AMRUT

AMRUT = Atal Mission for Rejuvenation and Urban Transformation, SMERA = SME Rating Agency of India.

Sources: CARE Ratings. 2017. *Pune Municipal Corporation Bond Rating*; CRISIL Ratings. 2022. *Rating Rationale for Vadodara Municipal Corporation*; Greater Hyderabad Municipal Corporation. *Budget 2021-22*; and Indore Municipal Corporation. 2022. *Draft Offer Document*.

Cities are incentivized to improve their creditworthiness for raising funds from municipal bonds through property tax governance and ring-fencing user charges on urban infrastructure.

Budgetary Allocation to Local Governments

Historically, India's municipalities have faced challenges in their fiscal capacity, often relying on state contributions to finance their budgets. As part of the devolution process through the 73rd and 74th Constitutional Amendments (indicated in the section on Local Governance System in India), state finance commissions were set up to formulate principles for disbursing adequate finances from the state to local governments. In addition to their own revenue handles, these ULBs were to be empowered through grants from the central government and respective state governments (which may or may not be tied) as well as transfers formulated by the Finance Commission. However, an important feature of transfers to municipalities in India is its discretionary nature. Unlike the constitutional provision that lays down the revenue-sharing arrangement between the central government and states, there exists no statutory provision in state municipal laws that define the conditions under which transfers should take place from the states to municipalities. Since local governments are a state subject, and spending responsibilities and taxation powers are determined by state governments, it is assumed that the state governments have the obligation of bridging the gap between what the municipalities are able to raise by way of taxes, charges, and levies, and what they need to implement given their spending responsibilities, with the provision that such a gap is worked out on normative considerations and not attributable to inefficiencies and fiscal profligacy.[120]

---

[120]   National Institute of Public Finance and Policy. 2010. *India Public Expenditure and Financial Accountability: Public Financial Management Performance Assessment Report.*

Credit Rating of Local Governments

Credit ratings for municipal bond issues have been in practice since 1998, focusing on evaluating a specific bond issue. Cities are also rated to raise bonds and have become eligible for various schemes announced by the central government.

The central government has also encouraged the credit rating of cities under the AMRUT reform agenda, which includes 11 reforms comprising 54 milestones. Credit rating for cities is one of them. As of December 2022, to make cities creditworthy, credit rating work has been completed in 470 cities. A total of 164 cities have received Investible Grade Rating (IGR).[121]

Case Study 1: City Bus Service on Public–Private Partnership—Surat, Gujarat

1. Background

Surat is one of the fastest growing cities in Asia, with its population having gone up from about 1.5 million in 1991 to 2.48 million in 2001, and to an estimated 3.5 million in 2007. This population explosion, combined with rapid economic development, has resulted in very high levels of vehicle ownership. The total vehicles registered with the Regional Transport Office in Surat went up from 761,000 in 2001 to 1.33 million in 2007, with almost 80% of these being two-wheelers. A study conducted by the Central Road Research Institute in 2004 reveals that, of the daily passenger vehicular trips in Surat, more than 40% were on two-wheelers, 20% by cycle, and 16% by auto rickshaw. This has contributed to traffic congestion and air pollution. Several measures have been undertaken to deal with these issues, such as expansion of road networks, construction of flyovers, traffic islands and road dividers, and conversion of all auto rickshaws to compressed natural gas fuel. However, the situation clearly indicates the dire and urgent need for a public transport system in Surat. Hence, the Surat Municipal Corporation (SMC) decided to implement a bus-based city transport system.[122]

2. Physical Infrastructure

The city of Surat had negligible public transportation system run by the State Transport Corporation, with 15 buses on city routes until 2006. Looking into the problems faced by the conventional models of operating such services, it was considered appropriate to adopt a PPP approach to creating a city public transport system in Surat. Accordingly, the SMC obtained the approval of the state government of Gujarat and has started operation of city bus services through private agencies in Surat since

---

[121]   Government of India, Ministry of Housing and Urban Affairs, Press Information Bureau. 2022. Status of AMRUT. Press release. 8 December.
[122]   Government of India, Ministry of Urban Development; Confederation of Indian Industry; and Ernst & Young Pvt. Ltd. 2008. *Compendium on Public Private Partnership in Urban Infrastructure—Case Studies*.

August 2007. Within a year, 102 buses have been deployed, carrying more than 45,000 passenger trips every day on 42 identified routes in the city. By the end of 2008, the number of buses was expected to reach 200.

3. Description of Public–Private Partnership Model

The key features of the project are as follows:

- The SMC obtained a statutory approval from the Transport Department of the state government of Gujarat to run the city bus service through private participation.
- In selecting the operators, the SMC adopted a transparent methodology by inviting tenders. Three operators were selected for running the city bus service.
- The selected operators make the entire capital investment with respect to purchase of buses, development of infrastructure, and operations (compressed natural gas fuel, drivers, maintenance, and control).
- The SMC has allotted two plots at token rent to the concessionaires for setting up workshop and fuel stations and four check post cabins as depots.
- The service parameters such as bus specifications, bus fares, and routes and frequencies of bus trips are decided by the SMC with the approval of the Regional Transport Authority.
- Service levels are being monitored jointly by private operators and the SMC. A system of weekly review by the SMC's Traffic Department has been put in place.
- The SMC will be paid a fixed annual premium of ₹10,500 per bus by operators for 200 buses for 5 years. The bus operators have been awarded the right to display advertisements on the buses.
- The pickup stands are being set up by the SMC on build–operate–transfer (BOT) basis or at its own cost. Private investment of about ₹95 million for the construction of 267 bus stands on BOT basis with advertisement rights is being sought, against which the SMC can expect to receive a fee revenue of up to ₹7.5 million as a premium per year from the successful bidders.
- All stakeholders like operators, traffic police, citizens, and nongovernment organizations are involved in the decision-making process.
- Innovative features such as daily passes, student passes, and free travel for freedom fighters, and announcements on bus and bus stations have also been introduced.

4. Risk-Sharing Matrix

Risk Category	Private	Public	Shared
Financing	✓		
Traffic	✓		
Revenue	✓		
Operation and maintenance	✓		
Approvals		✓	

5. Project Finance

Information on the project's financing mode is unavailable.

6. Project Construction

The project involves construction of pick-up point infrastructure, shelters for passengers, and procurement of buses.

7. Project Revenues

The above model for bus operations is called the net cost model, wherein the operator provides a specified service for a specified period and retains all the revenue. In lieu of this, the operator pays the authority a royalty per bus per month. Under a net-cost contract, the operator must forecast the cost incurred, the revenue, and the risk over the entire concession period. The contracting authority earns revenues by way of royalty from the buses and additional fee revenue from advertising rights provided to the PPP operator.

8. Further Developments in the Project—Post Award

The sole operator, who was awarded the concession in 2007, introduced more than 120 buses in various city routes. However, because of the issues between the SMC and the concessionaire, and associated inefficiencies, the concessionaire terminated the contract and its services in the city in 2013. Some of the key reasons for ending the contract included the following:[123]

- The concessionaire was unable to pass on the increase in fuel prices, leading to losses.
- Owing to losses, the number of buses decreased and maintenance deteriorated, leading to poor services—both in number and quality of services.
- Only 20 buses were operating at the end of the contract, which affected at least 80,000 commuters.
- Passenger experience was negatively impacted.

Owing to a high economic growth in the city, the SMC took over the responsibility of providing the services. The SMC issued tenders for 575 city buses and planned to increase services to 1,000 buses.

The city has subsequently implemented the Intelligent Transit Management System (ITMS). The ITMS has a cost outlay of about ₹489 million ($6.7 million), which is being financed entirely from the Smart Cities Mission funds by the central government.[124] The Command and Control Centre was developed under the project, along with a data center, and four bus depots have started utilizing the depot

---

[123]   M. Parikh. 2019. A Study of Failure and Rise of Surat City Bus and Its Impact on Surat Residents. *International Journal of Science and Research.* 8 (9). pp. 1557–1560.

[124]   Government of India,Ministry of Urban Development. 2017. *Intelligent Transit Management System (ITMS)—Surat. In India Smart Cities: Success Stories from Mission Cities.* pp. 42–44.

management system. After completion, the project covered 30 operational routes for bus services in the city. A total of 115 bus rapid transit system (BRTS) buses and 200 city buses are being tracked using the ITMS. A ridership of 85,000 per day for BRTS and 45,000 per day for other city bus services has been recorded. A total of 154 BRTS stations and more than 400 city bus stops have been integrated with the ITMS. While in November 2016, the initiative got only 3,000 riders per day, by August 2017, it increased to about 65,000 riders, which is more than a 20-fold increase in ridership.

A combination of savvy pricing and smart technology shows that the service launched less than a year ago by the municipal body has succeeded in attracting 93% passengers, many of whom were earlier using auto-rickshaws and two-wheelers. In 2018, the SMC was chosen for the Best City Bus Services Award by the central government at an urban mobility conference, and this award has led to many economic benefits. The operation and maintenance (O&M) of the ITMS is planned through PPP.

9. Key Learnings—Success Factors

Some of the factors that assisted in the smooth introduction of this innovative model for the first concession are the capability of the contracting agency, significant stakeholder involvement, and infrastructure readiness:

- Capability of the contracting agency
  - > vision and professionalism in selecting a financially prudent and sustainable model;
  - > past experience of the SMC in PPP-based services, such as construction of bus stands, and pay-and-use toilets; and
  - > selection of concessionaires after proper scrutiny of economic and technical aspects.
- Significant stakeholder involvement
  - > complete confidence of the elected wing in the administrative wing of the SMC with respect to operational matters—no interference in operational matters (such as selection of routes) by the political wing;
  - > full cooperation of the city traffic police in making the city bus service a success (e.g., training of drivers, traffic flow);
  - > cooperation of the Regional Transport Authority (district collector), which provided prompt approvals for stage carriage permits;
  - > free and frequent communication between the SMC and the concessionaire; and
  - > enthusiastic response of the citizens of Surat
- Infrastructure readiness
  - > wide roads on the city's major routes; and
  - > a mix of 18-seater and 36-seater buses to cater to inner-city areas with narrow roads

The following are some of the key lessons that could benefit subsequent projects:

- There is a need to manage uninformed opposition from auto-rickshaw associations with a firm hand and by assuaging their fears of being driven out.
- No-parking and no-hawking zones should be created near bus stops to allow easy access to bus stops.
- Constant supervision and traffic training for drivers are needed.

10. Key Learnings—Reinventing the Model

- The original contractor suffered losses because the SMC could not play a timely partnership role, causing the concessionaire to increase fares. Operational losses led to poor services, which in turn led to poor ridership, resulting in the undesirable end of contract and loss of service to end users.
- However, the municipal corporation became proactive in reinventing its role by actively participating in the Smart Mission Program and availing funds to develop intelligent transport systems, integrating them with city buses and BRTS services and offering a seamless experience to the commuters.
- The SMC is planning to bring in a PPP operator for O&M and contract management to continue the provision of efficient services.
- The partnership plays a critical role in the project's success. Corporations should keep in mind the importance of providing quality service to the public as the primary objective of any contract and allowing flexibility in the contracts in such a way that it leads to a win-win partnership.

Case Study 2: National Mission for Clean Ganga —Construction of Sewage Treatment Plants in Mathura Using a Hybrid Annuity Model

1. Background

In the state of Uttar Pradesh, the city of Mathura stands as an integral player in an ambitious mission to rejuvenate the Ganga River. Recognizing the extensive social and economic advantages of a cleaner Ganga for the 500 million inhabitants along its basin, the Government of India approved the Namami Gange or the National Mission for Clean Ganga (NMCG) in May 2015.[125] In January 2016, a hybrid annuity model (HAM) was introduced to facilitate the implementation of sewage treatment plant (STP) projects under the NMCG through PPP.

Simultaneously, the Ministry of Water Resources issued the River Ganga (Rejuvenation, Protection, and Management) Authorities Order, 2016 (Ganga 2016 Order),[126] establishing various authorities to support pollution control in the Ganga. The Ganga 2016 Order extended its jurisdiction to include all states within the Ganga basin, including Uttar Pradesh. Under this mandate, the NMCG transformed into an authority designated by the Environment (Protection) Act, 1996, responsible for implementing the Ganga 2016 Order.[127]

[125] National Mission for Clean Ganga.
[126] Government of India, Press Information Bureau. 2016. Cabinet Approves the River Ganga (Rejuvenation, Protection and Management) Authorities Order, 2016. Print release. 21 September.
[127] NMCG. Development of 50 MLD Sewage Treatment Plant at Varanasi under Hybrid Annuity Based PPP Mode.

Challenges facing the Ganga include the adverse effects of population growth, improved standards of living, urbanization, and industrialization on water quality. In some stretches, the river is unfit for bathing during lean seasons. Factors such as global climate change, glacier melt, and upstream infrastructure projects demand a comprehensive response.

Within the Ganga basin, about 12,000 million liters per day (MLD) of sewage is generated, against a treatment capacity of only about 4,000 MLD. About 3,000 MLD of sewage is discharged into the main stream of the Ganga River from the Class I and Class II towns located along the banks, while a treatment capacity of about 1,000 MLD has been established to date. To address this, the Uttar Pradesh Jal Nigam (Jal Nigam), empowered by the Uttar Pradesh Water Supply and Sewerage Act, 1975, collaborates with the NMCG to develop STPs and treatment technology package projects in Mathura. These projects, using a PPP HAM, aim to bridge the sewerage treatment gap. Jal Nigam oversees the execution and bidding, while the NMCG manages payment disbursement. The NMCG and Jal Nigam seek to

- intercept raw sewage flowing into the Yamuna River and divert the raw sewage to the Mathura STPs;
- treat the raw sewage at the Mathura STPs;
- treat the STP effluent for usage at the Indian Oil Corporation Limited premises;
- implement viable technologies and international best practices for development, operation, and maintenance of the Mathura STPs, treatment technology packages, and other facilities; and demonstrate large-scale private sector participation and mobilize private sector investment to further the national aim of rejuvenating the Ganga River and its tributaries.

The components of the Mathura project include construction, operation, and maintenance of a 30 MLD STP in Masani, the work for which has been awarded to the Triveni Engineering & Industries Limited and costs about ₹4,379.5 million ($53.42 million) under HAM mode.

2. Description of Hybrid Annuity-Based Public–Private Partnership Model and Financing Mode

Figure 60 presents a schematic illustration of the HAM-based PPP model and financing for the STP construction in Mathura.

Figure 60: Hybrid Annuity Model Public–Private Partnership and Financing Mode for the Construction of Sewage Treatment Plant in Mathura

CONSTRUCTION PERIOD (2 YEARS)	OPERATION AND MAINTENANCE PERIOD (15 YEARS)

GOVERNMENT/ AUTHORITY

40% of CAPEX

Inclusive of Mobilization Advance

60% of CAPEX paid back in the form of equal annuity payments + O&M payments as bid by the developer

Interest on the 60% CAPEX also paid to the developer (SBI MCLR + 3% or as per Project Agreement)

Assets transferred to the Government at the end of the Concession Period

HYBRID ANNUITY

PRIVATE DEVELOPER

SPV/ CONCESSIONAIRE

60% of CAPEX

Design, Construct, Finance

O&M for the period as per Project Agreement 15 years

Annuity and O&M Payments received from Government

CAPEX = capital expenditure, O&M = operation and maintenance, SBI MCLR = State Bank of India Marginal Cost of Fund Based Lending Rate, SPV = special purpose vehicle.

Source: Author's analysis.

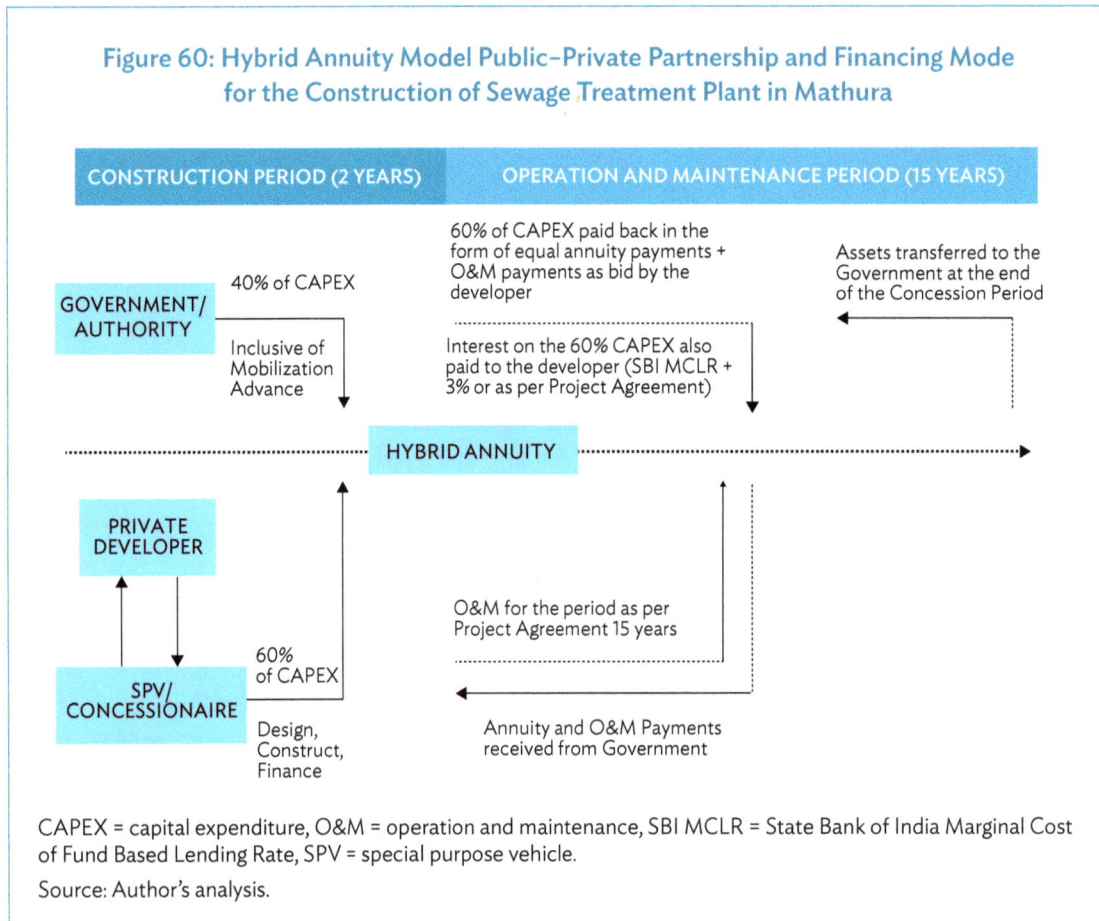

The key features of the concession structure are summarized in Table 61.

Table 61: Salient Features of the Concession Structure

Feature	Description
Performance-based contract	• 100% availability of the facilities • Quality of treated effluent (biochemical oxygen demand, chemical oxygen demand, total suspended solids, etc.) • Quality of digested sludge • Continuous online monitoring • Liquidated damages for nonavailability and noncompliance to discharge standards for treated water and digested sludge
Technological flexibility	• Offers the concessionaire considerable technology flexibility to encourage adoption of the most cost-effective and efficient solution for the sewage treatment plant

continued on next page

Table 61 *continued*

Feature	Description
Payment security	• Escrow mechanism: a minimum escrow balance of two capital expenditure milestones and 2 years of operation and maintenance (O&M) payments
Lock-in restrictions	• Each member's technical and financial capacity was evaluated for qualification, to hold a minimum 26% of the total capital and voting rights until 3 years into the O&M period. • After 3 years, members' O&M experience is used for qualification to stay or to be replaced with an equally qualified member or contractor.

Source: Government of National Capital Territory of Delhi. 2018. *Concession Agreement: Mathura STP Project.*

The risk-sharing matrix is as follows.[128]

Risk Category	Private	Public	Shared
Financing			✓
Operation and maintenance	✓		
Approvals		✓	

3. Project Finance

The government must make annuity and O&M payment to the concessionaire.

4. Project Status

Milestone dates of the construction of STPs in Mathura are listed in Table 62.

Table 62: Construction of Sewage Treatment Plants in Mathura —Project Status Based on June 2023 Monthly Progress Report

Milestone	Date
Commencement date	15 January 2019
Completion date (according to contract)	14 January 2021
Actual completion date of the Masani Zone	31 October 2021
Actual completion date of the Trans Yamuna Zone	30 November 2021
COD of the Masani Zone	25 March 2022
O&M commencement date for the Masani Zone	25 March 2022

continued on next page

---

[128] Examrace. What is HAM, BOT? What is HAM, BOT? India's First Sewage Treatment Plant under Hybrid Annuity (HAM).

Table 62 *continued*

Milestone	Date
O&M completion date for the Masani Zone	24 March 2037
Partial COD (up to STPs) for the Trans Yamuna Zone	11 July 2022
O&M commencement date for the Trans Yamuna Zone (up to STPs)	11 July 2022
O&M completion date for the Trans Yamuna Zone (up to STPs)	10 July 2037
COD (TTP) for the Trans Yamuna Zone	21 October 2022
O&M commencement date for the Trans Yamuna Zone (for TTP)	21 October 2022
O&M completion date for the Trans Yamuna Zone (for TTP)	20 October 2037

COD = commercial operation date, O&M = operation and maintenance, STP = sewage treatment plant, TTP = treatment technology package.

Source: Mathura STP Project. June 2023 Monthly Progress Report.

5. Key Learnings and Future Opportunities

- Promote and establish practices like reusing treated water, sludge, and other by-products.
- Mandate biogas power generation for larger plants.
- Initiate the incorporation of solar power generation.
- Demonstrate instances of contractual wastewater reuse.
- Provide incentives, like selling treated wastewater and sludge, to private entities (optional).
- Emphasize the feasibility and offtake assessment during project preparation for added momentum.
- Ensure guaranteed offtake to enhance project viability.
- Strengthen institutional and policy-level involvement to solidify implementation.

Appendixes

Appendix 1: Critical Macroeconomic and Infrastructure Sector Indicators for India

The following table presents the various macroeconomic and infrastructure sector indicators for India.

Parameter	Value	Unit
Total population (2023 forecast)	1,429	million
Average annual population growth rate over the past 5 years (2018–2023 estimates)	0.9	%
Population density (2023 forecast)	481	persons per km^2 of surface area
Urban population (2023 forecast)	36.0	% of total population
Surface area	3,287.26	'000 km^2
Unemployment rate (July 2023)	7.9	%
Proportion of population below $2.15 purchasing power parity a day	10.0	%
Nominal GDP (2022)	3,585	$ billion
Annual growth rate of GDP (2022)	6.8	%
Annual growth rate of GDP (2023 forecast)	6.4	%
Annual growth rate of GDP (2024 forecast)	6.7	%
GDP at purchasing power parity per capita (2022)	8,379.1	$
GDP at current market prices (2022)	3,385.0	$ billion
Gross fixed investment at current market prices (2022)	29.0	% of GDP
Per capita GNI, Atlas Method (2022)	2,380	$
Current account (2022)	2.9	% of GDP
External trade, goods, value of imports, CIF (2020)	367.98	$ billion
External trade, goods, value of exports, FOB (2020)	275.49	$ billion

continued on next page

Table *continued*

Parameter	Value	Unit
CPI % change	7.9	% of CPI in 2022
Real effective exchange rate (July 2023)	115.9	2005=100 (index)
Investment in energy with private sector participation (2022)	1,621.24	current $ million
Investment in transport with private sector participation (2022)	6,469.84	current $ million
Investment in water and sanitation with private sector participation (2022)	583.3	current $ million
Logistics Performance Index rank	38	number
Logistics Performance Index score	3.40	number
Customs rank	47	number
Customs score	3.00	number
Infrastructure rank	47	number
Infrastructure score	3.00	number
International shipments rank	22	number
International shipments score	3.50	number
Logistics competence rank	38	number
Logistics competence score	3.50	number
Tracking and tracing rank	41	number
Tracking and tracing score	3.40	number
Timeliness rank	35	number
Timeliness score	3.60	number
Net foreign direct investment inflows (2022)	1.5	% of GDP
Sovereign debt risk rating	BBB –	letter rating
Central government debt (2022)	55.1	% of GDP
CPIA quality of budgetary and financial management rating (2013)	3.5	1 (low) – 6 (high)
Structure of Output (% of GDP at current producer | basic prices)		
Agriculture	18.4	%
Industry	28.3	%
Services	53.3	%
CPI (national) (2021–2022)	6.7	% annual change
Wholesale price index (2022, base 2010 = 100)	6.7	% annual change

continued on next page

Table *continued*

Parameter	Value	Unit
Ease of Doing Business		
Ease of doing business	63	number
Starting a business	136	number
Dealing with construction permits	27	number
Getting electricity	22	number
Registering property	154	number
Getting credit	25	number
Protecting minority investors	13	number
Paying taxes	115	number
Trading across borders	68	number
Enforcing contracts	163	number
Resolving insolvency	52	number
Corruption and Sustainable Development Index		
Corruption Perceptions Index rank (out of 180, 2022)	85	number
Corruption Perceptions Index score (out of 100, 2022)	40	number
Sustainable Development Index rank (out of 193)	112	number
Sustainable Development Index score (out of 100)	63	number
Economist Intelligence Unit Infrascope Index Score[a]		
PPP regulations score (out of 100)	77	number
PPP regulations rank	4	number
PPP institutions score (out of 100)	94	number
PPP institutions rank	3	number
PPP market maturity score (out of 100)	58	number
PPP market maturity rank	11	number
PPP financing score (out of 100)	73	number
PPP financing rank	2	number
Investment and business climate score (out of 100)	81	number
Investment and business climate rank	1	number

ADF = Asian Development Fund; CIF = cost, insurance, and freight; CPI = consumer price index; CPIA = country policy and institutional assessment; FOB = free on board; GDP = gross domestic product; GNI = gross national income; km² = square kilometer; PPP = public–private partnership.

[a] The Economist Intelligence Unit Infrascope ranks are at regional (Asia) level.

Note: If the year is not explicitly mentioned for a figure or statistics, the year is 2023.

Sources: ADB. 2021. *Basic Statistics 2021*; Centre for Monitoring Indian Economy; Transparency International. Countries; World Bank. 2020. Ease of Doing Business in India; EPWRF India Time Series; IMF. Exchange Rates Selected Indicators; ADB. GDP Growth in Asia and the Pacific, Asian Development Outlook (ADO); Government of India, Ministry of Statistics and Programme Implementation; IMF. IMF Data: Access to Macroeconomic and Financial Data; CEIC. India Real Effective Exchange Rate. ADB. 2020. *Key Indicators for Asia and the Pacific 2020*; World Bank. Logistics Performance Index Rankings 2018; World Bank. PPP Knowledge Lab: India; Sustainable Development Report. Rankings: The Overall Performance of all 193 UN Member States; J. D. Sachs et al. 2021. *Sustainable Development Report 2021: The Decade of Action for the Sustainable Development Goals.* Cambridge University Press; and Economist Intelligence Unit. The Infrascope Archives 2009–19: India.

Appendix 2: World Bank's Ease of Doing Business Parameters for India

Table A2.1: India Basic Country Profile

Ease of Doing Business in India	Region	South Asia	Doing Business Rank: 63	Doing Business Score: 71
	Income category	Lower middle income		
	Population	1,352,617,328		
	City covered	Mumbai, Delhi		

Source: World Bank. 2020. *Doing Business 2020: Economy Profile, India.* Washington, DC.

Figure A2.1: Rankings on Doing Business in India by Categories, 2020

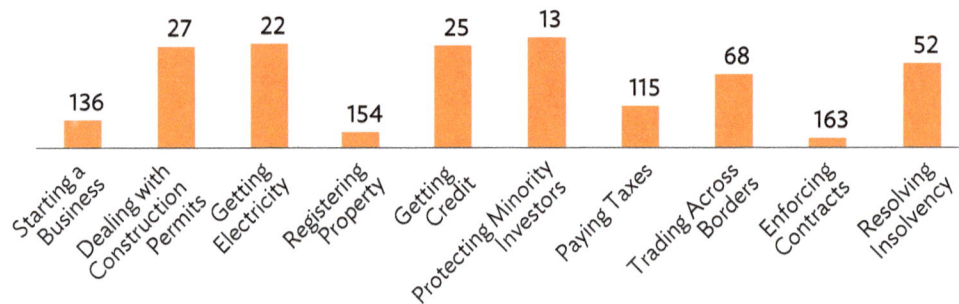

Sources: World Bank. 2020. Doing Business 2020: Comparing Business Regulation in 190 Economies; and World Bank. Ease of Doing Business in India (access 3 January 2024).

Figure A2.2: Scoring on Doing Business in India by Categories, 2020

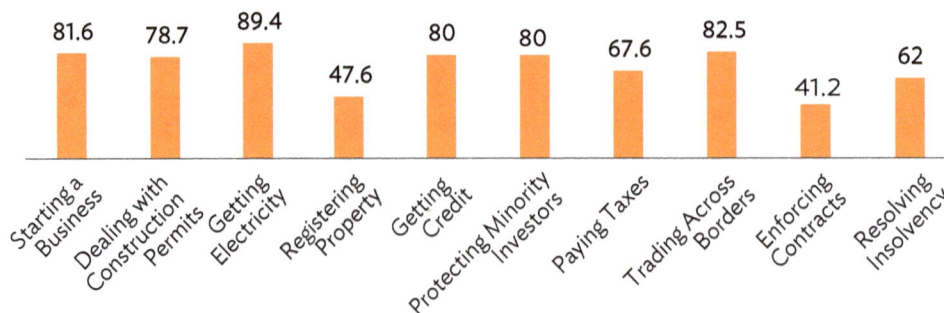

Sources: World Bank. 2020. Doing Business 2020: Comparing Business Regulation in 190 Economies; and World Bank. Ease of Doing Business in India (access 3 January 2024).

Table A2.2: Scores on Doing Business in India, by Categories and Subcategories

Starting a Business (rank)	136	Dealing with Construction Permits (rank)	27	Getting Electricity (rank)	22	Registering Property (rank)	154
Score of starting a business (0–100)	81.6	Score of dealing with construction permits (0–100)	78.7	Score of getting electricity (0–100)	89.4	Score of registering property (0–100)	47.6
Procedures (no.)	10	Procedures (no.)	15	Procedures (no.)	4	Procedures (no.)	9
Time (days)	18	Time (days)	105	Time (days)	53	Time (days)	58
Cost (no.)	7.2	Cost (% of warehouse value)	4.0	Cost (% of income per capita)	28.6	Cost (% of property value)	7.8
Paid-in minimum capital (% of income per capita)	0.0	Building quality control index (0–15)	14.5	Reliability of supply and transparency of tariff index (0–8)	6	Quality of the land administration index (0–30)	10.8

Getting Credit (rank)	25	Protecting Minority Investors (rank)	13	Paying Taxes (rank)	115
Score of getting credit (0–100)	80.0	Score of protecting minority investors (0–100)	80.0	Score of paying taxes (0–100)	67.6
Strength of legal rights index (0–12)	9	Extent of disclosure index (0–10)	8.0	Payments (no. per year)	11
Depth of credit information index (0–8)	7	Extent of director liability index (0–10)	7.0	Time (hours per year)	252
Credit registry coverage (% of adults)	0	Ease of shareholder suits index (0–10)	7.0	Total tax and contribution rate (% of profit)	49.7
Credit bureau coverage (% of adults)	63.1	Extent of shareholder rights index (0–6)	6.0	Post-filing index (0–100)	49.3
		Extent of ownership and control index (0–7)	6.0		
		Extent of corporate transparency index (0–7)	6.0		

continued on next page

Table A2.2 *continued*

Trading Across Borders (rank)	68	Enforcing Contracts (rank)	163	Resolving Insolvency (rank)	52
Score of trading across borders (0–100)	82.5	Score of enforcing contracts (0–100)	41.2	Score of resolving insolvency (0–100)	62.0
Time to export		Time (days)	1,445	Recovery rate ($ cent)	71.6
Documentary compliance (hours)	12	Cost (% of claim value)	31.0	Time (years)	1.6
Border compliance (hours)	52	Quality of judicial processes index (0–18)	10.5	Cost (% of estate)	9.0
Cost to export				Outcome (0 as piecemeal sale and 1 as going concern)	1
Documentary compliance ($)	58			Strength of insolvency framework index (0–16)	7.5
Border compliance ($)	212				
Time to export					
Documentary compliance (hours)	20				
Border compliance (hours)	65				
Cost to export					
Documentary compliance ($)	100				
Border compliance ($)	266				

Sources: World Bank. 2020. Doing Business 2020: Comparing Business Regulation in 190 Economies; and World Bank. Ease of Doing Business in India (access 3 January 2024).

Appendix 3: Assessment of Public Financial Management System in India, 2010

The latest assessment of the Public Financial Management System (PFMS), based on the Public Expenditure and Financial Accountability (PEFA) framework (2010), states that India has an overall rating of B+ (on a four-point scale, with A as the best and D as the worst) for the transparency of intergovernmental fiscal relations.

Parameter or Subparameter	Score	Justification for Score
Transfers to subnational governments	B+	Overall rating based on M2 methodology
System for allocating transfers	B	The transfers are based on the Finance Commission's recommendations, constituting 63% (average over 2005–2006 to 2008–2009) of total transfers. These transfers are rule-based and transparent. The plan transfers constituting about 30% (average over 2005–2006 to 2008–2009) of total transfers are a mix of rule-based and discretionary schematic transfers. The rule-based transfer in the plan transfers is about 30%.
Timeliness of information on transfers	B	The share of individual states in central taxes depends upon the tax realization of the central government. The grant recommended by the Finance Commission is fixed for a full 5 years. The state governments finalize their plans after deliberation with the central Planning Commission. Thus, before the state budget is presented, the states are aware of the likely flow of funds under these heads. The centrally sponsored scheme flow for the year is known and the actual release depends on the stipulated utilization of funds during the year.
Extent of collection and reporting of consolidated fiscal data for general government	A	Fiscal information (ex-ante and ex-post) that is consistent with the central government's fiscal reporting is collected for 90% (by value) of subnational government expenditure and consolidated into annual reports within 10 months of the end of the fiscal year.

Notes: The Public Financial Management and Accountability Assessment report, developed by the World Bank and other development partners, comprises scoring of various indicators and rates them from A to D. Ratings of A to D are based on the criteria stated in the Public Expenditure and Financial Accountability framework and are broadly interpreted as follows:

A = represents performance that meets good international practice—the criteria for the indicator are met in a complete, orderly, accurate, timely, and coordinated way.
B = typically represents a level of performance ranging from good to medium by international standards.
C = represents a level of performance ranging from medium to poor.
D = represents either that a process or procedure does not exist at all, or that it is not functioning effectively.

M1 method: The M1 method is applied for multidimensional indicators where poor performance on one dimension of the indicator is likely to undermine the impact of good performance on other dimension(s) of the same indicator. Under this method, the indicator is assigned the score of the lowest dimension, but a "+" is added if one of the other dimension scores is higher.

M2 method: The M2 method is applied for multidimensional indicators where a low score on one dimension of the indicator does not necessarily undermine the impact of higher scores on other dimensions of the same indicator. Because it applies equal weighting to each of the dimension scores within the indicator, the M2 method is also referred to as the "averaging method."

Source: National Institute of Public Finance and Policy. 2010. *India Public Expenditure and Financial Accountability: Public Financial Management Performance Assessment Report.*

Data is unavailable for the 2010 PEFA assessment of PFMS for India:

Parameter	Value	Unit
Central government transfers to subnational governments	UA	% of GDP
Actual budgetary allocation to subnational governments from national government	UA	% of total expenditure
Deviation of actual against the budgeted transfers to subnational governments	UA	% of budgeted transfers

GDP = gross domestic product, UA = unavailable.

Source: National Institute of Public Finance and Policy. 2010. *India Public Expenditure and Financial Accountability: Public Financial Management Performance Assessment Report.*

References

Acuite Ratings & Research. *Credit Ratings: India*.

Asian Development Bank (ADB). Cumulative Lending, Grant, and Technical Assistance Commitments (accessed 15 July 2023).

ADB. GDP Growth in Asia and the Pacific, Asian Development Outlook (accessed 15 July 2023).

ADB. 2019. *Public–Private Partnership Monitor.* Second Edition.

ADB. 2020. *Key Indicators for Asia and the Pacific 2020.*

ADB. 2021. *Basic Statistics 2021*.

Brickwork Ratings. About Brickwork Ratings: India.

Central Electricity Regulatory Commission. 2019. *Generic Tariff for RE Technologies for FY2019–2020*.

Charan, A. R. and R. Arora. 2020. India: Solutions to PPP Challenges in Infrastructure Sector. Hemant Sahai Associates. *Mondaq.* 27 February.

City Population. Airports (accessed 15 July 2023).

Commonwealth Local Government Forum. 2019. *The Local Government System in India*. CLGF Regional Project Office.

CRISIL Limited. CRISIL Ratings Limited. Mumbai.

CRISIL Risk and Infrastructure Solutions Limited. 2018. *CRISIL Infrastructure Yearbook 2018*. Mumbai.

Dedicated Freight Corridor Corporation of India Limited. About Us.

The Economic Times. 2020. Railways Rules Out Fare Regulator for Private Trains, to Allow Competition in Transport Sector. 13 August.

Economist Intelligence Unit. The Infrascope Archives 2009–19.

Economist Intelligence Unit. 2018. *Infrascope: India Country Report*.

Federation of Indian Chambers of Commerce and Industry, and 2030 Water Resources Group. 2016. *Urban Wastewater Public–Private Partnerships.* White Paper.

The Global Economy. Compare Countries with Annual Data from Official Sources (accessed 15 July 2023).

The Global Economy. Education Spending, Percent of Government Spending—Country Rankings.

The Global Economy. India: Energy Imports (accessed 15 July 2023).

The Global Economy. Health Spending per Capita—Country Rankings.

The Global Economy. Internet Bandwidth—Country Rankings.

The Global Economy. Internet Subscribers.

The Global Economy. Mobile Network Coverage.

The Global Economy. Mobile Phone Subscribers.

The Global Economy. Port Traffic—Country Rankings (accessed 15 July 2023).

The Global Economy. Railroad Infrastructure Quality—Country Rankings (accessed 15 July 2023).

The Global Economy. Railway Passengers—Country Rankings (accessed 15 July 2023).

The Global Economy. Railway Transport of Goods—Country Rankings (accessed 15 July 2023).

The Global Economy. Port Infrastructure Quality—Country Rankings (accessed 15 July 2023).

The Global Economy. Share of Clean Energy—Country Rankings (accessed 15 July 2023).

Goel, V. and M. Dhankhar. 2021. Indian Parties Can Opt for A Foreign Seated Arbitration. Singhania & Partners LLP. *Mondaq.* 29 April.

Government of Goa, Department of Finance, Public Private Partnership Cell. 2011. *Official Gazette.* Series I No. 52. 24 March.

Government of India. Airports Authority of India.

Government of India, Airports Economic Regulatory Authority of India. *Airports Economic Regulatory Authority of India (Amendment) Act, 2019.*

Government of India. Airports Economic Regulatory Authority of India.

Government of India, Airports Economic Regulatory Authority of India. Directions/Guidelines.

Government of India. Central Electricity Regulatory Commission.

Government of India, Department of Telecommunications. 2018. *National Digital Communications Policy, 2018*.

Government of India, Department of Telecommunications. FDI Policy for Telecom.

Government of India, Department of Telecommunications. 2019. *National Broadband Mission*.

Government of India. Department of Telecommunications.

Government of India, Department of Water Resources, River Development and Ganga Rejuvenation. Policy/Schemes – Policies.

Government of India. Directorate General of Civil Aviation.

Government of India, Directorate General of Hydrocarbons. Roles and Functions.

Government of India. Indian Railways.

Government of India, Ministry of Civil Aviation. 2016. National Civil Aviation Policy.

Government of India. Ministry of Civil Aviation.

Government of India, Ministry of Commerce and Industry, Department for Promotion of Industry and Internal Trade. 2020. *Review of FDI Policy on Civil Aviation*.

Government of India, Ministry of Commerce and Industry, Department for Promotion of Industry and Internal Trade, India Investment Grid. *Projects under NIP and Non-NIP* (accessed 15 July 2023).

Government of India, Ministry of Education. 2020. *National Education Policy 2020*.

Government of India, Ministry of Electronics and Information Technology. 2017. *Guidance Notes for IT PPP Projects*.

Government of India, Ministry of Electronics and Information Technology. Acts and Rules, Policies and Guidelines.

Government of India, Ministry of Finance. 2021. *Newsletter*. LXXX (IV). 31 March.

Government of India, Ministry of Finance, Department of Economic Affairs. 2010. *Government Guarantee Policy*.

Government of India, Ministry of Finance, Department of Economic Affairs. 2010. *PPP Toolkit for Improving PPP Decision-Making Processes*.

Government of India, Ministry of Finance, Department of Economic Affairs. 2010. *PPP Toolkit for Improving PPP Decision-Making Processes: Water and Sanitation*.

Government of India, Ministry of Finance, Department of Economic Affairs. 2011. *National (Draft) Public Private Partnership Policy*.

Government of India, Ministry of Finance, Department of Economic Affairs. 2013. *Appraisal and Approval Mechanisms for Central Sector PPPs*.

Government of India, Ministry of Finance, Department of Economic Affairs. 2013. *Scheme and Guidelines for India Infrastructure Project Development Fund*.

Government of India, Ministry of Finance, Department of Economic Affairs. 2015. *Guidelines for Post-Award Contract Management for PPP Concessions*.

Government of India, Ministry of Finance, Department of Economic Affairs. 2015. *Post Award Contract Management Toolkit for PPP Concessions*.

Government of India, Ministry of Finance, Department of Economic Affairs. 2016. *PPP Guide for Practitioners*.

Government of India, Ministry of Finance, Department of Economic Affairs. 2017. *Contingent Liability Management Tool*.

Government of India, Ministry of Finance, Department of Economic Affairs. List of All PPP Projects.

Government of India, Ministry of Finance, Department of Economic Affairs. 2019. *National Infrastructure Pipeline*. Volume 1.

Government of India, Ministry of Finance, Department of Economic Affairs. 2020. Scheme for Financial Support to Public Private Partnerships in Infrastructure Viability Gap Funding.

Government of India, Ministry of Finance, Department of Economic Affairs. 2020. *Updated Harmonized Master List of Infrastructure Sub-sectors (Annexure-I)*.

Government of India, Ministry of Finance, Press Information Bureau. 2012. Harmonized List of Infrastructure Subsectors. Press release. 1 March.

Government of India, Ministry of Health and Family Welfare. 2017. *National Health Policy, 2017.*

Government of India, Ministry of Home Affairs, Office of the Registrar General and Census Commissioner. 2019. *SRS Bulletin*. May.

Government of India, Ministry of Home Affairs, Office of the Registrar General and Census Commissioner. 2020. *Special Bulletin on Maternal Mortality in India, 2016-18*. July.

Government of India, Ministry of Housing and Urban Poverty Alleviation. 2007. *National Urban Housing and Habitat Policy, 2007*.

Government of India, Ministry of Housing and Urban Affairs. 2016. *Municipal Solid Waste Management Manual*.

Government of India, Ministry of Housing and Urban Affairs. 2017. *Public–Private Partnership Models for Affordable Housing*.

Government of India, Ministry of Housing and Urban Affairs. 2019. *Handbook of Urban Statistics 2019*.

Government of India, Ministry of Housing and Urban Affairs. *Toolkit for Public Private Partnership Frameworks in Municipal Solid Waste Management*.

Government of India, Ministry of Housing and Urban Affairs. Atal Mission for Rejuvenation and Urban Transformation.

Government of India, Ministry of Jal Shakti, Department of Water Resources, River Development, and Ganga Rejuvenation. 2011. *Comprehensive Mission Document for National Water Mission*. Volume 1.

Government of India, Ministry of Jal Shakti, Department of Water Resources, River Development and Ganga Rejuvenation. Namami Gange Programme.

Government of India, Ministry of Jal Shakti, Department of Drinking Water and Sanitation. Jal Jeevan Mission.

Government of India. Ministry of Ports, Shipping and Waterways.

Government of India; Ministry of Ports, Shipping and Waterways. Indian Port Rail & Ropeway Corporation Limited (IPRCL).

Government of India; Ministry of Ports, Shipping and Waterways. Inland Waterways Authority of India.

Government of India; Ministry of Ports, Shipping and Waterways; Sagarmala. 2020. Projects Under Sagarmala (accessed 15 July 2023).

Government of India; Ministry of Ports, Shipping and Waterways; Sagarmala. Background.

Government of India; Ministry of Ports, Shipping and Waterways. 2021. Model Concession Agreement 2021 for Public–Private Partnership (PPP) in Major Ports. 12 November.

Government of India, Ministry of Railways. 2020. *Draft Document for Discussion on Re-development of Railway Station*.

Government of India, Ministry of Railways. 2020. *National Rail Plan*.

Government of India, Ministry of Railways. 2021. *Reforms in Passenger Train Operations*.

Government of India, Ministry of Road and Transport and Highways of India. 2019. *Basic Road Statistics of India 2016–2017*.

Government of India, Ministry of Road Transport and Highways. 2000. *Central Road and Infrastructure Fund Act*.

Government of India, Ministry of Road Transport and Highways. 2021. *Annual Report 2020-21*.

Government of India, Ministry of Road Transport and Highways. Acts/Rules.

Government of India, Ministry of Road Transport and Highways. Bharatmala Phase 1.

Government of India, Ministry of Road Transport and Highways. Standard Documents (accessed 15 July 2023).

Government of India, Ministry of Road Transport and Highways. Setu Bharatam (accessed 15 July 2023).

Government of India, Ministry of Road Transport and Highways. National Highways and Infrastructure Development Corporation Limited.

Government of India, Ministry of Urban Development. 2017. Intelligent Transit Management System (ITMS)—Surat. In India Smart Cities: Success Stories from Mission Cities. pp. 42–44.

Government of India, Ministry of Urban Development; Confederation of Indian Industry; and Ernst & Young Pvt. Ltd. 2008. *Compendium on Public Private Partnership in Urban Infrastructure—Case Studies*.

Government of India, National Highways Authority of India. 2021. *Annual Bidding Plan 2020–21*.

Government of India, National Highways Authority of India. About NHAI.

Government of India, National Highways Authority of India. 2020. *Model Concession Agreement for BOT (Toll) Projects*. August.

Government of India, National Rural Health Mission, National Health Systems Resource Centre. 2019. *National Health Accounts 2016-17*.

Government of India, NITI Aayog. 2012. *Guidelines for Monitoring of PPP Projects*.

Government of India, NITI Aayog. Model Agreements (accessed 15 July 2023).

Government of India, NITI Aayog. Public–Private Partnerships.

Government of India, NITI Aayog. Public–Private Partnerships, Infrastructure (accessed 15 July 2023).

Government of India. Petroleum and Natural Gas Regulatory Board.

Government of India, Ministry of Civil Aviation, Press Information Bureau. 2018. New Transaction Structure for Future Greenfield Airports Proposed Under Nabh Nirmaan 2018. Press release. 14 August.

Government of India, Ministry of Health and Family Welfare, Press Information Bureau. 2020. Average Life Expectancy. Press release. 13 March.

Government of India, Ministry of Railways, Press Information Bureau. 2020. Ministry of Railways Invites Request for Qualifications (RFQ) for Private Participation for Operation of Passenger Train Services over 109 Origin Destination (OD) Pairs of Routes. Press release. 1 July.

Government of India, Ministry of Railways, Press Information Bureau. 2020. Indian Railways Issues Draft National Rail Plan. Press release. 18 December.

Government of India, Press Information Bureau. 2021. Cabinet Approves BharatNet Implementation Through Public Private Partnership Model in 16 States with Optical Fibre Connectivity to All Inhabited Villages. Press release. 30 June.

Government of India, Ministry of Finance, Press Information Bureau. 2021. Government to Step Up Funding for National Infrastructure Pipeline. Press release. 1 February.

Government of India; Ministry of Ports, Shipping and Waterways; Sagarmala. Projects under Sagarmala.

Government of India; Ministry of Ports, Shipping and Waterways; Tariff Authority for Major Ports. Establishment of the TAMP.

Government of India, Ministry of Railways, Press Information Bureau. 2021. Modernisation of Railway Stations. Press release. 10 March.

Government of India, Telecom Regulatory Authority of India. 2021. Consultation Paper on Validity Period of Tariff Offers. 13 May.

Government of Karnataka. Infrastructure Development Ports and Inland Transport Department.

Government of Rajasthan, Planning Department. 2020. Reg. Notice Inviting Public Consultation on Draft PPP Policy, 2020 for the State.

Government of Tamil Nadu. Tamil Nadu Infrastructure Development Board.

Government of Telangana, Mission Bhagiratha. Mission Bhagiratha: Inspiration.

Government of Uttarakhand, Uttarakhand Public Private Partnership Cell. 2019. Uttarakhand Public Private Partnership Revised Policy 2019.

Government of West Bengal, Finance Department, Audit Branch. 2012. *Notification*. No. 6523-F(H). 27 July.

ICRA Ratings India. Profile.

India Brand Equity Foundation (IBEF). 2019. Infrastructure Sector in India.

India Ratings and Research. Overview.

Indian Council of Arbitration. About Us.

Indian Council for Research on International Economic Relations. 2019. *State of Municipal Finances in India: A Study Prepared for the Fifteenth Finance Commission*.

India Development Review. 2020. IDR Explains: Local Government in India. 28 January.

Indian Ports Association. Profile.

Indian Railway Stations Development Corporation Limited. About IRSDC.

Infomerics Ratings. About Infomerics.

International Benchmarking Network of the World Bank (IBNET) Tariff Database. Tariffs for Hyderabad Metropolitan Water Supply & Sewerage Board, HMWS&SB (India) (accessed 15 July 2023).

International Benchmarking Network of the World Bank (IBNET) Tariff Database. Tariffs for Bangalore Water Supply and Sewerage Board (India) (accessed 15 July 2023).

International Monetary Fund (IMF). Exchange Rates Selected Indicators.

Invest India. National Investment Promotion and Facilitation Agency. FDI Policy of India (accessed 15 July 2023).

IMF. IMF Data Access to Macroeconomic and Financial Data (accessed 15 July 2023).

Jones Lang LaSalle. 2016. *Affordable Housing in India: Key Initiatives for Inclusive Housing for All*.

Joshi, A. and S. Talwar. 2017. *Infrastructure in India*. Economic Laws Practice.

Mankikar, S. 2018. The Impact of GST on Municipal Finances in India: A Case Study of Mumbai. *ORF Issue Brief*. No. 257. Observer Research Foundation.

Mathur, O. P. 2018. *The Financing of Urban Infrastructure Issues and Challenges*. Background note prepared for the Urban Development: Technological Solutions and Governance Challenges. 19–20 April.

Mufti, I. and R. Sampal 2019. Why Tejas is '1st Private Train' — Railways Owns It, Outside Vendors Provide Food and Clean It. *The Print*. 6 October.

National Institute of Public Finance and Policy. 2010. *India Public Expenditure and Financial Accountability: Public Financial Management Performance Assessment Report.*

Nidumuri, L. K. 2015. Whether Indian Parties Can Choose Foreign Law to Settle Disputes? *Indus Law, Mondaq.* 9 October.

Organisation for Economic Co-operation and Development, and United Cities and Local Governments. 2016. *Subnational Governments Around the World: Structure and Finance—Country Profiles.* OECD Publishing.

Parikh, M. 2019. A Study of Failure and Rise of Surat City Bus and its Impact on Surat Residents. *International Journal of Science and Research.* 8 (9). pp. 1557–1560.

PR Newswire, Research and Markets. 2019. The Waste to Energy (WtE) and Waste Management Market in India, 2019–2025: High Population Growth and Changing Lifestyles to Increase Waste Volumes in India. 28 November.

PRS Legislative Research. 2020. *Draft Electricity (Amendment) Bill, 2020.*

PRS Legislative Research. 2021. *The National Bank for Financing Infrastructure and Development (NBFID) Bill, 2021.*

Rail Land Development Authority. About Us.

Reserve Bank of India. 2015. Master Circular – Prudential Norms on Income Recognition, Asset Classification and Provisioning Pertaining to Advances. Master Circular DBR No. BP.BC.2/21.04.048/2015-16. 1 July.

Reserve Bank of India, Foreign Exchange Department. 2018. Foreign Exchange Management (Acquisition and Transfer of Immovable Property in India) Regulations. Notification No. FEMA 21(R)/2018-RB. 26 March.

Sachs, J. D. et al. 2021. *Sustainable Development Report 2021: The Decade of Action for the Sustainable Development Goals.* Cambridge University Press.

SCC Times. 2021. Arbitration and Conciliation (Amendment) Act, 2021. Blog. 16 March.

Securities and Exchange Board of India. *Names and Registered Addresses of Credit Rating Agencies.*

Sheikh, Y. A. 2017. Higher Education in India: Challenges and Opportunities. *Journal of Education and Practice.* 8 (1). pp. 39–42.

Singh, G. and A. Sahay. 2020. *Project Finance in India: Overview.* Thomson Reuters Practical Law.

Sustainable Development Report. Rankings: The Overall Performance of all 193 UN Member States.

Tax Management India.com. 2012. *Harmonized List of Infrastructure Sub-sectors*.

Transparency International. Countries.

United Nations, Department of Economic and Social Affairs. 2019. *Energy Statistics Pocketbook, 2019*.

World Bank. 2020. Doing Business 2020: Comparing Business Regulation in 190 Economies.

World Bank. Access to Electricity (% of population) – India (accessed 15 July 2023).

World Bank. Air Transport, Passengers Carried (accessed 15 July 2023).

World Bank. Current Health Expenditure (% of GDP).

World Bank. Doing Business. Getting Electricity (accessed 15 July 2023).

World Bank. Ease of Doing Business in India (access 3 January 2024).

World Bank. Infrastructure Finance, PPPs and Guarantees. Custom Query (accessed 3 January 2024).

World Bank. Investment in Water and Sanitation with Private Participation (current US$) - India. (accessed 15 July 2023).

World Bank. Logistics Performance Index Rankings 2018.

World Bank. PPP Knowledge Lab: India.

World Bank. Telephone Subscribers.

World Bank. Total Government Expenditure on Education (% of GDP) - India.